Advance Praise for

CRITICAL ISSUES IN

Anti-Racist Research Methodologies

"*Critical Issues in Anti-Racist Research Methodologies* is a remarkable contribution to the scholarship on race and educational reform. George J. Sefa Dei and his colleagues have written an important and timely book that charts a new course in the emerging field of anti-racist scholarship. This edited volume is radically eclectic: It covers a wide range of critical issues related to theory, methodology, and policy and foregrounds many of the pivotal tensions and contradictions in this area of education research. Many of these essays are path breaking, insightful, and refreshing in tone and direction. The volume is indispensable reading for students and general practitioners operating in the field of educational policy and reform." *—Cameron McCarthy, Professor, Institute of Communications Research University of Illinois at Urbana*

"This important book addresses, and advances, the theory, ethics, and methodologies of anti-racist education research. It raises timely and challenging questions about how anti-racist education can actually make (more of) a difference—both in academia and, even more importantly, 'on the ground.' This book also provides an exemplary model of the collaborative research approach that it espouses—presenting engaged, egalitarian, empirical, and critical research throughout." *— Stephen May, Professor of Education, University of Waikato, New Zealand*

"The authors courageously write about what can only be whispered at in the academy and the classroom about current racial ethnic studies. This provocative confrontation with racism is no defense of the conservative approach to anti-racist research. In this book, which is highly accessible across race, gender, and class, social inequality as well as critical social theory studies scores several points. The liberal left has always been trapped into using race instead of the intersection of race, gender, and class in anti-racist research to bring about social change. This book is the most compelling inclusive anti-racist research critical approach to the more liberal nuanced accommodation and celebration of racial ethnic studies. A must read!"*—Jean Ait belkhir, Founder and Editor of the Journal,* Race, Gender & Class; *Founder and Former Chair of the Journal,* American Sociological Association Race, Gender & Class; *Acting Chair and Chair Elect of American Sociological Association RGC*

CRITICAL ISSUES IN

Anti-Racist Research
Methodologies

Studies in the
Postmodern Theory of Education

Joe L. Kincheloe and Shirley R. Steinberg
General Editors

Vol. 252

PETER LANG
New York • Washington, D.C./Baltimore • Bern
Frankfurt am Main • Berlin • Brussels • Vienna • Oxford

CRITICAL ISSUES IN

Anti-Racist Research Methodologies

Edited by GEORGE J. SEFA DEI
GURPREET SINGH JOHAL

PETER LANG
New York • Washington, D.C./Baltimore • Bern
Frankfurt am Main • Berlin • Brussels • Vienna • Oxford

Library of Congress Cataloging-in-Publication Data

Critical issues in anti-racist research methodologies /
edited by George J. Sefa Dei, Gurpreet Singh Johal.
p. cm. — (Counterpoints; vol. 252)
Includes bibliographical references.
1. Racism—Research. 2. Race relations—Research.
3. Power (Social sciences). 4. Research—Methodology.
I. Dei, George Jerry Sefa. II. Johal, Gurpreet Singh.
III. Counterpoints (New York, N.Y.); v. 252.
HT1521.C75   305.8—dc21   2003007313
ISBN 0-8204-6800-2
ISSN 1058-1634

Bibliographic information published by Die Deutsche Bibliothek.
Die Deutsche Bibliothek lists this publication in the "Deutsche
Nationalbibliografie"; detailed bibliographic data is available
on the Internet at http://dnb.ddb.de/.

Cover design by Lisa Barfield

The paper in this book meets the guidelines for permanence and durability
of the Committee on Production Guidelines for Book Longevity
of the Council of Library Resources.

Contents

Acknowledgments

We would like to thank the students in George Dei's graduate course, SES 3910: 'Advanced Seminar on Race and Anti-Racist Research Methodology in Education', at the Ontario Institute for Studies in Education of the University of Toronto (OISE/UT), who provided the inspiration for putting together this much-needed collection. Our discussions exploring key epistemological questions and methodological concerns on race and anti-racism research, and the political and ethical implications of studying across difference (race, ethnicity, gender, class and sexuality) were germane to many of the ideas presented in this work. We appreciate the assistance of Bathseba Opini of the Department of Sociology and Equity Studies at OISE/UT for assisting with editorial work on a draft of the manuscript and helping respond to reviewers' comments. Also, we are grateful to Joe Kincheloe and Shirley Steinberg who have always been supportive and have nurtured critical scholarship on race and oppression studies. George Dei would like to thank Gurpreet for his assistance on this project and the many tireless conversations we had as we proceeded to bring this work to fruition. We would like to dedicate this work to the UHURU COLLECTIVE, made up of a group of academics, researchers and social activists at the Ontario Institute for Studies in Education of the University of Toronto (OISE/UT). The Collective is a diverse group of scholars from African, First Nations, Arab, Asian, and European backgrounds whose scholarship and community work are grounded in working for change to address social injustice and all forms of oppression. It is to the embodiment of the spirit of freedom, community and unity that we dedicate this work. We believe that academic work must be meaningful and firmly grounded in collective aspirations for equity and social justice. We believe that our politics must be informed by indigenous knowledges and anti-racism principles, critical feminism, and anti-colonial thought, not just as theories but as practice in our daily lives and in our work.

Chapter One

GEORGE J. SEFA DEI

Critical Issues in Anti-racist Research Methodologies
AN INTRODUCTION

I would like to begin this introduction in a very unconventional way. I wish to thank the students in my graduate level course at the Ontario Institute for Studies in Education at the University of Toronto for sharing their many ideas with me in class. These ideas have, over the years, been informed by thinking on anti-racist research. When I started thinking about this project and the possibilities of putting such a collection in print, I was moved by the knowledge and questions that I had encountered in my few years of teaching a course of this kind. While I was strengthened by the amount of past, current, and existing scholarship on anti-racism, I also felt that one of the means of moving the subject into other territories would be to produce a textbook that raises some key questions about anti-racist research. I have always sought and welcomed collaborative intellectual work and the opportunity to share thoughts and ideas with Gurpreet Johal, as co-editor of this collection has been extremely rewarding. Some of the views expressed in this introduction were presented in a keynote address to the Ryerson Polytechnic University, Spring Faculty Community Services (SRC) event on May 21, 1997, and I would like to thank the audience for their critical comments.

This introduction is purposely intended to raise questions rather than provide answers. Anti-racism studies have blossomed over the years with scholarship and political work reinforcing each other to cement anti-racist change, but how do we understand anti-racist research? How is anti-racist research methodology different from other methods of research investigation? What are the principles of anti-racism research? This edited collection attempts to provide some answers to these questions, and brings together works that examine the perils and desires of anti-racist research with a particular focus on the notion of *difference* by seriously looking at the race, gender, class, and sexuality intersections/implications of educational research.

Anti-racist research places the minoritized at the center of analysis by focusing on their lived experiences and the "simultaneity of [their] oppressions" (Brewer, 1993, p. 16). The research purpose is to understand social oppression and how it helps construct and constrain identities (race, gender, class, sexuality), both internally and externally through inclusionary and exclusionary processes. People of color (e.g., black women) experience oppression in a way that is different both in substance and intensity. Anti-racism research is not about becoming located or situated in another's lived experiences but is rather an opportunity for the researcher to critically engage his or her own experience as part of the knowledge search. While discussing such experiences in the research process, one must also ask, "how does this experience speak to me in terms of theorizing experiences and pursuing political action for change?" The belief in the power of ideas to change society requires that the anti-racist researcher explores ways and means of understanding the philosophy behind the social ideals and practices in which people are involved.

It goes without saying that an understanding of the simultaneity of oppression is essential if the educator/researcher is to understand the experience of oppression dealt with by minoritized individuals. The simultaneity of oppression always speaks directly to lived experience of the minoritized, but in order for this way of conceptualizing oppression to move beyond theory, it must inform practice through daily human [social] action, e.g., research, teaching). Research on race must touch on multiple subject identities and how these identities are intertwined, as well as how they inform political practice. Change in anti-racist attitudes depends on the ability to pursue a politics beyond our fragmented identities while concentrating on certain goals. The lessons of history suggest that in coalition building, when struggles have been fought, certain people will remain oppressed while others assume the mantle of power and privilege. Social-movement politics have also been known to ignore certain agendas and desires not deemed in the interest of their rank and file. These are the kinds of issues that prompt rethinking and revision of coalition politics to promote social change. There is strength in numbers, and this realization is important enough to cause anti-racist politics to cross borders and seek important allies.

It is important to reiterate that our goal is not to preach to anyone about the desires and perils of anti-racist work. In fact, we see ourselves as part of the topic of discussion, and bring with us ideas that are a reflection of our own individual and collaborative research practices. We present this discussion as a way to rethink collaboration and anti-racism research, and we begin by posing some basic questions that drive the need to rethink such research. Our intention is not to offer answers to these fundamental questions, but rather, to pose them in a way that helps to reframe anti-racist practice. While our focus is on anti-racism, we believe the issues raised in this text span many diverse concerns of academic researchers and community workers interested in decolonizing research in the academy (i.e., schools, colleges, and universities) (see Smith, 1999).

There are varied discursive approaches to anti-racist research. For example, what are the specific epistemological, ontological, and axiological assumptions underlying anti-racist research? What are the specific methods called for in such research? What distinguishes anti-racist research from other social science research methodologies? How do we look at collaboration among anti-racism researchers (e.g., collaboration with/between/among research institutes, universities, and other centers of learning; collaboration among research teams from different academic disciplines; and collaboration between anti-racist-'theorists' and local communities outside of the academies)? What are the specific political projects for undertaking this form of research? In this collection, we focus on many of these issues as we seek to unravel the politics and intellectual agendas behind anti-racist research and research methodologies. A key focus of the discussion is on collaboration among academic researchers and the subjects of their study, local communities and research.

The pursuit of ant-racist research raises a host of complex theoretical and methodological issues. There is a vast array of competing interests, tensions, and contradictions in thinking through the power relations of knowledge production in the broader context of anti-racism (see also Bulmer and Solomos, 2004; Twine and Warren, 2000). Anti-racism is about power relations. Anti-racism discourse moves away from discussions of tolerating diversity to the pointed notion of difference and power. It sees race and racism as central to how we claim, occupy, and defend spaces. The task of anti-racism is to identify, challenge, and change the values, structures, and behaviors that perpetuate systemic racism and other forms of societal oppression. Specifically, and as many have pointed out, anti-racism discourse highlights persistent inequities in communities, focusing on relations of domination and subordination (Thomas, 1984; Lee, 1985; 1991; Walcott 1990; Dei, 1996). Thus anti-racism troubles the manifestation of the social problems as simply bias and discrimination rather than hatred, exclusion and violence (see Price, 1993; Dei and Callieste, 2000). Anti-racism perceives prejudice as an integral part of the social order and views the mechanism of redressing societal inequities as being fundamental structural change. Anti-racism problematizes the position that we all start from a relatively level playing field, that we have access to similar resources, and that we have comparable values, aspirations, and concerns as far from the reality of those racially minoritized in our communities.

It is important to distinguish anti-racism from hegemonic notions of liberal multiculturalism. Liberal multiculturalism is an ideology that promotes cultural diversity as an intrinsic component of the social, political, and moral order. This ideology presents itself as a mosaic that cherishes difference and plurality and promotes an image of multiple, thriving, mutually respectful, and appreciative ethno-cultural communities. Liberal multiculturalism suggests that the primary issue of relevance in different cultural communities is that there is a lack of recognition of positive contributions, misunderstandings, and miscommunication. This is manifested in intolerance, and lack of goodwill among people. The primary mechanism of redress is education, cultural sensitivity, sharing and exchange. Within this paradigm, prejudice of individuals, rather than systemic inequity is the primary obstacle facing ethno-cultural communities. Perceived prejudices should be redressed through the language of democratic rights.

Anti-racism, on the other hand, suggests that the whole nation-building enterprise is suspect, as are assumptions underlying empathy, commonality, and goodwill. The Anti-Racism Secretariat (a government mandated body in the Ministry of Citizenship, responsible for development of policy on anti-racism initiatives in the province of Ontario) definition of anti-racism suggests that it is the practice of identifying, challenging, and changing the values, structures, and behaviors that perpetuate systemic racism. The discourse of anti-racism emphasizes persistent inequities among communities that are embedded in relations of domination and subordination. The primary issue is that of entrenched inequality and power imbalances. This is manifested in bias, discrimination, hatred, exclusion, and most importantly, violence. Mechanisms of redress outlined by anti-racism are fundamental structural and societal change. In this context, prejudice is perceived as an integral, rather than an anomalous, part of the social order.

Race, gender, class, and sexual identity consciousness influence what we see and interpret in race and anti-racism research work. Race and anti-racism studies, as a serious area of inquiry, present fundamental epistemological and theoretical challenges. Today anti-racism workers continue to search for appropriate ways to secure, interrogate, validate, affirm, and/or challenge pubic and commonsensical knowledge about race/and racism. Questions of ethics and human values continually resurface in anti-racist practice. Stanfield (1995a, 13) rightly observes that conventional research into race has been notorious for its passivity and degradation of racial minorities and particularly for its exclusion of researchers as subjects, from playing significant decision-making roles in research projects involving members of their own communities. It is no secret that legitimacy is accorded to race research and scholarship when produced by members of the dominant group (see Fine, 1994a; Fine, 1994b, 80; Stanfield, 1995b, 26). There are emerging issues concerning the relevance and the application of anti-racist research, and the effects of race research on subjects (e.g., pain, suffering, and material costs).

An emerging concern for contemporary anti-racist research is to move beyond the bland politics of inclusion to a new politics of transparency and accountability. Critical academic researchers are taking responsibility for what they do or fail to do, while ensuring that their subjects are continually informed about the process, objective, and goals of their research. Embedded in this concern is anti-racist researchers' awareness of reactions to their work as they seek to rupture the status quo. Our theoretical conception and political praxis of engaging in critical research is anchored in an integrative anti-racism discursive framework, a recognition of the pervasiveness of power and its dominance in a racialized, gendered, and classed society. There is a powerful connection between race identity and knowledge production. Every researcher must acknowledge the crucial impact of race identity and social difference. Our subjective identities and political locations inform how we produce knowledge and come to interpret and understand the world. Along with this important knowledge, antiracist research must acknowledge the inherent asymmetrical power relations that are structured along lines of difference.

At the conceptual level, the notions of power, social politics, community, change become crucial in discussing anti-racist research. Importantly, anti-racist research must problematize colonial practices. An anti-colonial approach theorizes colonial and neo-colonial relations and the implications of imperial structures on processes of knowledge production and validation, the understanding of indigence, and the pursuit of agency, resistance, and subjective politics. The approach critiques colonial imposition, where *colonial* is understood to be imposed and dominating and not simply foreign or alien. Pursuing anti-racist research in an anti-colonial framework (Dei and Asgharzadeh, 2001) means to critique the "shark phenomenon," (the practice of seeing subjects as merely "objects and subjects" of raw data) and the researcher's role as collecting data and then "theorizing" elsewhere apart from the subjects. This practice seeks only to reproduce colonial and power relations. Anti-racism change requires that research and researchers see local peoples/subjects as theorists of their own everyday lives and practices. Local peoples live and create theory. They are creators of knowledge not simply subjects of study. For many local peoples, what is theoretical does not stand in opposition to what is pragmatic.

Self-involvement and Asking Critical Questions

Anti-racist researchers are many things in addition to being researchers. Each has ethical, political, moral, and educative responsibilities that may be in conflict. Anti-racist research requires recognition of the contributions of the subjects of study to shaping theory, practice, and knowledge. A researcher's personality and ability to establish trust and open dialogue are also crucial to collaborative work with local subjects and communities. Trust allows for solidarity building in communities and dealing with the difficulty of learning from a distance (see Foster, 1994; Fine, 1994a, b).

A critical engagement of the self as a researcher means understanding the feelings subjects have about the research process. The researcher becomes a learner and must view research as a process of self-discovery and self-examination (see also Rogers-Huilman and Grane, 1999). More importantly, the self as a collaborative researcher must ask some basic questions in the challenge of knowledge production. For example, what is the fundamental challenge in anti-racist research involving multiple parties and subjects? How does a researcher define her or his relation to others? How does involving the self, assist us in rethinking the meaning of research within the anti-racist/anti-colonial paradigm (e.g., the search for a new model for research), while working with subjects to collaboratively produce critical knowledge? Do we define and operationalize the *how* of anti-racist research (are there specific models for such research)?

An important objective of anti-racist research is to challenge the unidirectional flow of information/knowledge from a source (i.e., subjects of study) to the "expert" (i.e., researcher) and then to an epistemic community (i.e., academic audience). Part of the challenge of decolonizing academic research is to rupture the conventional notion of *ethnographic authority*. As researchers, do we begin our studies by claiming certain knowledge and therefore the right to set about "proving we are right?" Do we have a right to seek research information, no matter the cost, in the name of knowledge production? What sorts of rationalizations do anti-racist researchers use concerning decisions about with whom to work (as knowers)? Why and how do we select subjects to work with and to what ends and purposes? How many of our subjects have input into the many decisions we make about our research? When we claim to *know*, is it because 'we were there' in the classic anthropological sense? or, is it because the paraphernalia of the academy and/or the trappings of academic membership have bestowed on us certain privileges and honors that may set us apart from the subjects we study? This claim of ethnographic authority, authorial control, and the privilege of the authorial voice may be assumed by us as researchers, but it is not necessarily lost on our subjects. In fact, this naked appropriation of voice and experiences is at the heart of the increasing suspicion that many local peoples have for academic research and researchers. Bramble (2000) interrogates this situation in the question, "Why do we think" (to quote one of my students) that the "natives have become their own researchers?" The challenge is for critical, anti-racist research to promote and uphold a discursive and interpretive space for our research subjects.

As academic researchers, we often enter the social space of research subjects "embedded in the context of [our] own scholarly environments" (Borland, 1991, 71). Our interpretations may or may not necessarily be an accurate reflection of what our subjects said. The task is not to argue for collaboration with research subjects in order to validate our research findings. It is more a question of our varied and differential responsibilities when it comes to producing and disseminating knowledge. Our personal histories, educational experiences, and scholarly training can shape our interpretations (as researchers). We need to be aware of this in critical research. Within our Eurocentric academies there is an undeniable history of racist, sexist, homophobic, and class bias teachings that fail to inform learners of the complete history of ideas and events that have shaped and continue to shape human growth and development. Anti-racist research calls for subverting the conventional processes of knowledge procurement, interrogation, validation, and dissemination. Anti-racism calls for renegotiating with our subjects the crucial issues of discursive power, control, and interpretive authority in research.

Today, local subjects are seeking to have a real and legitimate voice in the interpretation and interpretive process of social research. They are not simply the sources of raw data. They want to be able to create, tell, analyze, and interpret their own stories and experiences, and not simply have researchers assume that ethnographic, interpretive, and discursive authority. As Borland (1991) notes, there is not always this likeness of mind between subjects and researchers. There is always difference of thought that must be upheld in social research. Researchers cannot assume that their subjects will simply accept their interpretations. As researchers constantly construct their own identities through social interactions with research subjects, we must be cautious of how we "construct our notion of others" in field research (see also Borland, 1991, 70).

As noted elsewhere (Dei et al., 2002), anti-racism studies suffer from charges of being a fiercely partisan discourse and as unapologetically pursuing political ends, but the issue is not whether anti-racism claims to inform legitimately or not. It is a question of whether anti-racist workers (educators/learners/researchers/activists) will allow for the production of critical knowledge (through multiple knowings) in order to counter the corruption and invalidation of non-hegemonic ways of knowing as illegitimate/invalid knowledge.

Particularly for minoritized researchers and subjects, anti-racism affords possibilities for naming, narrating our own oppressions, and devising strategies of resistance through critical practice. Like all contested discourses, anti-racism sees the *authority to know* as contextual, situational, contestable, and problematic. While anti-racism may not necessarily create new epistemologies (through its focus on contestations, ambivalences, and ambiguities), at least it must not present itself through research practice as an imperialist project claiming to be a discourse with guarantees.

There are risks involved in pursing anti-racist research. There is no end to the constantly emerging questions about ethics and the ethicality of anti-oppression research. Anti-racist research does not claim that the only valid knower is one who has experienced the *fact*. However, anti-racism discourse problematizes any attempts to de-racialize the subject as a legitimate knower, particularly if the politics of de-racialization are aimed at subverting the power of subjectivity and subjective knowings in order to make room for a so-called objectivity and/or objective knowing. As Wahab notes in this collection, we cannot erase or bracket out subject(ive) knowings in the search for knowledge. Knowledge resides in the body and cultural memory. However, for many of us the Eurocentric gaze has influenced and determined what we see and do not see, and what we characterize as (in)valid and (il)legitimate. Anti-racism poses the question: How can we assign discursive authority and authorial control to experts (including researchers) who have no embodied connection to knowledge or to the particular experiences that produce the knowledge they seek? There is no definitive answer to this question unless we uncover what it means to have *embodied knowledge*. We must also not confuse this critical interrogation with a problematic position that, for example, color (race) simply determines what one knows. Having embodied knowledge means bringing personal feelings, emotional and spiritual connectedness, and a deep passion and commitment to seek knowledge and using these things to transform existing conditions as a noble cause that emanates from within the self.

Anti-racism research, by virtue of the dictates and politics of the discourse, bears a tremendous burden on researchers to find ways to resolve/address critical questions. Anti-racism research must deal with whether the collaborating parties in a research study necessarily share a common understanding of the nature and politics of research (e.g., definitions, boundaries, objectives). How do anti-racists work with their subjects in a genuine spirit of collaboration and power sharing in the context of an open and insidious denial of the privilege that comes with particular racial identities, e.g., white identity? The anti-racist researcher always stands accused of bringing up the issue of race and racism when and where it never existed. In a research study of minority youth disen-

gagement from school (Dei, Mazzuca, McIsaac, and Zine, 1997), we were
accused of bringing up race issues and fomenting divisions in schools because
black students began demanding black teachers and the teaching of
black/African history and culture in the school curricula. In other words, all
of a sudden students began reading their world in terms of color!

Today, we are faced with conflicting and complicated readings of power and
difference. How do diverse parties work together in social research in the context of the complexity of power of asymmetrical relations? Power hierarchies
and merit badges are a plague on institutions today (see Hatcher, 1998).
Academy power games can influence communities, and we must understand
the power relationships among research, researcher, and the so-called subjects
of study. How do we understand the power relationships between researchers
and institutional authorities, especially when they infringe upon the basic
tenets of academic freedom, free speech, and institutional autonomy? Other
considerations include how we deal with the parasitic nature of social research
knowing full well the implications of social research in terms of subjects' time
and effort. Research takes up people's time. We ask people to commit to our
projects and to give us their time and space, all in the name of searching for
knowledge, but we avoid burdening ourselves with asking whether research will
lead to meaningful change in the lives of our subjects (students and schools).
Will anti-racist research make a difference?

Similarly, there are the ethics and politics of collaboration itself. For example, how do anti-racist workers define the need to collaborate, and what are
the benefits and potential dangers? Let me use one particular study that I have
been involved in to illustrate this concern. Between 1992 and 1995, I worked
with a number of graduate students at the Ontario Institute for Studies in
Education of the University of Toronto (OISE/UT) on a three-year project
concerning the narratives of black students and school dropouts who discussed their experiences in the Ontario public school system, and in some cases
their reasons for leaving school. The Social Sciences and Humanities Research
Council of Canada (SSHRC) and the Ontario Ministry of Education and
Training (MET) funded the study. The findings of this study have since been
reported in two publications that I have co-authored with graduate assistants
(see Dei, Holmes, Mazzuca, McIsaac, and Campbell, 1995; and Dei, Mazzuca,
McIsaac, and Zine, 1997). The main research objective was to determine
what student narratives could tell us about the dropout problem, and particularly about the influence of race/ethnicity, class, gender, power, and social
structures on the decision to drop out of school. Specifically, our research was
designed to shed some light on how students understand and articulate the factors that affect their decisions to stay in school or leave school prematurely. As

in every study, a critical researcher must grapple with very pertinent ethical and political questions. For me, as the principal investigator, there were issues concerning my academic and political reasons for undertaking such a study. For example, in the search for and uses of research data, how would my research address the power issues and differences between myself as a researcher (supported by an academic institution), and my research subjects, who expressed a feeling of vulnerability with respect to their place in the institutions they attended? What motivated me to undertake this study and why, and what did I envision as its result? How would my research benefit my subjects, and how would I balance my responsibilities to my academic profession, funding agencies, and the local communities I have worked with? These issues could not be easily glossed over. Minoritized communities have for far too long born the brunt of academic research. A number of past educational research projects have focused on minorities, and particularly on black pathologies and alleged cases of failures and underachievement. Not many studies have dealt with the successes of the marginalized and particularly how people resist their marginality and domination. Minority communities have been blamed for their plight without any critical interrogation of the structures of schooling and the delivery of education (teaching, learning, and administration of education), which affect schooling and what has come to mean 'academic success'. The pertinent question for me was how to make this study different. Could I assure my subjects that my research would move beyond such conventional research and contribute to strengthening their knowledge base and sense and spirit of intellectual agency? Could my research make a difference in their lives? Would their voices be heard? When a study participant asked me what difference my study would make, I found it a very compelling question. After all, research takes up a lot of people's time!

Anti-racism research and praxis means challenging and rupturing the very structures one is trying to work with. This is not easy and it has tremendous personal and emotional costs. How do we ensure that working partnerships, including collaborative ones, do not lead to coercion, co-optation, and control? If borders are to be crossed, why, how, when, and at what cost? Also, as already noted, an anti-colonial approach to research necessitates centering on the question of how we work with local cultural resources and knowledge bases (e.g., privileging subjective knowing). What is the role and place of indigenous/local knowledge in critical anti-racist research? Oftentimes, research subjects challenge the way academic researchers know and interpret the world. How can anti-racist research be approached so that this body of knowledge can be taken into account? Furthermore, as alluded to elsewhere (Cruishank, 1992; Dei, 2001) written text and oral communication have their own power within the academy. There is the challenge of textuality and orality and the privileging of written text over oral communication. What happens in research when subjects refuse to have their voice written into text? There is historical precedent for this, stemming from the misrepresentation of the knowledges of local peoples by academic researchers as they sought to translate oral culture into textured and textual forms without the necessary safeguards. What happens to the spoken word when it is translated into text? These are additional concerns for the anti-racist researcher to deal with.

Conceptualizing Anti-racist Research: The Problem of Meaning, Definitions, and Boundaries

We operationalize *anti-racist research* as research on racial domination and social oppression, and proceed with an objective of providing local subjects with an opportunity to speak about their experiences within the broader contexts of structural and institutional forces of society. This form of research also focuses on the nature of local resistance to oppression, and the learning objective is to create healthy spaces in which subjects can collaborate with researchers to understand the nature of social oppression. This form of research also proceeds with some basic ideas about the working relations among subjects with a shared objective or common goal. Consequently, anti-racist research requires a new paradigm shift away from colonial research to a genuine relational approach with local subjects to uncover power relationships in knowledge production, interrogation, validation, and dissemination. Genuine collaboration in anti-racist research means working on a shared, collective vision based on mutual trust and respect and meaningful dialogue among all partners. It is research that does not infantilize, patronize, or denigrate subjects. It affirms the knowledge base of the subjects of study as creators of knowledge and also as subjects that resist oppression. It also means working with the idea of multiple and collective origins, as well as collaborative dimensions of knowledge. This approach supports the idea that all parties involved can make substantive contributions to research (even if not necessarily as equal partners). All research participants bring strengths and potential contributions to the research process.

Anti-racist research begins with the researcher developing an understanding that personal characteristics influence the success of research and meaningful partnerships with subjects of study. The racial identity of the researcher and the subjects of study are important considerations in the process of knowledge production. Anti-racist research links the issue of identity to knowledge production. This suggests that who we are, our educational and personal histories and experiences, all shape how we make sense of our world and interpret social reality. Anti-racist research also proceeds with a persistence and commitment to working co-operatively. The nature of the research relationships among different parties is to admit to and work with tensions and trade-offs. Research also means engaging in the process of negotiation concerning research agendas, the facilitation of entry, design and implementation, evaluation of research data, and the dissemination and use of research information. Research involves the local participants giving the researcher the right to go into their communities with the responsibility to work collectively to produce knowledge that speaks to the complexities of the lived experiences of the subjects of study. Anti-racist research is meaningful if the objective and process of research lead to social transformation and there is genuine power sharing among various stakeholders.

Quite often it is asked, if something is *against* something, then what it is *for*? If anti-racism challenges and opposes any and all forms of racism, then what does it support? The question is somewhat misleading. For example, if one uses the metaphor of a virus operating throughout the entire life's blood of the body, replacing it (the virus) with something else does not necessarily do anything to bring the body's health back to equilibrium. Only the complete rejection of the virus and strengthening of the body will allow this to occur. We are not trying to replace one flawed system with another; we do not want to replace the virus with the flu. Anti-racism seeks to constantly ensure that the body politic remains vigilant against any and all forms of oppression, especially given the fact that racism is often just like a virus; it mutates and tries to re-enter the body when the immune system is weak. In this sense, anti-racism is for holistic interconnection among all forms of life. It follows the aboriginal proverb, "All things are connected," and suggests that we must respect and cherish this principle. We must not replace the hegemonic order with one that suffocates life and does not allow each of us to flourish in ways that we may not even be able to begin to imagine.

How can this be achieved? There must be recognition of the history and context that underpin the nature of research. For example, the history of the (mis)application of research findings; (non)recognition of the contributions of subjects; and the context of using research information for academic imperialism and domination have created mistrust on the part of local subjects with regard to institutional research. A hegemonic way of knowledge production that accords unquestioned ethnographic and discursive authority to the researcher has served to deny local intellectual agency and disempower local subjects. Anti-racist research, by resisting imposed and dominating knowledge, helps to challenge colonial and imperial relationships. By addressing the researcher's responsibility to the subjects and to the uses and applications of knowledge, anti-racist research shifts conventional research away from its parasitic nature. This form of research places an obligation on the part of the researcher to assist subjects in resisting colonizing relationships and subverting hegemonic ways of knowing. It interrogates positivists' accounts of what constitutes credible, authentic, valid, empirical knowledge. It poses questions about who is speaking, on what, and for whom. It raises questions about the social and political contexts of knowledge production, as well as the sources and uses of research data.

Anti-racist research assumes that there is institutional racism in mainstream social science research. This is evident in the topics of study; the concepts and methodologies that are privileged; who is allowed, legitimated, and validated to research what and how; and how existing structures allow for the production and dissemination of certain knowledges (see Smith, 1999). Much of social science research has been rooted in a historical legacy of institutional racism, which governs the work of the academy. Therefore, there needs to be an ethical code for researching race and social oppression, and local marginalized communities, a code that acknowledges the impact of racism on the theoretical and conceptual frameworks, epistemologies, and research methodologies employed in so-called "scientific" studies. Therefore, the ethics and key concepts underlying the aims and purposes of research, and the ethos, design, conduct, application, and dissemination of research knowledge should be guided by antiracist principles of multiple ways of knowing and the need to seek full representation and the inclusion of varied experiences.[1]

Anti-racist research is research explicitly committed to promoting anti-racism objectives, and particularly to challenging domination and power relationships in society through the promotion of social justice, equity, and fairness. Such research includes giving saliency and centrality to minoritized peoples' perspectives on the issues of race, social justice, and oppression. It is research that also challenges exploitative relationships and, in particular, the tendency for dominant research to pathologize, stereotype, label, and re-victimize marginalized peoples. Anti-racist research also recognizes the idea of interlocking oppressions, differential privileges, simultaneity of oppressions and privileges, and the imbrications of race, gender, sexuality, and class identities as evidence of the complexities of our lived experiences. Anti-racist research also brings to the fore the power relations that govern the social interactions of researchers and their subjects of study, as well as the differential validation of research knowledge emerging from dominant and minoritized scholars. The epistemic saliency of minoritized bodies is maintained in anti-racist research, which values the contribution of multiple perspectives. Anti-racist research also acknowledges and respects the rights of individuals and groups to withhold or withdraw information.

Anti-racist research deals with the questions of transparency and account-ability. It argues that what we do, as researchers must always be transparent to our subjects if we are to rebuild trust with communities. Furthermore, researchers must be held responsible for their actions by the communities they purport to study, as well as by the disciplines of their academic training. The issue of relevance is key in anti-racist research. Relevance is defined in the eyes of those researched, not in the eyes of the researcher and the funders of the research project. Relevance and responsibility must go hand in hand, meaning researchers have a responsibility not to place their subjects in any oppressive or dominating situations, or disseminate knowledge that could cause injury or undue harm to communities and social groups. Thus there are limits to academic freedom; rights must be matched with appropriate responsibilities.

Affirming an Epistemic Community

Anti-racist research supports the idea of an *epistemic community* that shares certain basic principles and underlying ideas about racism and its manifestation in society. It is generally felt that racism is endemic in all societies, and that the objective of social research is not to prove or disprove the existence of racism but, rather, to seek understanding of the nature, extent, and consequences of racism and the myriad ways racism and other oppressions play out in different historical and contemporary contexts. Anti-racist research also works with the notion of *community* in terms of how identities and experiences are both shared and collective. As argued elsewhere (Dei, 1999), it is fashionable today in critical scholarship to offer a lucid critique of the essentialist discourses that cultivate and promote community, emphasizing its (community's) homogenizing tendencies. Critical academic engagement requires that we begin talking about how difference both fractures and enhances the community's political agenda. It is important for academic and political work to avoid presenting communities as static, homogenous entities, particularly when this becomes a starting point for critique. As Price (1998) notes, the term *community* can refer to different conceptions of social identity. The term can operate or function as an enabler or a mobilizing force in the fight for social justice and the redistribution of power and material advantage.

There are, even in the community, complex processes through which racial, class, gender, and sexual ideologies are produced and sustained. Such ideologies are linked to material conditions in order to produce particular discursive effects. In social movement politics, a community can be a vehicle for perpetuating ideologies of race, class, gender, and sexuality. Given the great complexity of our world today, academic and discursive practices must be sophisticated enough to account for the tensions, contradictions, and structural ambiguities that pervade claims for particular identities. To claim community is to engage in a powerful linguistic, cultural, and discursive practice.

As Price (1998, 3–4) further states, we can speak of community in some multiple, nonexclusive combinations of: (1) "spatial community" in which boundaries (as spatial, localized settings) are defined for the pursuit of socially meaningful interactions; (2) "affective/relational community" in which community draws on some bonds of affinity (community becomes a mutually shared experience of the values, attitudes, beliefs, concerns, and aspirations of a collective); and (3) "moral community" as defined in meaningful participation and belonging in a citizenry to achieve common goals defined as the collective good. Within these various conceptions of community, the tensions, struggles, ambiguities, and contradictions are captured and articulated, and yet the integrity of a collective membership is maintained. As members of a community or communities, individuals have multiple, rather than single, affinities and allegiances resulting in profound complexities that defy/challenge easy categorizations and designations. Yet, each community also maintains and reinforces certain processes of inclusion/exclusion in order to ensure that identities and histories are not obliterated.

As community is not an undifferentiated category, so also is the local community faced with competing interests, oppressions, and marginalities. Fortunately, it is within communities that local knowledges are nurtured and made relevant for daily human survival. To survive is to co-exist with other peoples. Learning to exist collectively demands a conscious attempt to redress multiple forms of oppression as they play out within and among communities. An important question to ask is: How do colonial and imperial relationships, social alienation, and cultural ideology interface in contemporary human experience? As has already been pointed out, there are multidimensional experiences of identity and resistance to oppression and subordination. The powerful correlation among racial, class, gender, and sexual exploitation and oppression demand the adoption of a collective approach to understanding human subjectivities and social resistance. Subjective experiences of human struggles against oppression are not simply diverse, they are intertwined. While we move away from the homogenizing tendencies of race, class, and gender discourses, we must simultaneously acknowledge the larger global, structural, and historical forces that account for commonalities in human experience. To this end, we must reject the liberal notion of individuality and, as well, interrogate the problematic postmodernist take on the autonomous, differentiated subject.

The Pursuit of Anti-racist Research: Specific Methodological Approaches

Anti-racist research calls for the full and active involvement of the subjects of study in initiating, designing, implementing, and evaluating the research study. This is more than collaboration. It is an approach to research that relies heavily on local peoples identifying the major issues of research interest and working with others to ensure a degree of local community initiation, linkage, and support. Through a team approach, researchers and their subjects can identify the problems of investigation, design multiple research approaches, and implement and evaluate research strategies.

The various parties/partners must also find research to be relevant to their causes if research is to be truly anti-racist in the sense of subverting colonial and imperial relationships in knowledge production. In any scholarly research there is a need to formulate key ideas of investigation by carefully delineating the specific learning and research objectives with study participants. Let me illustrate this with the study previously mentioned involving school dropouts (see Dei, Holmes, Mazzuca, McIsaac, and Campbell, 1995; Dei, Mazzuca, McIsaac, and Zine, 1997). I use this case not to imply that our research followed a perfect anti-racist research methodological approach, but to highlight some of the approaches that may be involved in anti-racist research. These steps were not linear, and the negotiations actually strengthened the process. In hindsight there were many things we could have done differently; there were also moments of tension and frustration as in all research that purports to be collaborative (involving the subjects of study).

The process of formulating ideas for the study emerged after several steps, which included an understanding of the personal experiences/perspective of the researcher. First, as a parent with children in the school system, and having heard many children speak at public gatherings about their schooling experiences, I found my personal and experiential knowledge about youth and the challenges of schooling very useful. Second, as a member of a local community group, I repeatedly heard other parents express concern with the problem of disengagement of black youth in schools. My prior discussions with parents involved identifying which questions needed to be researched and answered. There were also consultations with other scholars. The concern and fascination with school dropouts is not new. It was therefore important to follow an initial process of consultation with local experts, parents, and members of local organizations, particularly the Organization of Parents of Black Children (OPBC) and other local black groups in the city of Toronto (e.g., the Ghanaian-Canadian Organization, GCO) to identify some schooling issues as understood by parents, guardians, and community workers. Third, a critical review of the existing literature was undertaken in order to flesh what exactly was being written on the topic of investigation, what were the strengths and gaps in the existing literature, and what would be a point of departure for a new study. Following these steps helped me to grasp the dilemma of school dropouts or appropriately 'push outs' and what explanations have been and can be offered to account for the problem. There was also participation in scholarly academic exchanges with academics and other researchers in the Ontario public school system, and conversations regarding possible research topics relating to the dilemma of premature departure from school were seen as crucial steps leading to the formulation and strengthening of my learning and research objectives.

The question raised in our study was whether researchers and subjects of study have a common and shared understanding of community. What does a researcher do when there are competing theoretical and ideological interests? For example, who gets to be represented in research? Whose stories get told? How does research reflect the idea of community as multiple interests and desires? Anti-racist research must work with a community of differences that ruptures any monolithic meaning of community. Anti-racist research must benefit the local community. We must sell the idea of research as contributing to the enrichment of human lives, which requires allowing local communities (e.g., schools) to have some control or ownership of the research process.

In educational research, an anti-racist approach may be to identify different stakeholders (e.g., university researchers, a family of schools, school board and other bodies in the local communities) to come together as a working committee/team with shared representation to identify and suggest possible research ideas; to conduct their own studies in selected schools; to advise on potential research applications; and/or to provide knowledge of research findings to subjects of study. Such an approach to research can be tension ridden, especially when groups do not share the same understanding, politics, and so forth.

One model of anti-racist research is to focus on domination studies. This challenges the traditional role of research to merely interpret, provide an understanding, or even reproduces the status quo/existing relationships of inequality and inequities. This model of research formulates questions with input from subjects of study in order to allow them to talk about their experiential knowledge on domination and subordination, and the specific ways they understand how marginality and domination are maintained.

Anti-racist research also borrows from the idea of participatory action research by putting the theory into practice. It is not simply about researching social practice with community workers. It is about having a critical gaze on research and its relevance for politics. Theorizing and researching anti-racism issues does not insure anti-racist work. Anti-racist research is action oriented in the sense that it is not reactive but proactive in addressing racism and social oppression. So in anti-racist research (and while studying these initiatives), teachers engaged in genuine anti-racism initiatives (e.g., exemplary practices of inclusive schooling, or working with community members with a known history of educational and political activism) will be identified, and researching such initiatives will offer ways to strengthen political practice.

Research should be designed in a way that demarcates responsibilities and boundaries for researcher and study participants. Demarcating areas and roles for research communities and subjects to play may include such methodological approaches as allowing schools, local communities, and study participants to develop their own research ideas, and to share in the research design, implementation, and evaluation of research. Sometimes this requires turning the research relationship upside down, which may not be the conventional academic research style. For example, in schooling research, this may involve allowing the local community to determine the important issues worthy of investigation from their own understandings; allowing students some control over the research process; sharing information on the research with students; and students sharing in research interpretations and findings.

Anti-racist research seeks to open new lines of communication among interested parties and stakeholders. Research could seek alternative lines for communicating research findings to subjects and communities as the research process unfolds. Research participants from diverse backgrounds and interests could discuss questions about developing and designing problems/issues of study and implementation of research. In anti-racist research in schools, there could be some periodic meetings and briefings that would give some degree of ownership of research information to schools and local communities. The idea of site-specific reports could be promoted in such research. For example, school principals and school boards could be encouraged to respond to specific identified problems. Research could identify specific bodies and individuals for accountability purposes. Roles could be defined collectively for schools and local communities. Anti-racist research can be geared toward training local subjects/communities in research methods and building capabilities for initiating and conducting social research on a local level. Many research communities seek partnerships and collaboration with researchers, but these communities also want to strengthen their capacity to conduct their own studies through a decolonized research model.

As already alluded to, there is a political dimension to anti-racist research. Such research should challenge the extent of intellectual aggression to which racially minoritized communities have been subjected. Anti-racist research should challenge the recolonization of the intellectual space of those racially minoritized. To decolonize conventional research, anti-racist research must begin to ask significant political, theoretical, epistemological, and methodological questions about whose interests continue to be served by social science research. As noted, Gandy (1998) speaks of an epistemic community, one that shares a common core of critique and believes in the possibility of transforming a racist society. This community can be a partnership of the researcher and the local community. The epistemic community must work politically to understand and disrupt the ways in which race determines the unfair and unequal distribution of life's chances and opportunities. Critical race and anti-racism research must be presented as a critique, subversion, and unravelling of conventional research paradigms as "ideologically determined and culturally biased production of knowledge" (Stanfield, 1995a, 4). The argument is that dominant methodologies and epistemologies are incapable (by design) of capturing the experiences of the oppressed, or of capturing oppressive relations and dynamics (Stanfield, 1995a; see also Gandy, 1998; Scheurich and Young, 1997). This is because uncritical epistemologies and methodologies deny oppression exists in the first place. If the politics of representation and identity is to continually assert the marginalized as knowing subjects, then it requires that the anti-racist researcher find ways to collaboratively work with local communities. But collaboration must extent beyond partnerships to sustain the capacity of local communities to undertake their own research.

It is important to note that the strategies and models of anti-racist research outlined in this collection of essays are not mutually exclusive. Their success requires individual (self) and group criticism and reflection on the part of researcher(s) and subjects/community partners. Local community involvement is key to successful anti-racist research, whether in schools, homes and families, workplaces, union halls, churches, or other institutional settings. *Involvement* is a meaningful word if it leads to power sharing among partners. Local communities are increasingly becoming sceptical of academic research for many reasons, including a disturbing history of defensiveness and resistance to knowledge sharing. There is the failure of some academic researchers to develop sensitivities to the context of data gathering. The sources and uses of data are not apolitical. The effects and consequences of conducting academic research within a colonial and imperial paradigm, which denies local subjects a role as active theorists and knowers, and powerful narrators of their own histories and stories, can be disempowering for many local subjects and minoritized groups. For subjects from minoritized groups, most academic research has not sufficiently dealt with problems of social injustice, power, and domination in society. Anti-racist research must overcome these problems in order to be truly transformative and/or subversive of the conventional ways of producing knowledge about ourselves.

Scope of Collection

The essays in this volume address pertinent conceptual and methodological issues in anti-racist research. While the authors grapple with a host of issues in these chapters, each is informed by certain central questions as ideas are presented on anti-racist research. The strength of this collection is that it moves away from a prescriptive discourse to practical and pragmatic engagement in anti-racist research, touching on philosophical, methodological, political, and ethical questions for critical researchers. The tone of the discussion as a whole focuses on the academy, and particularly social science research and knowledge production. Exploring questions around (Eurocentric, counter- and non-hegemonic) knowledge production in the academy, the emphasis is on the processes of producing, validating, and disseminating knowledges. The subject/object binary is problematized as well as the body/mind split and the challenge of body/mind/soul connections or interface with(in) history and context. Amar Wahab's paper, "Consuming Narratives: Questioning Authority and the Politics of Representation in Social Science Research" offers a critical discussion of knowledge production in research practice. The author problematizes some key assumptions of social science research, *ethnographic authority, discursive authority, interpretive authority, self-representation and authenticity, and authorial control* over knowledge and knowledge production. He notes that traditional social science research and anthropology engage in a process of authenticating knowledge through the production of credible discourses and bodies. This construction of authority is, however, built on the othering of cultures and racially different groups, yet masked within discourses of validity and reliability. Through an anti-racist discursive framework, Wahab critiques concepts of ethnographic authority, interpretive authority, and discursive authority to situate race and embodiment in all knowledge-production projects. A particular strength of the discussion is the author's interrogation of how race and the politics of difference in ethnography can be used to re-articulate representation toward the situated, emancipatory projects of anti-racist discourse. He argues that through a troubling of authority, anti-racist discourse also serves to unwork the narratives that have consumed other discourses and bodies to represent themselves as God figures, rather than historically and culturally specific processes of hegemony.

Beverly-Jean Daniel's chapter, "Researching African Canadian Women: Indigenous Knowledges and the Politics of Representation" examines the invisibility of African Canadian females in the texts and literature. The chapter is particularly useful in terms of the exposition of the avenues through which we can begin to re-search minoritized women's lives and experiences. The author highlights some of the problems inherent in applying Eurocentric research paradigms to researching non-white bodies. She further interrogates the ways in which indigenous knowledges can be used to develop and analyze research that serves to respect the lives and the voices of local subjects. The strength of the chapter lies in shedding some light on the role that research plays in the individual and collective representation of self and the implications of these representations for African Canadian women.

Building on such epistemological and ontological questions, Karen Max's chapter, "Anti-colonial Research: Working as an Ally with Aboriginal Peoples," utilizes the lens of anti-colonial research to center Aboriginal worldviews, and the discussion is couched in a sustained critique of hegemonic research practices. The author outlines several anti-colonial research projects initiated by Aboriginal peoples, while pinpointing the urgent need to challenge Eurocentric research paradigms. An important question raised by the discussion concerns the manner in which white researchers can begin to work as allies with non-white study subjects in the research process.

In what other disciplines/fields of study does the Eurocentric gaze offer problematic readings and meanings of social research? Louise Gormley's chapter, "Some Insights for Comparative Education Researchers from the Anti-racist Education Discourse on Epistemology, Ontology, and Axiology," explores the philosophy-inspired theories of epistemology, ontology, and axiology with a specific focus on how these terms have been recently defined by anti-racists. She contends that a deeper understanding of these concepts will help comparative researchers to interrogate the presence of epistemological racism in their research. Drawing in particular from the writings of Scheurich and Young (1997), Stanfield II (1994), and other related literature, the author suggests that comparativists consider two pertinent issues: (1) the importance of researching primary sources in native languages and (2) using a conceptual framework that reflects the philosophical ideals of the regions studied. Locating and challenging the negative views held by classmates, the discussion highlights the seemingly sparse contact between the fields of comparative and anti-racist education.

In order to address the challenge of anti-racist research, we need to fully understand how racism works in society. A critical exploration and accounting of racism in varied institutional settings can help uncover the pernicious nature of systemic racism. In Paula Butler's "Shattering the Comfort Zone: Ethical and Political Aspects of Anti-racism Research in Churches," she poses the question: What does it mean for a Protestant church to claim to be engaged in an "anti-racist transformation of itself and society?" The chapter argues that such anti-racism commitments are not truly credible without an examination of white supremacy in the church, and makes the case for an anti-racism research agenda that examines the precise nature of white supremacy in the church today. The chapter is informative in laying out how white identities are produced and how in particular the church participates in the production and maintenance of a white settler society. The discussion also explores the ethical and political issues involved in being a racially dominant person engaged in anti-racism research, and the sensitivities required in supporting the importance of research focused on the nature of white supremacy in the church. The theoretical strength of this chapter lies in the discussion of the nature and extent of racism in society and why anti-racist research action is needed. The paper presents the history of racism and shows the extent to which racism is viewed as a social and political problem. The discussion is grounded in the acknowledgment of the role of the nation-state involvement/response in controlling or mediating the problem of racism.

Renu Sharma's chapter, "Re-searching the Spiritual: Applying Soul to Research Practice," analyzes current issues about researching the topic of spirituality through an engagement with Eastern and Western notions of spirituality and how they manifest in school systems. In Sharma's analysis, prominence is placed on understanding dominant and mythologized notions of spirituality and how this affects political legitimacy and practices in schooling and educational initiatives. In this chapter, the issue of institutionalizing spirituality as a means of transcending a holistic approach for education is addressed, and emphasis is placed on approaching research as a spiritual practice and how this enhances the research experiences of both researchers and participants.

Zeenat Janmohamed's "Rethinking Anti-bias Approaches in Early Childhood Education: A Shift Toward Anti-racism Education" considers the limited discussion on the existence of racism, homophobia, and class issues in curriculum content and textbook materials for early childhood education students. The author points out that students receive training in the limited form of anti-bias education that prepares them for establishing programs rich in cultural tourism, without extensive discussion or recognition of the significance of dominant relationships that are inherent to racism, homophobia, and class issues. By critiquing key teaching sources in the Early Childhood Program at a local college, the author raises the challenges faced by instructors in community college settings working with a complex population of students. In the end, she calls for a shift from anti-bias to anti-racist strategies in early childhood education.

Nuzhat Amin explores the challenges of conducting anti-racist feminist research in applied linguistics in her paper entitled, "Voices of Minority Immigrant Women: Language, Race, and Anti-racist Feminist Methodologies." She notes that applied linguistics is a field dominated by colonial discourses that promote white speakers of English from the predominantly English-speaking countries of the First World as legitimate speakers of English and construct non-white speakers of English from the Third World as speaking non-standard English with a non-standard accent. She argues that First World linguists are perpetuating a caste system among speakers of English based on accent, race, ethnicity, and national origin. Locating herself as an ethnic Pakistani middle-class woman with high investments in English, Amin describes her study of minority immigrant women who teach English as a second language to adult immigrants in Toronto. She grounds this study in the three ideologically similar research traditions of feminist ethnography, critical ethnography, and anti-racist ethnography, and discusses the methodological concerns that arose for her while she was conducting her study. She concludes by discussing the implications of her study for applied linguists, minority teachers, and anti-racist researchers.

The issue of social difference is central to anti-racism research. In line with the concept and understanding of *integrative anti-racism* (Dei, 1996) (how race, gender, class, and sexuality intersect through the saliency of race), Judy Hughes's chapter "Analyzing Women's Experiences: Race, Social Difference, and Violence against Women" offers a critical engagement with the complexities of race and social difference. She sees the understanding of social difference as a powerful means to disrupt, denaturalize, and ultimately change dominant discourses, practices, and structures. However, she carefully notes that invoking difference in anti-racist research requires consideration not only of the possibilities, but also delineation of the contradictions. The tensions and contradictions for dominant white researchers in studying race and difference demands some recognition of how social privilege locates dominant researchers in relationships of domination and subordination to research participants from minoritized groups. The discussion is located in understanding women's experiences through a feminist, anti-imperialist framework, and how differences among women create and shape experiences of violence and abuse. The author suggests that connection of women's experiences of violence and oppression to the social relations of dominance and subordination demonstrates how the severity and consequences of oppressions are different for different individuals and groups. In conclusion, Hughes calls for creative linkages between oppressions in order to create common ground to work toward social change. The chapter offers a reading of race and the multiplicity of oppressions through the lens of race—the saliency of race—and highlights the contextual and situational variations in intensities of oppression and draws out the implications for critical research.

What are the specific anti-racist research methods to be employed in educational research? Samina Jamal's chapter, "Critical Ethnography: An Effective Way to Conduct Anti-racism Research," undertakes a general discussion of research methods highlighting the distinctiveness of anti-racist research methods. The chapter interrogates the use of quantitative and qualitative approaches, emphasizing the "whats" and "whys" of qualitative approaches, and provides specific examples of studies that require such methods. There are significant epistemological and axiological questions of anti-racist research methodology. Jamal views methodology as the philosophy of method. The chapter is situated in a theoretical discussion of some key theoretical, epistemological, ontological, and axiological questions. On the specific political and ethical questions of research, Jamal raises issues about who, for whom, why, and what and the consequences and implications of research are for subjects, researchers, the academy, and other communities. The chapter also deals with the emotions of knowing and the power of not knowing, highlighting pertinent ethical and moral issues.

Andrew Okolie's chapter, "Toward an Anti-racist Research Framework: The Case for Interventive In-depth Interviewing," in many ways highlights the importance of positionality in anti-racist research. The key question explored concerns the meaning of subject position[ality] for social science and, specifically, anti-racist research. This paper makes important connections by contextualizing anti-racist research in other critical research agendas for social and educational transformation. It is important for critical research to build bridges by asking such questions as what kind of research will promote transformation? For example, the challenges of anti-racist research for social workers, educationists, practitioners, policy makers that will help us transform our collective existence. By drawing out connecting links, as well as the points of divergence between anti-racism and feminist research or anti-racism and participatory action research, we begin to learn about the similarities and the particularities of scholarly research.

Gurpreet Singh Johal's chapter, "Order in K.O.S.: On Race, Rage, and Method," ends the collection by pointing to new directions and questions for anti-racist research. The academic and political project of examining these new directions is imperative if we are to make anti-racist research meaningful. Part of the future challenge for anti-racist workers is collaborating with subjects in knowledge production and strengthening the capacity of local communities to undertake their own research. The goal should be anti-racist researching with, and not for or about, peoples. Such an approach and methodological perspectives help us to rupture colonial and imperial knowledges through anti-colonial approaches to research.

Traditional social science research has long worked with certain key concepts and ideas. The collection of essays presented here allow us to examine how anti-racist research can borrow some of these concepts and yet rework them in a way that addresses the main issues of anti-racism. In other words, how does anti-racist research move away from the conventional meanings attached to such words as validity, reliability, trustworthiness, credibility, confidentiality, anonymity, risks, and generalizability? How do we allow anti-positivist research to challenge positivist research through critical anti-racist scholarship (see also Twine and Warren, 2000)? There are crucial issues in minority schooling and educational research. This is one area that anti-racism can boast of critical scholarships attainment based on sound research. Of course, those who deny racism in society would see any research about racism in schools as unsound and not based on hard evidence. This book highlights the challenges, possibilities, and limitations of researching racism in institutional settings, and provides us with lessons on how research shapes or can shape anti-racist practice in schools and other institutional settings.

NOTE

1. See "An Ethical Code for Researching 'Race,' Racism & Anti-Racism in Scotland." Internet source: *http://www.sabre.ukgo.com/code.html*.

REFERENCES

Borland, K. 1991. "That's Not What I Said": Interpretive Conflict in Oral Narrative Research." In. Gluck, S. B., and D. Patai (Eds.), *Women's Words*. New York: Routledge, pp. 63–75.

Bramble, M. 2000. "The Natives Have Become Their Own Researchers." Essay for graduate course: SES1952: 'Indigenous Knowledges and Decolonization: Pedagogical Implications.' Ontario Institute for Studies in Education of the University of Toronto (OISE/UT). Spring, 2000.

Brewer, R. 1993. "Theorizing Race, Gender and Class: The New Black Feminist Scholarship." In James and Busia (Eds.), *Theorizing Black Feminisms*. New York: Routledge.

Bulmer, Martin and John Solomos, (eds.). 2004. *Researching Race and Racism*. London: Routledge.

Cruikshank, J. 1992. "Oral Tradition and Material Culture: Multiplying Meanings of 'Words' and 'Things.'" *Anthropology Today* 8 (3): 5–9.

Dei, G. J. S. James-Wilson, S., and Zine, J. 2002. *Inclusive Schooling. A Teacher's Companion to Removing the Margins*. Toronto, Canadian Scholars' Press.

Dei, G. J. S. 2001. "Rescuing Theory: Anti-Racism and Inclusive Education and the Lessons for the Educational Practitioner." *Race, Gender and Class Studies* 8 (1): 139–161.

Dei, G. J. S. 2000. "Rethinking the Role of Indigenous Knowledges in the Academy." *International Journal of Inclusive Education* 4 (2): 111–132.

Dei, G. J. S. 1999. "Why Write 'Black?': Reclaiming African Cultural Resources Knowledges in Diasporic Contexts." *Journal of Education* 23 (2): 200–208.

Dei, G. J. S. 1996. *Anti-Racism Education: Theory and Practice*. Halifax: Fernwood Publishers.

Dei, G. J. S., and Ashgharzadeh, A. 2001. The Power of Social Theory: Towards an Anti-Colonial Discursive Framework. *Journal of Education Thought* 35 (3): 297–323.

Dei, G. J. S., and Calliste, A. 2000. *Power, Knowledge and Anti-Racist Education: A Critical Readers*. Halifax, Fernwood Publishing.

Dei, G. J. S., Holmes, L., Mazzuca, J., McIsaac, E., and Campbell, R. 1995. "Drop Out or Push Out? The Dynamics of Black Students' Disengagement from School Report." Submitted to the Ontario Ministry of Education and Training, Toronto.

Dei, G. J. S., Mazzuca, J., McIsaac, E., and Zine, J. 1997. *Reconstructing "Dropout": A Critical Ethnography of the Dynamics of Black Students' Disengagement from School*. Toronto: University of Toronto Press.

Fine, M. 1994a. "Dis-stance and Other Stances: Negotiations of Power Inside Feminist Research." In. A. Gitlin (Ed.). *Power and Method: Political Activism and Educational Research*. New York: Routledge, pp. 13–35.

Fine, M. 1994b. "Working the Hyphens: Reinventing Self and Other in Qualitative Research." In N. K. Denzin and Y. S. Lincoln (Eds.), *Handbook of Qualitative Research*. Thousand Oaks, CA: Sage, pp. 70–82.

Foster, M. 1994. "The Power to Know One Thing Is Never the Power to Know All Things: Methodological Notes on Two Studies of Black American Teachers." In A. Gitlin (Ed.) *Power and Method: Political Activism and Educational Research*. New York: Routledge, pp. 129–146.

Gandy, O. H. 1998. *Communication and race: A structural perspective*. New York, Oxford: Arnold.

Hatcher, R. 1998. Social Justice and the Politics of School Effectiveness and Improvement. *Race, Ethnicity and Education*, 1 (2): 267–289.

Lee, E. 1985. *Letters to Marcia: A Teacher's Guide to Anti-Racist Education*. Toronto: Cross-Cultural Communication Centre.

Lee, E. 1991. "An interview with Educator Enid Lee. Taking Multicultural Education seriously" Rethinking Schools vol.6. No. 1. (Oct.-Nov.).

Price, E. 1993. "Multiculturalism: A Critique." Unpublished Paper, Department of Sociology and Equity Studies in Education, OISE, University of Toronto.

Price, E. 1998. "First Thoughts Toward a Thesis Proposal." Unpublished paper, Department of Sociology and Equity Studies in Education, OISE, University of Toronto.

Ropers-Huilman, B. and B. Grane. 1999. "Stumbling Toward Knowledge: Enacting and Embodying Qualitative Research". In. C. A. Grant (ed). *Multicultural Research: A Reflective Engagement with Race, Gender, Class and Sexual Orientation*. Philadelphia: Farmer Press. pp. 228–239.

Scheurich, J., and Young, M. 1997. "Coloring Epistemologies: Are Our Research Epistemologies Racially Biased?" *Educational Researcher* 26(4): 4–16.

Smith, L. T. 1999. *Decolonizing Methodologies: Research & Indigenous Peoples.* New York: Zed Books.

Stanfield, J. H. 1994. "Ethnic Modeling in Qualitative Research." In N. K. Denzin and Y. S. Lincoln (Eds.). *Handbook of Qualitative Inquiry* Newbury Park, CA. Sage, pp. 175–188.

Stanfield, J. H. 1995a. "Methodological Reflections." In J. H. Stanfield and R. M. Dennis (Eds.). *Race and Ethnicity in Research Methods.* Thousand Oaks, CA: Sage Publications, pp. 3–15.

Stanfield, J. H. 1995b. "Epistemological Considerations." In J. H. Stanfield and R. M. Dennis (Eds.). *Race and Ethnicity in Research Methods.* Thousand Oaks, CA: Sage Publications, pp. 16–36.

Thomas, B. 1984. "Principles of Anti-Racist Education." *Currents* 2(2): 20–24.

Twine, F. W., and Warren, J. W. 2000. (Eds.). *Racing Research, Researching Race: Methodological Dilemmas in Critical Race Studies.* New York: New York University Press.

Walcott, R. 1990. "Theorising Anti-Racist Education." *Western Canadian Anthropologist* 7(2): 109–120.

Chapter Two

AMAR WAHAB

Consuming Narratives

QUESTIONING AUTHORITY AND THE POLITICS OF REPRESENTATION IN SOCIAL SCIENCE RESEARCH

European and American anthropology . . . that cultural practice and intellectual activity carry, as a major constitutive element, an unequal relationship of force between the outside Western ethnographer-observer and the primitive, or at least different, but certainly weaker and less developed non-European, non-Western person.

—Said (1994)

The site of Whiteness is a site where privilege and domination seem normal, its structures invisible and its underpinnings and practices unmarked and unnamed.

—Arber (2000)

Power does not enter the anthropological picture only at the moment of representation, for the cultural distinctiveness that the anthropologist attempts has always already been produced within a field of power relations.

—Gupta and Ferguson (1992)

Introduction

A few years ago I was employed by an academic institution to conduct an ethnographic study of a community in Trinidad and Tobago. Apparently, part of the reason I was chosen was because I, like the community, was also Indo-Trinidadian. It was felt that I would be able to "gain access" without many problems and get to the real issues of people's lives. Once in the field, other issues, particularly class and spatiality became barriers to informant access and information gathering. However, the community spoke so generously about a previous white researcher from the United States who conducted research in the community. They helped him out without any suspicion and volunteered whatever information he required. Although at the time ethnography in the epistemological sense did not register as an ethically culpable and fraught process, I remember asking myself what this white male researcher represented to the people to "get access to all this information and entry," whereas the research process had to be so cautiously negotiated between the community, my colleague (an Indo-Trinidadian female), and myself (an Indo-Trinidadian male).

What remained normalized in the process and my readings of it post-experience was the normalcy of white, male, academic, Northern entitlement to the field/bodies/communities of the non-white, historically colonized South. Strongly woven into the white ethnographer's craft of telling seemed to be a sensibility that canonized representations of the people, the resources, the place, the community, and off course, the culture. My reading of this experience was that racialized difference is constructive of a systematic differentiation in credibility and authority/authenticity.

Particular canonized notions of reliability (replicability) and validity (accuracy) (LeCompte and Goetz, 1982), the main tenets of authority accepted in mainstream academia underpin the theory and praxis of similar scientific research. Although ethnographic research remains suspect by more positivist schools of inquiry regarding its replicability (LeCompte and Goetz, 1982), its construction of validity (i.e., "I was there so it is real"), has been a marker for establishing authenticity. Yet, from the above example it is evident that the notion of validity is not a static, unraced, unembodied one, but more a production of social reality based on culturalized, embodied constructions of representations of the field. Representation is, therefore, a political act that is historically contextualized and that is implicated by intersecting notions of race, gender, sexuality, place, and so forth, yet remains situated and contingent on particular material and imaginative boundaries.

In the opening case, a political economy of representation illustrates the importance of racialized constructions of authenticity, entitlement, and author/scribe in hegemonic performances of knowledge production. Social science research, like all forms of textual representation, is such a performance-situated, negotiated, and representative of particular gazes. Even so, the textual performances of the mainstream academy retain an emphasis on convincing itself and multiple audiences that the gaze of the text/author is universal, unsituated, neutral, ahistorical, acultural, and an unquestionable production.

In doing so, the academy builds on the constructed credibility of authors and discourses to establish itself as an intellectual fortress with the right and might of determining knowledge, the knower, and the known.

The construction of authority and bodies of authority has been a central part of the project of positivist social science research, in which a neutral observer separates him/herself from the object being researched to produce as objective a gaze/performance as possible (Fine 1994a; Narayan, 1993). Vidich and Lyman (1994, 23) state that a detachment between self and others has been important to authenticating qualitative ethnographic social research. This is what Haraway (1988) terms the "God-trick," the performance of seeing everywhere but from nowhere at once.

Although this sentiment (universalized as "fact") has performed in different social science disciplines in different ways (for example, in anthropology it is the assumption that the object possesses some intrinsic, unnegotiated essence, devoid of inter-subjective meaning), contemporary methodologies, particularly regarding critical and deconstructive research, highlight research as an inter-subjective process. The research is textualized by a landscape of power relations (mapping politics, interests, and desires), negotiated, contested, and politically situated. Within this epistemological turn, the concept, figures, and figurations of authority become destabilized and questionable. In the ambit of anti-racist studies, this articulation performs a crucial role in exposing the racialized politics of representation that has historically produced categories of "Other and Othering" performances.

In this chapter, I attempt to discuss the various forms of authority and their enabling or sanctioning of racist performances, not to dispense with the notion of authority, but to contest those that have been embraced by social sciences. The goal is to offer spaces to bodies and discourses that have been "Othered," minoritized, and ghettoized on the "standard" hegemonic maps of knowledge to challenge and change the landscape of power relations that overdetermine our representation. Since this conversation is working within an anti-racist discursive framework, a discussion of the latter is essential to the journey of this paper. Some of the questions that I believe provide crucial discursive junctures are: How do authorities/validities produce and perform maps of inclusion/exclusion and create categories of "Other"? Is authority/the authoritarian politically and socially vested? How does epistemological authority exclude on the basis of race, gender, class, sexuality, and other social constructs? What dilemmas emerge out of authorial performances for the subject/object? What are the roles of (un)marked bodies in racializing the performance of authority? And finally, (how) can anti-racist epistemology be used to implode/contest the hegemony of racialized authority?

What Do I Mean by Anti-racist Discourse?

Difference is not merely something oppositional, a series of dualisms reflecting margin and centre, but something that is never finished, something, which is always deferred. What is Us and what is different becomes distorted in a doubling where there is always a trace, an unfolding, an over or underdetermined something left over.

—Clifford (1983)

Theorizing race and racism should focus on both the acknowledgement and celebration of difference, as well as on the methods of collective political organizing (resistance) to over-turn the economic, political and social marginality of all subordinate peoples.

—Dei (1999)

Although issues of race and of anti-racist studies continue to be challenged by Eurocentric positivist/postmodern social science, and by even those articulating anti-Otherizing discourses, in different ways and for different political projects, anti-racist discourse constitutes a particular epistemological project, rife with agency and complexity (Troyna and Carrington, 1989).

Race and other markers of social construction are also embedded and implicate particular (readings of) histories, determining the contexts in which they are evoked. The goal of anti-racist research as I see it, is therefore to critically engage structures and practices of racialized domination, to expose their hegemonies and transform political economies in ways in which minoritized and "Othered" bodies and discourses exert greater autonomy in self-determination and relational/representational politics. In so defining, it is also meant to subvert conventional research, which is ideologically driven and culturally specific, yet presented as universal, neutral, and objective. Moreover, there is an emphasis on decolonizing representations and strategically invoking racialized difference to rupture and manoeuvre political economies of representation.

Anti-racist research is interested/vested in asking significant/critical political, epistemological, theoretical, and methodological questions about whose interests continue to be served by social science research (Scheurich and Young, 1997). It also affords minoritized bodies possibilities for narrating, naming our oppressions and strategies of resistance/survival. It is therefore an explicitly, unapologetically political project. In so being, it bears the stigma of ghettoized discourses, similar to feminism and anti-colonialism, relegated to the margins of mainstream "objective" liberal academic mega-projects. Troyna (1995) posits that the debate centers on the partisanship of the discourse, which can be interpreted as either "informing legitimately" or "corrupting or invalidating." Writing about critical race theory, Ladson-Billings (1998) asks the question: "just what is critical race theory and what's it doing in a *nice* field like education?" to underscore the degree to which the discourse bears the weight of contestation.

Experience is given value in this discursive terrain, recognizing that it is valid but contestable and needs to be linked to the larger macro-political structures in society, although advocates of post-structuralism may want to contend that structures are themselves fluid and instead flows and fluxes that change the landscape of contestation and readings of experience. Anti-racist research, by no means monolithic in its theoretical, epistemological, and methodological reach, views the researcher as occupying particular subject positions (Dei, 1999; Troyna, 1995) and engaged in research as a learner and change agent. At the same time there is contention as to whether race or culture are undergoing transformation in the process of research, especially when all subjects (researcher and researched) are multiple in positioning and voice. Re-articulating social science research as an anti-racist project means questioning the authority, a myth that traditional research has institutionalized, of the researcher as objective cartographer of knowledge and of the existence of an incontestable, unpositioned truth.

Yet, it is unclear how positioning can enact or facilitate the transformation of authority, and even more, the political economy of knowledge and praxis that cartographic research has entrenched. With this questioning of authority comes an implicit burden of taking responsibility for textual representations, despite anti-racist discourses' resonance with postmodern notions of fluidly and solidly situated bodies and discourses.

Crucial to the ability of anti-racist research to enact its own project are challenges to universal claims to voice and theory to suggest that discourses are situational and contextual and that the multivocality of subjects predispose multiple positionings. Working differently from neo-liberal sentiments within the folds of postmodern discourse, anti-racism probes whether the racialized inter-subjective space of research is always or can even be one of "negotiation," and the many ways that written text is racially coded.

Although very often uncontested, anti-racist research, like other discourses at the margins, is burdened with the responsibility of dealing with competing claims to truth (Troyna, 1995). It implies risk for both researchers and researched (Dei, 1999) as their knowledge projects bear consequences for each other. Often, voices of the minoritized, intended to rupture/interrogate processes and structures of domination remain ghettoized by a vortex of white academy insisting on having a conversation with itself. In other words, the academy grants token space-inclusionary sites to anti-racist discourse that dispenses with its complicity in imperial discourse. Dei (1999) states that racism, patriarchy, heterosexism, and classism perpetuate selective readings of the histories, cultures, and knowledges of minoritized groups, justifying the colonial and imperialist gazes of academia. Anti-racist research must therefore be cognizant of the interlocking nature of oppressions.

Some of the key questions of anti-racist research are: Whose voices and narratives are highlighted and what political projects do they anchor and promote? How is the relevance of the study defined? Whose interests are being served by the project? What are the researcher's responsibilities to other research participants? Should the anti-racist researcher be able to locate and make explicit a commitment to emancipatory politics? Liberatory goals of this research emerge in the context of recognition of inequities in the current social system, the importance of addressing moral issues, unprecedented global and transnational changes, and the problematic call to separate theoretical from practical.

Yet, does anti-racist research create new epistemologies in light of a continuity of contestations and ambivalences? These questions may seem necessary to investigate anti-racist research as a particular methodology, but at the same time they can be read as imperialist, in that they suggest a responsibility for bringing an "end to ethics," a place of safety, where no risks are impinging.

Punch (1994, 86) articulates that the "politics of research" is shaped by researcher positionality, geographic proximity, nature of the research object, the researcher's institutional background, gatekeepers, status of field workers, expectations in research teams, social and moral obligations, and other factors affecting research in the field. It is within the latter category that race and gender are marked as "closing certain avenues for inquiry, while opening others." Yet, what is popularly evident from articles on methodology and qualitative research is the absence of, or token homage to, race as implicated in the systematic coding of authority. Some of the ways in which authority is constructed in the production of knowledge will now be expanded on and critiqued to offer a more liberatory consciousness for anti-racist research.

Before I unpack some of the instrumentation of authority, I think it is important to engage in my own subjective positioning and some of my academic politics that metaphorically inscribe the thoughts in this paper. Race and anti-racism, as discursive and material realities for me, connote a very complex set of evocations, nuances, juxtapositions, and contestations. I am an Indo-Trinidadian male who recently immigrated to North America, and who has suddenly been faced with a crisis of reinterpreting categories of race, place, nation, gender, and so forth in a complex form different from the ways I interpreted them in Trinidad.

Having to subscribe to a "visible minority" and "people of color" politics, in a nation that naturalizes whiteness and Otherness (non-whiteness), has challenged me to search for and analyze a diverse spectrum of discourses that offer alternatives for re-imagining a survival politics to contest, talk back, and sometimes just plain evade the risk of violence inherent in the processes of reaffirming the nation as a white nation. At the same time, racialized representations have presented a chaotic stage on which I look south Asian, a term I never associated myself with in Trinidad, but perform as Caribbean. My body is a confusing marker of placelessness, yet, an embedded one in its racialized presence. At this early stage of immigrancy, I am not sure where/which is my community (apparently all minorities are supposed to have a particular one). I am writing therefore from a sort of border/transitional zone, a raging delta of racialized transnationalized currents in which there is push and pull from many directions.

Having said this, I share with minoritized communities a continuity of historical Othering of body, nation, place, and culture. I ascribe to a re-reading of history that is aimed at de-colonizing and subverting racialized hegemonic texts to re-ground for a strategic play of post-colonial, anti-colonial, postmodern, indigenous, and anti-racist politics. One of the stages on which I do such is in academia, a "thick" institution heavily complicit in the manufacture of colonial fantasies that have impressed racialized imaginations of "Self-Other" in knowledge production.

Academia and white expansionism have historically appropriated and bullied their right to name on "Othered" peoples through writing the representational hegemony. However, I prefer to work this hegemony against itself, to produce a metaphor for implosion, to invoke and convert structure into flow and interruption. I understand that there is a risk of conversing this way, of entrenching myself in the machine of discourse with the dominant tropes of authority. Yet, based on the positioning stated above, can I claim an absolutist organicism or afford to risk the consequences of blindness to difference and political economies?

I cannot afford to apologize for what may at times be perceived as an essentialist stance on body politics in which I believe that the presence and performances of racialized bodies produce racialized subjectivities that are constituted in the power plays of representational politics. I do invoke a strategic essentialism as a way of de-naturalizing the normalcy of white hegemonic discourse. In so saying, dominant white bodies always come into question regarding the suspicioning of authority and a discursive gaze on the politics of representation. This, because the history of intellectual production as it is trademarked by the academy, is a selective history in which white bodies have retained privilege to discipline and have entrenched a genealogy of de-racing knowledge production. I also believe that the presence of our racialized bodies operates with distinctly different but related ideological and material circumstances from our performances.

Racialized presence is a very important metaphor for deconstruction because it invites a conversation (not necessarily a negotiation) about the risks on both sides of the inter-subjective fence. I understand white researchers' claims that, an anti-essentialist perspective is more open to the intersections of gender, class, and so forth, but I also think that these other social categories become strategically foregrounded in white-washed political projects that stymie the saliency of race in the socio-historical construction of realities, and instead present a pluralist mindscape in which to hide racialized individual guilt. As a researcher, I do believe that my work must be caring and considerate, but not at the risk of historical insensitivity or erasure, and definitely not at the cost of the politics, interests, and desires of those of us on the margins.

Yet, I must admit that it is a really tiresome dance to work within anti-racism because it has so far been a discussion of subverting racialized hegemony, and this has meant subversion of white Euro-American universalizing narratives of truth. Anti-racism research and discourse have not yet become sites for interrogating the racialized differences within the margins, to rupture the power relations that exist among "people of color." Nor have they engaged in a conversation as such in the absence of an imperializing gaze that essentializes these differences into the straitjacket of culture "they are like that, that is their culture." I also say this because I wonder how anti-racism can work in the context of Trinidad, where the concept of ethnicity is more current as difference is invoked within the borders of the nation. Yet by positioning nation within the context of globalization and historical construction, anti-racism offers more possibility for analysis. Authority and representation form and reform in the political market of intellectual capital flows, a market that has existed and been entrenched in colonial expansionism. My taking up of these central figurations in knowledge production is therefore an imperative that is as much informed by my subjective (juxta)positioning and politics of questioning and renaming as it is an interruption of the flow of knowing.

Ethnographic Authority and the Anthropological Imagination

Historically, photographic images of black people all over the world have been captured by intrepid white photographers looking for the 'exotic,' the 'different,' the 'anthropological native types,' for 'local colour'creating myths, fictions and fantasies which have in turn shaped the nature of encounters between contemporary black and migrant settlers and the predominantly white populace of the metropolis.

—Parmar (1990)

What are the political considerations of particular bodies translating for and across cultures? Early ethnography grew out of the West's preoccupation with "less civilized/primitive cultures" that were thought to be reflective of earlier segments in the West's evolution (Vidich and Lyman, 1994, 25). Clifford (1983) casts his discussion/deconstruction of ethnography theory in a specific historicity of the making of authority (the knower) in European and American academic traditions namely anthropology. He claims that participant observation constructed the authority subject through the merging of the fieldworker and expert anthropologist subjectivities in the academy between 1900 and 1960. Like a vortex of interpretation, anthropology has evolved its claim to fuse the narrator and audience. Clifford expresses this sentiment as "you are there because I was there," as a means of coercing the audience/reader into sharing a standpoint with the lens of the ethnographer.

This technology, although indispensable, has worked to establish validity and authority in the theory, epistemology, and methodology of the author's gaze. In addition, it vests the body of the ethnographer with the power to know and determine the existence of the subject. Yet, Clifford (1983) reads this process as the ethnographer engaged in a complex hegemonic process of composing a particular fragment of reality for the "Other" a translation of the real. Edward Said in *Orientalism* (1979, 55) described this process as a poetic in the following quote: "For there is no doubt that imaginative geography and history help the mind to intensify its own sense of itself by dramatizing the distance and difference between what is close to it and what is far away."

In this process, ethnography vests the racialized "Other" with *culture*, which becomes a metonym for race. Invoking ethnographic authority therefore requires a de-racing of societies and their histories. Culture becomes a glaring metaphor for the erasure of racialized difference, while at the same time invokes race most pronouncedly and violently. In the field of development studies, this has been heavily institutionalized in the gaze of the white ethnographer/anthropologist turned development expert as a narrative of fictional maps that seek to frame, construct, cast, determine (I read these performances as "consuming") the subject of research with culture, implicating "Self-Other" assumptions of race, nation, gender, sexuality, and so forth. In many ways, the development industry is rife with conflations of these discourses, contingent on the power of international development organizations in the north to narrate the fictions, which it performs as universal fact. Clifford (1983) for example, locates this problematic in the discourse of cross-cultural representation. However, the dialectical scripting of authority (subject) and known (object) can also be differently read to encompass the politics of representing difference, recognizing that neither difference nor representation are fixed. In fact, what traditional ethnography has done is to create a legacy of indifference to the violence of constituting difference as "Other" as native and the self as civilized.

Ethnographic authority includes elements such as physically and culturally locating oneself in the locale of the research subject for an extended period
of time, acquiring and utilizing the language of the subject so as to gain
insight into the native processes, capturing their essence and producing an interpretation that is as close as possible to the real thing. This has been the pre-
occupation of the ethnographer: to produce factual, native, objective
cartographic mappings of "Other" cultures. The perceived professionalization
of the ethnographer as fieldworker and theorist allows for an authority designed
and vested by a particular culture of academia, as universal and therefore real.
Clifford states that the purpose of this authority is to "convince the audience
of readers that the facts were objectively acquired, not subjective creations."
Michelle Fine (1994b) writes about this process as ventriloquy, as dis-stance,
where the researcher retains the authority to narrate and speak for the "Other."
Van Mannen (1988) sees this dynamic in what he labels the "realist tale" in
which the words of the researched are taken/usurped by the god-like
researcher, without subject complicity, to author the research su(o)bject, which
Fine (1994b) interprets as a "romantic decoy." Authority therefore evacuates
a particular interpretation of its culpable subjectivity. Crapanzano (1986), on
the anthropologist's constructions of a substantialized authority says that, "it
represents a sort of asymmetrical we-relationship with the anthropologist
behind and above the native, hidden but at the top of the hierarchy of understanding." Even further, ethnographic authority operates as a powerful strategy and a "meta-tenet" of Western civilization's reification of its civil self
(ignoble, different, "Other").

In this tradition the praxis and the institutionalization of anthropology by
white experts has required non-white, non-Western su(o)bjects to map, enculture, know. Race as a constituting reality has been (un)marked in the making of this authority because legitimacy is based on attempts to "bracket out
the subjective" an invisible voice of authority (Crapanzano, 1986). It is by
speaking on behalf of bodies and societies of color that white researchers have
not only produced a hegemonic authority, but also advanced their professional careers. This is not to say that their work is not useful, but to deconstruct
the very underlying processes of racialized power relations that continue to
organize the political economy of knowledge in contemporary academia. I want
to argue that the process of making authority through a dialectical process of
authorizing/Othering has been a racialized project in which culture becomes
the textual marker and blinder of racial difference.

In Clifford Geertz's (1973, 9) naming of ethnography as "thick description" relating to an interpretive theory of culture, he articulates that anthropological writings are "our own constructions of other people's constructions,"

which through writing inscribe social discourse. Invoking the metaphor of the "invisible hand," I read the inscription of ethnographic authority as a sort of "ghost play." Rabinow (1986, 244) also recognizes the paradoxical strategy of naturalizing authority in which the ethnographer claims a unique authority through experience while at the same time vanishes from the text (discursively and dialogically). Rosaldo (1986, 81) posits that ethnographic authority is buttressed by novelistic realism (testimonies with titles, names, places, dates, etc.) and using Michel Foucault, Rosaldo claims that "the narrator invokes the will to truth in order to suppress the document's equally present will to power."

I believe that various racialized notions of bodies and their representations act as figurations in determining how the ethnographer manufactures consent and a runaway sense of entitlement to the lived/interpreted reality of another culture, in other words, a connived border diplomacy in representation. The object of this perceived entitlement is to study a different culture as opposed to another race. In so doing, unquestioned representation freezes the interpretation of context; canonizes, privileges, and universalizes selective readings of history; and reifies a panoptical heritage that relies on racial hegemony. This hegemony erases its written representation as a means of denying its responsibility and culpability in globalizing knowledge production. Unworking the silent hyphen in ethnographic research, the metaphor can be turned upon itself to name ethnographic authority as a fossilized authority. Why have white anthropologists authority figures such as James Clifford, Clifford Geertz, Paul Rabinow, Margaret Mead, Mary Louise Pratt, Edward Evans-Pritchard, and Bronislaw Malinowski, et al., who have made the study of other cultures their mainstream activity practiced this view outwardly? How has it afforded a representation of the body of ethnography as a sort of constituted, entitled, and omniscient subject, and how has this authorial subject been central to the Euro-American charts of civilization?

Gupta and Ferguson (1992) and Appadurai (1988) widened the critique of ethnographic authority to invoke space as a powerful textual and material metaphor for institutionalizing power relations. The authority of the ethnographer relies on the encultured capability to naturalize cultural and spatial divisions to contribute toward what Gupta and Ferguson (1992, 16) (extracting from Appadurai, 1988) term the "spatial incarceration of the native." They go on to contend that anthropology's understanding of culture has implied a "certain unity of place and people." According to Stam and Spence (1983), racial stereotyping and "pernicious" distortions of history and culture are productions of this "certain unity." In denouncing the spatial location of "culture," symbolic of a physical grid for mapping difference, Gupta and Ferguson (1992,

20) instead advocate "multiple grids that enable us to see that connection and contiguity more generally the representation of territory vary considerably by factors such as class, gender, race, and sexuality, and are differentially available to those in different locations in the field." Although postmodernists may contend with the notion of a connected, contiguous field, I feel that this spatial criticism reflects the imperialist construction of ethnographic discourse to highlight the import of race, space, and culture in the anthropological imagination of distance. Unquestioned representation therefore serves to naturalize and universalize this imagination and to build it as rhetoric for "Othering" and knowing the rational self.

Interpretative Authority

How, then, did we, who had a close, confidential, longstanding relationship, manage to misunderstand each other so completely?
—Borland (1991)

The shift to interpretive authority retains a common emphasis on the production of a textual subject, yet views cultures as assemblages of texts (see Clifford, 1983). It also shifts from a reliance on experience or being there, and attempts to move beyond translation to the recognition of textual production. This kind of authority engages a specific fiction-producing project in which the text is not required to be in the presence of the speaker. The assemblages of interpretations imply that text can travel and go through (be constituted by) multiple lenses and interpretations (Clifford, 1983). According to McCormack (2000), the situated accounts of both participants and researchers in the interpretive story open the reader to the possibility of multiple interpretations. She posits that narratives, language, context, and moments constitute multiple lenses that provide alternative modes of representations. In this way, narrative authority is shared and negotiated. Interpretative authority then goes beyond the authority claim of translation (a main tenet of ethnographic authority), but begins to recognize a positioning of gaze. Denzin and Lincoln (1994, 481) posit that interpretations are narrative, or storied accounts, that privilege particular positions. These positions may be situated in any of a number of paradigms (positivism, post-positivism, constructionism, critical theory, feminism, cultural studies, or ethnic models of inquiry).

Yet, without the raced presence of the body and history, to function as performative texts, the inability to track power relations in the multiple interpretations of text can produce a relativist process, which in many cases does not foreground the lenses that bring power to the process. Hence, the politics of whose interpretations become written and authorized remains unmarked and sidelined. Dei (1999) views discourses as presented in racialized bodies and contexts. Borland (1991) reflects on the contestations between her and her grandmother's stories of the latter's life through interview. Borland's narrative highlights an interpretive conflict that gives way to a continuous narrative negotiation in which interpretations are shared and there is reciprocal learning between researcher and researched. Yet, particularly when the interview process involves a narration across racial, gender, class, or sexual difference, the textualized ritual or event becomes divorced from its production by actors and becomes culture or what Clifford (1983) terms as "an englobing reality."

This is performed in development discourses in the concept of *community*, treated as a culturally homogeneous entity. Clifford (1983, 133) however locates this discourse in the wider ambit of colonial representation, critically emphasizing the politics of ethnographers/researchers "positioning the cultural realities of other peoples without placing their own reality in jeopardy." In analyzing Chicano struggles in the southern United States, Pulido (1996) talks about how the politics of representation across racial difference is heavily implicated in the interpretation of struggle, and even more relevant to the strategic agencies of minoritized groups. In her study, a Chicano social movement organization used stereotype representations of colonial fantasy as indigenous and having authentic claims to environmental preservation to leverage funding and U.S. support for the cross-border, racialized struggle. It suggests an understanding of representation that can be strategically evoked or utilized to manoeuvre in a political economy of representations.

I am, however, not convinced that the differentiation between experience and interpretation can be marked in terms of textual practices, because both practices are in different ways using textual strategies to invoke a constructed authority. The difference, as I see it, is that interpretive authority is shared, though still not historicized.

Discursive Authority

The mode of communication in which speakers/actors/subjects/interlocutors and their contexts or situations of dialogue are marked provides for what anthropologists now term *discursive authority* (Clifford, 1983). It represents the movement away from unembodied texts or texts that are not marked by their body/subjectivity (although this issue is rather slippery because the ways in which bodies/subjects mark their texts and the ways in which these markings are contested require more attention, which I do not further in this paper), and, according to Clifford (1983), cannot be interpreted in an open-ended, potentially public way that text is read. It seems to me that this rationalizing of actors, discourse, and contexts as separate and intrinsically stable is, however, simplistic and unconscious of the flux of text, which is itself a multiplicity, a consuming and producing dialectical machine that may in fiction, fuse the embodied subjects, discourse, and context. Dei (1999) supports the notion that knowledge resides in the body and cultural memory, but that the Eurocentric gaze has influenced and shaped what to see and what not to see as valid knowledge.

Underlying the articulation of discursive authority is the power of context to constitute a real dialogic text. Yet, this assumption forecloses the possibility that even contexts are subject to interpretation, subtext, and contestation. Discursive authority, therefore, although it embodies the text and gives it context, does not afford multiple re-readings of the dialogic representation. In this way, the racialization of text/discourse remains unmarked, and the power vested in the actors/subjects as bodies situated within institutions and historical processes to ground/interpret context and its power is not marked as a culpable technology in the dialogic machination. Dei (1999, 409) echoes this sentiment in the statement: "When discursive authority is assigned to scholars who have no embodied connection to knowledge or to the particular experience that produces such knowledge, then it is a testament to how privilege and power work, in mutually reinforcing ways, to legitimize scholarship in the academy."

Clifford (1983, 119) also offers critique of a purely dialogical authority that would "repress the inescapable fact of textualization." However, what I want to suggest is that these authorities are never constituted in separation of each other, but in fact arrange and emerge with each other. Their different politics of representation therefore constitute a dynamic, complex chaos of politics. The challenge in advocating this possibility is to reconcile the need to track power with the changing meanings of the research process. It presents an epistemological challenge for anti-racist studies and vice versa. In the frame of anti-racist research, dialogic representation and discursive authority can, however, be useful in providing a site for minority voice and power to name and textualize. It can also be a place where dis-enchantment with the liberatory impotence of traditional research can be investigated.

Race and the Politics of Difference in Social Science Research

The objective production and capture of an "Other" entity, culture, or englobing entity remains a central activity of knowledge production and authorization, regardless of the different ways authority is deconstructed into safety. Anthropology has been engaged in a long-time love affair with bodies/cultures

of "Other," particularly non-white and non-Western ones. With conceptualizations such as *ecumene* and *field*, the white anthropologist has had a particular investment in scripting history and culture in a larger global knowledge
project. Yet, one must argue that anthropologists in contemporary academia
are not only white, but also of various races, genders, nationalities, sexualities,
and so forth, bringing complex angles of thought on the theory and practice
of the discipline. And I might add that the productions are often useful to various groups. I have sat through many graduate classes and heard the sentiment
of white students that they do not possess any culture, a statement that automatically implies its possession by a racialized "Other." Arber (2000) res-
onates with this sentiment to articulate the mundane entrenchment of
whiteness as "the universal something, yet something so empty of content that
those situated within its ambit do not see it as there. Whiteness becomes
something beyond ethnicity, history, privilege or struggle." Radhika Mohanram
(1999), in her book *The Black Body*, unmaps this cartographic fiction to reveal
its technology of creating and presenting difference as an other/they category, to enable whiteness to know itself. Richard Dyer's (1997) deconstruction
of whiteness also does much to underscore the invisibility and perceived neutrality of white hegemony in everyday life.

Bakhtin's (1981) notion of *heteroglossia* (intersection of languages, cultures,
subcultures) is useful in that the field represents speaking subjects in a field of
multiple discourses. Attempts to enculture or englobe are viewed as constructs of monological power. He sees culture as a "concretely, open-ended,
creative dialogue of subcultures, of insiders and outsiders, of diverse factions,
a carnivalesque," (quoted in Clifford, 1983, 136). He does not, however, mark
the racialized culture of this deconstruction, not only in terms of the individual bodies in the research process, but in terms of the Western hegemonic norm
of whiteness expressed through academic discourse. Although this hinges very
closely on what some might consider a dangerous essentialism, I read it as a
project that is fraught with the culpability of "Othering" non-white texts.
Moving beyond realist narratives to imagine a polyphony would, however, only
"displace ethnographic authority, still confirming the final, virtuoso orchestra-
tion by a single author of all the discourses in his or her text" (Clifford, 1983,
139).

Arber (2000, 45) agrees with this quandary for narrative researchers studying politics of difference in her claims that "even as the other is encouraged to
speak, the researcher orchestrates their voices and is also positioned within the
research." She notices that even in the project of polyvocal textual representations, the author has the final voice. Yet, Clifford (1983, 141) states that, "the
multiplication of possible readings reflects the fact that self-conscious 'ethno-

graphic' consciousness can no longer be seen as the monopoly of certain Western cultures and social classes." Is the inclusion of native informants on title pages as "interpreters and corroborators of ethnographers' interpretations" (Clifford, 1983, 141) sufficient to assume that the West is still not complicit in a powerful vortex of consumption. Is there a power to (re-) create the carnivalesque, different voices that are spread evenly among subjects (implied by Clifford) in a unitary political project, or are there still political projects that ground a politics of difference? What the task of critiquing ethnography enacts is the disturbance of authority, unsettling its claims to represent and the technologies it uses to do so. It forces an ontological query of the notion of authority-signage that academia in its paradoxical existence has no choice but to continue this chaotic assemblage.

The conversation emerging between the politics of positioning and the politics of difference, in Arber's (2000, 46) interpretation, is that "positioning is both nothing, an invention, and everything, our everyday lives." In the context of anti-racist research, Arber highlights the marking of difference (an axis of differentiation) as an essentialist project based on racialized sub-projects of biology, experience, culture, and so forth. This technology works to solidify constructed categories of difference, giving way to the erasure of racialized violence (i.e., colonialism and instead discourses about multiculturalism, integration, and assimilation). Dei (1999), however, reiterates the powerful relationship between personal subjectivity and the operationalization of anti-racism knowledge and practice. The politics of difference can, in fact, be articulated from those on the periphery to strategically perform constructions that allow for sites of resistance and contestation. Race and difference can provide avenues for self-definition, self-naming, and a place for fighting back. To paraphrase Frankenberg (1993, quoted in Arber, 2000, 51), "far from being nonracial or neutral, whiteness, like otherness, refers to sets of locations that are historically, socially, politically, and culturally produced and linked to unfolding relations of domination." Positioning in the context of anthropology, however, has come to mean the difference of otherness rather than the complicity and particularity of whiteness.

Yet, Arber (2000) warns that the task of positioning is complex, as the barriers between real and unreal, symbolic and material, fluid and discrete, desirable and contemptible, seem permeable, parallel, intersecting, and fragmentary. She approaches this nexus by posing the question: "How do we re/position positioning and how do we negotiate the spaces in between?"(Arber, 2000, 46). Fine (1994a) also writes about working the hyphen between self and "Other" in the coherence of master narratives, to deconstruct it as a site of racism. She also posits that this site can also be recast with agency to utilize in-between sensibilities to rupture racially coded dialectics. This space of in-between has produced a varied degree of dialogue and contestation, as to its existence and its utility. It offers a site of perhaps limited autonomy to the "Other" to play with the solidity and fluidity of identity. Yet, the question remains: who (and where) has the power to fix this flux? I include *where* because I believe that spatialities are like bodies, raced and deeply implicated in the coding of text. Recognizing that ethnographic projects have been complicit in the "narration of colonialism," Fine (1994b) comments that the researchers/writers self-consciously carry no voice, body, race, class, or gender and no interests into their texts. This "narrative strategy," as she refers to "Othering," is embedded in the tradition of writing cultures, making difference apparent by the homogenizing, bounding, and fixation of an "Other" category, an "Other" body.

To what extent can the technologies of deconstruction, discourse, and psychoanalysis be set apart from the saliency of body politics? Fine (1994a, 74) opines that "when we construct texts collaboratively, self-consciously examining our relations with/for/despite those who have been contained as "Others" we move against, we enable resistance to, "Othering." Yet she co-opts the discursive alternatives/bodies of "Others" to do so. Her narratives foreground how white hegemony has boxed in the "Other" without attempting an in-depth deconstruction of how it institutionalizes its own dominance through this process. What emerges is a displacement of the same, in which the responsibility for anti-racism/counterhegemony remains contingent upon the discursive realm of non-white bodies and worlds. Fine opens her article utilizing a quote from bell hooks (1990) "I am waiting for them to stop talking about the "Other," a sentiment that Fine would do well to recognize.

The task of "writing against Othering" as Fine (1994a) puts it, can be placed with liberatory political projects that seek to write/authorize struggle, resistance, and counterhegemony. Denzin and Lincoln (1994, 481) see writing as interpretation, as representation, and hence as a form of inquiry. Lincoln (1997) and Rhodes (1994) view the author as being multivoiced and as choosing to represent a particular self/voice and participate in the interview process as a negotiable space. I feel that the concept of a negotiable space does not recognize that negotiations are always fraught with different parities of representation, different political projects that become foregrounded, various strategies that are themselves ambiguous, and various interests in participation and narration. This is for both researcher and researched. It means that negotiation does not necessarily account for nor address explicitly the fact that race is constructive of these forces, which play on the interview process. In addition, I do not necessarily support the assertion by Lincoln (1997) that the producer of text and the readers of text have to share some common framework for a text to be meaningful, constituting an interpretive community. Is the landscape of meaning-making uniform, homogeneous, and monolithic?

In the discussion of who researches whom, Rhodes (1994) articulates that in the British context, black interviewers with black subjects as a political strategy risks marginalization of both black issues and researchers. To some extent this is true across the Atlantic where authority becomes ghettoized, expressed in assumptions by the white academy of what types of research students of color should be doing. I agree with Lincoln (1997) that the ultimate decision/choice of representing remains with the researcher, irrespective of the levels of interpretation that the researched chooses. Here I am not speaking of neo-realist strategies where the interview is co-authored by both researcher and researched, but the way in which the co-authored text is cast as a narrative strategy to deploy various projects that are important to the author's credibility and authenticity.

Let's face it: Academia's pre-occupation on preserving authenticity and authority remains paramount yet unquestioned by those within. The challenge and costs of challenging this authority within this club holds greater weight and consequences for bodies that are not naturalized subjects of the knowledge institution, namely minority scholars. Whose work is branded as credible, fundable, and mainstream? These sorts of considerations play very important roles in the ways academia represents authority to the world outside. While acknowledging the postmodernist stance that all subjects are multiply positioned and in flux, there is a constructed and historical power to name realities, a power that I am convinced lives within the body itself, a powerful text in the interview process. I agree that there could be textual convulsions between the presence and performance of bodies, and that these can in many ways convolute the mapping of racial power relations in the space of interviews. This is further complicated by the mental maps that intersect based on constructions of race, gender, class, and so forth. Yet, I am not convinced that power can be evened out between researcher and researched. It boils down to the fact that each person occupies particular raced, gendered, and class positions and engage in inter-positioning in the research process. Disaggregation of constructing currents and positions are therefore useful to anti-racist research.

However, positioning is complicated by location, culture, language, histories, and cannot be frozen on paper. Writing as representation, in my view, is a selective yet hegemonic canon of power relations, instituting a particular authority, a legitimized eye, narrator, hand, author. In my own previous experience of development work in the Caribbean, I read the power to narrate, to make sense of or to name, although retained by bourgeois intellectuals, as a localized though universalized power. The choice of non-participation is also sometimes a very powerful, albeit fraught, source of communication and narration for individuals and groups who recognize that their participation is crucial to the projects of an imperializing different gaze and body. For the anti-racist scholar, it is therefore important to recognize that positioning is important to informing the political project and the praxis of research as enabling of change. It is a systematic, positioned stance of resistance and struggle against narratives that consume "Other" bodies and stories, to reflect the civility of the bourgeois subject. In recognizing the cultural, historical, and language specificities of research, race as a social construct can be made more visible and hence affect the ways in which power relations are analyzed and changed.

Within this context of racialized representational politics (premised on embodiment of knowledge and positioning), I believe that anti-racist research challenges and transforms (post)modernist and racist notions of authority. It offers multiple political sites, which translate into different reframings of authority, particularly based on agency and strategy, both associated with praxis. In doing so, the discourse affords multiple sites to contest and question the embodied (white researcher) and historical (colonial/liberal) constructedness of authority. One strategy is cooperative inquiry/co-authorship (Reason, 1994) where both researcher and subject negotiate the text of the interview and the text that is written. This offers an opportunity for a space in which to contest issues, in which the researcher is not only called upon to be reflexive, but critical of his/her own positioning, politics, interests, and desires, and therefore to deconstruct racialized currents in the process of textual negotiation/entanglement. Gupta and Ferguson (1992, 17), however, warn that, "there is thus a politics of otherness that is not reducible to a politics of representation. Textual strategies can call attention to the politics of representation, but the issue of otherness itself is not really addressed by the devices of polyphonic textual construction or collaboration with informant-writers, as writers like Clifford and Crapanzano sometimes seem to suggest."

In this chapter, I do not mean to force a simplistic binary between anthropology and anti-racist discourse. In fact, critical ethnography overlaps anti-racist discourse in so far as it suggests an emancipatory project that requires a deconstruction of positionality and a critical engagement with experience. Simon and Dippo (1986, 196) suggest that critical ethnography is both "pedagogical and political and is organized by a standpoint and implicates us in moral questions about desirable forms of social relations and ways of living." Ethnography and all social science research therefore allow us to register a "political moment," which Gitlin et al. (1989, 238) define as "the relation between method and what the researcher is trying to achieve through the method." Lu and Horner (1998, 257) state that critical ethnography "rejects the possibility of a politically neutral stance," but argue that the distinction between experience and discursive understanding must be maintained. It is within this tension between practice and theory that anti-racism discourse will need to own its rhetorical baggage and allow for critical thought that helps push the boundaries of the discourse. In fact, it will also provide an opportunity for the redefinition of discourse. Perhaps where anti-racist research offers something different from critical ethnography is its specific focus on critiquing the racialization of experience, interpretation, positioning, authorial control, researcher-participant relationship, and discursive production. In doing so, anti-racist discourse rearticulates a narrative of power that transgresses critical ethnography's goal post of reflexivity. Anti-racist research therefore poses a legitimate challenge to the fields of international development and comparative education. As a cross-cultural enterprise these disciplines are embedded in colonial discourses of saving and civilizing through categories such as community, capacity, participation, sustainability, and development, and will all require deconstruction to unveil their racialized imaginings of native "Other."

To question whether a white ethnographer can ever be reflexive enough to properly apply anti-racist methods in fields where the objects of the study are natives, is to assume a simplistic and liberal notion of discourse where the issue of safety and security seems more paramount for a meta-discourse of racialized privilege. At the level of embodied knowledge, racial imaginaries are specific but not confined to body politics, whereas in the inter-subjective space between researcher and participant, different and more complex notions of race and knowledge production are layered onto the research process. In addition, both traditional social science and more critical reflexive methods have inscribed a momentum of white privilege to knowledge production. I mean here to invoke a notion of racialized strategy in which individual and collective constructions of social projects hinge on strategies that affirm and contest racial politics. White researchers will have to deal with this racial imaginary to disturb the place of safety they occupy in traditional and alternative discourses. For once it may mean sharing the fear of not knowing. Yet, white researchers have come to this moment out of choice. What determines that choice and how it manifests as a political strategy will push the boundary of reflexivity and the anti-racist discourse to new imaginings.

Anti-racism research, which is grounded in the discourse of embodied knowledge (politically and historically positioned), calls for authority to be embodied, situated, and raced for authority itself to be englobed and cultured. In so doing, antiracist research requires a shift from ethnographic to discursive and interpretive authority. Subjects choose particular voices, ranges, and registers based on how they are played by the researcher. As a result, the construction of authority in anti-racist research is tantamount to offering space and developing the capacity for voice among bodies/voices of color that have been historically silenced and muted by the flow of social science.

Like all discourses, anti-racist research approaches to knowledge production are positioned and particular to political projects. The discourse does not offer a relativist space that guarantees safety in representation. What may be represented as "uninclusive and anti-white" by those threatened by this openly racialized, embodied, strategic, and historical discourse is also emancipatory for us, bodies of color, who have historically occupied multiple sites of exclusion in colonial discourse. It helps us to question the claims of bodies that do not see race in everyday social science, yet interpret anti-racism as reverse racism. Anti-racist discourse is a strategic incitement to contestation, while at the same time offering rupturings and suturings to imagine a self-determined, indigenous political economy of representation. The only guarantee is that anti-racist discourse is a place where bodies of color can work the hyphen and remake self-representation. There are also risks to both white bodies and bodies of color, but these risks must be historically informed and formulated.

The field of anti-racist discourse therefore offers a strategic, emancipatory space for people of color, especially in the context of a historically imperial present and a neo-globalizing Western dominance. If we are to *own* our own representations of self, community, and culture, anti-racism must function to give ground to sites of interrogation and must itself be questionable in boundary.

What is needed, then, is more than a ready ear and a deft editorial hand to capture and orchestrate the voices of 'others'; what is needed is a willingness to interrogate, politically and historically, the apparent 'given' of a world in the first place divided into 'ourselves' and 'others.'

—Gupta and Ferguson (1992)

REFERENCES

Appadurai, A. 1988. "Putting Hierarchy in Its Place." *Cultural Anthropology 3*, 36–49.

Arber, R. 2000. "Defining Positioning within Politics of Difference: Negotiating Spaces 'In-between.'" *Race, Ethnicity and Education 3*(1): 25–44.

Bakhtin, M. 1981. "Discourse in the Novel." In Michael Holquist (Ed.), *The Dialogic Imagination: Four Essays by M. Bakhtin.* Austin and London: University of Texas Press. pp. 259–442.

Borland, K. 1991. "That's Not What I Said: Interpretive Conflict in Oral Narrative Research." In S. B. Gluck and D. Patai (Eds.), *Women's Words.* New York: Routledge.

Clifford, J. 1983. "On Ethnographic Authority." *Representations 1*, 118–146.

Crapanzano, V. 1986. "Hermes' Dilemma: The Masking of Subversion in Ethnographic Description." In J. Clifford and G. Marcus (Eds.), *Writing Culture: The Poetics and Politics of Ethnography.* Berkeley, Los Angeles, London: University of California Press, pp. 51–76.

Dei, G. J. S. 1999. "Knowledge and Politics of Social Change: The Implications of Anti-racism." *British Journal of Sociology of Education 20*(3): 395–409.

Denzin, N. K., and Y. S. Lincoln (Eds.). 1994. *Handbook of Qualitative Research.* Thousand Oaks, CA. Sage Publications, pp. 83–97.

Dyer, R. 1997. *White.* London: Routledge.

Fine, M. 1994a. "Working the Hyphens: Reinventing Self and Other in Qualitative Research." In N. K. Denzin and Y .S. Lincoln. *Handbook of Qualitative Research.* Thousand Oaks, CA: Sage, pp. 37–55.

Fine, M. 1994b. "Dis-stance and Other Stances: Negotiations of Power Inside Feminist Research." In A. Gitlin (Ed.), *Power and Method: Political Activism and Educational Research.* New York: Routledge, pp. 13–35.

Frankenberg, R. 1993. *The Social Construction of Whiteness: White Women! Race Matters.* London: Routledge.

Geertz, C. 1973. "Thick Description": Toward an Interpretive Theory of Culture." In C. Geertz, *The Interpretation of Cultures* New York: Basic Books, pp. 3–30.

Gitlin, A., Siegel, M., and Boru, K. 1989. "The Politics of Method: From Leftist Ethnography to Educative Research." *Qualitative Studies in Education 2*(3): 237–253.

Gupta, A., and Ferguson, J. 1992. "Beyond 'Culture': Space, Identity, and the Politics of Difference." *Cultural Anthropology 7*, 6–23.

Haraway, D. 1988. "Situated Knowledges: The Science Question in Feminism and the Privilege of Partial Perspective." *Feminist Studies 14*(3): 575–597.

hooks, b. 1990. *Yearning: Race, Gender and Cultural Politics.* Boston: South End.

Ladson-Billings, G. 1998. "Just What Is Critical Race Theory and What's It Doing in a 'Nice' Field Like Education?" *International Journal of Qualitative Studies in Education 11*(1): 7–24.

LeCompte, M., and Goetz, J. 1982. "Problems of Reliability and Validity in Ethnographic Research." *Review of Educational Research 52*(1): 31–60.

Lincoln, Y. S. 1997. "Self, Subject, Audience, Text: Living on the Edge, Writing in the Margin." In W. Tierney and Y. S. Lincoln (Eds.), *Representation and the Text.* New York: State University of New York Press, pp. 37–55.

Lu, M., and Horner, B. 1998. "The Problematic of Experience: Redefining Critical Work in Ethnography and Pedagogy." *College English 60* (3): 257–277

McCormack, C. 2000. "From Interview Transcript to Interpretive Story: Part 2–Developing an Interpretive Story." *Field Methods 2* (4): 298–315.

Mohanram, R. 1999. *Black Body: Women, Colonialism, and Space.* Minneapolis and London: University of Minnesota Press.

Narayan, K. 1993. "How Native Is a 'Native' Anthropologist?" *American Anthropologist 95*, 671–686.

Parmar, P. 1990. "Black Feminism: The Politics of Articulation." In J. Rutherford (Ed.), *Identity: Community, Culture, Difference.* London: Lawrence and Wishart Limited, pp. 101–126.

Pulido. L. 1996. *Environmentalism and Economic Justice: Two Chicano Struggles in the Southwest.* Tucson: The University of Arizona Press.

Punch, M. 1994. "Politics and Ethics in Qualitative Research." In N. K. Denzin and Y. S. Lincoln (Eds.), *Handbook of Qualitative Research.* Thousand Oaks, CA: Sage Publications, pp. 83–97.

Rabinow, P. 1986. "Representations Are Social Facts: Modernity and Post-Modernity in Anthropology." In J. Clifford and G. Marcus (Eds.), *Writing Culture: The Poetics and Politics of Ethnography.* Berkeley, Los Angeles, London: University of California Press, pp. 234–261.

Reason, P. (Ed.). 1994. *Participation in Human Inquiry.* Thousand Oaks, CA: Sage.

Rhodes, P. J. 1994. "Race-of-Interviewer Effects: A Brief Comment." *Journal of Sociology 28*(2): 547–558.

Rosaldo, R. 1986. "From the Door of His Tent: The Fieldworker and the Inquisitor." In J. Clifford and G. Marcus (Eds.), *Writing Culture: The Poetics and Politics of Ethnography.* Berkeley, Los Angeles, London: University of California Press, pp. 77–97.

Said, E. 1979. *Orientalism.* New York: Vintage Books.

Said, E. 1994. *Culture and Imperialism.* New York: Vintage Books.

Scheurich, J., and Young, M. 1997. "Coloring Epistemologies: Are Our Research Epistemologies Racially Biased?" *Educational Researcher 26* (4): 4–16.

Simon, R., and Dippo, D. 1986. "On Critical Ethnographic Work." *Anthropology and Education Quarterly 17*, 195–202.

Stam, R., and Spence, L. 1983. "Colonialism, Racism and Representation." *Screen 24* (2): 4.

Troyna, B. 1995. "Beyond Reasonable Doubt? Researching 'Race' in Educational Settings." *Oxford Review of Education 21*(4): 395–408.

Troyna, B., and Carrington, B. 1989. "Whose Side Are We On? Ethical Dilemmas in Research on 'Race' and Education." In R. Burgess (Ed.), *The Ethics of Educational Research.* London: Leves Falmer, pp. 205–223.

Van Mannen, J. 1988. *Tales of the Field: On Writing Ethnography.* Chicago, IL: University of Chicago Press.

Vidich, A. J., and Lyman, S. M. 1994. "Qualitative Methods: Their History in Sociology and Anthropology." In N. K. Denzin and Y. S. Lincoln (Eds.), *Handbook of Qualitative Research.* Thousand Oaks, CA: Sage Publications, 23–59.

Chapter Three

BEVERLY-JEAN DANIEL

Researching African Canadian Women

INDIGENOUS KNOWLEDGES AND THE POLITICS OF REPRESENTATION

To acquiesce is to lose ourselves entirely and implicitly agree with all that has been said about us. To resist is to retrench in the margins, retrieve what we were and remake ourselves. The past, our stories local and global, the present, our communities, cultures, languages and social practices all may be spaces of marginalization, but they may have also become spaces of resistance and hope.

—Linda Tuhiwai Smith (1999)

Textual, oral, and visual representations influence the way in which people discern and interpret their world and experiences. It also informs the manner in which people interact with the world and understand their individual selves (Ellsworth, 1994). The particular cultural representations to which people are exposed, however, are primarily based on the position that their specific ethnic, racial, or cultural group occupies in society. In addition, depending on whether one is a member of a dominant or minoritized population affects the level of control one has over the particular manner in which one is represented and the positive or negative associations that are implied in these portrayals.

African Canadian women occupy spaces that are framed by race and gender, two socially constructed categories that are situated in a position that appears to be diametrically opposed to the white, European, male paradigms. These paradigms are presented as the norm in both the public and private spheres, wherein the reigns of power are contained. The representations of the

African Canadian woman are fraught with contradictions; she is simultaneously invisible and visible. Their visibility lies in the negative stereotypes that have pervaded the writings and the imaginations of white males. Her invisibility (Moses, 1997; Henry, 1998) lies in the fact that the reality of the lives and experiences of African Canadian women, with all its intricacies, strengths, and abilities, remains missing from the texts and the public domain.

What are the factors that have rendered the lives of African Canadian women invisible within the public and academic realms of society? In what ways have the hegemonic, racist, and sexist research methodologies ensured the silencing and erasure of the lives and experiences of black women? What particular methods and methodologies can be employed in the process of centering and recording the lives of African Canadian women in a manner that serves to ensure that the stories are true reflections rather than appropriations of their voices designed not to improve their circumstances, but rather to reinforce the negative images that have so pervaded their histories? How do we begin to engage in research that is not designed to buttress the credentializing machine of white academics that is as much located in the academic politics as in the politics of the body? What is the role of research in the social construction of identities of African Canadian women?

This chapter seeks to address the invisibility of black females in the texts and literature, and to examine avenues through which we can begin to *re*-search their lives and experiences. I will briefly discuss the problematics inherent in applying Eurocentric research paradigms to researching nonwhite bodies. Second, I will explore the manner in which indigenous knowledges can be used to develop and analyze research that respects the lives and the voices of the participants, rather than engaging in the destruction that research historically has levied at colonized bodies, physically, mentally, and socially. Finally, I will discuss the important role that research plays in the individual and collective representation of self and the implications of these representations for African Canadian women like myself whose experiences in this society are impacted in significant ways by the manner in which we are reflected to the world, which are seldom based on our understandings of our histories and knowledges.

The experiences of African women have often been collapsed within the crisis of black masculinity (Gilroy, 1993) or subsumed in the experiences of white women. The crisis to which Gilroy refers emerges in conversation with bell hooks and highlights the historical manner in which issues of the black family and the community have been structured around the patriarch. The construction of the black man as "sources of pleasure and sources of danger" (Gilroy 1993, 228), feeds the voyeuristic tendencies of the white majority and further intensifies the objectification of the "Other." In contemporary times, this focus on the black male continues to be the visual aesthetic with which the white world remains most comfortable. These are, therefore, the images that pepper the landscape of popular culture, highlighting the role of power in constructing the images of minoritized bodies.

Given the focus on the situation of black males, the forms of oppression to which black women are subjected are often rendered invisible. The extreme sexual, physical, and mental violence that marks the lives of black women become marginal issues seldom worthy of discussion. Analyzed through a feminist lens, the erasure of black women reflects the patriarchal structure of society as well as the power of the dominant group to determine the manner in which the black community is represented. It also speaks to the second-class status to which women have been relegated. Additionally, the construction of black masculinity as separate from patriarchal structures of domination (Wright et al., 1998) serves to render gender-based oppression of black females at the hands of black males, nonexistent. A comprehensive analysis of the politics of the black community and family that accounts for issues related to gender continues to be limited.

The crisis of black masculinity is developed beyond the conceptual level. The contemporary reification of this crisis becomes evident in the manner in which black men are treated in the Canadian media. A striking example of this is what has been commonly referred to as the "Just Desserts" case in which a black male was suspected of killing a white female. The attendant political, immigration, and media maelstrom stands in direct contrast to the case in which a white man killed a black woman who was selling newspaper subscriptions. Whereas the Just Desserts case has been indelibly carved on the Canadian landscape, the death of the black woman has become nothing more than a blip on the underbelly. An exhaustive search for information on this case in an attempt to, at the very least, unearth the name of the victim, came up empty. However, the search for information on the Just Desserts case was readily available. This search highlights the continued decimation of black womanhood, deemed unimportant, barely newsworthy, and continually marginalized.

This chapter was developed as an attempt to move the lives of black women from the margins of academia and society in general, to begin to understand the centrality of their experiences to the sustenance of the African Canadian community. Positivist research methods have reinforced the negative images that have been so pervasive. An example of this would be the notion of the black matriarch and the resulting emasculation of the black male. I believe, therefore, that I would be remiss in making the erroneous assumption that the "crisis of black masculinity" emerged within our community and to use this term as a fact of the history of black male/female interactions. The concept of the "crisis of black masculinity" becomes important in this context given the power of naming and representation that is so inherent in researching the lives of the Other. For example, the concepts of the black matriarchal family or the image of the black community as being deficient in particular forms of cultural capital, has not emerged from within our community (hooks, 1992). I believe that as we begin to engage in research that decolonizes, we have to become acutely aware of the terms we use given the external forces that have determined these representations of us as blacks.

Questioning these "truths" becomes significant in understanding the emergence of African-centered feminisms and the influence of the outside hegemonic forces that can benefit from not only the engagement of our feminism, but also the issues that we deem important and how they are taken up. If African feminist epistemologies become reified in ways that mimic white feminism, clearly, we as African peoples do not benefit, but rather serve to reinforce the current structures of oppression and domination.

African feminism departs from the historical engagement of white feminism in the degree to which the issues that are deemed important within the community become an aspect of the expression of African-centered feminism. For example, the manner in which black males are treated in society is a reality that impacts not only on the males themselves, but also on the community as a whole. Therefore, within an African-centered feminist approach, our feminisms cannot divorce themselves from these issues. Rather, the ways in which our feminisms become reified are reflected in the application of the particular brand of feminisms at a given time. There exists no set grocery list that outlines what the specific issues are, and most certainly our feminism is not set up as being diametrically opposed to the issues of the males in our community.

With all of this being said, however, there still exists the need for spaces wherein we can focus on the issues that are relevant to us as women, which are informed by gender but not devoid of our racial, sexual, and class affiliations. As African women it is necessary for us to name our issues and identify when and where those spaces should be created. Many authors have effectively created spaces within which African women can be heard and can also name their realities. Filomena Chioma Steady (1985) in her book *The Black Woman Cross-Culturally*, brings together the words of many women who collectively name and engage African feminisms within theoretical and applied spaces. Obioma Nnamaeka (1998), in her more recent works, also provides an exciting lens through which we can draw upon our ancestral pasts to create contemporary ways of being in the world. Christine Barrow, in her analysis of Caribbean feminisms, draws a distinction between the manner in which Caribbean women live and name their feminisms, which can be contextually unique in significant ways from some of their counterparts. According to Barrow, "Caribbean women just did not fit received images and rhetoric. They were not 'marginalized' in the same way as their Third World counterparts . . . and though constrained by patriarchal ideology and practice, they did not suffer the same subordinate status in relations with their kinfolk" (1998, xi).

What becomes important within these discussions of African-centered feminisms are the specificities that inform their practices, which, though formed within particular spaces and locations, have shared historical contexts. African women share histories of race, gender, colonization, imperialism, and slavery, factors that have all served to clearly demarcate our feminisms whether through struggle or resistance.

Definition of Terms

There are several terms being used in this discussion, and the meanings and usages within the current contexts should be defined. *Indigenous knowledge* is defined as "knowledges associated with long-term occupancy of a place. It refers to the traditional norms and social values, as well as mental constructs which guide, organize and regulate people's way of living and making sense of their world" (Dei, Hall, and Rosenberg, 2000, p 6). Although I work within a paradigm that centralizes the application of indigenous knowledges, for the purposes of this chapter, I specifically focus on the indigenous knowledges related to African Canadian peoples. Focusing on the lives of African Canadian women is by no means an indication that I am unaware of the need to also acknowledge and discuss alternative forms of indigenous knowledges such as aboriginal, north and south Asian communities, and so forth. However to focus on the indigenous knowledges of other groups belies the original intent of this paper, which seeks to specifically address the invisibility of black women in the literature rather than collapsing them within the folds of larger discussions. Within this chapter, I use the term *African Canadian* to refer to women living in or born in Canada whose ancestral homeland is Africa. This includes women from the Caribbean, Africa, the United States, Canada, and the diaspora. The term *black women* will be used interchangeably with African Canadian women. Although I ground my study within the experiences of African Canadian women in Canada, this should not be seen as a narrow analysis. This spectrum of the African diaspora is the focus of this study because it has been so heavily understudied. By examining African Canadian women, this study intends to not only extrapolate the specificity of such a standpoint, but also allows for others to ponder the similarity and differences of experiences across borders.

The term *African Canadian woman* entails a specificity and generality in its application. Even so, one can easily argue as to the essentializing quality of the term. Inherent in its usage is the strategic invocation of a global community of women whose experiences, as earlier indicated, of racialized and gendered oppression, colonization and imperialism, serves to unite them and frames their political agency. I believe that junctures exist where we as African women, by necessity, form strategic alliances that can serve to challenge the hegemonic and patriarchal systems of domination that inform our existence, irrespective of our geographical positioning.

Throughout the discussion I wish to highlight the importance of research in the process of black women in Canadian society creating and reclaiming their representations and determining which aspects of their histories they can privilege or discard. Elizabeth Ellsworth uses the term *representation* "to refer to the processes that people and social groups use to interpret and give meaning to the world, and to the mediation of those meanings by and through language, stories, images, music, and other cultural products" (1994, 100). She goes on to say that "all knowledge is socially constructed and linked to power and its interests. . . . meanings are not direct reflections of the world or of people, but are actively made and always mediated by interests and histories of dominant groups and by previous and current cultural representations" (Ellsworth, 1994, 101). These meanings, knowledges, and representations are not static. Rather they are dynamic manifestations influenced by specific contexts, experiences, politics, agency, and a host of other factors that influence our subjectivity.

In addition to using Ellsworth's definition of the word, the discussion will centralize the process of naming as a form of empowerment as well as a means through which we as a community of women can begin to ensure that the lives of the young girls and women in our community are no longer silenced and erased, while simultaneously challenging the hegemonic male discourses that have for so long informed and dominated our sense of self.

History

Inherent in the act of identifying the places from which the African Canadian woman has originated, points to a significant aspect that makes research difficult. The histories of these women are vast and varied; this in part informs the reasons for migration, the manner in which their history has developed, and the spaces they are permitted to occupy. In addition, it points to the pitfalls inherent in attempting to essentialize the term *black women* and expect that the research will speak to the lives and histories of all who are embodied within blackness. However, as highlighted in the earlier discussion, there are times when we, through necessity, engage in strategic essentializations.

The African American woman has had a long-standing history in the United States and the Caribbean. In examining the bits of history of the African presence that has not been erased, one can also see that they have also had a long history here in Canada, contrary to the popularized content of Canadian history, which begins and ends with the British and the French invasion and subsequent domination. The histories of the Aboriginal peoples of Canada have suffered significant erasures. In a conversation that occurred among a group of preservice teachers in a classroom, one member of the group commented that if people migrate to Canada they should be expected to learn one of the original Canadian languages (either English or French) a statement with which the rest of the group heartily agreed. At this point I also agreed with him, but proceeded to ask him which one of the Aboriginal languages he believed we should have all Canadians learn, given that they were the original Canadian people. The original speaker's reply was that he never thought about the issue in that way, while the rest of the group remained silent.

Such commonplace conceptions and glaring chasms in people's understanding of history speak to the nefarious manner in which European history has presented itself as the only true history. In situations where the histories of other groups are presented, the information is the colonizers' version of that history, designed to meet the needs of the colonizer and to ensure that the colonized bodies and minds embrace an inferior concept of themselves, while privileging whiteness over their own cultures and histories.

Many of the earliest Africans in Canada settled in parts of Nova Scotia, a history which the Black History Society has done an excellent job of documenting. The significant numbers of those who currently live in Ontario are here as a result of migration primarily during the late 1970s and early 1980s, when they were allowed to enter Canada to work in the homes of white families as domestics. Linda Carty and Dionne Brand (1991) have written on the lives and experiences of some of the women who came as domestic workers and Annette Henry (1998) has written on the lives of African Canadian teachers. Adrienne Shadd (1994) has written on the history of African women and their journeys via the Underground Railroad. These writers all need to be celebrated for the work they have done, but our journey does not end there. According to Sheila Radford-Hill (2000) we have "further to fly."

There are many facets of the lives of African Canadian women that have yet to be explored. One of the factors that have served to make this exploration difficult is the inability to effectively document the lives and experiences of these women within the positivist Eurocentric conceptions of research.

Eurocentric Research Paradigms

Eurocentric paradigms have positioned themselves as universalizing principles of human behavior and concerns. Added to this, these discourses have been built on a foundation of neutrality and objectivity that allows them to speak to all human concerns, irrespective of the variables of race, gender, class, or sexuality. With the continuing analysis and interrogation of these theories by the more critical theories and discourses, such as anti-racism, feminism, and Afrocentricity, for example, this fallacy of neutrality is increasingly laid bare. What has become more evident as these canons are stripped of their shell of neutrality, are the issues of power, control, racism, and sexism inherent in the development and institutionalization of their practices. It is evident that these theories have been developed to support the interests, desires and politics of one particular social group—white, European, heterosexual males.

Delving into many of the research texts that are employed within academia, one is presented with in-depth coverage of the particular research methods one can employ in developing and designing a research project. Glaringly absent from these texts are research methodologies that deviate from the presumed norm of white maleness and that serve to challenge the conventional modes of knowledge production. More recently there has been some discussion of critical research methods, such as feminist and postmodern research methods (Neuman, 1991). However, when one attempts to engage a research project that is not structured linearly (Smith, 1998), as the dominant theories, there are many difficulties with which one is faced. Additionally, as one begins to strip away the veneer of many of these theories that have positioned themselves as challenging the dominant icons, there lies the realization that they replicate that which they claim to challenge. This becomes a glaring reification of Audre Lorde's (2001, 39) infamous comment, "the master's tool will never dismantle the master's house." Feminism and some of the other critical theories have developed in ways that serve to reinforce the dominance of the master's house and reinforce the process of Othering minoritized groups and voices (Fine, 1994).

Indigenous research paradigms provide the lens through which we can begin to challenge prevailing research discourses while also providing an analysis of the issues of power that are inherent in them. The power imbalances evident within the researcher/researched paradigms, mirrors the structures within the colonizer/colonized dichotomy. In much the same way that colonizers have regarded their role as civilizing the natives through the provision and control of knowledge and information, much of what has been accomplished has been through various forms of violence (emotional, physical, and mental) directed at the colonized bodies; the traditional researcher/researched structure has functioned in much the same way. The researcher enters into communities not in search of information in conjunction with the participants, but to find information that can reinforce and buttress existing ideas and divisions of power by "giving" the subjects the information "they need to know."

This control over the production, valuation, and dissemination of information and knowledge serves to ensure that the dominant groups maintain their control over the information market, while determining who and what type of data gains access to or is prohibited from entering the market sphere. Research becomes another capitalistic endeavor in which knowledge is bought and sold to the highest bidder. The researcher becomes the scout who searches for exoticized information that can be sold in the market. The white, heterosexual male becomes the primary consumer of the information and knowledge products that are developed.

The predominant research paradigms focus on the reliability and validity of the results of the research findings that address whether the research can be repeated and the degree to which the findings can be generalized to the larger population. There is the constant search for grand theories, as Barbara Christian (1987) refers to them, or meta-narratives (Lyotard, 1984), which can serve to explain human behavior. These grand theories fail to account for race, gender, and class variables that significantly influence the manner in which people are treated in society, thereby influencing their reactions to various situations.

Another problem in applying these theories to researching nonwhite populations is the way in which these populations are constructed and analyzed, and the way the resulting information is interpreted. Non-white populations are perceived as problems or defined in terms of deficits and pathology (Brewer, 1997), and research projects on these populations are often structured in ways that seek to explain the nature of the problem. In addition to this, the apparent degree of behavioral deviation from the "norm of whiteness" is analyzed as an apparent indication of deficit.

This form of research ignores the multiple centered representations of social life (Brewer, 1997), i.e., the many facets of the lives of the research populations. Rather, the research focuses on the identified problem without developing either a historical or social analysis that would serve to explain the etiology of the problem. Such research serves to ensure that nonwhite groups continue to be represented in stereotypical ways, while contributing much to their continued marginalization and little to the uplift of the communities in question.

In the process of writing this paper, I have examined writings on white feminist research epistemologies (Fonow and Cook, 1991; O'Brien, 1999) in an attempt to determine whether the erasure of black women's experiences had, in some small part, been reversed. However, the lack of inclusion is ever present. In books where there exists some discussion, it is limited to a few pages wherein some of the primary names associated with black feminist thought, such as bell hooks, Patricia Hill Collins, Audre Lorde, and Barbara Christian are cited, and their basic philosophical thrust regurgitated.

At most, one is able to locate a few articles by African women cited in these edited works (St. Pierre and Pillow, 2000). This reality seeks to reinforce the importance of choosing frameworks that respect the lives of the participants rather than frameworks that, although they are positioned as being in opposition to the dominant research paradigms, significantly reinforce the exclusion of non-white bodies in the discussions.

In addition, white feminist ascription to the liberalist notion of color blindness (Powell, 1999) has remained relatively constant. Notions of sexuality have emerged as viable areas of discussion and focus (Nnaemeka, 1998), while race remains buried within white liberalist conceptions of equality, and has been replaced with the more socially acceptable tropes of ethnicity and diversity. Therefore, while white feminist theories have lauded the importance of making gender visible, they have primarily remained race-blind (Henry, 1998). Within white feminist discourses, as with many of the canonical theories being applied within academia, African women continue to be invisible.

Research and Indigenous Knowledges

Research that is being conducted on the lives of African Canadian women in Canada is limited or at best remains in the private realm of student scholarship, and is seldom published. A cursory glance at the public libraries and the academic journals reveals a shocking erasure of their lives and experiences. Feminist literature, in both its historical and contemporary manifestations has also provided little coverage of their experiences (Amos and Parmar, 1997). In much the same way that African American women within the American context historically, have had their lives collapsed within and subsumed under either the discourse of race or gender, contemporary Canadian scholarship subsumes African Canadian women within the trope of women of color (Dua, 1999; Leah, 1999; Robertson, 1999).

This type of naming is problematic on many fronts, most especially within the politics of representations. Living in a racist society in which African Canadian women are both objectified and "Othered," the manner in which we are represented is determined within the racist structures that control the production, dissemination, and value that is attached to those representations of knowledge. Women from differing racial, ethnic, religious, and sexual groups have begun to claim and define the right to their accurate representation, given the important role this plays in the development of self-identity. Within the American context, African American women have been rewriting their histories and claiming the right of self-representation on many fronts, including within the academy and the media, two significant sites of cultural knowledge production. The application of indigenous knowledges becomes a significant site from which this struggle for self-representation is staged.

Engaging indigenous paradigms can be regarded as a form of opposition to the domination and universalizing tendencies of Eurocentric white male discourses. Research paradigms that respect participants' connection to the earth and nature are diametrically opposed to the dominant paradigms currently being espoused within academia. Drawing therefore from the implications inherent in adopting indigenous paradigms that speak to the importance of diverse perspectives, respecting people's connections to their particular ways of living and ensuring that processes are neither invasive nor destructive becomes paramount.

Indigenous paradigms also allow for the reclamation of the values, practices, and beliefs, the ontological underpinnings that inform existence and survival of African Canadian women. These values and conceptions provide a foundation upon which people's identities and ways of interacting with the world develop. These historical influences also impact on particular "historical memories" (Amadiume, 1997) that have helped to shape the contemporary political stance and the manner in which African Canadian women produce and interpret these knowledges. Indigenous knowledges inform the development and enactment of our feminisms.

The manner in which African women keep moving from one space to another, one role to another, and one activity to another, is representative of the polymorphous character of our feminisms. Similarly, our skill and behaviors are engaged in constant motion; sliding amongst and between roles and responsibilities, and our feminisms reflect that movement; movement that is not limited by particularistic notions, but very much grounded in our senses as woman. Mother, daughter, wife, sister, worker, teacher, friend, all of these roles are simultaneously enacted within the space of any given moment in our day. These many roles speak to the hybridity of the concept of woman, as do our feminisms.

However, it would be problematic to speak of forms of critical or oppositional research methodology without highlighting the possible drawbacks and shortcomings of adopting these approaches. As mentioned earlier, feminist research that positions itself as being a form of critical theory, falls within the same exclusionary space as the modernist conceptions of research, given its limited inclusion of issues of race within its premises. In many ways, therefore, it serves to mimic conventional research paradigms.

Rutledge M. Dennis (1993), in discussing the relevance of participant observation in race-relations research, situates his argument within the positivist conceptions of Hobbes, Kant, and Locke and their "philosophy of science." This argument becomes specious on many levels. First, the notions of race relations being discussed that serve to heighten one's interest, however, given that the argument is developed within a limited frame, I believe its applicability within the realm of critical or oppositional research paradigms is restricted. Dennis, I believe, falls within the trap of buttressing his argument by quoting the canons of the field. However, research paradigms developed within these frames serve primarily to replicate the existing notions of acceptable research and tend to be masked by the notions of validity and reliability.

Issues of validity and reliability refer to the ability to reproduce the study and the degree to which the research can be generalized. Therefore, researchers who position themselves as engaging in oppositional research while applying these limited notions of study, limit the spectrum wherein which knowledges can be produced and disseminated. Adopting these restrictive methods of engaging research limits the audience for which it is intended (typically an academic audience), and further limits the application of the research findings, given that much of it is inaccessible to the population that has been researched.

Another factor to be considered within this discussion is the manner in which indigenous research tends to be restricted through technologies of control, such as the ethical review guidelines and the strict research codes that are implemented by the academy. An excellent example of this is the notion of having signed consent on the part of the participants. Given the painful history to which indigenous peoples have been subjected because they have "signed" documents they did not understand or that were written in a language different from their own (as in the case of the Canadian Aboriginal populations), many people are wary of placing their signature on paper. In addition, this process of signing papers changes the nature of the relationship that we have traditionally had with our elders and other community members.

We as researchers are effectively placed in a border zone (Anzaldua, 1987; Brah, 1996) between our community norms and the expectations of the university environment. This border zone becomes a space of conflict that is highly problematic for the researcher who is interested in engaging research that respects the indigenous community when, in the eyes of our community, we are regarded as outsiders (Hill-Collins, 1991), given our academic requests and affiliations. This becomes a difficult bridge to cross, effectively strangling us in limbo and leaving the narratives of our communities unrecorded because these systemic constraints also limit the particular techniques we may employ in conducting our research.

Constructing the Research Question

Following the structure of Eurocentric research paradigms that are noted for being steeped in scientific objectivity, the research questions have to be clearly defined prior to entering the field to conduct the research. Conventional researchers know what they are looking for and often wear blinders, eliminating any information that does not conform to or support the research question. Indigenous research methodology allows for the research project to be one of discovery in which researchers are open to what they find. The questions are not structured prior to the interviews, but rather there are some questions that are used to guide the interview while most of the questions emerge out of conversations with the participants. The participants exercise their agency in determining the route the conversation will follow.

Researching the lives of African Canadian women demands their participation in the structuring of the questions and issues that frame their existence. Entering the field with pre-set notions of what is to be found limits the collection of the data as well as the analysis, which tends to be grounded in the particular theoretical paradigm being employed rather than being based on the subjects' understanding of their circumstances. Conventional theoretical paradigms provide boxes into which the data must be trimmed to fit, and any extraneous bits of data that fail to support the initial quest are eliminated.

Allowing the research participants the opportunity to define the nature and application of the research, and therefore the research questions, respects their role as active subjects in their own development, informs the manner in which the resulting information is represented. The participants become subjects in the research rather than objects of a modernist research project. Adopting such practices allows the researcher to enter the field as a learner rather than a knower, and serves to neutralize the power imbalances inherent in traditional researcher-participant relationships. The relationships become symbiotic rather than parasitic.

Theoretical Frameworks to Ground Our Research

As mentioned earlier, race continues to be erased in both dominant and so-called critical discourses. This erasure of race speaks to the importance of applying frameworks that allow for the research to highlight the particularity of the experiences of black women who are bound within the social constructions of race, gender, and other forms of difference including class and sexuality. African feminism as an indigenous research framework allows for the development of an understanding of the uniqueness and specificities of women's experiences and allows the researcher to develop living theories. These living theories serve to explain the occurrences within a specified context and situation rather than subscribing to the notion of universalistic explanations of behavior developed primarily to control the behaviors of colonized bodies.

The application of indigenous research methodologies allows for the development of experience as research, and permits the possibility of moving the knowledges gained in the research from the individual level to the larger macrostructures. This is not equivalent to the generalizability of findings that is an important aspect of validity within Eurocentric theories. Rather it speaks to the need for the participants to make connections to the larger social structures that impact on their life circumstances. For example, a research project that examines issues of colonization within the Caribbean region can be connected to similar questions and issues on a larger or global scale. Recognizing the similarities in the experiences of various groups is significantly different from attempting to predict reactions to the colonizing process simply based on their race. Such an understanding allows researchers to begin to search for processes that allow the research participants to become creators of knowledge rather than being positioned as replicators of the social structures and systems that have reinforced their domination of others. It opens up spaces in which the participants can begin to exercise some degree of control over their representations. To ensure that research becomes transformative, we as researchers must be aware of the theoretical paradigms that ground our research.

"Anti-racism is a critical discourse of race and racism in society and of the continuing racializing of social groups for differential and unequal treatment. Anti-racism explicitly names the issues of race and social difference as issues of power and equity rather than as matters of cultural and ethnic variety" (Dei 1996, 25). Anti-racism research highlights the issues of power and the manner in which power dynamics inform the research project and provides alternatives to the racist paradigms that inform normative research projects.

In addition to this, anti-racism discourses allow for the examination and discussion of the manner in which varying levels of oppression intersect, while providing a basis for analyzing the real material manifestations of these oppressions. This particular theoretical framework provides the foundation for examining the impact of oppression at the level of the individual project, but also the tools for moving the project from local concerns to larger social, institutional, political, and economic structures that have been involved in the development of these problems. For example, within an anti-racism framework, one is able to conduct a research project that addresses the erasure of black women from Canadian literature and histories, while at the same time providing an examination of the manner in which historical and social factors such as power, racism, and institutionalized racist practices (such as schooling), have served to reinforce those practices within contemporary Canadian society.

Working within an anti-racist and African-centered feminist framework, for example, allows the researcher to develop an understanding of the manner in which the intersections of race and gender impact on the manner in which African women are researched. An African-centered feminist perspective provides a framework through which the lived experiences of African women can be used as sources of knowledge and ways of knowing, as well as a format through which living theories are created. Both of these discursive frameworks provide spaces within which minoritized bodies can be heard, and additionally provide multiple centers and sites of knowing through which the world can be understood. Using the canonical theories is, at best, limiting in its application to the lives of African Canadian women, and at the very least serves to re-center whiteness within the discussion of their lives. This therefore serves to replicate the concept of whiteness as the norm, reinforce hegemonic relations, and continues to push the lives of non-white bodies to the margins not only within society but also within academic discourses.

Multiculturalism, for example (the foundation theory upon which much of Canada's treatment of diversity issues is built) fails to address the institutionalized and historical factors that inform the manner in which the society's non-white citizenry is treated. The focus of multiculturalism remains rooted in the ideology that much of the conflict among diverse groups results from groups' lack of knowledge of each other. Therefore the focus has to be on providing positive stories and snippets of information regarding Canada's diverse populations.

Canada's liberalist multicultural ideology and policies have developed as a carnivalistic display (Daniel, 2001) of cultural foods, costumes, and various markers of different cultural groups including music and musical instruments. It is structured around the "add and stir" ideology in which diverse cultural practices are exoticized and included in the traditional Eurocentric curriculum as interesting information about diverse groups. Multiculturalism does not provide a space wherein one can begin to interrogate the manner in which whiteness fails to be included in the discussion of culture, or the fact that it continues to be considered the normative culture.

Shrouding discussions of racism and sexism in the coat of multicultural-ism provides an escape route for Canadian society to avoid addressing the impli-cations inherent in the adoption and application of the dominant paradigms. Multiculturalism's simplistic view that in the process of changing the curricu-lum (May, 1999) one has addressed the systemic and structural violence expe-rienced by minoritized social groups, makes its application problematic; it also fails to address the issue of power relations in society.

Attempts have been made in the contemporary literature to restructure the context of multicultural education rather than throwing out the proverbial baby with the bathwater. The emergence of critical multiculturalism discourses has heralded an attempt on the part of theorists to deconstruct the practice of mul-ticulturalism (May, 1999; Kanpol and McLaren, 1995; Nieto 1999), and to analyze the issues of diversity within a wider social context.

Discursive Framework

There are specific strengths that each of the frameworks brings to bear on this discussion. African-centered feminist epistemology combines the focus of fem-inisms applicable within an indigenous framework that focuses on research issues relevant to the subjects. Therefore, the outcomes of the research can be more applicable to the subjects and their specific contexts. For example, research that involves examining the ways in which Caribbean women become involved in small business can be used to enable the participants to improve their business strategies or develop new ways of advertising.

Another benefit of this discourse is the spaces that are opened up to allow for the unique expressions of the lives of women who are being researched. African-centered feminism allows for the participants to be involved in the ways in which the research is produced and the resulting knowledges disseminated. This level of control over the development of the research process plays an important role in the way in which the resulting knowledges are represented. Anti-racism research, with its ability to examine the social and institutional sys-tems that reinforce and buttress the systems of oppressions, illustrates the ways in which oppressions operate at differential levels for groups based on issues of race, gender, class, sexuality, and other forms of difference.

Another significant advantage of indigenous research paradigms lies in the ability to remain grounded within the particular community or context that is being researched.

A combination of these frameworks results in a theoretical discourse that allows for research to be developed that respects the specificities of the con-texts that inform the lives of the participants. The application of indigenous discourses also allows the research to move from the level of local concerns to global connections through a comprehensive analysis of the systemic and structural issues that inform the local contexts. The application of indigenous research methodologies provides for the application of research methods that are grounded in the particular communities that are being researched, and builds on the knowledges of the communities, while respecting the historical and ancestral ideologies that form its foundation.

Positioning of Self

According to Arber (2000), researchers must begin to question their position in the research project. The researcher's positioning can affect the questions that are being asked, the theoretical paradigms that are adopted, and the interpretation of the research data. A particular subjectivity informs that which is known, the knowledges that a person develops with regard to social and structural issues, and the manner in which power impacts on structural relationships. I believe that there is a world of difference between the acts of naming versus positioning oneself. Naming oneself becomes an act of stating a specific place in society that one occupies by virtue of belonging to a particular ethnic, religious, or sexual group. Positioning, by contrast, deals with the understanding of the material and social consequences or rewards that accompany the particular location or space that one occupies. For example, to name oneself as a Jewish woman is in no way an indication that the researcher has engaged in an analysis and interrogation of the meanings inherent in occupying that location.

Positioning comes with the understanding that as a Jewish woman, one is still located in white skin, and there are specific rewards that are accrued by virtue of being white. Therefore, it is important to analyze not only the idea of being female and Jewish but also the inherent implications of power that are intricately linked to whiteness and the impact that positioning can have on the research process.

Another example of naming that is problematic is the usage of the term *woman of color*. The term, which excludes white women, is an indication that whiteness is not a color. A further problem inherent in the usage of this term is the manner in which it serves to collapse the experiences of minoritized women. The naming of women within this terminology provides no indication as to the positioning of the subject or the particular politics they represent.

Carty and Brand (1993) in their piece titled "Visible Minority Women: A Creation of the Canadian State," discuss the manner in which the usage of such terms serve to group the experiences of minoritized women in an attempt to address their shared oppression. According to the authors, the unification of the oppression of differentially racialized bodies is "not only absurd but impossible, precisely because their racial histories cannot be unified" (1993, 207). According to the authors, the term *visible minority* emerged as a state initiative, designed to address the factors affecting immigrant women. Given the origin of the term, the benefits to women at the grassroots level are minimal. However, the state was able to tap into rapidly increasing groups of constituents. The resulting impact of such state-initiated frames of reference is the delegitimating of the ability of minoritized women to name and define themselves.

The efficacy of using the term *woman of color* has also been questioned by other authors such as Bannerji (1999) and Dua (1999). Dua, for example, questions whether the usage of the term serves to homogenize multiply located women's experiences of racism while simultaneously failing to address the issue of class. The universalistic and essentializing principles of the term is another level on which Dua questions its applicability.

Agnew (1996) posits that the term serves to categorize people with varied histories and experiences under one umbrella, based on the fact that they share a history of oppression and colonization. The term woman of color then serves to deny the uniqueness of their identity, traditions, and histories. The term is further problematized as it locates white women as the center and serves to marginalize nonwhite women.

I believe that it is difficult to engage a discussion regarding self-identification without critically interrogating the issue of who has the power to name these groups. An important aspect of the process of defining one's subjectivity is the power to name and define the issues that are important within one's community. According to Agnew, "Women are concerned about their identity and wish to name themselves. . . . However it is not just the identity imposed by these terms that is being challenged but also the political and social relations that such terms encode and attempt to obfuscate. Analyzing these terms exposes the power relations embedded in them and suggests strategies for resistance" (1996, 106).

The research implications inherent in this externally imposed naming are multifaceted. The issue of naming falls within the context of generalizability of the results, given that the manner in which the specific contexts that inform the unique experiences of women who are multiply located, are lost within the usage of the term *women of color*. The implication is that the research results gleaned from one particular project, designed to examine the experiences of women in a specific location, will apply to other women simply based on the assignation of the generic phrase. Therefore, being called a "woman of color," can serve to limit the degree to which minoritized women can exercise control over their representations.

As an African Canadian woman born in the Caribbean, I believe that I have been given a unique worldview that has allowed me to question and interrogate the manner in which black women and the black community have been represented. Growing up in a society where black skin was the norm and where there were doctors, lawyers, teachers, and all manner of professionals who looked like me, provided me with a clear sense that having black skin was in no way a type of pathology. However, having said that, I also remember the resistance I had not only to whiteness, but to the concepts that were being provided to us within, what I can now call a product of the colonial schooling system. As a child I could not verbalize my discomfort with the manner in which whiteness was revered, but as an adult in an academic environment, I continue to question and challenge the manner in which whiteness is centralized, and seek to identify ways in which I can respect and pass on the indigenous knowledges and teachings of my ancestors.

Another factor that affects my positioning is the issue of class, which significantly impacts on my experiences as an African Canadian woman. The opportunity to pursue higher education tempers the level of class-based discrimination than I will be subjected to. In my research I have to be aware of the manner in which I have been privileged, and to ensure that the privilege is not used as a tool of condemnation.

Additionally, I have to remain ever vigilant of the impact that a colonial education, such as the one that currently exists in graduate schools, continues to have on my understanding and reading of the world. Brewer, in discussing the discipline of sociology and the manner in which it informs the research practices of African American female intellectuals states that, "Even as its specialties include race relations, sex and gender and social stratification, the field is embedded in a masculinist, Eurocentric context in epistemological assumptions, research practice, and sociological training. . . . Yet, sociology as a field is problematic because it does not treat African American women as subjects in the world" (1997, 71)

Therefore, although I am engaged in a process of mentally decolonizing myself, the impact of colonization is ever present and at times debilitating, but most importantly it can be blinding. Its mental stranglehold on colonized subjects blinds us to the damaging effects and the manner in which we as subjects have become complicit in our own domination. Therefore, it is my responsibility to my participants to ensure that I am aware of the particular damage that can be inflicted upon them through my research, and ensure that I make every attempt to be fully aware of my fallacies, shortcomings, and the manner in which they inform my analysis of the information as well as the questions I ask. Further to this, I have to be aware of the implications of the manner in which I represent my participants and their knowledges.

In the process of positioning myself, I must begin to question my own location within the African Canadian community. Although I may share the realities of race and gender with African Canadian women, thereby making me an insider, my location within academia as well as my class affiliations serve to simultaneously position me as an outsider. Linda Tuhiwai Smith (1999) and Patricia Hill-Collins (1991) both speak to the difficulty inherent in this double-bind situation. Hill-Collins refers to this situation as the "outsider within."

Analyzing the Data

African-centered feminisms provide alternative lenses through which the information obtained from the research project can be analyzed. The theories we choose, the questions we ask, and the manner in which we position ourselves all impact on the way in which the data is analyzed. As mentioned earlier, Euro-masculinist discourses with the focus on validity and reliability as well as the search for the grand theories that can be used to speak for the entire group being researched, are of limited usefulness. African-centered feminisms provide multiple centers from which the data can be analyzed.

The goal of the research projects framed within both anti-racism and African-centered feminist discourses, is to analyze the data based on the specificities of the context in which the phenomenon is occurring. The transformative nature of these indigenous paradigms lies in their ability to not only allow the space for the participants to be involved in the development of the project, but also in how the data is presented. Additionally, the opportunities for participants to make connections with the larger social structures that affect their circumstances, allows them to develop a heightened sense of agency in determining the application of the particular research project.

An added factor that is of importance in the discussion of the analysis of the data is the determination of whether the discourses allow for an analysis based on the interlocking nature of the oppressions that function in the lives of black women. For example, research that involves the experiences of black women in academia cannot be effectively analyzed within a white feminist framework that centers gender as the main cause of women's oppression. African Canadian women should not be placed in a position where they are forced to privilege one form of oppression over another when they are simultaneously present in their lives, and it is difficult if not impossible to separate the effect of one from the other. An effective analysis within such a research project will have to interrogate the impact of race, gender, class, sexuality, and the multiple "isms" that frame our lives. The analysis should examine the way that these social ascriptions work and uniquely inform the lives and experiences of African Canadian women and the manner in which we are represented in academia.

Within the African Canadian community, the issues of class and sexuality are also very real aspects of the daily lives of women, and any attempts to erase these real issues, which have significant material consequences, belies the results of the research project. Race and gender are the two main issues that provide a shared history of oppression, and they significantly impact the manner in which we are represented in society. However, one should resist making the assumption that our race and gender are the only factors that impinge on our lives in Canada.

Research and Representation

As a group African women have been labeled in ways that have run from one end of the spectrum to the other, and in ways that appear to have mutative powers that allow them to change dramatically from one situation to the next. For example, the ascription of the mammy, loving when interacting and caring for white children, changes and becomes the dominating and welfare-trapped mother when dealing with her black family. The loving asexual figure that has been the wet nurse for generations of white families becomes the hypersexualized black Sapphire when she enters her own community. The representations of African womanhood have been created in the white imagination, and black women have had limited power in determining the manner in which these images have evolved. These images have pervaded our psyches for generations and have affected us in many ways that have yet to be examined. What has become increasingly clear is the importance of ensuring that we as African Canadian women continue to assume responsibility for the development of those images.

I think of the many times I have been subjected to the stereotyped images of who I am expected to be and been aware of the subtle and almost invisible manner in which these negative stereotypes emerge in conversation with those whites who would vehemently deny any racist notions or intentions. When the comments are made about my being too young to have children as old as I do, the image of the black teenage mother becomes wrapped up in that "compliment." Being placed in a position in which my apparent age impacts on my credibility and becomes a marker of my approval within academia is a contested space that few whites occupy or have to defend.

Nellie Y. McKay, in her discussion of the experiences of black faculty in predominantly white institutions, indicates that, "our location is always contested space even though it is as rightfully our space as that of others in the academy" (1997, 15). Research becomes a forum through which we can begin to reaffirm our right to occupy these spaces and others that have been denied to us through the exclusionary practices of racism and sexism.

African women in academia are all too often labeled as being angry when we dare to speak passionately about an issue. The white woman on the other hand, will be regarded as knowledgeable of her particular area of interest. Significant amounts of our energies are directed toward self-preservation and fighting the invectives that are constantly hurled at us. This is but one context wherein the importance of positioning our experiences and ourselves, is highlighted.

The experience of African women in academic circles is often discussed as a privilege that serves to highlight the distance that we have traveled. Inasmuch as this is true, it is a significantly skewed version of the picture, and it is used to highlight the quality of the Canadian education system. At every point in time, our experiences are being used in ways that continue to be detrimental to us and to future generations of African Canadian women. Using our experiences and our ability to attain this level of work as a way of showing that the school system is a good one, serves to blind one to the atrocities that are being committed against us in that very system. Additionally, it dismisses the necessity of conducting serious investigations into the experiences of black girls in the school system and the coping mechanisms they develop in order to allow them to remain afloat in the system.

As researchers we have to begin to ask questions such as: How are the images of African women in the texts being used in the curriculum impacting on the experiences of black girls in the schools? What coping mechanisms are African Canadian female students adopting that have allowed them to be successful? How do the images of African Canadian women inform the relationships between black girls and their teachers? And most importantly, how do these images inform the African Canadian female students' self-concept? Lewis indicates that "Any viable approach . . . must focus first on deconstructing contrived history, demystifying the false scientific basis of subjective knowledge, uncovering the hypocrisy and special interests that undergird it, and presenting it clearly and forcefully to those who are paralyzed by the controlling paradigm" (1997, 49). She goes on to say that "Once black women in the academy situate themselves within the global struggle against racist/capitalist patriarchy, they are positioned to build a bridge for youth and others in the academy and are poised to serves as both catalysts and resource leaders for empowering the community of the oppressed" (49).

One primary rationale that has caused non-white bodies to resist the infringement of research into their lives and communities is the knowledge that most of the information they provide is lost and their voices and words are often changed. Oftentimes white researchers enter indigenous communities, engage in research projects, return to the academy to write their theses, and leave with their degrees. Non-white voices and experiences are used to feed the credentializing process of the academy. This leads us to question who speaks on behalf of the participants and who owns the voices and the knowledges that are produced. Within traditional Eurocentric discourses, the author and the academy own the information, and little thought is given to the authorial capacity of the participants. According to indigenous ways of interacting with the world, no one owns knowledge.

Engaging in research that respects African Canadian women allows us to resist the essentialization and commodification of these experiences and resist the creation of our identities through the media and other forms of cultural socialization. Rather, we as women can reclaim the histories, representations, and indigenous knowledges of African Canadian women, while simultaneously resisting the application of Eurocentric principles in these research projects.

There are political implications inherent in incorporating African-centered feminist frameworks. In addition to allowing us the space to see our own interests and desires reflected in the research being conducted in our communities, we reclaim the right to determine who engages in the research as well as the application of its results. Reclaiming the power to name and define from the hands of white males and females is an act of empowerment in and of itself.

Perhaps the difficulty that many of us a black women face is that, while we have been sojourners in this world, we are also on an internal journey that includes a search for ourselves. I believe that the very act of questioning speaks to our agency in trying to determine the particular epistemological groundings that best meet our needs rather than subscribing to that which has been imposed upon us. Ifi Amadiume (1997) speaks of the sense of power that comes from that naming, and to that I would add the sense of privilege, given that as minoritized women we are often identified within Western scholarship as being without power or privilege.

REFERENCES

Agnew, V. 1996. *Resisting Discrimination: Women from Asia, Africa, and the Caribbean and the Women's Movement in Canada*. Toronto: University of Toronto Press.

Aidoo, A. A. 1998. "African Woman Today." In Obioma Nnaemeka (Ed.), *Sisterhood, Feminisms and Power: From Africa to the Diaspora.* Trenton, NJ: Africa World Press.

Amadiume, I. 1997. *Reinventing Africa: Matriarchy, Religion and Culture.* London: Zed Books Ltd.

Amos, V., and Parmar, P. 1997. "Challenging Imperial Feminism." *Black British Feminism*, Routledge, pp. 54–58.

Anzaldua, G. 1987. *Borderlands: The New Mestiza? La Frontera.* San Francisco: Aunte Lute Books.

Arber, R. 2000. "Defining Positioning within Politics of Difference: Negotiating Spaces 'In Between.'" *Race, Ethnicity and Education 3* (1): 45–62.

Bannerji, H. 1999. A Question of Silence: Refelctions on Violence against Women in Communities of Colour. In E. Dua and A. Robertson (Eds.), *Canadian Anti-Racist Feminist Thought.* Toronto: Women's Press, pp. 261–277.

Barrow, C. 1998. *Caribbean Portraits: Essays on gender ideologies and identities.* Kingston: Ian Randle Publishers.

Brah, A. 1996. *Cartographies of Diaspora: Contesting Identities.* London, New York: Routledge.

Brand, D., and Carty, L. 1991. *No Burden to Carry: Narratives of Black Working Women in Ontario, 1920s–1950s.* Toronto: Women's Press.

Brewer, R. M. 1997. "Giving Name and Voice: Black Women Scholars, Research, and Knowledge Transformation." In Lois Benjamin (Ed.), *Black Women in the Academy: Promises and Perils.* Florida: University of Florida Press, pp. 68–80.

Carty, L., & Brand, D. 1993. "Visible Minority Women: A Creation of the Canadian State". In H. Bannerji (Ed.), *Returning the Gaze: Essays on Racism, Feminism and Politics.* Sister Vision Press, pp. 207–222.

Christian, B. 1987. "The Race for Theory." *Cultural Critique 6* (Spring): 51–62.

Daniel, B. J. 2001. "Merging Theoretical Paradigms: Discussing Race, Class and Gender in Teacher Education." Unpublished paper, Ontario Institute for Studies in Education, University of Toronto.

Dei, G. J. S., Karumanchery, L. 2001. School Reforms in Ontario: The 'Marketization' of Education and the Resulting Silence on Equity. In. J. Portelli & R.P. Solomon (Eds.), *The Erosion of Democracy in Education: From Critique to Possibilities.* Calgary: Det Selig Enterprises Ltd. pp. 189–215.

Dei, G. J. S., Hall, B. L., Rosenberg, D.G. 2000. *Indigenous Knowledges.* University of Toronto Press.

Dei, G. J. S. 1996. *Anti-Racism Education: Theory and Practice.* Halifax: Fernwood Publishing.

Dennis, R. M. 1993. "Participant Observations." In J H. Stanfield and R. M. Dennis (Eds.), *Race and Ethnicity in Research Methods.* Thousand Oaks, CA: Sage Focus Editions, pp. 53–74.

Dua, E. 1999. "Canadian Anti-Racist Feminist Thought: Scratching the Surface of Racism." In E. Dua and A. Robertson (Eds.), *Canadian Anti-Racist Feminist Thought.* Toronto: Women's Press, pp. 7–34.

Ellsworth, E. 1994. "Representation, Self-Presentation, and the Meaning of Difference: Questions for Educators." In R. Matusewicz and W. Reynolds (Eds.), *Inside/Out: Contemporary Critical Perspectives in Education.* New York: St.Martin's, pp. 99–108.

Fine, M. 1994. "Working the Hyphens: Reinventing Self and Other in Qualitative Research." In N. K. Denzin and Y. S. Lincoln (Eds.), *Handbook of Qualitative Research*. Thousand Oaks, CA: Sage, pp. 70–82.

Fonow, M., and Cook, J. 1991. *Beyond Methodology: Feminist Scholarship as Lived Research.* Bloomington, Indiana: University Press.

Gilroy, P. 1993. *Small Acts: Thoughts on the Politics of Black Cultures.* London: Serpents Tail.

Henry, A. 1998. *Taking Back Control: African Canadian Women Teachers' Lives and Practice.* Albany: State University of New York Press.

Hill-Collins, P. 1991. "Learning form the Outsider Within: The Sociological Significance of Black Feminist Thought." In M. Fonow and J. Cook (Eds.), *Beyond Methodology: Feminist Scholarship as Lived Research.* Bloomington: Indiana University Press, pp. 35–59.

hooks, b. 1992. *Black Looks: Race and Representation.* Toronto: Between the Lines.

Kanpol, B. and MacLaren P. 1995. *Critical Multiculturalism: Uncommon Voices in a Common Struggle.* Westport, Conn.: Bergin & Garvey.

Leah, R. J. 1999. "Do You Call ME "Sister"? Women of Color and the Canadian Labour Movement." In E. Dua and A. Robertson (Eds.), *Canadian Anti-Racist Feminist Thought.* Toronto: Women's Press, pp. 97–126.

Lewis, S. 1997. Africana Feminism: An alternative paradigm for Black women in the academy. In, B. Lois (Ed.), *Black Women in the Academy: Promises and Perils.* University of Florida Press, pp. 41–52.

Lorde, A. 2001. "The Master's Tool Will Never Dismantle the Master's House." In Kum Kum Bhavnani (Ed.), *Feminism and Race.* Oxford: Oxford University Press, pp. 89–92.

Lyotard, J. F. 1984. *The Postmodern Condition: A Report on Knowledge.* London: Penguin Books.

May, S. 1999. *Critical Multiculturalism: Rethinking Multicultural and Antiracist Education.* Philadelphia, PA: Falmer Press.

McKay, N. Y. 1997. "A Troubled Peace: Black Women in the Halls of the White Academy." In Lois Benjamin (Ed.), *Black Women in the Academy: Promises and Perils.* Gainesville: University Press of Florida.

Moses, Y. T. 1997. "Black Women in Academe: Issues and Strategies." In Lois Benjamin (Ed.), *Black Women in the Academy: Promises and Perils.* Gainesville: University Press of Florida.

Neuman, W. L. 1991. *Social Research Methods: Qualitative and Quantitative Approaches.* Boston, MA: Allyn and Bacon.

Nieto, S. 1999. *The Light in Their Eyes: Creating Multicultural Learning Communities.* New York: Teachers College Press.

Nnaemeka, O. 1998. "Introduction: Reading the Rainbow." In Obioma Nnaemeka (Ed.), *Sisterhood, Feminisms and Power: From Africa to the Diaspora.* Trenton, NJ: Africa World Press, pp. 1–29.

O'Brien, H. L. 1999. "A Postmodern Caring: Feminist Standpoint Theories, Revisioned Caring and Communications Ethics." *Western Journal 63,* 32–56.

Powell, J. A. 1999. The Color-Blind Multiracial Dilemma: Racial Categories Reconsidered. In R. D. Torres, L. F. Mirón & J.X. Inda, (Eds.), *Race, Identity and Citizenship.* London: Blackwell Publishers, pp. 141–157.

Radford-Hill, S. 2000. *Further to Fly: Black Women and the Politics of Empowerment*. Minneapolis: University of Minnesota Press.

Robertson, A. 1999. "Continuing on the Ground: Feminists of Colour Discuss Organizing." In E. Dua and A. Robertson (Eds.), *Canadian Anti-Racist Feminist Thought*. Toronto: Women's Press, pp. 309–329.

Shadd, A. 1994. "The Lord Seemed to Say 'Go': Women and the Underground Railroad Movement." In *"We're Rooted Here and They can't Pull us Up": Essays in African Canadian Women's History*. Toronto: University of Toronto Press, pp. 41–68.

Smith, T. L. 1999. *Decolonizing Methodologies: Research and Indigenous Peoples*. New York: St Martin's Press.

Smith, V. 1998. *Not just Race, Not just Gender: Black Feminist Readings*. New York: Routledge.

St. Pierre, E. A., and Pillow, W. S. 2000. "Inquiry among the Ruins." In Elizabeth St. Pierre and Wanda Pillow (Eds.), *Working the Ruins: Feminist Poststructural Theory and Methods in Education*. New York: Routledge, pp. 1–24.

Steady, F. C. 1985. "The Black Woman Cross-Culturally: An Overview." In Filomina Chioma Steady (Eds.). *The Black Woman Cross-Culturally*. Rochester, Vermont: Schenkman Books, Inc.

Wright, C., Weekes, D., McLaughlin, A., and Webb, D. 1998. "Masculinized Discourses within Education and the Construction of Black Male Identities amongst African Caribbean Youth." *British Journal of Sociology 19*(1): 75–87.

Chapter Four

KAREN MAX

Anti-colonial Research

WORKING AS AN ALLY
WITH ABORIGINAL PEOPLES

Introduction

The term "research" is inextricably linked to European imperialism and colonialism. The word itself, "research," is probably one of the dirtiest words in the indigenous world's vocabulary.

—Linda Smith (1999)

Anti-colonial research must be initiated, directed, and controlled by Aboriginal peoples.[1] Research must do more than avoid harm to participants, it must benefit those involved (Battiste and Henderson, 2000). If non-aboriginal researchers are to collaborate effectively with aboriginal peoples, it is important to understand how Eurocentric belief systems maintain colonial relationships and undermine self-determination. From this place of awareness and understanding it becomes possible to work for change.

While it is not appropriate for non-aboriginal people to do research on aboriginal peoples, we can work to become allies in collaborative research projects. As we work to become allies, we begin to turn our gazes from the "Other" (Razack, 1998) onto ourselves. As we reflect critically on our own positions of privilege, we become better able to work collaboratively and respectfully.

This chapter will highlight some initiatives that aboriginal peoples are taking to reclaim research through an anti-colonial lens. Through reflections on my work in northern Canada I will also explore the tentative path of beginning to work as an ally, from a position of privilege as a white woman.

Re-defining Racism

Racist ideologies have been used to justify colonization and subjugation of peoples, lands and continents. By way of racism, entire communities, languages and cultures have been eradicated.

—George Dei (2001)

The Ontario Anti-Racism Secretariat of the Ontario Ministry of Citizenship defines racism as: "A system in which one group of people exercises abusive power over others on the basis of skin color and racial heritage; a set of implicit or explicit beliefs, erroneous assumptions and actions based upon an ideology of inherent superiority of one racial or ethno-cultural group over another." For many aboriginal peoples, racism also has another layer, which relates to land and treaty rights.

North American aboriginal opposition to systemic racism is grounded in economic claims to land mass; timber, mineral, and fishing rights; the right to regulate their economies, including high-stakes bingo and importing cigarettes; and in political terms to sovereignty and self-determination (Regnier, 1995, 75).

The Chippewas of Nawash outline a new definition of racism that encompasses individual, institutional, and cultural racism as they relate to self-determination for aboriginal peoples.

> Racism is any communication, action or course of conduct, whether intentional or unintentional, which denies recognition, benefits, rights of access or otherwise abrogates or derogates from the constitutionally recognized rights and freedoms of any person or community on the basis of their membership or perceived membership in any racial, ethnic or cultural community. The fostering and promotion of uniform standards, common rules and same treatment of people who are not the same constitute racism where the specificity of the individual or community is not taken into consideration. The public dissemination of any communication or statement which insults a racial, ethnic or cultural community or which exposes them to hatred, contempt or ridicule also constitutes racism. (http//www.bmts.com/~dibaudjimoh /page14.html)

The process of colonization uses racism as a tool, a justification to exist. In their book, *Protecting Indigenous Knowledge and Heritage*, Battiste and Henderson (2000) outline Memmi's four strategies, which have been used to exert colonial control over indigenous peoples.

> (1) stressing real or imaginary differences between the racist and the victim; (2) assigning values to these differences, to the advantage of the racist and the detriment of the victim; (3) trying to make these values absolutes by generalizing from them and claiming that they are final; and (4) using these values to justify any present or possible aggression or privileges. (Memmi, as quoted in Battiste and Henderson, 2000, 134)

An understanding of racism and aboriginal peoples, needs to include an understanding of the colonial process that is a part of imperialism. Reconciliation must involve recognition of treaty rights and land claims, and will only occur through the recognition of self-government and self-determination of Aboriginal peoples. Denying these rights adds another layer to individual and institutional racism.

Dei and Asgharzadeh (2001) defines colonization as not simply "foreign" or "alien" but rather as "imposed and dominating." They urge us to "redefine the term colonial to include all forms of dominating and oppressive relationships that emerge from structures of power and privilege inherent and embedded in our contemporary relationships" (7). If research is to move away from its colonial history with aboriginal peoples, it is essential to center aboriginal worldviews.

Locating Myself

One must know and understand the self in order to pursue politics for anti-racism change. Subjectivities are contradictory sites of privilege, domination and subordination.
—George Dei (1999)

My social location, class, skin color, gender, sexuality, race, and level of ability all conspire to form the lens through which I make sense of the world. However, understanding our social position and naming our subjectivity should not merely begin and end with a litany of "I am a white heterosexual . . ." in order to name our biases and let ourselves off the hook, while we continue our oppressive practices (Patai, 1994). It is important to recognize that skin color is a powerful marker that attaches privileges to white skin and punishment to dark skin (Dei, 1996). Different bodies take different risks and reap different rewards in naming their subjectivities. It is safe for me to say who I am, but many people do not experience this sense of safety. I believe that locating ourselves should be an ongoing reflexive process that requires an openness to critique from others, as well as our own critical reflection of ourselves and our work.

I was born in Denmark and am writing as a white, heterosexual, female, mother, and university student, working toward a master's degree. My work in northern Canada at a women's shelter was what compelled me to come back to school and explore aboriginal epistemologies and Aboriginal worldviews. Through my work in the north, I had many questions about working cross-culturally, as an ally with aboriginal peoples. As the program co-ordinator at a women's shelter, I was asked to conduct training with aboriginal women who were looking to create a safe home for abused elders, women, and children in their community. While working with these dedicated and inspiring individuals, I learned that often my view and perspectives did not mesh with the work of the community.

For example, I was taught to see violence in relationships from within a critique of patriarchy primarily perpetrated by men against women. From this perspective, the solutions involved a narrow focus of working with women alone, helping them leave their community to go to a safe shelter in another town. The aboriginal women that I worked with repeatedly asked who would help the men in their community. Their focus was much more holistic as they looked toward healing for the entire community. While it was not seen as a justification for violence, their was a recognition that the causes of violence were complex and any analysis needed to include an understanding of the oppressive policies of the Indian Act, the residential schools, and centuries of devastating colonial practices that still exist today.

After several years of working within a system that seemed to be making the lives of many aboriginal peoples worse instead of better, I began to question my framework for understanding violence. By talking to aboriginal women and reading the work of leading scholars, I was able to expand my feminist analysis to include an anti- colonial perspective on violence (LaRocque, 1993; Comaskey and McGillivray, 1999). This shift in thinking reverberated throughout my work in the north as I began to question the policies, power structures, and philosophies under which the shelters operated. I began to see colonization not just as something that happened in the past and was now over, but as an ongoing practice playing itself out in everyday acts of racism and sexism within the system.

For example, when I decided to move north to look for work in the counselling field, I was warned by many people about the serious problems of violence and alcohol abuse in "native communities." The people who issued these warnings never spoke about how the centuries of colonization have devastated the lives of many aboriginal people and forever changed their communities. I found after working for several years with aboriginal peoples that much of the victimization I saw was occurring within the white systems they turned to for help.

Many of the non-aboriginal people that I worked with had no knowledge of the impacts of colonization and therefore perpetrated stereotypes about aboriginal communities. Often I heard police and judges blame an aboriginal woman for her partner's abuse because she may have been drinking. They had no understanding of why women may use alcohol as a coping mechanism.

An aboriginal woman involved in a Winnipeg study about domestic violence described her experience:

> There were a lot of times when I did call (the police), I don't think they believed me. Or else they would take one look at me and say, well, I got a lot of smart comments from them like 'you probably deserved it, look how drunk you are . . . If I had an old lady like you that was as mouthy I would slap her around too.' (Comaskey and McGillivray, 1999, 100).

I often heard social workers and police blame women for choosing to return to their communities, even though they might have been returning to try to get custody of their children or they may have had nowhere else to go. There was also very little understanding of the importance of the support of family members and extended family. It was assumed that aboriginal women would be safer outside of their communities, but many aboriginal women who came into our shelter were not safe when they left home to move to larger cities. For many of these women, the isolation, poverty, racism, and sexism experienced while living in shelters or on the street were new and different forms of violence and abuse.

I found that judges and police often became frustrated with the lack of reporting of domestic abuse, and they would comment; "Why should we press charges when she never testifies anyway?" While the reasons for this are complex and multilayered, many women that I worked with had no faith in the justice system. They were not willing to go through the disruptive court process to see their partner get a ridiculously short sentence. A Winnipeg study of domestic violence found a similar experience among their participants.

> One or more partners of nine respondents received a jail term of less than one year. One got six months for a reign of terror of repeated assaults, in which he broke the respondent's nose and eardrum and knocked out her teeth. (Comaskey and McGillivray, 1999, 118)

In the shelter where I worked we did an intake when a woman first arrived. We asked whether she was Status First Nations (status, or legal recognition as an "Indian" is granted or withheld according to the dictates of the Federal Indian Act) or not and recorded her band number so that social services could bill the DIA (Department of Indian Affairs) for her stay. We did not record race statistics for any other group of women. I became concerned that these statistics could then potentially be used to portray domestic violence as an aboriginal problem, when in reality we worked with women from many different racial and cultural backgrounds.

While working as a women's advocate, I noticed that aboriginal women received less social assistance through DIA than non-aboriginal women did through Social Services. This formed a huge barrier for women with several children who were attempting to find housing in the community. I also noticed that many more aboriginal women lost custody of their children when they left an abusive partner than non-aboriginal women did. Some women had a difficult time accessing legal aid or got lawyers who were incompetent.

By working closely with aboriginal peoples, I began to have an inkling that their worldviews, their epistemologies, may hold some of the answers to research that could be inclusive, empowering, and relevant for all peoples. Through living in the north and learning about the worldviews of aboriginal peoples, I have started a paradigm shift where I am beginning to think in circles instead of hierarchies. This has opened my eyes to the importance of diversity and the inclusive nature of aboriginal worldviews.

Shifting the Gaze and Becoming Allies

> Within complex and ever shifting realities of power relations do we position ourselves on the side of the colonizing mentality? Or do we continue to stand in political resistance with the oppressed . . . where transformation is possible?
>
> —bell hooks (in Fine, 1994, 71)

While white researchers debate about whether it is appropriate to conduct cross-cultural research, aboriginal peoples, are taking control of their own research. At the same time, a huge void exists in the study of whiteness and white privilege as it relates to working with aboriginal peoples. Much of the writing about white people working cross-culturally in aboriginal communities focuses on learning cultural norms, while it ignores glaring power imbalances and oppressive histories. It is much easier to focus on the "Other" and how to work with "them." However, what I am proposing is that we shift the gaze to ourselves, our biases, and what we bring to our research.

The *gaze* refers to how white people look at those who are not white and how we construct them in our minds as different, subordinate, and primitive as compared to whites (Dei, 1996; Razack, 1998). Creating an "Other" is part of creating an identity that allows white people to see ourselves as helpers, generous and giving. At the same time we construct "those less fortunate" who "need our help" (Smith, 1999).

Constructions of the "Other" are not some deep dark secret left behind in the past. They are constantly reformed in our day-to-day interactions. For example, when I left the north to return to school in Toronto, I would mention to people that I had been working at a women's shelter up north. The first reaction from other white people was usually a sort of knowing look and the comment, "Wow, lots of problems with the natives up there, eh?"

It seemed that when whites got together and talked about "working in the north," a sort of one-upmanship would occur as each of us tried to come up with a more ghoulish story about what we saw. This allowed us to construct people as victims with sites of agency erased or portrayed as deviance. At the same time we positioned ourselves as altruistic and generous.

The stories we tell each other, along with constant media images flashing us glimpses of the social problems in aboriginal communities, allow us to create "their problem" while we, as white people, avoid looking at our own complicity. We rarely see examples of agency or resistance, and when we do, aboriginal peoples are portrayed as violent warriors. We see ourselves as generous helpers instead of as part of the problem.

The irony is that while we slot the "Other" into the space below us in our hierarchical configuration of the world, we also mystify and commodify the "Other" as someone exotic who holds the key to something missing in ourselves. As happens in a capitalist society, we try to buy what we have called mystical and a new age market for dream-catcher air fresheners and collector talking-sticks is born. As bell hooks states in her essay "Eating the Other";

> The commodification of Otherness has been so successful because it is offered as a new delight, more intense, more satisfying than normal ways of doing and feeling. Within commodity culture, ethnicity becomes the spice, seasoning that can liven up the dull dish that is mainstream white culture. (hooks, 1992, 21)

Sometimes knowledges become commodified as well, something we pull out and share as if to prove that we are enlightened. For example, last winter the Indigenous Education Network (IEN) at the Ontario Institute for Studies in Education (OISE) organized several speakers including roundtable sessions with local elders and a book launch displaying the works of aboriginal authors. A friend of mine, who is Cree, gently chastised me for writing down the elders' stories. She reminded me to listen fully and completely with my heart, and not focus on remembering the story. I have struggled to do this and I ask myself why I was so intent on taking the stories home with me, by writing them down or remembering them. I know that the stories seemed so powerful to me, with many hidden layers of meaning. My mind was racing and I wanted to hold onto that moment. It was not enough to learn from the teaching and enjoy the moment; somehow I wanted to keep it.

When white people work with aboriginal peoples, we must be ever vigilant of this tendency in ourselves. I have heard white students, myself included, question whether we should include cultural practices, such as smudging or circle work, into our research with Aboriginal peoples in order to be culturally appropriate.

When we appropriate these practices we are taking and using something cultural out of context, while avoiding the critical interrogation of power and privilege. Through a constant focus on the "Other" we avoid looking at the complicity of our own privilege. Exploring whiteness also means critically examining our own histories, understanding that which had been destructive and revisiting our own rituals and cultural practices. Shifting the gaze means that we critique constructions of the "Other" that place white people and our knowledge at the center of our Western hierarchy, while we see other knowledges as inferior.

I am not advocating that white researchers never do research with aboriginal peoples. I am interested in a new direction in research where we problematize our own privilege and our complicity in the colonial system. I do not personally feel that it is ethical for me to conduct research on or about Aboriginal peoples. Although I may learn about Aboriginal worldviews and perspectives, I know that I still view the world through a Eurocentric lens. Any research that I conduct in Aboriginal communities would be influenced by my different values, cultural beliefs, language, structures of power, and a different conceptualization of things such as time, space, and subjectivity (Smith, 1999). When we turn the lens on ourselves, it is imperative that we learn how to act as allies with Aboriginal peoples. Positions of power are not given up when we merely critique our own privilege while refusing to engage with Aboriginal peoples. Refusing to work together gives us a privileged way out of dealing with difficult issues (Patai, 1994). We must learn to work cooperatively and respectfully.

Acting as an ally involves educating ourselves about the impact of colonization in the past, as well as the current processes of colonization. Anti-colonial work is not about understanding differences but is about a deeper analysis of power and privilege. This includes an understanding of agency and complicity. In her book *Decolonizing Methodologies* (1999), Linda Smith offers the following guidelines for cross-cultural research:

> Researchers must go further than simply recognizing personal beliefs and assumptions, and the effect they have when interacting with people. In a cross-cultural context the questions that need to be asked are ones such as: Who defined the research problem? For whom is this study worthy and relevant? Who says so? What knowledge will the community gain from this study? What knowledge will the researcher gain from this study? What are some likely positive outcomes from this study? What are some possible negative outcomes? How can the negative outcomes be eliminated? To whom is the researcher accountable? What processes are in place to support the research, the researched and the researcher? (Smith, 1999, 173)

These critical questions are not put forth as a blueprint for cross-cultural research, but as a part of the questioning that must be part of an ethical process. Other questions that Smith (1999) advocates relate to challenging the assumption that researchers can find *the truth* as if one truth exists out there somewhere.

Linda Smith (1999, 177) offers four models of culturally appropriate research developed by Graham Smith, for non-indigenous researchers working with the Maori people. One model is called *tiaki*, where the Maori people guide and sponsor the research through a mentoring process with the researcher. In the *whangai* model the researcher becomes a part of the day-to-day lives of the Maori people and sustains lifelong relationships that become a part of the research. The third involves a "power-sharing model" in which "researchers seek the assistance of the community to meaningfully support the development of a research enterprise." The fourth model, the "empowering outcomes model," focuses on the questions that Maori people have themselves and would like to research in order to improve social conditions. Linda Smith cautions that, as Russell Bishop argues, "espousing an emancipatory model of research has not of itself freed researchers from exercising intellectual arrogance or employing evangelical and paternalistic practices" (Smith, 1999, 177).

Collaborative research is another possibility for anti-racist research with aboriginal peoples. Jo-Anne Archibald and Celia Haig-Brown explore the use of critical ethnography in their (1996) article, "Transforming First Nations Research with Respect and Power." Their example uses storytelling and constant critical reflection to develop research that can be transformative.

Ethical guidelines are being developed to protect indigenous knowledges and practices. In 1993 when the Royal Commission of Aboriginal Peoples was doing research in aboriginal communities, they developed extensive ethical protocols to guide this research. Collaborative processes ensured that Aboriginal community members would be involved in meaningful ways at all stages of the research process (Battiste and Henderson, 2000). Community protocols must be respected so that key community members are not excluded from the research process. Sometimes it may not be appropriate to ask one member of the community to speak as a representative of the whole community (Battiste and Henderson, 2000). Reporting back to the community and sharing any knowledge gained is also an important part of ethical research (Smith, 1999).

Research institutes, universities, and funding bodies must work creatively to find ways to strengthen the local communities' capacity to do their own research on their own terms. One example may include specific research grants for communities interested in doing their own research. Partnerships between universities or colleges and communities may be another way to strengthen local research. To do this work, power inequities between universities and communities must be interrogated. If we remain stuck in a hierarchical framework, universities often place the value of their knowledge production at the top, with other forms of knowledge falling below. However, if we embrace a circular approach, we see the equal contributions of different forms of knowledge.

As collaborative partnerships emerge, interested community members may be able to mentor with more experienced researchers. As more aboriginal peoples engage a decolonization process and become professors in mainstream institutions, more opportunities are created for these mentoring partnerships. Having said that, the work of a mentor should be granted equal status to the research and writing of other professors. It is important that Aboriginal professors do not have the added burden of mentoring others in communities, while they are expected to publish, research, plan events on campus, and teach.

Aboriginal Peoples and Anti-colonial Research

We don't need anyone else developing the tools, which will help us come to terms with who we are. We can and will do this work. Real power lies with those who design the tools—it always has. This power is ours.
—Kathie Irwin (in Smith. 1999, 38)

Over the last year, I have been privileged to learn about some initiatives that Aboriginal peoples have taken to define and shape research from within their own epistemologies. While I will outline several projects, I recognize that this is not a complete list of Aboriginal or indigenous research initiatives.

In her book *Decolonizing Methodologies* (1999), Linda Smith outlines twenty-five indigenous projects. These research projects revolve around the themes of self-determination, healing, cultural survival, restoration, and social justice. The projects are:

[C]laiming, testimonies, story telling, celebrating survival, remembering, indigenizing, intervening, revitalizing, connecting, reading, writing, representing, gendering, envisioning, reframing, restoring, returning, democratizing, networking, naming, protecting, creating, negotiating, discovering and sharing. (Smith, 1999, 143–161)

These projects, in different ways, all involve "the survival of peoples, cultures and languages; the struggle to become self-determining, the need to take back control of our destinies" (Smith, 1999, 142).

Smith also describes an indigenous research methodology called "Kaupapa Maori Research." This type of research methodology reflects a movement toward taking control of research as the Maori people move from objects being researched to subjects doing the researching. The process involves centering the concerns and worldviews of Aboriginal peoples. Kathy Irwin characterizes Kaupapa Maori as research that is "culturally safe"; involves the mentorship of elders; is culturally relevant and appropriate while satisfying the rigors of research; and is undertaken by a Maori researcher, not a researcher who happens to be Maori (Smith, 1999, 184).

Empowerment can only come through having control over the research process. Decolonization cannot be given as a gift, it must be part of a process that involves struggle, conflict, and a changing social order (Dei and Asgharzadeh, 2001). While non-Maori people may act as allies or support people, these projects are conceptualized through a Maori worldview. Kaupapa Maori research has taken a strong anti-positivist stance and is envisioned as something "both less than and more than a paradigm" (Smith, 1999, 190). It defines what will be studied and what questions will be asked, while it builds on its own set of distinctly Maori assumptions, values, and knowledge. At the same time, it establishes sites of struggle that "weave in and out of Maori cultural beliefs and values, Western ways of knowing, Maori histories and experiences under colonialism, Western forms of education, Maori aspirations and socio-economic needs and Western economics and global politics" (Smith, 1999, 191). Kaupapa Maori research is concerned with improving the lives of those who are researched. For this reason, control of the research lies within the community doing the researching.

Some community members have developed clear ethical review procedures for research that occurs in their communities. Maori people are also developing their own lists of priorities for future directions of research from within their own value systems and cultural beliefs (Smith, 1999, 192).

The training of indigenous researchers is one of these priorities. It is clear that "when Indigenous peoples become the researchers and not merely the researched, the activity of research is transformed. Questions are framed differently, priorities are ranked differently, problems are defined differently, people participate on different terms" (Smith, 1999, 193). Other priorities that have been identified are collaboration, developing culturally appropriate ethical guidelines, developing indigenous writers, educating the wider research community, and developing local ethical review processes for research (Smith, 1999; Battiste and Henderson, 2000).

Battiste and Henderson (2000) explain that proficiency in indigenous languages is essential when conducting research with indigenous peoples. English can be seen as one of the "master's tools" (Lorde, 1984), which mirrors a Eurocentric view and bias. As Battiste and Henderson write, "Indigenous languages offer not just a communication tool for unlocking knowledge, they also offer a theory for understanding that knowledge and an unfolding paradigmatic process for restoration and healing" (Battiste and Henderson, 2000, 133). They make it clear that to fully understand indigenous worldviews, one must be competent in understanding indigenous languages. This reminds me of Freire's (1987) belief that those who have the power to name the world also have the power to claim the world, and their knowledge is seen as legitimate.

Currently, Eurocentric thought is often deemed, by those with power, to be the only legitimate view of the world. However, a Eurocentric lens clouds our understanding of Indigenous knowledges and can cloud research. I remember an exercise involving making assessments, which a professor did in a counselling class I took. This professor brought a ball of clay into the room and passed it from student to student. She asked us to examine it and write down what it was on a piece of paper. Each student had a different assessment of the object, as useful or not, depending on his or her worldview and history. Some students found it ugly and useless, while others saw its potential and beauty. The same applies to research as we use our own lens to assess communities, people, and cultural practices. Can we learn a different worldview to replace the lens we have now? I don't know, but I understand now why the research that Aboriginal peoples engage in may be significantly different from other forms of research.

The danger comes in assigning less value to that which is different. As a Western perspective tends toward a hierarchical view, we place Eurocentric knowledges clearly at the top while others are deemed inferior and primitive. This issue needs to be examined. We must create space for multiple knowledges. I believe that it is time to bring Aboriginal peoples' knowledges into the center as a way of working toward sustainability and critiquing our patriarchal capitalist society.

As aboriginal peoples' knowledges come to the center, protection becomes an issue of utmost importance. Western conceptions of knowledge and ownership are clearly different from the way in which Aboriginal peoples understand the concept of who owns knowledge. Indigenous peoples' knowledge and heritage are not commodities, nor are they the property of the nation-states and their researchers. Indigenous knowledge and heritage are sacred gifts and responsibilities that must be honored and held for the benefit of future generations (Battiste and Henderson, 2000, 144).

In order to protect indigenous knowledges, Battiste and Henderson advocate "the establishment of community-based institutions for supervising research, promoting education and training, and conserving collections of important documents" (142). As they develop, these institutions will provide a gateway to the community for researchers. All researchers will be required to prove that their research is ethical before they gain access to community members. In this way sacred knowledge will be protected and preserved while the community decides collectively what to share and what to protect.

Conclusion

'We know we are dying', someone said, 'but tell me why we are living?' 'Our health will not improve unless we address the fact that we have no sovereignty', 'We're sick of hearing what's wrong with us, tell us something good for a change', or 'Why do they think that by looking at us they will find the answers to our problems, why don't they look at themselves?'
—in Linda Smith (1999, 198)

This speaker clearly encapsulates the essence of what I have been trying to articulate in this chapter. While anti-colonial research uncovers the atrocities of the past, it is also important to search for seeds of hope and possibilities for future generations. Anti-colonial research addresses current social conditions from the root up, working from within a philosophy of hope.

As a society we must make a commitment to strengthening local capacity by supporting, funding, and encouraging research initiatives of Aboriginal peoples. At the same time it is essential that we continue to critique positivist research methodologies that claim neutrality and cover up hidden political agendas.

The journey into anti-colonial research offers many challenges and opportunities. I believe that the positive outcomes resulting from centering Aboriginal peoples' knowledges are immense and will impact positively on all of us. Our current global crisis demands new paradigms as it becomes more and more apparent that our Western value system is destroying the earth and its inhabitants. As Dr. Vandana Shiva states in the foreword to *Indigenous Knowledges in Global Contexts*, "The future of indigenous knowledges will not simply determine whether the diverse cultures of the world evolve in freedom or are colonized; it will also determine whether humanity and diverse species survive" (2000, ix). It is essential that we disrupt the current hierarchy of knowledge systems if we are to benefit from the vast diversity of knowledges in our midst.

As aboriginal treaty rights and land claims negotiations progress forward, we have an incredible opportunity to redress the atrocities of the past and work toward positive future relationships with Aboriginal peoples. As we do this, we begin to live authentically as we put the guilt and shame that immobilize positive action behind us.

As researchers, we are challenged to think about old terminology in new and creative ways. How will concepts such as reliability and validity be defined from within an anti-positivist stance? What about replicability? If one person believes passionately about something, does it matter to a researcher? Does it make it "true"? Can research itself ever be radically transformed from within the institutions that fund it? What about holistic research? How can we embrace the spiritual, the emotional, the physical, as well as the mental when we do research? The challenge will be in creating research that is inclusive, creative, empowering, and relevant to the lived experiences of people as it moves beyond the realm of a mere academic exercise or a tool to justify oppressive policies.

On a more personal level, when I left the north to return to school I was looking for answers, a guidebook to use when working cross-culturally with Aboriginal peoples. I know now that such a guide can never exist because just as each community is unique, each researcher brings different beliefs, values, and biases to the work that she or he does. What I found in returning to school are more questions to ask myself before doing work with Aboriginal communities, questions such as: What lens of understanding am I working through? Was I invited here and what can I offer this community? Who benefits from the work that I'm doing and what are the risks involved in doing this work? How do we walk the fine line of centering Aboriginal worldviews respectfully, while not appropriating and using that, which is not ours? As we move away from research that reduces human interactions to numbers, these questions can be explored and highlighted within the research project.

If I do future work with Aboriginal communities, I am committed to working collaboratively, which means that the community guides the process at each stage of the project. I know now that it is not appropriate or expected that I incorporate spiritual practices into my work. Many resources exist in the community if the group that I am working with decides that they would like prayer or smudging to open the meetings.

Having done this work on anti-racist research, I see my research taking a different direction, away from the north and toward myself. I am curious about my own racist and sexist socialization and upbringing, particularly how that translates into my work as a counselor and facilitator.

I have noticed that if I use an anti-racist lens to critique my own work and the practices of other white people, I have often been taken more seriously than my Aboriginal colleagues who offer similar critiques. It is almost as if those living within the oppression are seen as biased. I find this curious, as obviously those living within oppressive circumstances are the best people to understand and articulate the impact of that oppression.

My future work involves trying to understand what it means to work as an ally with Aboriginal peoples, how to stand as part of a circle, not ahead or behind, but alongside Aboriginal peoples as equal partners in the research process.

I like the idea of becoming an ally because it recognizes that working together is a process that is never complete. When I become overwhelmed by everything that I still don't know, I remember a saying by Rabbi Tarfon in Paul Kivel's book, *Uprooting Racism:*

> *It is not upon you to finish the work.*
> *Neither are you free to desist from it.*
> —Paul Kivel (1996)

NOTES

1. For the purposes of this paper the term *Aboriginal* is meant to encompass people categorized as non-status, status, Inuit, and Metis. While recognizing that one term cannot encapsulate the diversity found within Aboriginal cultures and languages, I will follow the direction of the Royal Commission of Aboriginal Peoples and uses the term Aboriginal peoples. When I quote or paraphrase authors, different terms may be used throughout the paper as I respect the right of people to name themselves.

REFERENCES

Archibald, J., and Haig-Brown C., 1996. "Transforming First Nations Research with Respect and Power." In *Qualitative Studies in Education 9* (3): 245–267.

Battiste, M., and Henderson, J. 2000. *Protecting Indigenous Knowledge and Heritage.* Saskatoon, Saskatchewan Canada: Purich Publishing Ltd.

Comaskey, B., and McGillivray, A. 1999. *Black Eyes All of the Time.* Toronto: University of Toronto Press.

Dei, G. J. S. 1996. *Anti-Racism Education.* Halifax: Fernwood Publishing.

Dei, G. J. S. 1999. "Knowledge and Politics of Social Change: The Implication of Anti-Racism." *British Journal of Sociology of Education* 20(3), 395–409.

Dei, G. J. S., and Asgharzadeh, A. 2001. "The Power of Social Theory: The Anti-colonial Discursive Framework." *Journal of Educational Thought 35*(3): 297–323.

Fine, M. 1994. "Working the Hyphens: Reinventing Self and Other in Qualitative Research." In N. K. Denzin and Y. S. Lincoln (Eds.), *Handbook of Qualitative Research.* Thousand Oaks, CA: Sage, pp. 70–82.

Freire, P. 1987. *Literacy: Reading the Word and the World.* London: Routledge.

hooks, bell. 1992. "Eating the Other." In *Black Looks, Race and Representation*, Boston: South End Press, pp. 21–39.

Kivel, P. 1996. *Uprooting Racism.* Gabriola Island, B.C.: New Society Publishers.

LaRocque, E. 1993. "Violence in Aboriginal Communities." *Report to the Aboriginal Justice Inquiry.* Ottawa: Inquiry.

Lorde, A. 1984. *Sister Outsider.* Freedom, CA: Crossing Press.

Patai, D. 1994. "When Method Becomes Power." In A. Gitlin(Ed.). *Power and Method.* New York: Routledge.

Regnier, R. 1995. "Warrior as Pedagogue, Pedagogue as Warrior, Reflections on Aboriginal Anti-Racist Pedagogy." In R. Ng, P. Staton, and J. Scane (Eds.), *Anti-Racism, Feminism, and Critical Approaches to Education.* Westport, CT and London: Bergin & Garvey, pp. 67–86.

Razack, S. 1998. *Looking White People in the Eye: Gender, Race, and Culture in Courtrooms and Classrooms.* Toronto: University of Toronto Press.

Shiva, V. 2000. Foreword. In G. J. Sefa Dei, B. Hall, and D. G. Rosenberg (Eds.). *Indigenous Knowledges in Global Contents.* Toronto: University of Toronto Press.

Smith, L. 1999. *Decolonizing Methodologies.* London, New York, Dunedin: Zed Books.

Chapter Five

LOUISE GORMLEY

Some Insights for Comparative Education Researchers from the Anti-racist Education Discourse on Epistemology, Ontology, and Axiology

This essay explores some possible ways in which comparative international researchers can benefit from a deeper consideration of the philosophy-inspired theories of epistemology, ontology, and axiology, with a specific focus on how these terms have been recently defined by anti-racists. While some comparative education scholars have already addressed theory-building aspects of these three philosophical constructions (Masemann, 1990; Hayhoe, 2000), I suggest that a stronger focus on such concepts, in particular how they have been analyzed in the writings of anti-racist scholars Scheurich and Young (1997) and Stanfield II (1994), will lead to a more demanding and self-critical inquiry. Covering much geographical ground, I draw on examples from the Chilean, Canadian, Mexican, and Taiwanese contexts, places I have lived in or in the case of Chile, read about somewhat extensively. Weaving my lived experiences of such locations into my discourse on anti-racist research methods assists me to more concretely grasp the hidden complexities inherent in many comparative research efforts. Reflections on varying definitions of knowledge (epistemology), reality (ontology), and value (axiology) may shed a little light on the discursive location wherein anti-racist methods and comparative education research can meet.

I devote the first half of this essay to a rather lengthy theoretical discussion of these three philosophical constructs (epistemology, ontology, and axiology). Of course my analysis is not at all sufficient to explore their countless intricacies, some of which have been partially unravelled and then knitted together again within the literature of philosophy and its related disciplines (Duran, 2001; Ginsberg, 1993; Marsonet, 1997; Neville, 1989; Scheurich and Young, 1997; Stanfield II, 1994). Nonetheless, I hope that my opening discussion will move the paper beyond an overly trite explanation of three important ideas. Next I comment on issues relating to the purported binary locations of comparative and anti-racist studies, and speculate on the lack of continuous contact between the two fields. Then, I draw upon other academic monographs in order to offer two practical suggestions for comparative researchers. I believe that a comparativist who follows such advice is less likely to unintentionally produce racist research. Finally, I suggest that in an environment of critical and supportive dialogue, the fields of comparative and anti-racist education can learn something from each other.

As a Ph.D. student of comparative international education at a prominent Canadian university, I recently completed a summer 2001 course entitled Advanced Seminar in Race and Anti-racist Research Methodology in Education. I was drawn to this course because I aspire, like many of my comparative education classmates, to produce work that does not harm. I was probably also lured into enrolling by my unexamined acceptance of the false "division into 'good' whites who address racism and 'bad' whites who do not" (Stanfield II, 1993, 26), and of course I would much rather see myself as a good person than a bad one! While I had some inkling that the course was likely to become intense at times, I did not realize how unsettling I would find a few of the concepts that surfaced throughout the discussions, especially those arguments put forth by the Sociology and Equity Studies (SESE) graduate students in the class. To my dismay, most SESE students enrolled in this advanced seminar course saw comparative international research as inimical to anti-racist endeavours. I soon realized that not all people hold the field of comparative education in as high regard as I do. Adding to my confusion were some anti-racist authors, such as the aforementioned Scheurich and Young (1997) and Stanfield II (1993, 1994), to name two, who forced me to examine my prior assumptions. My challenge soon became to find ways to reconcile (a) my ideological affinity to the field of comparative education with (b) some of the perspectives from the field of anti-racism studies. Arising in part from the criticisms of these outsiders to the comparative education field, this paper mainly represents my efforts to provide a partial solution to the perceived division between the two locations. I will demonstrate that three constructs in philosophy, epistemology, ontology, and axiology, may lead us toward a beneficial union of these two disciplines of inquiry. I now begin my discussion to unfold the meanings of the three philosophical terms.

> Epistemology is the branch of philosophy that studies knowledge and attempts to answer the basic question: what distinguishes truth from error? On a practical level, this question translates into contentious issues regarding research methodologies. For example, how can one discern theories that are "better" at describing a particular phenomenon or experience than existing or competing theories? (Principia Cybernetica Web, n. d., 2)

While epistemology is traditionally described as having ancient Greek origins, many cultures around the world and over the course of history have widely debated *what* constitutes valuable knowledge.

> Epistemology is derived from the Greek word *episteme*, which means knowledge, and *logos*, which means theory. It . . . addresses the philosophical problems surrounding the theory of knowledge. It answers many questions concerning what knowledge is, how it is obtained, and what makes it knowledge. (Rhetoric and Epistemology Resource Page, 2001, 1)

Epistemology has been differentially interpreted over the centuries, and diverse peoples have constructed various definitions of what constitutes knowledge. However, anti-racists and feminists stress that the white male's version has traditionally held sway in the Western world, resulting in knowledge generally being framed within a narrow lens (Duran, 2001; Scheurich and Young, 1997; Stanfield II, 1993, 1994). It is only very recently that 'Other' voices have been permitted to either make a contribution or to challenge the ingrained status quo. The inclusion of multiple standpoints is a relatively new phenomenon that is still not widely practised; nevertheless it has been influential in initiating a reformulation of some theories of knowledge (Collins, 2000; Dei, 1999; DeVault, 1999; Reinharz, 1992).

> When we look at the history of epistemology, we can discern a clear trend in spite of the confusion of many seemingly contradictory positions. The first theories of knowledge stressed its absolute, permanent character, whereas the later theories put the emphasis on its relativity or situation dependence, its continuous development or evolution, and its active interference with the world and its subjects and objects. The whole trend moves from a static, passive view of knowledge toward a more adaptive and active one. (Principia Cybernetica Web, n. d., 2)

Ontology is a philosophical study that is very much intertwined with epistemology but is primarily concerned with reality and humankind's conceptual schemes of that reality. It is "the science of *being* in general, and embraces such issues as the nature of *existence* and the categorical structure of reality" ("Xrefer-

Ontology," 2001, 1). "Conceptual schemes provide us with the means for thinking about, and speaking of, a reality which includes ourselves" (Marsonet, 1997, 23). Ontology refers to a set of worldviews consisting of socially constructed beliefs by which people interact with each other and with their surrounding environment. Operational perspectives based in ontological frameworks provide us with thought structures through which society organizes itself (Marsonet, 1997). Egon G. Guba and Yvonna S. Lincoln define the ontological question as "What is the form and nature of reality, and therefore, what is there that can be known about it?" (1994, 108). It is interesting to note that the term *ontology* has been adopted by developers of artificial intelligence computer systems, but in this essay the focus is on ontology's philosophical uses for researchers of human behavior and learning.

> The term ontology has some additional special uses in philosophy. In a derivative sense, it is used to refer to the set of things whose existence is acknowledged by a particular theory or system of thought: it is in this sense that one speaks of *the* ontology of a theory. ("Xrefer-Ontology," 2001, 4)

Most academics enter into their research with perceptions of reality that, to a greater or lesser degree, have been influenced by mainstream beliefs. Therefore, the ontologies of the theories espoused by the researcher are pivotally positioned throughout the entire research process. Anti-racists, as well as a substantial number of feminists, write of the racist conclusions that have resulted from the application of theories whose essential ontological structures were inappropriate or in many cases injurious to the groups under investigation (Collins, 2000; Dei, 1999; Patai, 1992, 1994; Scheurich and Young, 1997; Stanfield II, 1993, 1994; Tuhiwai Smith, 1999). Thus, an important point to grasp regarding the concept of ontology is its relative and subjective nature, born of a multitude of creating agencies as opposed to being sculpted in the image of a sole progenitor. In "Ontology and Conceptual Schemes," Michele Marsonet (1997) succinctly describes the genesis:

> Conceptual schemes [of reality], thus, are neither born out of nothing nor established on aprioristic bases . . . I wish to rule out from the outset, any attempt . . . to conceive of them as self-subsistent and metaphysical entities which exist independently of human subjects and social structures . . . They are primarily tied to the dimension of human action, and must be seen as elements of the agent/environment interaction. (Marsonet, 1997, 24)

The third philosophical concept to be addressed in this paper is axiology, which similarly is "tied to the dimension of human action" and affected by interpersonal interaction. Like epistemology and ontology, axiology is relational because "people are at the heart of knowledge and value" (Ginsberg, 1993, ix). As the science inquiring into values, "axiology inquires into goodness which is a condition of inquiries into existence and knowledge" (Bahm, 1993, 4). Axiology delves into that which is deemed good and, therefore, must also explore the meanings of its counterpart, that which is branded as unworthy.

> "Axiology" [is] from the Greek *axios*, meaning "worth something," "worthy, deserving," or "fit for its place," . . . 'Axiology' meant the study of the ultimately worthwhile things (and of course of the ultimately counterworthwhile things) as well as the analysis of worthwhileness (or counterworthwhileness) in general. (Neville, 1989, 30)

The ancient Greek philosopher Plato saw axiology as absolute with "the Good" being fairly easily identifiable. Axiology, thus conceived, laid the perceptual framework for the majority of historical Western research efforts. However, there was a smaller and less vocal group of other Western intellectuals (again, mainly white) who championed values as context dependent and variably defined from person to person.

> Axiology [is] the theory of values in ethics and aesthetics, particularly the search for the good and its nature. Axiology investigates basic principles governing moral judgment and the place of values (or norms) within the frameworks of philosophical systems. Plato held to an absolute theory of the Idea of the Good, while Hume and others believed that values were relative, depending on persons making value judgements. ("Xrefer-Axiology," 2001, 1)

As noted in the definition above, anti-racists are among those who believe that values are "relative, depending on persons making value judgements." They argue against the stance that research transcends individual or societal value and can be presented as if occurring in a vacuum. An erroneous interpretation of *objectivity* turns a blind eye to the axiological bases that provide the foundation of all research efforts. In *Cultures of Inquiry* (1999), John R. Hall disputes the claim of value-free research:

> No research proceeds independently of individual and institutionalized value interests, but the positivist assumption is that such interests . . . do not affect the conceptualization . . . in its causally relevant aspects. The cultural significance of a phenomenon presumably counts for nothing in its conceptualization. (Hall, 1999, 46)

Axiology, whether stated or left unsaid, is the driving force propelling all research efforts. However, numerous anti-racist and feminist scholars view the hegemonic discourse of Eurocentric superiority as obscuring its own associated value system. They assert that its narrowed path has caused too many academics to approach their research in an unexamined manner, appearing oblivious to its inherent axiological "truths" (Collins, 2000; Dei, 1999; hooks, 2000; Scheurich and Young, 1997; Stanfield II, 1993, 1994).

These relative truths, as defined in a society's epistemology, ontology, and axiology, can be examined from numerous standpoints in order to form a more comprehensive understanding of various research methods. In a survey article, Val D. Rust, Aminata Soumaré, Octavio Pescador, and Megumi Shibuya (1999) reviewed 427 studies in comparative education journals for the years 1985, 1987, 1989, 1991, 1993, and 1995. Their analysis revealed that 88.5% of the studies fell into one of two major paradigms in social science research: qualitative or quantitative. The remaining studies were classified into those that were a qualitative/quantitative combination (10.8%), and those that were neither qualitative nor quantitative but some other type of research (0.7%). Rust et al. state that these two main traditions (qualitative and quantitative) held immense consequences for the types of knowledges, realities, and values implicated in the research. They offer one author's interpretation of the philosophical assumptions behind the different types of paradigms, but it is worth noting that the following passage does not include a consideration of how knowledge might be framed within qualitative/quantitative combination studies.

> According to Creswell, a number of philosophical assumptions are behind the two different types of paradigms. Ontologically speaking, quantitative researchers tend to argue that reality is objective and singular, existing apart from the researcher, while qualitative researchers tend to see reality as being subjective and multiple. Epistemologically speaking, quantitative researchers tend to claim that they are outside their sphere of research, while qualitative researchers tend to believe that they are continually interacting with the subject matter being researched. Axiologically speaking, quantitative researchers usually claim that they are operating in a value-free and unbiased fashion, while qualitative researchers usually believe their values and biases come into play in their research activities. (Rust et al., 1999, 104)

Thus, according to Creswell (as cited in Rust et al., 1999), the empirical, experimental tradition found in quantitative research will yield much different findings than the constructivist, interpretive paradigm found in qualitative bodies of work, and these differences arise from their contrasting philosophical assumptions.

Norman K. Denzin and Yvonna S. Lincoln (1994) speak of the differences between quantitative and qualitative researchers with respect to their philosophical viewpoints. Denzin and Lincoln argue that all qualitative researchers, whether they realize it or not, conduct their research according to a paradigm that contains the researcher's epistemological, ontological, and methodological premises. These beliefs make particular demands on the researcher, including the questions that are asked and the interpretations that are brought to them.

All qualitative researchers are philosophers in that "universal sense in which all human beings . . . are guided by highly abstract principles" . . . These principles combine beliefs about ontology (What kind of being is the human being? What is the nature of reality?), epistemology (What is the relationship between the inquirer and the known?), and methodology (How do we know the world or gain knowledge of it?). These beliefs shape how the qualitative researcher sees the world and acts in it. (Denzin and Lincoln, 1994, p. 13)

I find both Denzin and Lincoln (1994) and Creswell (as cited in Rust et al., 1999) to have presented an overly essentialist dichotomy between qualitative and quantitative research. Not all qualitative researchers see research as multiple and subjective, and not all quantitative researchers claim to be operating within value-free frameworks. I would also argue that the previous quote from Denzin and Lincoln, describing how philosophical beliefs shape qualitative researchers, could also be extended to include quantitative researchers. In my view, not only qualitative researchers, but *all* researchers of every discipline of human inquiry, quantitative, qualitative, combination, and other, are shaped by their epistemological, ontological, and methodological beliefs, and these beliefs directly affect their research. According to Denzin and Lincoln, qualitative researchers emphasize the value-laden nature of inquiry, while quantitative researchers purport to do their inquiry within a value-free framework. I would contest Denzin and Lincoln's position since in my view, neither quantitative researchers nor qualitative researchers, by and large, place *enough* stress on the value-laden aspect of their work because only a relative few take into account how their race, gender, social class, and other factors influence their interpretations. Thus, I suggest that epistemological, ontological, and axiological dissonance between races and cultures can occur in all unexamined research in any field, regardless of whether it be qualitative, quantitative, a combination, or other.

Epistemological, ontological, and axiological dissonances are the main themes of some anti-racist writings. In "Coloring Epistemologies: Are Our Research Epistemologies Racially Biased?" Scheurich and Young (1997) tackle the contentious issues surrounding the concept of epistemological racism. They argue that race is an often ignored yet critically significant epistemological dilemma in educational research. Their analysis divides racism into five levels: individual (including both overt and covert), institutional, societal, and civilizational (out of which arises epistemological racism). Epistemological racism is grounded in the belief that our assumptions and our theoretical constructions about the world arise out of concrete cultural and racial experiences. Most members of a civilization are not typically conscious of how they think and name their world (Foucault, 1979, 1988 as cited in Scheurich and Young,

1997). Therefore, Scheurich and Young challenge academics to become more aware of the ways in which "the dominant group" and the epistemological level of racism affect their research. While I cannot provide a precise definition of Scheurich and Young's dominant group, their stress on race implies that any conception of class politics that does not include considerations of racial power and privilege is "an ideological failure" (Gilroy, 2002, 250). Anti-racists understand race to be an intrinsic and determining component of the meaning of the terms *dominant class* or *dominant group* (Gilroy, 2002).

> When any group within a large, complex civilization significantly dominates other groups for hundreds of years, the ways of the dominant group (its epistemologies, its ontologies, its axiologies) not only become the dominant ways of that civilization, but also become so deeply embedded that they typically are seen as natural or appropriate norms rather than as historically evolved social constructions. (Stanfield, 1985, as cited in Scheurich and Young, 1997, 7).

Scheurich and Young seek to reveal how "deeply embedded" Western epistemologies are when they ask the reader to consider the conceptual paradigms employed in most academic research. They list various white males, such as Kant, Flaubert, Churchill, Henry Ford, Weber, Dewey, to name a few, who have historically dominated as the Western world's major and most influential philosophers, writers, politicians, corporate leaders, social scientists, and educational leaders, and argue that Euro-American intellectuals' explanations of the world can make for an uneasy (and usually unequal) congruence when such theories are applied to peoples of other races, cultures, or genders. Scheurich and Young state that the ill-fitting applications of legitimated research epistemologies cast a distorted (and oftentimes harmful) gaze on members of an "Other" culture.

> It is they [historically influential white males], who have developed the ontological and axiological categories or concepts like individuality, truth, education, free enterprise, good conduct, social welfare, and so forth, which we use to think (that thinks us?) and that we use to socialize and educate children. This racially exclusive group has also developed the epistemologies, the legitimated ways of knowing (e.g., positivism, neo-realisms, postpositivisms, interpretivisms, constructivisms, the critical tradition, and postmodernisms/poststructuralisms) that we use. And it is these epistemologies and their applied ontologies and axiologies, taken together as a lived web or fabric of social constructions, that make or construct "the world" or "the Real" (and that relegate other socially constructed "worlds" like that of African Americans or the Cherokee, to the "margins" of our social life and to the margins in terms of legitimated research epistemologies). (Scheurich and Young, 1997, 8)

The authors hasten to add that they are not arguing that these prominent individuals were involved in a racial conspiracy or that they were morally corrupt, but rather that such intellectuals can only name and know from within the social milieu in which they live. I concur with Scheurich and Young that epistemological racism, as it is experienced by many people, is often simply a state of unknowing beyond one's intellectual milieu. However, their stance turns a blind eye to those researchers who single-mindedly choose dominant paradigms (with an intent to diminish Others' experiences) specifically because such researchers truly believe in the inherent racial superiority of these paradigms (G. Dei, personal communication, September 2001; Rose, 2001; Wells, 2001). And, as pointed out to me by an anonymous reviewer (personal communication, December 2001), some researchers employ dominant academic paradigms because of the personal material benefits that may accrue from such actions. Scheurich and Young's aim is to unearth the unintentional (and in some cases, purposeful) racism created when researchers use dominant race epistemologies to interpret the experiences of marginalized groups.

While not incorporating the term *epistemological racism*, as did Scheurich and Young, John H. Stanfield II's work spoke to the same dilemma by critiquing traditional approaches to research involving African Americans. "The tendency for Western researchers to impose even their most enlightened cultural constructs on Others rather than creating indigenized theories and methods to grasp the ontological essences of people of color is, of course, legendary" (Stanfield II, 1994, 176). The following statement summarizes an immensely broad issue into a gross oversimplification; nonetheless, it captures the essence of the arguments presented by Scheurich and Young, and by Stanfield II, that is, studying a minoritized group using the epistemologies, ontologies, and axiologies of the dominant class is a racist research act, even if the authors of the study had the noblest of intentions toward their participants. Their examples of unintentional epistemological racism include researchers who "claim to be producing knowledge sensitive to the experiences of African-descent peoples as a unique cultural population even as they insist on using Eurocentric logics of inquiry" (Stanfield II, 1994, 182). According to Stanfield II, cultural scholars who receive most of their inspiration from distinguished European thinkers, then go on to insularly interpret their research subjects by applying mismatched reality constructions onto unrelated groups who diverge from the leading populace.

> This love affair with European-derived theorizing about the nature of human beings and their collective inventions, institutions, communities, societies, socialization, and so on has resulted in the failure of even the most astute cultural studies theorists to realize how culturally limiting the work of otherwise brilliant thinkers, such as Alfred Schutz, Karl Marx . . . is when applied to . . . the experiences of populations . . . who deviate from what we used to call mainstream. (Stanfield II, 1994, 182–183)

Scheurich and Young and Stanfield II thus promote educational reform directed *away* from holding Eurocentric knowledge as the ideal/only form of learning. (Note that a number of comparativists (Farrell, 1987; Masemann, 1990, 1999) have also argued for greater legitimization of multiple, indigenous knowledge forms.) Some "anti-anti-racists" (Gilroy, 2002) would hotly contest Scheurich and Young and Stanfield II, defining anti-racism as a "mania" (Lewis, 1988) and as "an assault on education and value" (Palmer, 1987). Such critics oppose "the dictatorial character of anti-racism" (Gilroy, 2002, 249) and question whether or not "the terms 'black' [as well as other minority labels] and 'European' remain categories which [mostly] mutually exclude each other" (Gilroy, 2002, 253). However, the views held by Scheurich and Young and Stanfield II against powerful Western epistemologies resonate strongly with most scholars of the anti-racist literature. "[Anti-racism] should encourage all students to challenge any existing Eurocentric and patriarchal knowledges about their own societies and communities (Casey, 1991, cited in Dei, 1994, 11). Prominent anti-racists join Scheurich and Young and Stanfield II in their rally against the privileging of Western knowledge: "Anti-racism must challenge hegemonic Western discourses" (Dei, 1999, 406). Gilroy refers to "the problematic intellectual heritage of Euro-American modernity" (Gilroy, 2000, 491). Therefore, a central theme that runs through Scheurich and Young and Stanfield II, which is reverberated in most anti-racist works, is an impassioned plea for practices that diverge *from* mainstream Western thought.

Anti-racists and some feminists have written on the practice in many academic monographs of unknowingly imposing mainstream Western concepts onto the minoritized bodies being researched, and such scholars declare that through this imbalance, our collective vision of each other has become blurred (Collins, 1999; Dei, 1999; Patai, 1992, 1994; Scheurich and Young, 1997, Stanfield II, 1994; Tuhiwai Smith, 1999). In light of the points raised by Scheurich and Young and by Stanfield II, is it at all possible to study systems of education without imposing my Western-trained intellectual traditions? Others have asked questions in a similar vein (Cook, 1998; Farrell, 1987; Geertz, 1995; Hoffman, 1999; Masemann, 1990). Scheurich and Young and Stanfield II claim that the majority of white western scholars do not examine the bias of the frameworks of their thoughts, and therefore do not fully realize the extent to which privileged experiences have influenced the philosophical paradigms within which they construct their analysis. "The experiences that construct paradigms in sciences and humanities are derivatives of cultural baggage imported into intellectual enterprises by privileged residents of historically specific societies and world systems" (Stanfield II, 1994, 181).

However, here I feel compelled to point out that those who have not kept abreast of intellectual movements in the comparative field may not realize that cultural baggage is an issue that has been explored at great length by current comparative researchers. My summer classmates who stated that comparative researchers devote little time to the research implications of different cultural and racial interpretations have clearly not had much access to the academic comparative discourse of this past decade. At the cusp of the 1990s, in a paper delivered at the 1989 World Congress of Comparative Education in Montreal, Hans Weiler stated that there was "an erosion of consensus over epistemology" (Weiler, 1989, cited in Masemann, 1990, 471), and referred to the growing importance of valuing alternative paradigms arising from cultures located outside the status quo. In her 1990 Comparative International Education Society (CIES) presidential address, Vandra Masemann analyzed "our conception of knowledge itself, by our culturally created conception of ways of knowing, or epistemology" (Masemann, 1990, 465), and spoke of the necessity of recognizing indigenous, context-dependent ways of knowing. Clifford Geertz, reflecting on a lifetime of comparative research that broke from traditional forms in anthropology (Inglis, 2000), writes of the complexities surrounding cultural schemes and casts doubts on ever "grasping so vast a thing as an entire way of life and finding the words to describe it" (Geertz, 1995, 43). Joseph Farrell, in "Cultural Differences and Curriculum Inquiry," writes that cultural and racial differences are more than just superficial differences in classroom behavior but encompass "questions of what knowledge is, how it is to be acquired, for what purposes it is to be used, and how 'meaning' is to be derived from one's experience" (Farrell, 1987, 2). In *"Culture and Comparative Education: Toward Decentering and Recentering the Discourse,"* Diane M. Hoffman offers an intricate analysis of culture because it is "critically important for comparativists to consider how and why concepts of culture can enhance or impede understanding, research, and action in education" (Hoffman, 1999, 465). These afore-mentioned works, which represent only a fraction of the cross-cultural comparative work that has been done, intertwine race and culture.

Furthermore, race is the prime focus of some comparative studies. For example, I look forward to reading an upcoming special issue of the *Comparative Education Review*, entitled "Black Populations Globally: The Challenges and Promises in Their Educational Experiences" (2001, Call for Papers), and I wonder whether authors will draw upon insights from anti-racist sources. By making the effort to list the above works, I run the risk of belaboring my point, but my hope is to demonstrate to my colleagues that, with respect to discussions of race and culture, not all comparative researchers are ostriches with their heads firmly buried in the sand.

There are, however, some very basic and fundamental differences in the treatment of race between the two areas of inquiry. While the main purpose of this chapter is not to compare anti-racist and comparative education, I will briefly touch upon a few ways in which the two fields contrast. What distinguishes comparative education research from anti-racist education research is that the latter concentrates race, and sometimes epistemological racism, *at the forefront of all research*, with a main emphasis on the conflict/resistance that arises from racial privilege versus racial oppression, hence, all further discussion disseminates from that original position (Gilroy, 2000, 2002). In contrast, my interpretation of comparative research is that yes, race (and its subsequent social inequities) is very often incorporated into our discourse, but race tends to be one variable considered among many. For example, race may be addressed in comparative works, but often within a consideration of numerous phenomena such as school quality (Fuller and Heyneman, 1989), teaching/learning philosophy (Masemann, 1999), and state policy decisions on educational infrastructure (Schmelkes, 2000). The *Comparative Education Review*'s 2000 Bibliography (Raby, 2001) cites numerous individual comparative studies on racial implications, but in the comparative field as a whole, the focus on race is more apt to become diluted (in comparison to anti-racist research), partly because there is a wider array of factors competing for attention in the analyses. Furthermore, some comparative educators use the term *culture* as a blanket expression that covers both the concepts of culture and race (Hoffman, 1999), which suggests that the terms can be interchangeable, while antiracist educators denounce such practices as avoidance of the taboo word *race* (Dei, personal communication, May 2001) that leads to a narrow understanding of such terms (anonymous reviewer, personal communication, December 2001).

In addition, it is almost imperative to position oneself with respect to race, gender, social class, and so forth in anti-racist research (Kamler, Reid, and Santoro, 1999), creating a situation that practically demands that most anti-racist researchers employ "I" in their writings (or "we" in the case of co-authorship). Comparativists, on the other hand, sometimes position themselves in their research (Farrell, 1996; Robertson, 1984) and sometimes do not (Fuller and Heynemann, 1989; Noah and Eckstein, 1998), resulting in a more varied usage of the personal "I" or the more formal third party "It." (This difference in writing styles is outwardly superficial, but can sometimes reflect very different ontological schemes. The deeper implications of visible or invisible positioning cannot be fully explored here, but one obvious outcome is that a reader must dig deeper to discern the biases of an omniscient author.) Both disciplines conduct much research on the topics of race and culture, but generally speaking, the two fields approach the analysis using quite different angles of inquiry. It is as if there were two separate groups of people, who at some surface level are talking about the same sorts of things, but who, it seems to me, rarely speak to each other.

My hunch regarding the lack of continuous contact between the two fields is somewhat confirmed by an incomplete literature review of recent comparative theory. Rolland Paulston (1993, 2000), Rolland Paulston and Martin Liebman (1994), and Val D. Rust (1996) are comparativists who have attempted pictorial "macro-mappings of paradigms and theories in comparative and international education texts" (Paulston and Liebman, 1994, 224). Anti-racist literature is not among the paradigms and theories represented in these visual tools, unless one permits it to be categorized under the more general knowledge positions of conflict theory and critical theory. Rust builds upon Paulston and Liebman's (1994) work and refines the discourse by adding arrows between theoretical orientations. These thin or thick lines are visual indicators of the direction and amount of dialogue (both supportive and critical) between theoretical orientations (Rust, 1996). Comparative research is an eclectic field that draws from many intellectual traditions, but since anti-racism literature is absent from these pictorial diagrams, I am inclined to conclude that very little anti-racist dialogue enters into our theoretical orientations.

I believe I can explain part of the reason for this lack of either critical or supportive dialogue. I am not the first to note that some aspects of the anti-racist literature on minorities are overly entrenched in a United States of America version of reality. For example, the whole concept of the *Hispanic* race, a term often found in anti-racist literature, is steeped in American racial politics. Even in the United States, the meaning of the word is ambiguous at best (V. Masemann, personal communication, February 2001). First of all, Hispanic is a linguistic category referring to persons of Spanish-speaking origins regardless of their racial backgrounds. Thus, a white, Spanish-speaking Argentinean and a black, Spanish-speaking Cuban would both be identified as Hispanic if they were domiciled in the United States, even though their lived experiences of that term are highly likely to be vastly different. To continue with my critique, comparative researchers who interact with Latin American participants (who have never lived in the United States) would be ill-advised to build their study around this term. Hispanic is a positivistic construct that crumbles when one tries to apply it outside the United States. I have yet to meet a Spanish-speaking person not living in the United States who self-identifies by this term. Rather, each individual sees himself/herself as Mexican, Panamanian,

Peruvian, Bolivian, Uruguayan, Chilean, and so forth. Because being a Hispanic is a United States-centric experience, it would be unsuitable to apply Hispanic ontologies to, say, an ethnography of an elementary school in northern Mexico. Therefore, certain aspects of American-based, anti-racist studies do not transfer well to a comparative international context.

However, as I argue in this chapter, other insights from the field of anti-racist studies, especially those concerning philosophical constructs, offer comparativists a wealth of insights. I, for one, will be a comparative researcher who now asks herself a more demanding set of questions each time I embark on a study. My intellectual travels last summer are the journey of only one person, yet the implications of my experience indicate that antiracist studies and comparative studies are not reaping as full a harvest as possible, mainly because researchers are working in relative isolation from each other. Increasing the flow of conversation between the fields is the best way for comparative researchers and anti-racist researchers to learn from each other's critiques.

This call for informed critical collaboration leads me to the most crucial question in my paper. How can a comparative researcher, especially a privileged one, produce work that is anti-racist? Or to play devil's advocate, is this question riddled with oxymoronic reasoning? Can an outsider *ever* become more aware of the axiological system that grounds his or her efforts? My stance is that ontological dissonance between races is *always* present and can only be reduced rather than completely eliminated. A researcher who understands (and who does not downplay) the concept of epistemological racism *can* reduce the bias within his or her research. Yet almost no one can *totally* refrain from allowing epistemological racism to influence their work, simply because every person views the world from their unique intersections of race, culture, gender, social class, as well as their accumulated repertoire of life experiences. By this line of thought I do not mean that all comparative researchers should relinquish the field and give up doing comparative research since it will be inherently racist and inevitably doomed to failure. Permitting research only within one's racial and cultural milieu could very well lead to an unfortunate ghettoization of topics that would ultimately paralyze all educational research. I remain committed to the "immense value that can be derived from a disciplined study of foreign systems of education" (Cook, 1998, 94) which provides a window to the world. So in the ameliorative spirit typical of many educators, I gather here some hands-on ideas, first introduced elsewhere by other scholars who likewise hope to make an anti-racist contribution, albeit a small one, to the field of comparative education. If put into actual practice by more researchers, these practical ideas may increase the possibility that the concepts of epistemology, ontology, and axiology will become more frequently intertwined into the research method.

First Suggestion

The first suggestion arises from William Pinar, a curriculum scholar, who does not specifically use the terms epistemology, ontology, or axiology, but who nevertheless speaks to these issues. Pinar stresses the importance of using primary sources *in native languages* when doing international research because insider publications are more likely to possess epistemological resonance. Avoidance of those sources written in the language of the region studied, usually due to the linguistic limitations of the researcher, often results in serious ontological misunderstandings.

> The problem becomes acute when English-speaking scholars limit their international research to secondary English sources . . . This matter illustrates a tendency towards ethnocentrism in the First World, especially English-speaking nations. The significance of employing primary sources in the study of education internationally must be emphasized. (Pinar, 1995, 795)

I see a complementary relationship between Pinar's advice and the Sapir-Whorf hypothesis, which states that some elements of language, for example, in vocabulary or grammatical systems, influence speakers' and listeners' perceptions of the world, rendering language as a strong determinant of their attitudes and behaviors (Bonvillain, 1997).

> Human beings do not live in the objective world alone, nor alone in the world of social activity as ordinarily understood, but are very much at the mercy of the particular language that has become the medium of expression for their society. The fact of the matter is that the real world is to a large extent unconsciously built up on the language habits of the group. (Sapir, 1949, as cited in Bonvillain, 1997, 52)

From an ontological point of view, a comparative researcher (from a dominant or a marginalized position) must listen/speak/read/write (as applicable) with participants in their mother tongue to understand their real world. Since language shapes our lives and determines our views, it is only through the native language that any outsider can catch a glimpse, however fleeting, of this reality. Objects or forces in the environment become labelled in language only if they command the attention of the community, and once a language provides a word for an object or activity, it becomes culturally significant (Bonvillain, 1997).

When a group of participants speak a language that does not employ a script, a comparative researcher may find himself/herself in a situation wherein no written texts in the primary language are available. Perhaps only historical and/or current English texts are to be found, and so it would be tempting to rely almost exclusively on these more accessible sources. However, in such an oral culture, dominant researchers are less likely to misrepresent indigenous ontologies if they do expend the necessary time and effort into native language communicative competence beyond a few simple formulaic expressions. Nuances and subtleties of meaning can only be teased out from participants' words in their native language. (In the above case, a linguistically fluent researcher who hails from the participants' racial and cultural background would very likely be much more adept at understanding the viewpoints presented than would a dominant researcher who cannot adequately communicate with the participants in their own language.)

Furthermore, it is important that the process from native language to English (for the benefit of an English-reading audience) represent, as much as possible, the intended meanings of the participants. Sometimes translations into English do not convey the original message because the same linguistic label used by one group may hold different meanings when translated for the benefit of another group. Pinar quotes Ivor F. Goodson to demonstrate that commonly studied school subjects in formal educational systems around the world (i.e., mathematics, history, etc.) actually represent different epistemologies in other cultures, but their shared labels mask this difference: "common subject labels override different patterns of knowledge formation" (Goodson, 1983, as cited in Pinar, 1995, 793). However, although it is wise to be cautious with respect to translated and English-language sources, one cannot assume that native language text is necessarily *authentic* and that any text in the English language is *foreign*. Such a simplistic dichotomy nullifies the vast potential of viewpoints, including those native writers who choose to express themselves, for a wide variety of reasons, in the English language. Perhaps one solution is for comparative researchers (of all backgrounds and races) to keep the Sapir-Whorf hypothesis in mind, so that they place great importance on using native language sources/texts, but do not completely dismiss the potential of English-language ones.

A telling incident of the Sapir-Whorf hypothesis arose from my recent experience conducting a literature review of Chilean systems of education accessing both English-language and Spanish-language texts. I was struck by the dramatic difference between the conceptions of the Chilean reality as portrayed by English-language secondary sources versus Spanish-language, Chilean-originating primary sources. While English sources tend to locate Chile within a Latin American paradigm and therefore rank Chilean educational accomplishments highly, Chilean scholars often place themselves outside of the

Spanish-speaking nations' framework when measuring scholastic achievements and therefore voice much stronger dissatisfaction with their own progress (Arnove, Franz, Mollis, and Torres, 1999; *Comisión Nacional para la modernización de la educación*, 1995). In the aforementioned literature review, my purpose was only to read about Chile as an interested learner, but had I been an actual researcher of Chilean education who used only English language sources, my work would have become even more heavily weighed down by its epistemological racism. I offer this example to emphasize the fact that in spite of the inability of most outside comparative researchers to grasp the ontologies of a given group as well as an insider can, there are nevertheless a few ways in which such an outsider can at least climb a little higher in order to see more of the landscape.

I reiterate that I am not advocating outright avoidance of English language sources. As described by my experience with the Chilean texts, a variety of information including some telling discrepancies can sometimes be gleaned from a comparison of English and primary sources. Instead I am pointing out that research based *only* on English sources runs a much greater risk of being epistemologically racist. To combat this "tendency towards ethnocentrism in the First World, especially English-speaking nations," (Pinar, 1995, 795) the conceptual framework of comparative studies should consist as much as possible of primary sources. Reading and writing (when applicable), as well as speaking and listening in the primary language, are vitally important if one aspires to a less racist comprehension of a specific culture's epistemologies, ontologies, and axiologies.

However, I caution that although fluency in the primary language is a required tool for nonbiased comparative research, it is no guarantee of nonracist findings. Even when using a common language such as English, ontological perceptions vary dramatically between texts as well between sources when they represent the values of competing social interests. For a comparative researcher conducting an educational study, it should be a constant given that he or she must use multiple sources from both the marginalized and privileged groups because "the group to be 'represented' is not always internally homogeneous and is rarely democratically organized" (Atkinson and Hammersley, 1994, 253). A researcher who relied too heavily on say, the mainstream English-language Canadian media as a primary source would be unaware of how hegemonic discourse distorts reality and supports the traditional white axiologies (Stanley, 1998). For example, the headline on the front page of the *Toronto Star* on Canada Day 2001 was "*Citizens, old and new, share pride in our land*" (van Rijn and Barahona, 2001). The accompanying photograph depicted smiling visible minorities who were sporting face-painted maple leafs while carrying Canadian flags. Such displays of civic pride in ethnic diversity may lead to some festive celebrations but they also hide the ugly truths of racism that restrict too many citizens' lives. I will preface my statements by indicating that I believe I am indeed fortunate to live in this northern land. Yet I also recognize the limited viewpoint of mainstream journalists who proclaim countries such as Canada as nations already completely converted to racial tolerance and who denounce anti-racist educators as crazed people "who continually see this bogeyman beneath the Canadian bed" (Blatchford, 2001, A17). The journalist, who penned those words, though eloquently able in the English language, hardly represents the views of *all* English-speaking marginalized groups presently residing in Canada. Therefore, while fluency in a region's language helps to reduce a researcher's epistemological bias, it cannot produce anti-racist work alone. Pinar's (1995) stress on the importance of the primary language must be heeded along with Atkinson and Hammersley's (1994) advice on finding multiple sources within both privileged and oppressed groups. A caveat is issued against taking refuge in native language sources in order to naively assume that one's research will consequently be unbiased.

Second Suggestion

I draw my second suggestion from the previously discussed articles by Scheurich and Young and Stanfield II, and it is a very ambitious, or perhaps I should say lofty, goal for a Western-trained individual to attempt to achieve. When engaged in the initial steps of contemplating and designing one's research, a comparative education researcher should seek out primary works reflecting some of the philosophical assumptions of the region as opposed to non-reflectively imposing mainstream Eurocentric ideals. I propose that a Western-trained comparativist interrogate his/her own thinking by asking: "Am I weaving the thoughts of Dewey, Marx, Kant, (substitute any prominent, Western, probably male intellectual here) into my writing about such-and-such non-Western group mainly because *I personally* am most comfortable/familiar with these forms of knowledge? How much authentic relevance do such works really have to my participants' lives? This rigorous self-examination must be simultaneously accompanied by active interaction with the community and vigorous learning on the social and philosophical constructs, which frame participants' lives. Perhaps comparativists who have been mostly educated outside the Western tradition may be less inclined to frame non-Western groups through Eurocentric lenses. Nevertheless, many Western-trained researchers (both those from dominant groups and from marginalized ones) are more familiar, as a result of their schooling, with Western intellectual concepts than with indigenous ones, and so the above questions can help them to search their own thought processes for bias. Comparativists who learn from anti-racist scholars about how to critically reflect on the presence of epistemological racism in their work will ask themselves a new set of questions every time they begin a study. Ultimately, such questions will lead comparative researchers toward a more demanding and self-critical inquiry.

I am not suggesting a straitjacket approach in which it is heretical to ever quote a Euro-American intellectual in one's writing. But intuitively, does it not make sense to place the greatest faith in the potential of an *indigenous* work to guide one toward the most appropriate ontological paradigm? In other words, if I were to research, say, a specific educational phenomenon as it is experienced in Mexico (my second native country), then it is pointless to quote popular and historical mainstream Euro-American writers who very likely never set foot south of the American/Mexican border, and whose concept of the world encompasses nothing of *la realidad mexicana*. Rather, I must begin from a perspective that acknowledges a Latin American philosophy "with strong human and social interests [which] has been consistently affected by scholastic and Catholic thought" ("Xrefer-Latin American Philosophy," 2001, 1) as well as a Mexican philosophy that interweaves both the Spanish-derived and indigenous components (Quiroga, 1999). How ridiculous it would be to apply definitions created by Eurocentric intellectuals to a country whose chaotic "birthplace was a battle. The meeting between the Spaniards and the Indians was simultaneously, to use the poet Jáuregui's lively, picturesque image, burial mound and marriage bed" (Paz, 1990, 23). The Mexican versions of reality, historically influenced by Spanish colonial powers and Indian sufferings, would provide a more apt conceptual framework for my future analysis.

> Why speak of the Mexican essence as a philosophical problem in the first place? . . . Western philosophy has always spoken about man in general. This philosophy was "authentic" because the European was looked upon as Universal man . . . Anything that did not fit was simply excluded from that concept . . . [The Mexican] was now caught between two cultures. He no longer feels himself part of Europe, that "world" par excellent. He now felt left out and inferior to the culture he was trying to emulate . . . In fact, Mexican philosophy can be said to have begun with an inquiry into the nature of the Indian." (Zea as cited in Lipp, 1980, 67)

While far from eliminating racism in my research, drawing upon the works of Mexican *pensadores* (instead of the academy's favored Anglophone intellectuals) as the major point of reference for my future writings would at the very least provide a somewhat less inappropriate conceptual framework (Duran, 2001). Instead of positioning an analysis within, for example, John Dewey's frequently referenced North American democratic educational aims, my research would be better served by considering the writings of historical and current Mexican thinkers. One possible source to draw from would be the writings of world-renowned Mexican scholar Jose Vasconcelos. His works are somewhat dated now, but his impact on the development of Mexican educational systems was far greater than that of any European or North American educator. Taking "issue with the Anglo-Saxon philosophy of education" (de Beer, 1966, 323), Vasconcelos' version of knowledge formation describes the philosophical basis informing numerous past and current teaching practices in Mexico:

> Nature is subordinate to the spirit and every beautiful manifestation of nature is subjected to a rigorous process of selection and care. The child as a growing object cannot be left to follow his own inclinations and caprices; the teacher cannot passively stand by and observe and respect his every whim. If this were the case, the child would dominate his teacher and that would be an absurd situation. (Vasconcelos, as translated by and as cited in de Beer, 1966, 323)

To sum up my argument, a comparative researcher would be led astray by using, say, Dewey's famous and prevailing "My Pedagogic Creed" (1997), in which "the child's own instincts and powers furnish the material and starting-point for all education" (17) to analyze Mexican values regarding systems of education. Vasconcelos' passage above more succinctly captures a traditionally held version of the Mexican philosophy of education for children, and would be a more authentic source from which to start building a theoretical framework.

Now that I have shown how an anti-racist insight into epistemological racism holds the potential to influence comparative researchers, I will argue that the broad international scope of comparative education can inform anti-racist efforts. As previously discussed, there is a widespread critique of Western hegemonic discourse in most anti-racist analyses. As far as I have been able to deduce, the anti-racist movement is active primarily in such countries as United States, Britain, Canada, Australia, and South Africa; in France; in a few non-English-speaking countries wherein numerous authors are able to publish for an English language readership; and to a less visible extent (or at least less visible to mainstream North American society) in various regions of the Black African diaspora. This means that there are countless peoples living outside these locations, whose lived experiences with race have not yet contributed to the larger anti-racist efforts.

> Perhaps the race and ethnicity area requiring the most work is that of cross-national comparative studies. Except for the prospering international migration field, few race and ethnicity researchers conduct cross-national research. Indeed, as many scholars have

noted, the study of race and ethnicity has tended to be nation-bound in contexts such as the United States, Great Britain, France, and South Africa. (Stanfield II, 1993, 25)

Just as comparative researchers can interrogate their thought processes through anti-racist insights on epistemological racism, anti-racists may consider the benefits of taking a comparative international approach. As I embark on a career specializing in comparative studies and gradually become more familiar with the idea of epistemological racism, I have begun to see its re-enactment in numerous studies on various regions of the world, especially when I reflect upon those places in which I have lived, such as Taiwan. As I will discuss in further detail later, I am sure there are many insights to be acquired from the experience of racism in Taiwan. Therefore, there exists an expansive world of comparative understandings regarding anti-racism, but it presently lies largely untapped.

While many Western academics from many disciplines tend to frame their research within restricting Eurocentric paradigms, there are times when non-Western epistemologies are used to dominate other populations. Studies of Taiwan, for example, are currently and historically framed within a mainland pro-China conceptual view of the world (Kuo, 2000). Due to reasons arising mostly from the political instabilities between Taiwan and China, "Taiwan itself was rarely viewed as a legitimate subject for research. The island was treated as China in miniature. For many scholars, it existed as a 'laboratory' for the study of Chinese society and culture" (Hsiau, 2000, 155). Thus, "any academic study that emphasized Taiwanese particularities, especially in the humanities or the social sciences" (Hsiau, 2000, 155) was silenced and viewed as threatening to national security. This resulted in most researchers of Taiwan, including those who researched its educational systems, being practically forced to use epistemological frameworks that fit the values of the dominant Chinese government, but did not usually represent Taiwanese realities. I detail this example to show that contrary to the substantial anti-racist discourse against privileged Euro-American knowledge, it is not necessarily Western epistemologies in themselves that are problematic. Indisputably hegemony restricts, but the crucial point is that hegemony is not always Western. Rather, the dilemma of epistemological racism arises when researchers use the social and theoretical constructions of any dominant group, of any race or nationality, when studying peripheral populations. Therefore, I argue that "a fundamental change in intellectual culture . . . toward a broad comparative understanding of the world" (Farrell, 2000, 30) would contribute to fuller anti-racist education understandings. Anti-racists need to use a broad comparative perspective to more fully understand both Western and non-Western forms of hegemony, which will expand the definition of epistemological racism to include the lived experiences of more peoples. A wider, more global conceptual paradigm of the philosophical constructs of epistemology, ontology, and axiology within an anti-racist critique could offer us a wealth of insights.

Bringing these philosophical points down to a more intimate level, are there ways in which a better understanding of these three concepts could reduce the conscious and subconscious biases in *my* own perspective as a white researcher? In Stanfield II's article, "Ethnic Modeling in Qualitative Research," to which I frequently refer in this essay, he prefaces his arguments with the eloquent introduction "My thoughts in the next section were influenced mostly by . . ." (1994, 181). Borrowing from his example, I hope to acquire the ability to identify the things that have influenced my thoughts. In fact, such a realization is a necessary prerequisite for the reply to the question that I pose to myself at the beginning of this paragraph. Curiously, though, this self-interrogation creates an odd sense of disequilibrium within my inner soul because, although I am a researcher from the dominant social class, my lived experiences draw from other contexts. *Tengo doble nacionalidad–la mexicana y la canadiense* (I am dually Canadian and Mexican in my citizenship). While benefiting from all the privileges that society bestows on an Anglo appearance (I resemble my Irish-descent Canadian father in coloring), I also derive great pride in my additional identification as a Latin-heritaged woman through my Spanish-speaking Mexican mother (who incidentally, happens to be light-complexioned and have medium-dark-brown hair, contrary to stereotype). Sharing some of the emotions of other persons of mixed ethnic backgrounds (Fernandez, 1996; Root, 1992, 1996), to situate oneself as wholly within the paternal status-quo feels like a negation of the maternal voice in one's own body. So while I acknowledge that my constructions of the world may have been immeasurably constricted by mainstream European/North American epistemologies, I also know that my interpretations cannot be neatly categorized as *solely* springing from such sources. Instead I perceive my personal reality to be an ever-changing and at times conflicting melding of Anglo and Latin ontologies. As a child, I occasionally sensed the sharp juxtaposition of the different value systems held in Canada and Mexico (the two countries in which I grew up) but at the time I did not know how to verbalize my thoughts on these axiological inconsistencies. Then as an adult, I gradually learned about other ways of knowing by becoming more familiar with several Asian "meta-narratives of value and ethical purpose" (Hayhoe, 2000, 439) during my eight years of living in Japan and Taiwan. Mothering my mixed race (Taiwanese/Canadian/Mexican) children has also brought about shifted ground in my definitions of the truth. Yet up until very recently, my insights on the Anglo, Latin American, and Eastern ways were expressed as superficial observations of cultural and racial lifestyle differences. It is only now in the graduate school context that I am beginning to gather the words to discuss how the mind-altering concepts of epistemology, ontology, and axiology have influenced my thought patterns, and how they will ultimately bear weight on my actions in future research endeavors. Far from being abstract and powerless word games, these philosophical concepts are the springboard for the entangled and complex interrogation of an academic woman whose critical introspection of her non-marginalized status is still very much in its infancy.

However, the above self-disclosure on my inner journey with these philosophical terms does not change the way epistemologies, ontologies, and axiologies are differentially experienced by mainstream versus minoritized groups. My intellectual wanderings are of little consequence to anyone besides myself and perhaps those dearest to me. "Taking account of my own position does not change reality. It does not, for example, redistribute income, gain political rights for those who don't have them, alleviate misery or improve health" (Patai, 1994, 67). Feminist scholar Daphne Patai questions current methodologies incorporating "extreme personalization" (67) and asks "Does all this self-reflexivity produce better research?" I am compelled to answer her "No and yes." No, it will not lead to better research when I simply state my multi-positioning and leave it up to the reader to imagine why and where I tread. But yes, it just might make a semi-useful contribution, or at least less of a harmful one, if I actually can learn to approach my research already more deeply cognizant of the fact that my epistemologies, my ontologies, and my axiologies may or may not be the same as the participants in my study, depending upon their ethnic, racial, sexual, and social-class background. If this self-reflexivity helps me to realize that, although my research may seem perfectly ethical to a university research ethics review board, it could very well be epistemologically racially biased, then this dawning of awareness is a tentative first step toward a so-called "better" research method. I am acutely aware that by including sections on doing educational research in Chile, Mexico, and Taiwan, this essay will be denounced by some as the pompous reflections of a privileged white academic female who is casting her imperialistic gaze on Others. As I alluded to in the introductory paragraphs of this essay, I have discovered that there appears to be a stereotype among some (many?) educators in the field of anti-racist research, that comparative education researchers are mostly whites who go abroad, overtly or covertly identifying themselves as "white saviors," trying to "fix" developing countries. The image is of self-aggrandizing comparative researchers on personal missions to glory, whose studies have ultimately caused great damage to the minority groups studied (G. Dei, personal communication, June 2000; Patai, 1992, 1994; Tuhiwai Smith, 1999). Criticizing the field of comparative international education, a minority classmate passionately exclaimed during a class discussion, "Why do these people have to go and solve the problems in other people's backyards, why don't you concentrate on the problems in your own backyard first?" (personal communication, May 2001). However, while I cannot speak on behalf of all the numerous comparative education studies that are presently being conducted all over the world, my own analysis of the four doctoral dissertations nominated or awarded the Comparative International Education Society's (CIES) prestigious Gail Kelly Outstanding Dissertation Award for the year 2000 reveals work that does not fit into the repressive "trying to fix developed countries" stereotype. These four comparative researchers used descriptive-based, ethnographically oriented research methodologies, including one that employed online Web medium resources, to contemplate various educational phenomena as they are played out in Morocco, the United States, France, and globally. It bodes well for the field that the four authors of these award-winning and current comparative studies considered how their own racial/ethnic positioning influenced their interpretations, and did not play the role of omniscient healers who could diagnose and prescribe remedies (Boyle, 2000; Langan, 2000; Skachkova, 2000; Stone, 2000). It is also heartening that within my graduate comparative education classes, a large chunk of the class discussions focus on issues stemming from various forms of societal inequalities and racial inequities. Yet, I must admit that within my anti-racist education, classmates' negative assessments of the field of comparative studies is a point that must not be brushed off lightly, because any person who approaches comparative research with a mind-set brimming with epistemological, ontological, and axiological distortions will undoubtedly produce racist interpretations in his/her work. My classmate's words challenge all of us comparative researchers to introspectively examine our most subconscious thought processes. Although not often a comfortable activity to engage in (at least not so in my experience of it), listening thoughtfully to a third party's disconcerting critique is a potentially golden opportunity to start travelling toward researcher self-awareness. And it just may lead to research that is less likely to be epistemologically racist, but only whenever we try hard enough and ask ourselves the toughest of questions.

The solution is not for dominant researchers to stop learning about world issues and to remain mired only in domestic concerns or for white academics living in the north to research only other white residents. During class discussions within the afore-mentioned "Advanced Seminar in Race and Anti-Racist Research Methodology in Education" course, such propositions were implied or proposed to me, but would certainly represent a step backward for the field of comparative international studies. I see the answer revealing itself somewhere within the active contemplation of the philosophical concepts discussed earlier. Two practical but extremely ambitious suggestions put forth in this essay and which originate from the theories presented, are for researchers to use primary sources in the native languages as often as possible, and for Western-trained researchers to simultaneously engage in self-reflection and in vigorous learning on the social and philosophical constructs that frame participants' lives. Such research practices help to slightly reduce the epistemological racism that arises from different paradigms of realities, knowledges, and values. When there is increased and better informed dialogue between the two fields of comparative education and the anti-racist education, I am sure that others can and will add many more suggestions to my meagre list. I reiterate that it is an almost untenable destination for any outsider to completely cast off the epistemologies, ontologies, and axiologies with which he/she grew up, and that map his/her outlook on the world. Nonetheless, critical self-reflection on the power of these three philosophical abstractions to fuel our research, and drawing on some of the anti-racist discourse of its surrounding problematics, may possibly navigate us into some other waters.

Acknowledgments

I wish to thank the following persons for their comments and criticisms of various versions of this paper: Eynolah Ahmadi, Jemille Chu, Leroy Clarke, Dr. George Dei, Dr. Joseph Farrell, Mary Therese Hirmer, Liao Chin-Lung, Adela Martinez Guajardo, Dr. Vandra Masemann, Patricia Slobodian, Jacob Young, and several anonymous reviewers.

REFERENCES

Arnove, R., Franz, S., Mollis, M., and Torres, C. A. 1999. "Education in Latin America at the End of the 1990s." In R. F. Arnove and C. A. Torres (Eds.), *Comparative Education: The Dialectic of the Global and the Local.* Lanham, MD: Rowman & Littlefield, pp. 305–328.

Atkinson, P., and Hammersley, M. 1994. "Rethinking Critical Theory and Qualitative Research." In N. K. Denzin and Y. S. Lincoln (Eds.), *Handbook of Qualitative research.* Thousand Oaks, CA: Sage, pp. 138–157.

Bahm, A. J. 1993. *Axiology: The Science of Values.* Amsterdam: Editions Rodopi B.V.

Blatchford, C. October 20, 2001, "$2.4M to Preach to the Converted." *National Post Newspaper,* p. A17.

Bonvillain, N. 1997. *Language, Culture, and Communication: The Meaning of Messages.* (2nd ed.). Upper Saddle River, NJ: Prentice Hall.

Boyle, H. N. 2000. *Quaranic Schools in Morocco: Agents of Preservation and Change.* Unpublished doctoral dissertation. University of Pittsburgh, Pittsburgh, Pennsylvania.

Call for papers for a special issue of the Comparative Education Review. (2001, September). *CIES Newsletter: Comparative and International Education Society 128,* 1–6.

120 | *Critical Issues in Anti-racist Research Methodologies*

Collins, P. H. 2000. *Black Feminist Thought: Knowledge, Consciousness, and the Politics of Empowerment.* (2nd ed.). New York: Routledge.

Comisión nacional para la modernización de la educación designada por S. E. el Presidente de la Republica (National commission for the modernization of education). 1995. *Los desafíos de la educación Chilena frente al siglo XXI* (The struggles/challenges facing Chilean education in the XXI century). Santiago, Chile: Editorial Universitaria.

Cook, B. J. 1998. "Doing Educational Research in a Developing Country: Reflections on Egypt." *Compare 28* (1). 93–103.

de Beer, G. 1966. *Jose Vasconcelos and His World.* New York: Las Americas.

Dei, G. J. S. 1994. "The Challenges of Anti-Racist Education Research in the African Context." *Africa Development XIX*(3): 5–25.

Dei, G. J. S., 1999. "Knowledge and Politics of Social Change: The Implications of Anti-Racism." *British Journal of Sociology of Education 20* (3): 395–409.

Denzin, N. K., and Lincoln, Y. S. 1994. "Entering the Field of Qualitative Research." In N. K. Denzin and Y. S. Lincoln (Eds.), *Handbook of Qualitative Research.* Thousand Oaks, CA: Sage.

DeVault, M. L. 1999. *Liberating Method: Feminism and Social Research.* Philadelphia, PA: Temple University Press.

Dewey, J. 1997. "My Pedagogic Creed." In. D. J. Flinders & S. J. Thornton (Eds.), *The Curriculum Studies Reader.* New York: Routledge, pp. 17–23.

Duran, J. 2001. *Worlds of Knowing: Global Feminist Eepistemologies.* New York: Routledge.

Farrell, J. 1987. "Cultural Differences and Curriculum Inquiry." *Curriculum Inquiry 17*(1): 1–8.

Farrell, J. 1996. "Narratives of Identity: The Voice of Youth." *Curriculum Inquiry 26*(3): 235–243.

Farrell, J. P. 2000. "Review Essay: Why Is Educational Reform So Difficult? Similar Descriptions, Different Prescriptions, Failed Explanations." *Curriculum Inquiry, 30*(1): 83–103.

Fernandez, C. 1996. "Government Classification of Multiracial/Multiethnic People." In M. P. P. Root (Ed.), *The Multiracial Experience: Racial Borders as the New Frontier.* Thousand Oaks, CA: Sage, pp. 15–37.

Fuller, B., and Heyneman, S. 1989. "Third World School Quality: Current Collapse, Future Potential." *Educational Researcher, 18*(2): 12–19.

Geertz, C. 1995. *After the Fact: Two Countries, Four Decades, One Anthropologist.* Cambridge, MA: Harvard University Press.

Gilroy, P. 2000. "The Dialectics of Diaspora Identification." In L. Back and J. Solomos (Eds.), *Theories of Race and Racism: A Reader.* London: Routledge, pp. 490–502.

Gilroy, P. 2002. "The End of Antiracism." In P. Essed and D. T. Goldberg (Eds.), *Race Critical Theories.* Malden, MA: Blackwell, pp. 249–264.

Ginsberg, R. 1993. Foreword to *Axiology: The Science of Values* by A. J. Bahm. Amsterdam: Editions Rodopi B. V., p. ix.

Guba, E. G., and Lincoln, Y. S. 1994. "Competing Paradigms in Qualitative Research." In N. K. Denzin and Y. S. Lincoln (Eds.), *Handbook of Qualitative Research.* Thousand Oaks, CA: Sage, pp. 105–117.

Hall, J. R. 1999. *Cultures of Inquiry: From Epistemology to Discourse in Sociohistorical Research.* Cambridge: Cambridge University Press.

Hayhoe, R. 2000. "Redeeming Modernity." *Comparative Education Review* 44(4): 423–439.

Hoffman, D. 1999. "Culture and Comparative Education: Toward Decentering and Recentering the Discourse." *Comparative Education Review* 43(4): 464–488.

hooks, b. 2000. *Where We Stand: Class Matters*. New York: Routledge.

Hsiau, A. 2000. *Contemporary Taiwanese Cultural Nationalism*. London: Routledge.

Inglis, F. 2000. *Clifford Geertz: Culture, Custom and Ethics*. Malden, MA: Polity Press.

Kamler, B., Reid, J., and Santoro, N. 1999. "Who's Asking the Questions?: Researching Race, Ethnicity, and Teachers." *Australian Educational Researcher,* 26(1): 55–74.

Kuo, J. 2000. *Art and Cultural Politics in Postwar Taiwan*. Seattle, WA: University of Washington Press.

Langan, E. 2000. *The European Union's Erasmus Mobility Policy: A Case Study of Three French Higher Education Institutions*. Unpublished doctoral dissertation. New York University, New York.

Lewis, R. 1988. *Anti-Racism: A Mania Exposed*. London: Quartet.

Lipp, S. 1980. *Leopoldo Zea: Mexicanidad to Philosophy of History*. Waterloo, Canada: Wilfrid Laurier University Press.

Marsonet, M. 1997. "Ontology and Conceptual Schemes." In M. Sainsbury (Ed.), *Thought and Ontology*. Milano, Italy: FrancoAngeli s.r.l., pp. 23–41.

Masemann, V. 1990. "Ways of Knowing: Implications for Comparative Education." *Comparative Education Review* 34(4): 465–473.

Masemann, V. 1999. "Culture and Education." In R. F. Arnove and C. A. Torres (Eds.), *Comparative Education: The Dialectic of the Global and the Local*. Lanham, MD: Rowman & Littlefield, pp. 115–133.

Neville, R. C. 1989. *Recovering of the Measure: Interpretation and Nature*. Buffalo, NY: State University of New York Press.

Noah, H. J., and Eckstein, M. A. 1998. *Doing Comparative Education: Three Decades of Collaboration*. Hong Kong: Comparative Education Research Center at the University of Hong Kong.

Palmer, F. 1987. *Anti-racism: An Attack on Education and Value*. London: Sherwood Press.

Patai, D. 1992. "US Academics and Third World Women: Is Ethic Research Possible?" In S. Gluck and D. Patai (Eds.), *Women's Words*. New York: Routledge, pp. 137–153.

Patai, D. 1994. "When Method Becomes Power." In A. Gitlin (Ed.), *Power and Method: Political Activism and Educational Research*. New York: Routledge, pp. 61–73.

Paulston, R. 1993. "Mapping Discourse in Comparative Education Texts." *Compare* 23(2): 101–114.

Paulston, R. 2000. "Imagining Comparative Education: Past, Present, Future." *Compare* 30(3): 353–367.

Paulston, R., and Liebman, M. 1994. "An Invitation to Postmodern Social Cartography." *Comparative Education Review,* 38(2): 215–232.

Paz, O. 1990. *Itinerary* (J. Wilson, Trans.). London: Menard.

Pinar, W. 1995. *Understanding Curriculum: An Introduction to the Study of Historical and Contemporary Curriculum Discourses*. New York: Peter Lang.

Principia Cybernetica Web. n.d. "Epistemology, Introduction." Retrieved June 22, 2001 from http://pespmc1.vub.ac.be/EPISTEMI.html.

Quiroga, J. 1999. *Understanding Octavio Paz.* Columbia, SC: University of South Carolina Press.

Raby, R. L. 2001. "Comparative and International Education: A Bibliography (2000)." *Comparative Education Review 45*(3): 435–474.

Reinharz, S. 1992. *Feminist Methods in Social Research.* New York: Oxford University Press.

Rhetoric and Epistemology Resource Page (n.d.). Retrieved June 22, 2001 from http://www.lcc.gatech.edu/gallery/rhetoric/terms/epistemology.html.

Robertson, C. 1984. "Formal or Non-formal Education? Entrepreneurial Women in Ghana." *Comparative Education Review 29*(4): 639–658.

Root, M. P. P. 1992. "Within, between, and beyond Race." In M. P. P. Root (Ed.), *Racially Mixed People in America.* Newbury Park, CA: Sage, pp. 3–11.

Root, M. P. P. 1996. "The Multiracial Experience: Racial Borders as a Significant Frontier in Race Relations." In M. P. P. Root (Ed.), *The Multiracial Experience: Racial Borders as the New Frontier.* Thousand Oaks, CA: Sage, pp. xiii–xxviii.

Rose, A. 2001, September 15. "What Is This Thing We Call the West?" *National Post Newspaper*, pp. B1, B4.

Rust, V. D. 1996. "From Modern to Postmodern Ways of Seeing Social and Educational Change." In R. D. Paulston (Ed.), *Social Cartography: Mapping Ways of Seeing Social and Educational Change.* New York: Garland, pp. 29–51.

Rust, V. D., Soumaré, A., Pescador, O., and Shibuya, M. 1999. "Research Strategies in Comparative Education." *Comparative Education Review 43*(1): 86–109.

Scheurich, J., and Young, M. 1997. "Coloring Epistemologies: Are Our Research Epistemologies Racially Biased?" *Educational Researcher 26*(4): 4–16.

Schmelkes, S. 2000. "Education and Indian Peoples in Mexico: An Example of Policy Failure." In F. Reimers (Ed.), *Unequal Schools, Unequal Chances.* Lanham, MD: Rowman & Littlefield, pp. 319–333.

Skachkova, P. 2000. *The Ethnic Teaches Back: Identity Formation and Academic Status of Foreign-Born Women Academics in the U. S.* Buffalo: State University of New York.

Stanfield, J. H., II. 1993. "Epistemological Considerations." In J. H. Stanfield II & R. M. Dennis (Eds.), *Race and Ethnicity in Research Methods.* Newbury Park, CA: Sage, pp. 16–36.

Stanfield, J. H., II. 1994. "Ethnic Modeling in Qualitative Research." In N. K. Denzin and Y. S. Lincoln (Eds.), *Handbook of Qualitative Inquiry.* Newbury Park, CA: Sage, pp. 175–188.

Stanley, T. 1998. "The Struggle for History: Historical Narratives and Anti-Racist Pedagogy." *Discourse: Studies in the Cultural Politics of Education 19*(1): 41–52.

Stone, K. M. 2000. *A Cross-Cultural Comparison of the Perceived Traits of Gifted Behaviour.* Loyola University, Chicago, Illinois.

Tuhiwai Smith, L. 1999. *Decolonizing Methodologies?Research and Indigenous Peoples.* London: Zed Books.

van Rijn, N., and Barahona, F. 2001, July 2. "Citizens, Old and New, Share Pride in Our Land." *Toronto Star*, pp. A1, A7.

"Xrefer-Axiology." n.d. Retrieved from Xrefer.com, Digital Reference Library on August 22, 2001, http://www.xrefer.com/entry.jsp?xrefid=497177&secid=.-

"Xrefer-Latin American Philosophy" n.d. . Retrieved from Xrefer.com, Digital Reference Library on August 22, 2001, http://www.xrefer.com/entry.jsp?xrefid=552571&secid=.-

"Xrefer-Ontology." n.d. Retrieved from Xrefer.com, Digital Reference Library on August 22, 2001, http://www.xrefer.com/entry.jsp?xrefid=553052&secid=.-

Wells, P. 2001, November 17. "English Canada Racist: New Book." *National Post Newspaper*, p. A6.

Chapter Six

PAULA BUTLER

Shattering the Comfort Zone

ETHICAL AND POLITICAL ASPECTS OF ANTI-RACISM RESEARCH IN CHURCHES

Introduction

This essay explores some of the political and ethical dimensions of carrying out research on white supremacy and anti-racism within the mainline[1] Protestant Church sector. While other sectors of society, and other major national institutions (schools, media, immigration, legal system, police, etc.) have been the focus of considerable anti-racism research, there has been relatively little contemporary research on race, racism, or white supremacy within the churches as national institutions or as a sector of society. I am interested in this sector because I am part of it, and because the Protestant Church, historically and presently, has a particularly intense relationship with the production of racism as well as with the eradication of racism.

Throughout this paper I will refer to the politics of a focus on white supremacy as part of an anti-racism agenda for the church. I need to clarify my use of the term *white supremacy* because its meaning throughout this paper is much broader than is connoted in popular culture (Ku Klux Klan, neo-Nazi, ultra-right images). In *White Lies*, Jessie Daniels (1997) examines how the images and concepts used by white-supremacist organizations in the United States can be understood as manifestations of what she calls a "white supremacist context." "White supremacy in the United States," she writes, "is *a central organizing principle of social life* rather than merely an isolated social movement. My aim . . . is to place the analysis of White supremacist movements and their discourse within a broader context of White supremacy as a social system" (11, italics added).

In anti-racism thought, white supremacy refers to the broad, pervasive phenomenon of economic, cultural, and epistemological white-skin hegemony, which operates on a global as well as a local scale, a product of European colonial expansion and contemporary patterns of Euro-American neo-colonialism (economic and cultural). Charles Mills (1998) names white supremacy as an "at least partially autonomous" global political-economic structure which was consolidated in the nineteenth century and which institutionalizes white power (100). He also notes that, "the privileging of whites is compatible with a wide variety of political and institutional structures" (101). Mills asserts that while the term *racism* is often reduced in popular usage to individual prejudice and attitudes, the term *white supremacy* emphasizes the systemic political, economic, and epistemological nature of white-skin hegemony, and insists on making visible the whiteness of global power structures. Unless a white settler society (like Canada) explicitly recognizes how white supremacy is produced and reproduced, and establishes mechanisms to redress the material, political, and discursive power imbalances, the society will by default continue to function in support of white hegemony.

I want to assert that for any Protestant church to address racism, part of the project needs to be an examination of the role of the church, both historically and presently, in producing and reinforcing white-supremacist privileges, power structures, and ideologies in the context of the production of a white settler nation.

Historically, the Christian Church played an important part in legitimizing European imperialism and disseminating ideas of white cultural superiority (Davies, 1988; Dyer, 1997; Wright, 1991). The role played by churches (along with the federal government) in violently assimilating Native children to white ways through the residential school experience has gradually been publicly exposed and documented, rendered visible in the official historical record, and named as genocide. Yet, many of the ways in which Canadian churches have contributed to the production of ideologies of white racial superiority are forgotten or not seen; this is a point to which I will return in the final section of this paper. The Christian Church has also produced radical ecumenical voices and movements, emanating from diverse bodies and diverse parts of the globe, drawing on core tenets of Christian doctrine to agitate for dignity and justice (including the eradication of racism) for all people. Given these profound contradictions, I want to make a case for the importance of developing a research agenda to examine the production of racism and the nature of anti-racism initiatives within the church today. My particular focus will be on my own denomination (the United Church of Canada), a prominent mainline Protestant Canadian church.

I want to emphasize at the outset the exploratory and tentative nature of my comments. With the exception of some limited examination of archived reports on the "mission to the Indians" between 1920 and 1980, I have not carried out primary research in this field, nor have I been much involved (except quite recently) in internal initiatives to address racism within my own denomination. I have followed the emergence of national anti-racism policy and anti-racism education initiatives in my denomination, without having been directly involved in the development of this work. What I do bring to this chapter is more than a decade of employment in the national office of my church, where my responsibilities included facilitating education on global justice issues. The issues I will explore in this paper therefore draw on personal work experience, textual analysis of key national policy documents on anti-racism, some historical/archival research, and familiarity with some of the academic literature on methodological issues in anti-racism research.

In the sections that follow, I explore some of the ethical and political issues related to researching and analyzing white supremacy, racism, and anti-racism in my church. The paper concludes with an identification of some of the key areas of research that I think are needed in order to expose and rupture white supremacy in the Protestant Church.

Negotiating the Politics of Pain

I begin with the question of my own subject position as a racially dominant person, and attempt to consider what is at stake for me, especially in carrying out research within an institution in which I am also a member.

My interest in better understanding the nature of racism within the church and the possibilities for anti-racism work was finally catalyzed by the experience of working as an adult educator on global development issues. In the context of this educational work I became more acutely aware of the depth of paternalistic attitudes on the part of many white church people with regard to people in "the South" ("the South" here being the latest euphemism, replacing "developing nations" and "Third World," for the geographical, economic and cultural Other). As I began to reflect on and seek understanding of this phenomenon, I also became more cognizant of my own racialized privilege and power, and of the extent to which I had a deep sense of myself as a normative or quintessential Canadian.

This awareness, and the critique I already had of racism within the church and in mainstream Canadian society generally, did not prepare me for the acute pain I experienced as I began to encounter trenchant critiques of the Christian Church in the writings of anti-racism scholars. One day, for instance, I read the statement, "racism is fully entrenched in dominant White Christian ideology regardless of who is perpetuating it" (Dei, 2000, 27), and found myself so emotionally overwhelmed that I was unable to read farther. Until that moment, I had not realized how much was at stake personally for me in examining and coming to terms with the church's profound entanglement in the production of ideologies of white superiority. My own identity was deeply invested in a Christian faith community as a source of an ethics of justice, "right relations" among people, ecological well-being, and hope. Involvement in this ecumenical community also gave me an identity of moral superiority and innocence. An anti-racism critique of the church as a primary bastion, for centuries, of white Eurocentric domination and colonization was something I could understand intellectually, but which had the psychological effect of leaving me suddenly disoriented and destabilized, the familiar ground under my feet jerked away. It was as though something I had known, but somehow avoided really seeing, was thrust into my face. This reaction was not just disorientation, but the intense pain and shame of becoming more cognizant of the racial atrocities that had been, and continue to be, committed, and of my own implication in this violence.

In my case, the pain I experience is that of a dominant-group person having to acknowledge the brutalities of my own faith/cultural tradition and faith community which is simultaneously a racialized tradition and community even while this faith tradition and community remain important to me and, by choice, a primary source of identity. I try to make use of this (relatively) small experience of trauma to gain some insight into the emotional costs for racially minoritized persons whose daily experiences may regularly contain assaults on fundamental aspects of their identities, aspects that cannot be chosen or unchosen, and who may belong to a community which for generations has experienced the deep psychological wounds of racism what A. K. Wing calls "spirit injury" (1997, 28–29). My own reaction also indicates to me how much is threatened in terms of identity for most dominant-group people, and the level of resistance to be encountered from those who are much less prepared than I was to grapple with the truths of the Christian Church's long complicity in producing and maintaining racist hegemonies.

I lay out these emotions because it seems impossible to carry out anti-racism research without experiencing pain. Politically, it is crucial to ask how pain will be distributed and *who* will suffer the pain, racially dominant people or racially minoritized people who, in addition to experiencing racism, are so often invited to "tell their stories" of racism? There is an enormous resistance among most racially dominant people to think of themselves as racist or to be confronted about our racism. This resistance can be understood as a deep (but historically and socially constructed) desire to view ourselves as good people. We will make all kinds of psychological moves and shifts to maintain our sense of innocence and inherent goodness (Heron, 2000; Razack, 1998). Yet because racism is inherently violent and ugly, the "race to innocence" has to be at some point abandoned in favor of a deep, painful confrontation. Thus, an ethical issue facing researchers of white supremacy is to ask what responsibility should be taken, and by whom, for the pain that will be generated? Without addressing this issue, there may be a temptation to do anti-racism research in a manner that tries to avoid producing (more) pain. In considering my own interest in carrying out research with white church members to better understand the nuances of white supremacy and how ideologies of white supremacy are produced and articulated in the church, I need to both challenge myself not to avoid potentially painful avenues, as well as to think strategically about when and how to ask questions or raise issues that catalyze a confrontation with the brutality of white supremacy.

However, I also want to critically interrogate the purpose or effects of such individual experiences of discomfort, dislocation, and pain. Is there an assumption here that anti-racism change at least partially depends on affective/psychic shifts within racially dominant individuals? In my view, there is always a danger in reducing socio-historical, systemic injustices to matters of individual change. I need to understand more precisely the connection between acute experiences of affective or psychological dislocation/pain in racially dominant individuals who begin to see white supremacy for what it is, and broader processes of social change toward a racism-free society. The personal experience of identity disruption has to translate into real shifts in how power is distributed. With some individuals, experiences of psychic dislocation or threatened loss of identity/power may intensify white-supremacist behavior (Daniels, 1997).

A final comment on the politics of pain is to note that within Protestant Church settings, ideas of community are quite central, and there are likely to be high barriers to any language or inquiry perceived as overtly painful or damaging. Notions of community, inclusion, respect, and welcome are key elements of the institutional culture and discourse, and while these concepts may themselves be used very effectively to protect white dominance and to muzzle critique, their operative and theological power is considerable. There is a Catch-22 here that is difficult to negotiate: Anti-racism seeks to rupture hegemonic race-based power structures in order to create space for the existence of respectful, diverse communities of people. It is exactly this kind of society that churches often claim to, or genuinely attempt to, model, and yet which anti-racism may insist needs to be ruptured in order for genuine power shifts and epistemological shifts to occur. In many church settings, there will be a strong instinct, even on the part of some racially minoritized members, to work for transformation (i.e., issues of redistribution of power) while preserving "*koinonia*" a Greek word the church uses to refer to community or the "communion of all members," irrespective of status or condition. In my view the notion of *koinonia* can be profoundly spiritual and humanizing and is not inherently in opposition to the goals of anti-racism, but its saliency and its effects as a basic theological tenet need to be more fully interrogated and explored in the context of a racialized society.

On Not Re-inscribing White Dominance

Occupying the subject position of white middle-class Canadian female raises immediate dilemmas for me with regard to my interest in carrying out anti-racism research within my own church. Anti-racism work, both at the national church level and within the local congregation, is perhaps the one place within church structures where there is heightened attention to racialized bodies and representation. Who takes the initiative to develop anti-racism programming? Who defines the meaning and content of *anti-racism*, and how is the content negotiated? What bodies are represented on committees? What bodies are paid to staff anti-racism work? Who represents the organization at national or international meetings and conferences on racism?

These questions need to be placed in the context of a church that may still have a dominant white Anglo-Saxon heritage, culture, and membership, but which is also the church of First Nations congregations, other so-called ethnic congregations (Japanese, Korean, Chinese, Ghanaian, Jamaican, Trinidadian, Congolese, etc.), and generations of members of non–Anglo Saxon heritage. Demographic changes in the ethnic makeup of the Canadian population have been slowly and partially reflected in the church membership, with growing pressure from racialized minorities for the church to change to reflect its diverse membership. This pressure has included demands for racism to be addressed within the church, and to a lesser extent, for the church to work more seriously at addressing racism in Canadian society.

Given this context, it is crucial for white people with commitments to anti-racism to think very carefully about how to avoid re-centering ourselves on the stage of anti-racism work. At the same time, anti-racism scholars such as Dyer (1997), Fine (1997), Dei (2000), and Frankenberg (1993) have insisted on the importance of keeping part of the anti-racism agenda focused on addressing how white identities and white superiority are produced. White people are being challenged to address racism as *our* issue, rather than merely being in solidarity with racialized minorities in "their" struggle, and without at the same time colonizing or appropriating the anti-racism work. (Even as I write this, I agonize over the persistent us/them dichotomy; it seems to reify difference associated with skin color, yet it also seems necessary in order to acknowledge the power imbalances that result in a racialized society.)

As a racially dominant researcher, how does one not colonize or re-secure dominance in the very process of carrying out research on white dominance? One important stance is to be able to acknowledge the primacy of the agency and priorities of racially minoritized peoples in their resistance to, and struggles against, racism, colonization, and neo-colonialism. I have used the example of the Esgenoopetitj First Nation in the area of Burnt Church, New Brunswick, who, as recently as August 2001, refused to sign a fishery management agreement with the Federal Department of Fisheries. Such an agreement was regarded by the First Nation as an expression of a hegemonic colonial relationship with the Canadian state, a relationship they contested and refused to reify. In this case, the actions of the Esgenoopetitj people, which they carried out at great material and psychological cost, nevertheless produced an actual anti-colonial effect in manifesting their own power of self-determination. While it might be an important initiative for me to carry out research among racially dominant church people in the Burnt Church area to gain an understanding of how white supremacy is constructed and how it might be deconstructed, such work must be seen as taking place distinctly in the margins of the anti-racism/anti-colonial actions of racially minoritized groups, whose efforts are central and foregrounded, and whose actions also have a discursive and pedagogical anti-racism effect.

Racially dominant persons engaged in anti-racism research and action can always use anti-racism commitments to secure our own innocence, goodness, and essentially our moral superiority. This too can be a way of maintaining privilege and acquiring status. There is no easy way out of this dilemma. We have to be continuously self-reflective and open to critical feedback; we have to develop an ability to discern when our views/actions are important and when they are irrelevant, when to be present and when not to be present, when to speak and when to keep quiet. Humility is key, balanced with an ability to effectively use the power we do have.

The Place of Whiteness and White Supremacy Research within an Anti-racism Agenda

Within my own church, anti-racism work, primarily as it is articulated in the national policy statement of August 2000, does not focus much on questions of the nature of whiteness and the production of white identities and white domination. Certainly, the term *white supremacy* never appears, although white privilege is mentioned and discussed briefly. Racialized minorities within the church have given priority to creating epistemological or cultural space for themselves within the church, often through developing separate organizational structures (All Native Circle Conference; Ethnic Ministries Council); to gaining access to decision-making structures by calling for more diverse representation; and by working to diversify church culture to be more inclusive and representative of diverse languages, traditions, and faith expressions.

An important research question would be to discover to what extent racially minoritized persons within the church view attention to whiteness and a critical understanding of (and response to) the production of ideologies of white superiority and practices of white domination as important tasks in a broader anti-racism action agenda. Is it possible for such work to be done without it becoming or being perceived as a colonization of anti-racism work? Can it be done without detracting from a focus on issues of representation of minoritized persons, and on the assertion of non-Western cultures and epistemologies? While anti-racism scholars identify all of the above as falling within the rubric of anti-racism, different components of anti-racism do generate different action priorities and may have very different implications in terms of who becomes the key actors or key subjects of anti-racism efforts. For instance, very different priorities may be assigned to the need to research the working conditions of racially minoritized pastors within the church, or to research barriers to ordination among racially minoritized women as opposed to, for instance, researching the production of white identity in the context of church youth group activities, or in the context of responding to emergency appeals for humanitarian crises overseas.

Given the care needed to find an appropriate balance among these various elements, it seems to me essential that a discussion be engaged within the church on appropriate roles of people of differing racial identities and subject positions in carrying out anti-racism work, including research. This is important not only to ensure that anti-racism does not itself become a site of reproduction of racial hierarchies and white domination, but also to establish parameters for anti-racism research by white scholars. This is particularly important for any research findings to be considered valid by racially minoritized persons within the church.

Researching Race in One's Own Institution:
Questions of Validity, Confidentiality, and Impact

Finally, there is a set of ethical and political issues related to doing an exposé of a particular institution. What is appropriate to expose about an institution about which one has privileged, intimate knowledge? Raising unpleasant issues and challenges internally about the church's history, values, and practices will be, for some, bad enough. To publicly expose the nature of white supremacy in the church through publishing research may constitute an even more serious form of "treason." Obviously, the political risks and consequences for a researcher who tells a different, unflattering story about his/her own community are very high, although there will also be some insiders who will welcome the courageous telling of nonofficial stories and histories.

However, the more important strategic question for me is whether shifts in the racial distribution of power within the institution are more likely to occur through internal processes of education, policy change, and incremental reform, or to what extent change is likely to be catalyzed by an external (in my case, insider-outsider) critique and analysis. Perhaps ways will always be found to discredit research that reveals too much dirt and calls for too radical changes.

My own sense is that both strategies can play important roles at different moments, but who determines when a particular strategy is appropriate, and what is the process for doing so? Researchers, especially racially dominant researchers, need to have sensitive and collaborative working relationships with a carefully selected and diverse group of allies within the church. This will greatly enhance the possibility of the research having some anti-racism impact. Accountability is important, but not usually to the official structures of the church. Accountability of researchers to a small group of like-minded insiders is, I would assert, enough. A sense of involvement, ownership, and input to the research from even a small insider group will directly increase the probability of the research contributing to transformative processes.

Case Study: Deconstructing a National Church Anti-racism Policy

This brings me to the politics of an anti-racism agenda. Here I want to consider a recent major national policy statement on anti-racism produced by my denomination. This comprehensive policy statement contains some thirty-two action recommendations emanating from a statement that the church "is committed to the anti-racist transformation of itself and Canadian society" (United Church of Canada, 2000, 6). This in itself is quite a remarkable assertion! Without having been involved in the production of this policy or having had access to minutes of meetings, I do not know the details of the negotiations that took place during the production of this text. However, contestations and negotiations undoubtedly occurred. For instance, while there is an explicit statement rejecting the use of the term *inclusion* as referring to practices that leave intact the power of the dominant group in the church, many of the specific recommendations attest to an underlying conceptual paradigm of inclusion. This suggests to me that even within the group drafting the policy statement there were different views and sensitivities. The policy states that it "encourages the full participation of Aboriginal and First Nations peoples and people of racial and ethno cultural minority . . . at every level of the church, particularly decision-making bodies . . ." (16). The policy promises to "ensure that various types of resources (i.e., human, media, and financial) are in place to support Aboriginal and First Nations peoples and people of racial and ethno cultural minorities as *they* assume these responsibilities" (16, emphasis added). This may seem to be too subtle a point, but does not the use of *they* recenter whiteness and white church members as normative? What would be the effect of using *we* throughout the document? And what is encoded in the term *ethno cultural*? Does it provide any possibility that Anglo-Saxon might eventually be recoded as an ethno cultural category and thus decentered from its present position of privilege?

Many other critiques of the policy statement could be made. There is minimal treatment of the church's history on racism, which is essentially glossed over and possibly falsified.[2] There is no explicit recommendation to address origins, expressions, and practices of white superiority or white privilege, although this might, in practice, occur in the context of what the text calls "training and continuing education in anti-racism education," which is to be widely provided at all levels of church governance and leadership. In the text of the policy statement, racism is narrowed to a set of individual and institutional practices with little recognition or acknowledgment of the broader historical and systemic nature of racism. There is no recognition of how racism interfaces with other hegemonic systems such as patriarchy or capitalism. The question as to how the church has theologically rationalized racism is not engaged.

I want to locate this brief critique of the policy statement within a paradigm of the church as a liberal institution of mainstream Canadian society, drawing on an article by Carl James and Joy Mannette entitled "*Rethinking Access: The Challenge of Living with Difficult Knowledge*" (2000). Many of the authors' observations about the effectiveness (or otherwise) of "access programs" (affirmative action) in Canadian universities to respond to the needs of historically disadvantaged groups are extremely relevant to an understanding of the church's anti-racism efforts. According to James and Mannette (2000), "Post-secondary access initiatives . . . can be understood as liberal 'quests for social justice'" within the context of what are seen as "essentially reformable social systems" (Burton and Carlen, 1979, 75). In the analysis by James and Mannette, Canadian universities develop access programs to respond to charges that they are sites where racial, ethnic, gender, and class hegemonies are reproduced.

> Official discourse in the form of policy documents serves to assign blame in terms of the temporary failure of essentially reformable systems . . . Once the institution has been seen to take charge publicly and authoritatively in the assignment of blame, the institutional process of official discourse instructs on the kind of institutional change required to obviate the problem. . . . Interestingly, the representative individuals from hitherto excluded groups, who animated the critique through claims of institutional bias, get invited to participate in the fact-finding, report-writing and ongoing administration of access programs. (James and Mannette, 2000, 76–77)

What James and Mannette point to, however, is the fact that the experiences of members of historically disadvantaged groups attest to continuing marginalization and racialization even with access programs in place, and even in the process of making use of access programs. Such programs constitute "one moment in hegemonic renegotiation following ideological disruption" (76). I would suggest that the anti-racism policy of my church might constitute a similar phenomenon. James and Mannette refer to the crucial differences between anti-racism and multiculturalism, asserting that, "the key issue with anti-racism politics is that, unlike multiculturalism, its ethos cannot be renegotiated or accommodated in and by the hegemonic elaborations and discourses that currently characterize the fabric of these institutions" (88). In other words, anti-racism by its very nature requires new institutions and new social arrangements, not internal reforms and accommodations that leave core power structures intact within the same institutions. In a short article on the experiences of black female teachers in Ontario schools, Annette Henry (2000) recalls that, "anti-racism, by definition, is political, transformative and oppositional" (97).

Reflecting on these definitions of anti-racism, I would need to ask whether my church's policy statement on anti-racism is actually an anti-racism initiative or much more an expression of multiculturalism, which in fact fits far more comfortably in the paradigm of a liberal institution. In other words, an agenda for change is undertaken that may push out the margins of the comfort zone of the dominant group, but that does not provide an adequate basis to fundamentally rupture structures and ideologies of domination.

A set of research questions could be posed to elicit a better understanding of the contestations that occurred in the production of this policy statement. Which bodies and which perspectives were influential, and which were marginalized? Did the style of working reflect Eurocentric culture or other ways of being, knowing, and producing knowledge? Was there any attempt to address the historical role of the church in imperialism and cultural assimilation, and the legacy of such actions? Is it possible to pursue elements of an anti-racism agenda within a paradigm that is essentially multiculturalism? Does this anti-racism policy respond to the self-articulated needs of racially minoritized people within the church, or does it primarily meet the needs of the dominant group to feel it is being progressive and sensitive?

Stepping back from a direct analysis of the policy text and process, I want to examine the political effects of a critical deconstruction of an institutional policy on anti-racism. Can such a critique catalyze a debate that could engender a more oppositional approach to anti-racism in the church? Or does such analysis move into the danger zone of intellectualizing transformative political projects such that elegant theoretical perspectives discredit the imperfect, gritty work of social change? Activists and (some) bureaucrats who work hard at the tasks of mobilizing, educating, disseminating information, networking and developing policy (all in the interest of working for change) will often be impatient with and dismissive of academic critiques. There is nevertheless a very important place for such critical and theoretical reflection. The activist work of social change can be so focused on immediate goals that it is not able to see the ways in which it may be functioning to *stabilize* the very structures and hegemonies it claims to be subverting.

What political sensibilities do I need to engage as a white researcher in relation to the range of responses there may be from different racially minoritized church members to this anti-racism policy? To the extent that it is actually implemented, the policy may represent a significantly improved possibility for all church members to experience the church as a place where different languages, music, forms of spirituality, experiences, and knowledge are fully valued, and where racially minoritized members no longer experience barriers to participation in any aspect of church life. If all this happened, it would indeed be significant. Yet without a deeper analysis and attention to white supremacy in the church and in Canadian society, I am not convinced that even these goals can be achieved in a form that goes much beyond tokenism. Nevertheless, I need to be able to respect and support those who are committed to implementing this national anti-racism policy, yet at the same time advocate constant attention to the manner in which the church as a liberal institution will tend to co-opt and "de-claw" a radical anti-racism agenda.

Elements of a Research Agenda on White Supremacy and Protestantism

Whiteness is also a refusal to acknowledge how white people are implicated in certain social relations of privilege and relations of domination and subordination. Whiteness, then, can be considered a form of social amnesia. (McLaren, 1998)

In this section of the paper I want to ask what avenues of inquiry are necessary for the church to genuinely engage in anti-racism? I propose several aspects of an anti-racism research agenda that particularly interest me, and that reflect the specificity of my own subject position and experiences. These are: (1) production of moral narratives or narratives of cultural superiority in the form of mission outreach, social reform/social gospel, and imperial saving; (2) interconnections among current understandings and practices of charity, paternalism and racism, which also come together in the concept of *imperial saving*; (3) history of church-state relations in the context of the production of a white settler society; and (4) constructions of theological correctness as a means of re-securing the dominance of white Anglo-Saxon Protestantism.

I have used Peter MacLaren's terminology "Whiteness as social amnesia" because I believe the church's approach to anti-racism must be grounded in an attempt to recall, tell, and come to terms with the stories from its own history that have been forgotten. What are the stories that need to be remembered so that we move out of social amnesia? What are the missing pieces or the different tellings of Canadian history that can serve to challenge and reveal the bias in the dominant official history? For the church, part of this is a matter of acknowledging who we have been, in order to understand more honestly who we now are.

White Supremacy in the Production of White Settlers

For the church to be credible in its anti-racism work, I suggest that it needs to begin by remembering the role played by Canadian Protestant churches since the formation of the country in producing a normative white (British, imperialist) Canadian national identity. To be Canadian was to be of British heritage, Anglophone, white, and Protestant. The alleged characteristics of Protestantism (industriousness, discipline, self-reliance) were considered to be productive of civilization and progress.

In *A World Mission: Canadian Protestantism and the Quest for a New International Order, 1918–1939* (1999), Robert Wright traces contestations of racism and Eurocentric cultural arrogance in the context of international mission work. Despite the efforts of a number of radical visionaries, the liberal church leadership and the majority of members maintained what was at best an ambiguous attitude toward other races and religions. Wright observes that "missionaries were capable of supporting indigenization while holding condescending opinions of non-Western cultures" (147) and that "the view that it was entirely reasonable for Canada to prevent any erosion of its historic Anglo-Saxon character was deeply entrenched in the mainline churches, even among those who called themselves friends of the Japanese" (203). Thus, he concludes, "Canadian efforts to forge an internationalist agenda for Protestant Christendom in the 1920s and 1930s were circumscribed not only by many church leaders' Victorian world-view but by a vision of Canada as a Protestant and Anglo-Saxon nation" (252).

My own foray into church archives for the period 1920 through 1980 to examine how white identities were articulated and constructed, as well as how the Other was constructed, revealed much that I found shocking. Going through official reports of regional and national church meetings on "Mission to the Indians," I found the tone, language, and concepts so disturbing that, concerned about the ethics of allowing such ugly terminology to find its way into print again (i.e., not from the perspective of protecting the church but rather in an effort to avoid re-exposing First Nations readers to such abusive language), I finally just summarized what I found as follows:

> [C]lear integration/assimilation agenda; pejorative stereotypes of Native people; 'through our courageous efforts, they can be helped to be Christian citizens'; some genuine concern on the part of white missionaries about economic conditions on reserves; unabashedly paternalistic; no indication of guilt, shame, complicity or analysis concerning the role of white settlers/settlement on Native lands; and overall a real belief in the validity of the project of improving and assimilating 'the Indians.'

What I found in these church documents was undoubtedly a typical expression of Canadian Protestantism's racist ideology of cultural superiority. Elements of this ideology show up in the "home missions" practices of aiding destitute, needy, non-white immigrants to survive and assimilate, and it shows up in the church's historical approach to "ethnic churches" (congregations of non-English-speaking peoples), contrasting these to the "regular" churches. Clearly, there is a deep and long tradition within the Canadian mainline Protestant churches of centering and rendering normative white Anglo-Saxon identities and practices (Lochhead, 1991).

Contemporary anti-racism research needs to test the extent to which such ideas are still deeply held among dominant group members of the church, and to what extent such ideas have given way to new understandings. Anti-racism research will also want to look at what paradigms most commonly appear as new understandings of Canadian identity. Research needs to be carried out to determine whether such racist ideologies as those I encountered in the archives as recently as the 1960s have actually been ruptured and eradicated, or whether they are lurking just below the surface in the worldviews of racially dominant Canadian church members. Research could also help identify the discursive unities, or disunities, between racist constructions of the past and new understandings of Canadian identity. For those in the church addressing racism, a precise and nuanced understanding of the history of the church's role in generating a white Anglo-Saxon normative identity for Canadian citizens is essential in order to know where the work of deconstructing white normativity needs to start.

Constructions of White Supremacy in the Figure of the Social Reformer

One of the most typical figures within white Canadian Protestantism (particularly in my own denomination, and I personally have played this role during much of my adulthood) is that of the social reformer. During the 1920s and into the 1930s church activists played lead roles in critiquing rampant capitalism for its effects on workers, women, children, the elderly, and poor people, and for promoting specific policy reforms. Their advocacy (known as the *social gospel movement*) contributed significantly to the establishment of a publicly funded comprehensive social welfare system or *social safety net*. This radical social reform work, focused on what would today be called economic justice, nevertheless coexisted with the church's involvement in forced removals of Native children from their communities in order to assimilate them into a white world through the residential school system. The social gospel movement also coexisted with the heyday of British colonialism and imperialism, during which the churches provided ideological and theological support for the great civilizing enterprise, and expanded their own overseas mission involvements. From an anti-racism perspective, it is significant to trace the connections between the process of individual Protestant Christians gaining social status and moral identities as social reformers, at the same time as white Christian Anglo-Saxon domination (rooted in a sense of moral and cultural superiority) enabled and legitimized both colonial imperialism abroad and genocidal assimilation of First Nations at home. In these narratives, the white Christian is always a good person (moral, industrious, a social reformer), and it is, ironically, the social construction of his/her very goodness, interchangeable with his/her whiteness, which lends ideological legitimation and impetus to global imperial expansion as well as to the colonization of First Nations.

A more contemporary manifestation of this imperial saving/colonizing phenomenon can be seen in acts of humanitarian aid, emergency relief, giving to charities, to the needy, to the Third World. I define paternalism as a propensity, produced by patriarchy and imperialism, to take care of those who are regarded as incapable of providing for themselves and in need of rescue or help. It is a fundamental denial of agency and adulthood to those whose lives are circumscribed by various forms of oppression. While there is a strong inclination in Canadian culture and Canadian churches to help the needy, this paternalistic helping (*imperial saving*) re-inscribes white racial privilege and dominance while directing the gaze away from structural and systemic causes of poverty and inequity.

For the church, these programs constitute a major site of reproduction of white superiority. Yet to critique such work is fraught with political pitfalls. Given how very long it will take to transform societal understandings of the historical context and social relations of charity, it will be argued that there is a need to continue giving because even wholly inadequate resources may, at minimum, save lives and, at best, enable some oppositional and anti-colonial work. Still, I contend that for a church constituency to exclude research on paternalism and charity from an anti-racism agenda is to leave intact one of the primary discursive foundations of White supremacy in the church. What is at stake here for white people and for the Protestant Church as a Canadian institution is something that touches on a deeply rooted sense of self and identity as moral and innocent.

Producing White Supremacy through Theological "Correctness"

The last anti-racism research theme I want to discuss briefly is what I have called *theological correctness*, a concept drawn from the idea of political correctness. Within mainline Protestant churches, particular theological ideas and practices have come to dominate theological thinking and form a set of ideas considered to be "theologically correct." Core tenets are: full participation of women in the life of the church; respectful interaction and dialogue with other religious faiths and spiritualities rather than efforts at evangelism or conversion; and the centrality of social justice action or social gospel. Of course, such ideals may not be fully realized or enacted in all parts of the life of the church. However, this "theologically correct" point of view may enable the construction of other faith traditions as sexist, patriarchal, evangelical, fundamentalist, or charismatic and thus backward, inferior, and unenlightened.

These categorizations become more complicated when race, ethnicity, and class are traced. In most countries that were subjected to European colonialism, there exist numerous small "independent" or "indigenous" church-es. Many of these were "splinter groups" from European-established church-es; they splintered often over a desire to incorporate indigenous worship traditions or to gain indigenous (as opposed to foreign missionary) control of the church. There are also ancient indigenous churches such as the Ethiopian Orthodox Church or the Egyptian Coptic Church, which now have branch-es. However, the established churches of European heritage, more affluent, vis-ible and with established relations with the state, effectively marginalize and ignore these "other" churches. I am suggesting that research needs to be car-ried out to explore the extent to which an ideology of theological correctness masks racism and is used by white establishment denominations to maintain white settler dominance. Rather than foregrounding perceived doctrinal dif-ferences and de-contextualizing racialized social relations and histories, anti-racism approaches could foreground global white supremacy and then engage a discussion of theological, political, and cultural differences.

Conclusion

This chapter has focused on some of the political and ethical aspects of anti-racism research in particular, research on white supremacy within a prominent Protestant Canadian church. I allege that the church has barely started to grap-ple with its own racist legacies or with current manifestations of racism. Research on the nature of and production of white supremacy within the church will be provocative. It will challenge and disrupt the comfortable para-meters within which the church as an institution may have hoped to be able to confine its approach to anti-racism. It will pose a strong challenge to the church's attempt to self-identify as well meaning and progressive. In other words, an analysis of white supremacy within Canadian Protestantism will potentially push the church to a more profound self-interrogation and a map-ping out of needed internal transformation, work that could heighten atten-tion to the nature of dominant subject-positions and to the role of the church in producing a white settler society. Such work could generate the production of different identities, different discourses, different practices, programs, and policies. Although there will be great resistance from many parts of the church to doing so, there is also a sense that for the church not to do so will consti-tute a profound theological failure to be a church in one of the most common-ly recognized senses of the word a sign of the presence of the spirit of life in the world.

142 | *Critical Issues in Anti-racist Research Methodologies*

NOTES

1. The term "mainline" churches typically include the Anglican, Baptist, Lutheran, Mennonite, Methodist, Presbyterian, Roman Catholic, and United churches. Mainline connotes White establishment churches; churches with long histories, European heritage, and significant membership (i.e., in the thousands and, for Roman Catholics, the millions). The term may also be used to distinguish the churches mentioned above from more evangelical churches (e.g., Pentecostal), although there is considerable ambiguity about the meaning of evangelical and some members of mainline churches consider themselves evangelicals. In the final section of the paper, I explore the question of the racialized naming and categorization of various Christian faith groups.

2. The policy states, "the church was active in aiding Japanese Canadians interred during the war." Another source, however, states that, "Notwithstanding the protests of individual clergymen . . . the churches at large "did nothing" (Wright, 1991, 213–214).

REFERENCES

Burton, F., and Carlen, P. 1979. *Official Discourse*. London: Routledge.

Daniels, J. 1997. *White Lies*. New York and London: Routledge.

Davies, A. 1988. *Infected Christianity: A Study of Modern Racism*. Kingston and Montreal: McGill-Queen's University Press.

Dei, G. 2000. "Toward an Anti-racism Discursive Framework." In G. Dei and A. Calliste (Eds.), *Power, Knowledge and Anti-racism Education: A Critical Reader*. Halifax: Fernwood Publishing.

Dyer, R. 1997. *White*. London and New York: Routledge.

Fine, M., Weis, L., Powell, L., and Mun Wong, L. Eds. 1997. *Off White: Readings on Race, Power and Society*. New York: Routledge.

Frankenberg, R. 1993. *The Social Construction of Whiteness: White Women, Race Matters*. Minneapolis: University of Minneapolis Press.

Henry, A. 2000. "Black Women Teachers' Positionality and 'Everyday Acts': A Brief Reflection on the Work to be Done." In G. Dei and A. Calliste (Eds.), *Power, Knowledge and Anti-Racism Education: A Critical Reader*. Halifax: Fernwood Publishing.

Heron, B. 2000. *Desire for Development: The Education of White Women Development Workers*. Doctoral dissertation. OISE/University of Toronto.

James, C., and Mannette, J. 2000. "Rethinking Access: The Challenges of Living with Difficult Knowledge." In G. Dei and A. Calliste (Eds.), *Power, Knowledge and Anti-Racism Education: A Critical Reader*. Halifax: Fernwood Publishing.

Lochhead, D. 1991. "The United Church of Canada and the Conscience of the Nation." In R. E. Vandervennen (Ed.), *Church and Canadian Culture*. New York and London: University Press of America.

McLaren, P. 1998. "Unthinking Whiteness, Rethinking Democracy: Toward a Revolutionary Multiculturalism." In P. McLaren (Ed.), *Life in Schools: An Introduction to Critical Pedagogy in the Foundations of Education*. Los Angeles: Allyn and Bacon.

Mills, C. 1998. *Blackness Visible: Essays on Philosophy and Race.* Ithaca, NY: Cornell University Press.

Razack, S. 1998. *Looking White People in the Eye: Gender, Race and Culture in Courtrooms and Classrooms.* Toronto: University of Toronto Press.

United Church of Canada. 2000. "That All May Be One: Policy Statement on Anti-Racism." Toronto: United Church of Canada.

Wing, A. K. 1997. "Brief Reflections Toward a Multiplicative Theory and Praxis of Being." In A. K. Wing (Ed.), *Critical Race Feminism: A Reader.* New York: New York University Press, pp. 27–34.

Wright, R. 1991. *A World Mission: Canadian Protestantism and the Quest for a New International Order, 1918–1939.* Montreal and Kingston: McGill-Queen's University Press.

Chapter Seven

RENU SHARMA

Re-searching the Spiritual

APPLYING SOUL
TO RESEARCH PRACTICE

This chapter discusses three issues: (1) the relevance of research that pertains to the notion of difference and spirituality in education, (2) why approaching one's research agenda from a spiritual stance enhances and enriches ethnographic research work, and (3) elaboration toward understanding that the topic chosen to research is, in and of itself, a spiritual exercise and reflective of the kind of spiritual values that are held by the respective investigator.

Defining the Undeniable

In assuming that research is a spiritually driven exercise, research practitioners should first be sentient to their own form of spiritual expression. Subsequently, this leads to the notion of typologizing spirituality and creates a point from which a prospective researcher departs in an attempt to define his or her own version of spirituality. This means recognizing the shifting nature of spiritual experience and how this influences conceptualization:

> In recent years we have seen, a major shift has taken place in spirituality which has influenced the question of unity and diversity, that is that human experience [is] increasingly accepted as a valid context for serious reflection. The acceptance of experience means that spirituality has moved away from a deductive process (from first principles to specific instances) towards a realization that spiritualities arise within particular and therefore different contexts. (Philips, 1995, 197)

Thus, defining boundaries based on the type of spirituality one practices becomes a challenging task. The concept is vast in its cultural, religious, and philosophical meanings. Spiritually placed education must assume grounds for personal definition, not ones contingent upon structures. Nevertheless, a working definition in terms of developing a point of foci for a perspective study must be in place whether religious or non-religious. For this project, the definitional framework for spirituality is partly derived from David Ray Griffin's (1988) analysis of what spirituality may presently mean. This definition, however, is by no means exhaustive or exclusive and leaves space for malleability:

> For many people, the term spirituality has otherworldly connotations and implies some form of religious discipline. The term is used [here] in a broad sense however to refer to the ultimate values and meanings in terms of which we live, whether or not we consciously try to increase our commitment to those values and meanings. The term does have religious connotations, in that one's ultimate values and meanings reflect some presuppositions as to what is holy, that is of ultimate importance. But, the presupposed holy can be something very worldly, such as power, sexual energy, or success. Spirituality in this broad sense is not an optional quality, which we might elect not to have. Everyone embodies spirituality even if it be a nihilistic or materialistic spirituality. It is also customary to use spirituality in a stricter sense for a way of life oriented around an ultimate meaning and around values other than power, pleasure and possession. [Restrictive religious uses of spirituality which are imposed and not chosen may lead to nihilism and materialism for they are pseudo-spiritualities even anti-spiritualities]. Spirituality as used here refers to a person's ultimate values and commitments regardless of their context. (Griffin, 1988, 2)

Griffin's version is valid for research because the reference to holy spirituality does not limit it to *religious holiness* but rather *holistic holiness*. Holistic holiness respects the sacred relationship between mind, body, and soul, which plays a role in personal spiritual formations. With this in mind, a researcher can move from respecting the relationship of synergy in his or her own life and extend this to research participants. Second, the notion of the spiritual can be derived from the values individuals deem to be important; different people regard different experiences as important. For example, a politician's quest for political power can be seen as having a spiritual foundation in that he may not feel complete until ultimate acquisition of a high level of political power, while an artist is driven by emotional pangs to express a facet of his or her life or the world at large in a piece of artwork. So too, students are driven in school by spiritual expressions that accord differential importance to different things.

One's spirituality can be passionately or affectionately driven by a sense that spiritual completeness depends on finding a soul mate or lover. A researcher can be driven spiritually to pursue inquiry into an area that she values as spiritually important to her, where it may not be for another. Third, and most relevant, Griffin's definitional framework recognizes that true spirituality can only manifest in terms of freedom. Imposed forms of spirituality or pseudo-spirituality (whether religious or otherwise) are not spirituality in a true sense because of the imposed quality. For example, religious groups may fight to gain spiritual completeness by religious power impositions on a civil society. Politicians who gain spiritual completeness from a dictatorship do not leave room for others to experience completeness because of a political party's dictatorial tendencies or cohesiveness. Thus, a politician or religious group who attains power for their own completeness may not be doing it for the society at large, but personal or cliquish gains. If a society is constrained by the quest for power-driven spiritual completeness of others or groups, the society may experience pseudo-spirituality (this can be construed as another form of false consciousness, to use Marx's term) because the society did not choose its own course; it was subtly imposed upon them.

The issue of pseudo-spiritual development is also relevant in terms of schooling and research because a pseudo-spirituality can be seen as a defense mechanism leading to false consciousness of students. For example, students whose needs are not fully met at school may assume pseudo-forms of spirituality that best befit their school's political structure rather than their personal values. In so doing, the students are living in a state of false awareness or denial of their own spiritual place.

Griffin's (1988) definition becomes useful because, while it is seemingly abstract, it does suggest a foundation based on personal definitions of spirituality, calling stricter forms of impositional spirituality anti-spirited or pseudo-spirited. This means that imposed spirituality is not real. The point in terms of investigative work is that researchers cannot impose their version of spirituality or their definition of it onto their participants. This could lead to pseudo-spirituality and spiritual injury as personally defined spirituality is closer to reality yet not necessarily total reality. This is a crucial criterion for understanding foundations of research on spirituality. In cases of falsification, the truth manifests eventually, and even if it is kept hidden, it always destroys something in its efforts to hide behind reality. Thus, the notion of pseudo-spiritual development is an important consideration for research because it deals with unraveling masked forms of spirituality and for understanding the underlying clarity of the data collected.

An analysis of what is to be gained from research on spirituality in schooling argues that if spirituality becomes an effective part of research practice *and* is respected as a researchable dimension, then the experience of ethnographic work will be valuable for both investigator(s) and participant(s). This means moving toward a set of spiritual criteria of measurement. Relating research work as a spiritual observance that respects identities, cultural differences, and expression of researchers and participants alike would be a worthy explorative goal for altering discriminatory educational practices.

Spiritual Research Principles

Including notions of the spiritual would transform research into an evocative expression of oneself. Attempts to place research or ethnographic studies in the realm of spirituality would be a task that many may embrace as necessary and timely, while others of the scientific community may feel that it would be impossible to scrutinize, measure, observe, or research the spiritual. My task here is to explore what it means to research using spiritually based conceptions and their relevant importance in the realms of educational practice, initiative, and movement toward equality in schools and research principles.

Complimentarity of the spiritual and scientific means that rather than attempts to separate the spiritual and the rational, writers like Vivekananda and Tata (1993) deeply believe that the spiritual and scientific are actually "complementary to, if not necessary for each other's development in modern life" (cited by Tulasiewicz and To, 1993, 45).

Atavistic tendencies to separate spirituality from rationality (linking it specifically to religion) or mythologizing from a seductive analytical standpoint negate an underlying assumption that science can only be effective without a spirited view. Rather, science without spirit is futile and obsolete; in the first place, it is the spirited driving force that a scientist has that encourages his or her drive to investigate or search out a phenomenon. Without this spirited belief and experiences befitting this belief, a scientist cannot pursue passionate research work. For example, Ernest Zebrowski (cited by Miller and Cook-Greuter, 2000) has found that:

> Science is seldom done in a social vacuum. Scientific progress is *intimately* dependent on communication for no human has time to observe first hand everything that may be related to his/her interests. (Zebrowski cited by Miller and Cook-Greuter, 2000, 159, (emphasis added)

While scientists may have many interests and cannot possibly perform enquiry into all of them, the ones they choose to investigate must have a spiritual closeness to their heart; otherwise why would they contemplate such inquiry? Thus, the personal and spiritual are certainly reflected in scientific inquiry and deepened in the analysis and interpretation of data collected, and this could even happen with a respectful attempt to be as objective as possible. To exemplify this point, it has been documented that in 1928

> [a] young Indian physicist S. I. Chandrasekhar traveled to England to propose that the laws of general relativity predicted the existence of massive singularities in space which are known as "black holes." This time it was Sir Thomas Eddington who ridiculed the young, visiting scientist, and so devastated him that he left the field of astrophysics. In

1983 Chandrasekhar won the Nobel Prize in physics. (Zebrowski cited in Miller and Cook-Greuter, 2000, 160)

The significance of this passage is the notable point of spirit injury that scientists can experience when their ideas for research are felt deeply. This may very well support the point that scientific research is a spiritual exercise. It can be said that Chandrasekhar's spirit was damaged by the ridicule of his peers so much so that he left the field. However, his second attempt to sell his idea displayed the close spiritual relationship he shared with his scientific beliefs and his work. His perseverance was certainly not driven by rationality alone.

Spiritual Attribution

The appeal of aesthetic perceptions combined with spiritual purpose is not detrimental but uplifting to research work. Attributing spirituality to myths and mores is a culturally derived sensibility that has become universal, thus taking it further from the scientific. From East to West one finds a certain paranormal or hazy, mystic attribution to spirituality, thus ensuring that it is perceived as having limited researchability. Our hesitancy to research spirituality and its mystical qualities and elements is actually the precise reason it should be studied like any other scientific phenomena. Timothy Arthur Lines (1992) suggests that just as the scientist is interested in "discerning basic verifiable information, so too, the mythologist, [or sociologist studying spirituality] is interested in the nature of information" (234). He goes on to further state:

> But in the case of the [researcher] the nature of the information is divergent. Where generally the evangelist and historian [or scientist] choose to begin their investigation with facts they ascribe, at least initially to hold some historical reality, the mythologist is not nearly as concerned with factual historicity. The [researcher investigates] and analyzes the *interpretive* story itself searching for the meaning that it communicates in a manner that is too deep for bare facts or objective data to convey. (Lines, 1992, 234)

There are two main issues of validity here. Research on spirituality and its mythical realm is divergent. Research findings cannot only aim to converge and direct limited explanations of spiritual phenomena. Second, as the researcher analyzes interpretations, while the spiritualist researcher looks at others' interpretations of their spiritual life as a valid form of knowledge that goes deeper than simple objective data. Research that attempts interpretations of students' spiritual lives should be done with caution because reinterpreted information dilutes the quality, context, and validity of the respective participant's perspective. Interpretational tendencies are looked upon as a positive quality. A scientist able to interpret a spatial occurrence interprets from his own knowledge, perhaps using physical science jargon and vocabulary. The same phenomenon may be described aesthetically from an artist's standpoint, but the artist may focus on shapes, textures, feelings, colors, and the emotions surrounding the occurrence, and look for ways of placing the scene on canvas. Therefore observations of a phenomenon, scientific or spiritual, must leave room for flexibility. For example, Colin Biott (1996) discusses the importance of researchers' beginning their explorations from a photographic image:

> Practitioner insights [or interpretations of a photograph] resulting from research into day to day experience are likened to 'the picture we were not aware of when we pointed the lens.' (Biott, 1996, 1).

Biott (1996) further strengthens this position by drawing on Barthes' notion of a "Punctum Point":

> [In a] photograph the 'point that disturbs' and becomes a focus for the whole picture is the Punctum point.

> The disturbance should actually facilitate an important contribution to our understanding of practitioner researchers' sense of self-identity. (Biott, 1996, 1).

The ultimate goal of a disturbance stemming from unique perceptions actually facilitates synergy and collaboration. For example, a picture of a tall tree with its limbs standing upright toward a sunset sky is perceived differently depending on who takes in the image. One may focus on the tree itself, seeing its upright limbs as a symbol of striving toward greater heights, perhaps signifying ambition. Another may focus on the sky at sunset as representative of the dawning of life. Still another may look at the display of colors as an explosion of human moods (anger, love, frustration, happiness, sadness, sympathy, etc.). If all the interpreters shared their perspectives, the divergence of their perceptions would actually facilitate collaboration toward understanding the whole picture. Thus, while everyone has his or her own spiritually oriented take on the picture, sharing of these impressions leads to a spiritually holistic understanding of the image.

When a scientist presumes to observe and research some phenomenon that exists, there is a rational belief (in his mind) about that phenomenon before he/she even begins. Even if there is a question of its existence, the phenomenon *does* exist in a limited but realistic way within the scientist's mind. Therefore, the thought of something that is material or immaterial, observed or unobserved, even if it is not a proven fact, exists by simply being thought of.

Spirituality as a thought process has profound effects in terms of universal research and practice because spirited research will aim at sundering restrictive educational norms. It will importantly question the culturally authoritative status quo of foundations in Western society. Speaking to this point, Butler (2000) asserts:

> The task of postfoundationalism is to interrogate what the theoretical move that establishes foundations authorizes, and what precisely it excludes or forecloses. (Butler, 2000, 5, cited by St. Pierre and Pillow).

In questioning authority, a spiritual application to research provides an opportunity for courageous analysis by investigators who go beyond what is normal to what has been authoritatively and structurally excluded. Thus, the spiritualist researcher would not aim at trying:

> [T]o convince others of her/his position . . . and does not arrange, select and interpret facts in the manner of the [scientist] instead, s/he focuses on a *sacred story* [or spiritual story] which is handed down because it contains a profound message for its hearers. (Lines, 1992, 234)

Similarly Parker J. Palmer (1994) passionately speaks of recovering "sacredness" in education. At one time, education and sacredness were seemingly opposed to each other. The current to look at education and research education in terms of its sacred dimension is now gaining momentum. Sacredness is linked to wholeness, and increasingly in today's society there is a quest to achieve a holistic approach for schooling, which should be reflected in research practice. To research the sacred means to attempt to understand wholeness. Application of sacred ideals and spiritual values to research sees the research process as a holistic, engaging exercise, and not only a rationalistic one. This pushes individuals to look deeper than the surface.

The sacred dimension provides depth in relation to meaningful practices:

> If you go deep, to the depths you go when you seek that which is sacred, you find the hidden wholeness. (Palmer, 1994, 28)

Linking the sacred to education and research means a shift from application of a hidden curriculum to the stimulation of the wholeness of students:

> A good teacher invites students to form community that weaves and re-weaves [their] lives alone and together. (Miller 1994, 243)

The teacher or researcher seeking to apply sacredness to their work must be a trailblazer because of possible negativity from colleagues and peers. Their stance will ensure the virtue of courage; so too, spiritual research takes courage. Courage to prove or attempt to standardize what it is seemingly not possible to standardize. Courage is important as it may foster elements of inspiration in cases of individuals' attempts at spiritual research:

> True courage is knowing as much as possible about the cost and then having the willingness to pay it. For example, like a gentle breeze that blows and infuses the body with coolness and calmness, so too a feeling of courage (by researcher and participant) flows through them with sensitivity and opens them to the kind of reception that courage instills upon students' spirits. (Lines, 1992, 331)

When researchers view their work on spirituality as a courageous endeavor, practices stemming from researched knowledge will also have the space to infuse education. Educators may come to a deeper understanding of what it means to teach and provide spaces that enable students to be courageous and challenge discriminatory norms, rather than conform to normative dominant values.

Research in the interest of spirituality will give credence to the transference of spiritually based ideology in schools. Currently, the intellectual community and general public cannot speak of health, social, or class issues without making reference to research. For example, in conversation one may say to a colleague: "walking a mile a day is good for the heart. Do you know that a recent research study has found that 1 in 4 over forty who walk a mile a day are less likely to have a heart attack?" Even if this notion is a commonsense one, the informal or formal reference to a research finding provides support for one's point. When done in daily conversations and interactions, this gives informal credence to points made.

Similarly, researching spirituality will enable those wanting to introduce the concept into educational practice to have a *re*-searched frame of reference as proof of success or failure. Why does anything have to gain credence through research? Although there is an abundance of biases and issues involved in research, it is the dominant force by which ideologies and societal and institutional governances are legitimated, and therefore cannot be ignored. Hypothesizing on the spiritual in education or attempting to apply the spiritual to research could be seen as going against scientific norms, but this has to be challenged. For Leonie E. Jennings and Anne P. Graham (1996) this means a move from latent research practice to action research:

> Attention [should be] drawn to the possibility of opening up [a] subject's [spiritual] positions which allows the modern and postmodern to 'speak,' so that heterogeneity and the recognition of difference might be better accommodated in the action research process. (Jennings and Graham, 1996, 86).

Legitimating Researchable Topics

Though medical institutions conduct research on parts of the body and funding is readily available, it is perhaps considered irrelevant for a researcher to ask for money to study the spirit(uality) or emotional state of humankind. Those who determine policies and allocate research monies may not deem spirituality as an important research topic. What is widely ignored is that the diseases being researched and those affecting much of humankind are directly attributable to the emotional health of the individual and his/her collective spiritual and political state. For example, a recent study in the *Journal of Family Practice* has found that seventy-seven percent of hospitalized patients believe that doctors should inquire about the role spirituality plays in their patients' lives (Jones, 2001).

This belief is relevant because many patients feel that doctors would better understand their physical ailment if they recognized the underlying spiritual reason for it. To look at the physical manifestation alone or the disease, only separates the patients' bodies from their spirits. Dr. Pat Fosareli at Johns Hopkins Medical School notes "We cannot ignore the research and the patient's desire for healing to include both body and soul." (cited by Jones, 2001) Here, one sees a clear culmination and compliment of spirituality in research and physical science. The physical is inextricably linked to the spiritual. If a person's spiritual state becomes broken, bruised, fractured, injured, or sick, such as when one is under stress (the unseen non-physical dimension) from work, the stress of the broken spirit or lowered confidence that originates in the mind goes on overtime to affect the senses of the body and finally the spirit and soul. Yet, attention is paid much less to this emotional and spiritual dimension of sickness because it is difficult to observe. Thus, the predisposition of research to pay attention to what has physical manifestations and can be seen is not always valid. One must also realize that the unseen dimension of a phenomenon is perhaps even more reason for it to gain researchable status. The Dalai Lama (1999) tells of how negative emotions (negative emotions in this sense means negative or spiritually injurious feelings) are detrimental to body and spirit:

> Negative emotions can be very harmful for one's self, one's body and one's mental well-being. Negative emotions can destroy or spoil all of our opportunities for the future. On the other hand, an open heart, a warm heart will bring more smiles, more friends more reliable friends and in that way more good fortune in life. (Dalai Lama, 1999, 89)

This leads to research flavored with emotions rather than dismissing those same emotions as irrational.

> In the postmodern World, with its plethora of choices, pluralism can become a new Meta value. Recognizing the worth and dignity of our fellow humans implies that we do not seed to colonize their chosen spiritual paths and shape them into conformity with our own. (Voice of the Unitarian Universalist Advance, 1998, 2)

Is the world supposed to be a better place in terms of postmodern research values if respect is given to all spiritual values? The answer may well be placed not in what is believed about postmodern philosophy but *how* the acceptance of the plethora of values is practiced. If all spiritual values are supposedly legitimate, but there are prevalent structural practices that persist in otherizing certain minority spiritual ideologies, values, and their sacredness, then postmodernism in terms of research certainly carries expected gaps. As Dei (2001) has pointed out, "anyone can theorize" and any postmodernist can sing the glories of legitimating everything, but practices, rules, laws and values that govern a society, its cultural structures, and its peoples are what leads to acceptance of spiritual ideas nationally, globally, and universally. Thus, postmodernist approaches to research conjure up a deeply felt questions in terms of investigating the spiritual: Which criteria should one take, or for that matter does one even have to choose a spiritual criterion for research?

> The postmodern horizon of spiritual recovery proceeds on a different basis: [It is] a dispersion of spiritual energy that is associated with the sacredness of the whole universe and a related feminization of political life that finds power in relations, rather than in capabilities for dominance and destruction, in earthborne more than skyborne energy. Unity without centralization of hierarchy provides the only firm constraint upon the design of desirable world order arrangements for the future. (Griffin, 1988, 83)

The postmodern stance is by no means perfectly befitting for research and comes with its own negativities and biases. It is, however, valid in the following particular instances: If one follows the logic set forth by Griffin (1988), postmodernism acknowledges spiritual energy as dispersal and sees all humans as being affected collectively and universally by spiritual energy worldwide. A "feminization" of political life sees spirituality as holistic, encompassing valid spiritual knowledge of the sexes, their bodies, and spirits. This in turn will influence power structures and universal politics. These validities of postmodernism and spiritual research dimensions can, however, only be taken at face value because the changes in society caused by postmodernism mean that new repressive structures will arise. Research that is identified from a spiritual stance has to move from notions of mere tolerance toward acceptance. The postmodern tendency to tolerate does not instigate. This implies the important action toward synergy and not spurious acceptances of values.

A researcher holding her own spiritual value system may not agree with the variant spiritual values held by those practicing paganism or Buddhism to the point of fully understanding their practices, but still she wants to research the practices. In this case the researcher must

> [a]t least sincerely encourage them [participants] in their own journey, and release any defensive anxiety about their lapsing into error. This is the spirit behind trying to move

from tolerance to acceptance as [a] motto for dealing with diversity. Acceptance refers to a full-hearted empathy for the methods and discoveries that guide another's spiritual life. It is not just becoming more tolerant; it is a qualitative change of attitude with respect to differences. With it we become truly synergistic. Learning to replace tolerance with acceptance can itself be a profound spiritual transition. (Voice of the Unitarian Universalist Advance, 1998, 2).

In terms of postmodern investigation, this passage first claims that tolerance only excuses marginality. Being empathetic and not dismissive of sacred reasonings for spiritual mores is important. Researchers need to work with notions of empathetic acceptance of spiritual differences. Acceptance of differences also gives an inner spiritual strength to participants and researchers because it proclaims a synergy in relationships and is thus immanent. The value of the research being done is not simply toleration of a group in order to gain groundbreaking information, but accepting what they spiritually are as they spiritually are this is uplifting for the research provider and her participants. While such empathies may also beg the question of ambiguity (*where* are the distinctions of spirituality made), looking at ambiguity of information positively rather than negatively leaves room for spiritual development of both the participant and researcher. The process of embracing ambiguity means that the research agenda acknowledges gray-area gaps and data information that may not fit politically with the initial hypothesis. However, it is precisely the ambiguous gaps that lead to new, variant, and valuable paths to spirited research initiatives.

In terms of schooling, research on spirituality will supply a repertoire of knowledge on which teachers, administrators, and educators can draw in altering practices of discrimination in educational systems. Many books have been written on the religious beliefs of separate theology based schools and the role faith plays in these schools, but little research has been done on delving deeper into the spiritual realm of mainstream schooling. It is likely that there exists limited research or ethnographic studies in the area because this is a topic that is only now gaining momentum. Studies that do exist are valuable sources. For example, a study by John P. Miller and Aya Nozawa ("Meditating Teachers: A Qualitative Study") found that forms of meditation can give a sense of peacefulness to preservice teachers. This form of spiritual exercise is valuable because

[w]hen introduced in an academic setting it can have positive long-term effects on both the personal and professional lives of educators. Most participants felt that meditation helped them become calmer and more grounded in their life and work. (Miller, 2002, 190)

Qualitative research studies like the one outlined above are strong sources for introducing values of the spiritual, emotional, and interpersonal realm into education; moreover, future works should also include the spirited aspects of students' emotional and academic life. Positive effects elicited from the *mindfulness* gained by educators when spiritual practices such as meditation are used to relieve the stress of daily activity are indeed valuable as the positive effects are released to the students themselves because the educators feel good about the work they are doing, but this is secondhand spiritual enforcement in terms of the students' spiritual development. The student may feel good because the teacher feels good. However, there is no guarantee that students will feel spiritual positivity when the teacher feels it. In this particular study, spirituality was seen as a way for educators to become *de-*stressed and experience a sense of physical and mental well-being. Future research should also center on student spirituality.

Interview and case-based studies that spiritually center students and their spiritual identities (e. g. the one conducted by Dei, 1999, "Spirituality in African Education: Issues and Contestations from a Ghanaian Case Study") provide evidence of the positive effects that spiritually formulated practices have in schools and on students themselves. The work concluded that values of spiritual conceptions and the meanings of self are nurtured through the fabric of the curriculum, *not merely added* onto curriculum. The study cited actual feedback from students on the positive sense of self they gained from teachers using a holistic approach. The study mainly focused on students, and future studies should center on both teachers and students. However, a strength of the study is its understanding that the spiritual dimension was not limited to spiritual practices of teachers alone, but a nurturance of the spiritual dimension was provided from the collective spirit of the entire school body.

Both Dei's (1999) and Miller and Nozawa's (1997) studies are progressive sources with valuable information relating to spirituality-based research in education. One focuses on teachers and the other on students. Future research needs to also recognize the spiritual synergy felt by students and teachers as one group. Initiatives to incorporate spirituality at all levels of education is becoming increasingly common. In some postsecondary cases it is the students who have expressed and identified such a need. A recent study found that medical schools are increasingly responding to the student demand for spirituality to be a part of the medical curriculum.

> In 1992 only a [few schools] taught spirituality. Now 50 of the 125 medical schools in the United States have [a] dedicated curricula. Students want to [be taught to] communicate with people so they can care for them. They want to do it with soul. (Strohl, 2001, 68)

Similarly, students in elementary and secondary schools have the spiritual will to express themselves and their spiritual needs to others. While they may not be in an independent position to make such decisions, policies of educational institutions need to reflect spiritual needs of students from elementary to postsecondary levels. The spiritual dimension should be nurtured soulfully and consistently at all levels of education. Thus, ethnographic studies that examine spiritual values using feedback from both teacher and student will assist in furthering knowledge of spiritual issues in education because there is a need being expressed for this from both students and educators. In turn, research practices have to consider both student and teacher perspectives on spirituality. Initiatives around researching spirituality in schools do exist. However, the majority use religion-based schools and usually categorize spirituality in relation to separate religions. It should be mentioned that religion-based spirituality and research are legitimate in their own right, but the main concern here is to have spirituality in its myriad forms, be they emotional, personal, ardent, passionate, fervent, and religious researched in mainstream schools. Such research should be solely concerned with providing respect and space to students so that they can develop an individual, collective, and flexible understanding of spirituality.

Spirituality as an Institution

Legitimating spirituality as an institution could render it acceptable for research; in considering this one can look to the common institutions of a given society for example, the political, economical, educational, familial, and cultural, as these become legitimated through the process of institutionalization. To incorporate institutional values into a system is to sanction them as the norm. To institutionalize is to politicize. Hence, religion is seen as a momentous organized and politically driven institution in Western society, spirituality is not institutionally driven or politically sanctioned, but is rather mystified and treated as a virtuous form of the supernatural. Until ideas of spiritually placed education are institutionally and politically sanctioned, they may lack credence. Thus, the main difference between a scientific approach to research and a spiritual approach is that the former is politically recognized, institutionalized, and thus (considered to be) legitimate, while the latter is mystified. The institutionalized treatment of spirituality is seemingly unequal to that of science, although "[t]he two greatest forces in human history are science and religion [spirituality]" (Schachter-Shalomi and Smith, 1999, 220).

The spiritual dimension ensures obstacles at every step toward legitimate institutionalization, and this is reflected in educational institutions:

> The main obstacle we face toward spirituality in education is that there is nothing in the world right now that has the power to stop scientism. [This power bestowed

upon science and reflected in education] is most unfortunate because it is untrue, and it diminishes our understanding of ourselves. (Schachter-Shalomi, 1999, 221)

The economic dimension was perhaps not as strongly legitimated or given astounding import until Marx placed it as the institutional infrastructure upon which all other superstructures (cultural, political, class, educational, religious) are placed upon in a given society. This is not to say that the ideas of Marx were new, but while they may have existed in the consciousness or superconsciousness of individuals and political societies of the time, it is Marx's synthesis and articulation of the ideas (in *Das Capital*) that brought about the notion that it is the economic infrastructure that drives societies.

Similarly, Emile Durkheim, Max Weber, and Mahatma Gandhi philosophized religion as an institutional basis of societal organization and attempted to establish religion as an institution. The call to institutionalize spirituality, whether different or parallel to religion, will be a timely one. To adopt spirituality as an educational standard by incorporating it into the fabric of education and curriculum will legitimate the spiritual, which may, in turn, mean legitimacy in terms of research agendas and institutionalization.

The Spiritual Taken for Granted in Research

The problem with the concept of research is that it begins with the letters "re." The prefix re means to go back, check, recheck, redo, alter, reify, remix, remit, allocate, displace, search out, find, look, examine, inspect, hunt, probe, take apart, separate, and scrutinize, all of which are counter to the principle of the spiritual, which is synthesis. If research searches out what is or is not existent, why is it the main form of legitimization and institutionalization of an intellectual questioning of a topic? Once a question occurs in a scholar's mind, the only legitimate way to answer it is to research it. We take for granted that we understand exactly what *re*-searching a question means.

In terms of doing research as a spiritual vocation or spiritual action, the researchers must first define their own place from a spiritual viewpoint (already pointed out at the beginning of this paper). With definition comes a deep understanding of the interrogator's self. If she first knows herself, then she is in a better position to understand her informants. As Dei (2001) points out however, one does not "always know the self totally." Experiences and cultural values cloud attempts at self-knowledge, and while this is a valuable criticism, self-knowledge even in its limited form is a beginning for understanding of the ethical, spiritual, and moral values of research and educational practice. Self-knowledge aids in beginning to understand others' views, and research that centers spiritual values of self and others may arrive at more valid and reliable results than research that does not.

Spiritual Reification, Laws of Science, Laws of Karma

According to the laws of science every action has a reaction. As an example, consider the commonsense notion that as temperature warms, water boils and as temperature cools, water freezes. If there is an action, there must be a reaction. This is an equal and synergistic relationship.

> The reaction will be of equal force and of similar nature. Every thought, desire, imagination, sentiment causes reaction. Virtue brings its own reward; vice brings its own punishment. This is the working Law of reaction. (Sivananda, 1974, 303)

Three Elements of Karma and Researching the Spiritual

Karma is a Sanskrit term signifying action or deed. In turn, deeds are classified as good or evil and are determined by man's nature, which is threefold: *Ichha* (desire or feeling); *Jnana* (knowing); *Kriya* (willing). These ambient factors are in accordance with an elemental synthesis that constitutes Karma. Such a synthesis of mind, body, and spirit causes a fusion by working in the following way: Persons know objects (chair, tree, star, moon), this is Jnana. They feel joy, sorrow, and sentiments about objects, this is Ichha. They will to perform particular actions, this is Kriya. Together, these create a relationship of synergy and depending on decisions made Karma is conceived. Spiritual sentiments are formed by actions with objects and persons and this renders experience. Similarly, a researcher in the decisional process to undertake a particular work uses their mind, body, and soul in making their judgment. The researcher has a desire to do a particular work because of her experiential knowings and karmic actions accorded in a cultural group or topic. She physically sets out to do her work and is willing to undertake it because a passion prevails due to a specified spiritual knowledge base (about the topic). She may also decide not to pursue a certain line of research due to a lack of desire or her knowings of the topic are limited, and thus, willingness is restrained. Her decisional actions are *spiritually* and *rationally* guided by the three elements of karma, as Laws of science guide the universe.

> There is nothing chaotic or capricious in this world. Things do not just happen in this universe by accident or chance in a disorderly manner. They happen in regular succession [reacting]. There is a certain definite connection between what is being done now by you and what will happen in the future. Sow always the seeds which will bring pleasant fruits and which will make you happy herein and hereafter. (Sivananda, 1974, 305)

Thus, the researcher in quest of accumulating data may take her role as a spiritually centered one and view that her actions as setting the groundwork for reactions of tomorrow. In taking action, researchers attempt to approach their work in an ethical, moral manner. Foresight and events are historically specific so that a particular work may seem positive now, but in the future may become negative. This recognition of consequences on the researcher's part will decide the reactions to the work. Thus, a moral grounding has to be considered, which ties in with a spiritual grounding.

If research from a spiritual standpoint considers active and reactive notions of the subject's and researcher's actions, with relevant consequences or reward, then attention could well be paid to effectiveness and truthfulness of fieldwork. For example, if a researcher has the mind-set that her ethnographic work will indeed reflect back on her, this may alter a potential for deceit. However, she must believe that the actions of the work will result in a reaction. With such an understanding, the researcher would approach her work believing that her *Karmic actions* during the work will have meaning when the work is done or data has been collected, written up, published, disseminated, and publicly recognized. Indeed the content and moral approach to the work will have reactions of similar value in the future.

Conclusion

Colin Biott (1996, 1) has contributed to the understanding "of practitioner researchers' sense of self identity." Self-identity of practitioners is derived from a perception that they (the researchers) belong to two worlds. This causes a constant tension or strain that can be accepted by researchers in their quest for an identity. There exists "tension between professional and personal identities. This should be used to draw out latent power and meaning in the Other." Such a tension afflicts the spirit of researchers, but if the tension is directed so that reactions are considered, then less stress is caused. In terms of safeguarding researchers' feelings and actions, data summation, and the writing up of data where necessary can include both the subjective and objective realities. Again, using the law of action/reaction, a researcher, when writing with freedom of mind may hope to elicit a future reaction, one that centralizes the notion of freedom as it connects to the writer's particular topic of focus. The notion of freedom, but freedom without a price, is what will facilitate a spiritually based ideology of research. Without freedom, the spirit of a researcher (or the researched) is not able to amply express itself. Constraint is a result of loss of freedom in a researcher's work. It leads not only to spirit injury of the investigator, but frustration from being constrained (by an academy, or internal or external factors) can eclipse important realities of a work in negative ways, resulting in, for example, falsification of data or methodological inconsistencies. It is important to point out that in terms of this work, freedom does not mean the ability of researchers to do anything at their whim; all research must be bound by moral and ethical values.

An awareness of ethics coupled with respect for others, along with the freedom to pursue a work on spirituality based upon spiritual values is what research advancement in a spiritualistic sense means. Such advancement considers the bodies, minds, and spirits of all involved.

REFERENCES

Barthes, R. 1993. *Camera Lucida*. London: Vintage.

Biott, C. 1996. "Latency in Action Research: changing perspectives on occupational and research identities." *Educational Action Research* 4(2): 1–36.

Dalai Lama. 1994. "Education and the Human Heart." In S. Glazer (Ed.) *The Heart of Learning: Spirituality in Education*. New York: Jeremy P. Tarcker.

Dei, G. 1999. "Spirituality in African Education: Contestations from a Ghanaian Case Study." University of Toronto/ Ontario Institute for Studies in Education. Unpublished Paper.

Dei, G. 2001. Lecture Notes. Advanced Issues in Anti Racist Research, University of Toronto/Ontario Institute for Studies in Education.

Hulmes, E. 1979. *Commitment and Neutrality in Religious Education*. London: Geoffrey Chapman (Cassell Ltd.).

Glazer, S. (Ed.). 1999. *The Heart of Learning: Spirituality in Education*. New York: Jeremy P. Tarcher.

Griffin, D. R. (Ed.). 1988. *Spirituality and Society*. Albany: State University of New York Press.

Jennings, L. E. and Graham, A. P., 1996. "Postmodern Perspectives and Action Research." *Educational Action Research*. 4(2): 86–99.

Jones, G. 2001. "Healing Spirit: Can Religion Play a Role in Treating Disease." April 2 C-Health Website.

Lines, Timothy Arthur. (1992). *Functional Images of the Religious Educator*. Birmingham: Religious Education Press.

Miller, J. P. and Ayo Nozawa. 2002. "Meditating Teachers: A Qualitative Study." *Journal of In-Service Education*. 28(1): 179–192.

Miller, M. E., and Cook-Greuter, S. R., 2000.*Creativity, Spirituality and Transcendence*. Stamford: Ablex Publishing Corporation.

Miller, R. 1999. "Holistic Education for an Emerging Culture." In S. Glazer (Ed.) *The Heart of Learning: Spirituality in Education*. New York: Jeremy P. Tarcher.

Palmer, P. J. 1999. "The Grace of Great Things: Reclaiming the Sacred in Knowing, Teaching and Learning. In S. Glazer (Ed.) *The Heart of Learning: Spirituality in Education*, New York: Jeremy P. Tarcher.

"Postmodernism and the Unitarian Universalist Diversity." (1998). Voice of the Unitarian Universalist Advance, "Postmodernism and the Unitarian Universalist Diversity." Newsletter January: 1–4.

Schachter, Shalom, Z. and H. Smith. 1999. "Spirituality in Education: A Dialogue." In S. Glazer (Ed.) *The Heart of Learning: Spirituality in Education*. New York: Jeremy P. Tarcher.

St. Pierre, E., and Pillow, W. S. (2000). *Working the Ruins*. New York: Routledge.

Strohl, I. (2001 July), "How Faith Heals." *Reader's Digest*. July. 61–65.

Tulasiewicz, W., and T., C. Y. (Eds.) 1993. *Religious and Educational Practice*. London: Cassell.

Chapter Eight

ZEENAT JANMOHAMED

Rethinking Anti-bias Approaches in Early Childhood Education

A SHIFT TOWARD ANTI-RACISM EDUCATION

Introduction

Although attention is paid to anti-bias education or curriculum ideas in early childhood settings (Derman-Sparks; 1989, Kilbride 1997; Tabors, 1998, with a particular emphasis on cultural awareness rather than empowerment Yeates, 2001), there is little discussion of the existence of racism, homophobia, or class issues being addressed in curriculum content and textbook materials for early childhood education students. The recognition of dominant power has received little attention to date, silencing the reality of racial minorities and the experiences of economically disadvantaged students (Dei, 1996). Students receive training in a limited form of anti-bias education, which prepares them for establishing a program rich in cultural tourism. Unless early childhood educators are taught to recognize the dominant relationships inherent in racism, homophobia, and class issues, they will be stuck in the notion that early childhood work is charitable, rather than becoming agents of social change. The latter is most significant because a fundamental premise of early childhood education is that it should lead to cultural/racial tolerance and harmony, an opportunity for inoculation against racism.

Although it is imperative that early childhood educators are trained to work with a variety of children and families recognizing the growing racial, economic, ethnocultural, and linguistic diversity in our community, there is little evidence in the existing literature on how to better prepare early childhood educators to critically evaluate their ability to work within an anti-racist framework that goes beyond decorating classrooms for special occasions. Instead, early childhood education students are trained to be culturally aware and free of bias in their work with children. They are encouraged to utilize materials that represent the diverse population they work with. They are encouraged to decorate classrooms with pictures of families from a variety of racial backgrounds. They are also encouraged to celebrate festivals such as Diwali and Hanukkah in an effort to be representative of the changing community in which they work. There is a growing body of evidence recognizing the diversity in developmental patterns of young children, and former assumptions about universal development are rightly being questioned and challenged (Bernhard and Gonzalez-Mena, 2000). Minimizing the value of a child's history with a "tourist approach" is obviously not effective.

In this chapter I will provide a critique of two key resources utilized in the Early Childhood Education (ECE) Program at George Brown College, commenting specifically on how anti-racist education principles are addressed by the authors. *Developmentally Appropriate Practices* (Gestwicki, 1999), used primarily in the Foundations of ECE and curriculum-related courses, explores the principles of developmentally appropriate practices in ECE and program curriculum. The book also describes teacher roles in planning appropriate curriculum. *Partnerships: Families and Communities in Canadian Early Childhood Education* (Wilson, 2001) is used for courses related to working with families. It explores the changing face of Canadian families and addresses issues related to families led by single parents, families living in poverty, racially diverse families, families experiencing divorce and families with lesbian and gay parents. It pays close attention to creating early childhood environments that are inviting to parents and children and respectful of the racial and cultural diversity of Canadian families.

I will then focus on the increasing number of challenges faced by instructors of students in community college settings, specifically related to working with a complex population of students within the context of cultural, linguistic, and racial differences. In the latter part of my paper, I will comment on some of the suggestions made by other educators with respect to integrating anti-racism principles and education strategies in early childhood education programs. The primary focus of my paper is the training needs of early childhood educators, who are being trained to work in regulated early childhood settings.

In an effort to provide an inclusive approach to early childhood education, college faculty at George Brown College has made a concerted effort to create learning environments that address the necessity to teach within an anti-bias framework, although the definition and delivery of such an approach is inconsistent. In some courses, faculty members prefer to integrate teachings on anti-bias education into the course work. Other faculty members separate anti-bias education as a specific discussion. However, there is no clear formula on how or what the direction of the teaching should be or to what extent the students are being challenged in their understanding of anti-bias education. I use the term *anti-bias education* to describe the general emphasis ongoing beyond multiculturalism because it acknowledges that race, class, sexual orientation, and ability present possibilities for prejudice. I also use it to explicate the emphasis on recognizing diversity in early childhood education rather than challenging the value systems that discriminate based on race, sexuality, class, and ability. This shift toward anti-racist education is an area of discomfort and challenge in the early childhood community.

In early childhood settings, despite the diversity in racial and cultural background, I make the assumption that the majority of individuals who work with children see themselves as being free of bias, based on their commitment to improve the lives of children and families. Although there are different philosophical approaches integrated into early childhood environments, many of these approaches share a commitment to providing a bias-free program to children and families. Anti-bias programming can range in practice from including culturally diverse books for children, to making an effort to recruit more "minority" parents on management boards, or displaying pictures of children that represent diverse cultural communities and backgrounds. A bias-free approach can be minimized to include a cultural artifact in the entrance area of the program or a welcome sign in a language other than English. In my experience, early educators without a thorough understanding of the principles or the practices that define an inclusive program utilize terms such as inclusive approaches, multicultural education, anti-bias education, or diversity training. Although early childhood educators receive some basic training in how to implement an anti-bias program, they continue to struggle with simple ideas such as offering a variety of books to children exploring different family structures. A key part of my responsibility as a faculty advisor is to supervise student practicum in childcare programs. During my observations of students, I take the opportunity to peruse the book area. I am pleasantly surprised by the diversity of authors and illustrators that tell stories of children from different racial backgrounds, but I cannot recall the last time I saw the children's book "Heather Has Two Mommies" (Newman, 1989) on the book shelf in a child care program. Although early childhood professionals claim to have a commitment to anti-bias approaches, it is apparent to the observant eye that the commitment does not necessarily go deeper to include an ability to articulate the principles and practices of antiracist education strategies. I deliberately make reference to anti-racist instead of anti-bias to exemplify the ongoing limited discussion as it relates to the power imbalance in early childhood programs. To provide a context for the paper, the following is an overview of early childhood services and training.

Early Childhood Care and Education Services

The care and education of young children has shifted significantly in the last fifty years. In 1933 there were about twenty day nurseries serving approximately 2,500 children. Today there are almost 1.5 million children from infants to school-aged children, being cared for and educated by people other than family members and outside the regular school system (Gestwicki and Bertrand, 1999). Today almost 70% of women with young children work or study and have their children cared for by both licensed and unlicensed caregivers, extended family members, and child care programs. Licensed childcare programs are accessible to only 12% of children (Beach, Bertrand, and Cleveland, 1998).

There are no national standards of regulation or training for early childhood educators. While there are provincial and territorial variations, regulations generally determine child-to-staff ratios, training for educators, program curriculum, health and safety standards, staff qualifications, funding, nutrition, governance, and the protection of children.

The Role of the Early Childhood Educator

The role of an early educator is infused with the responsibility of providing a holistic emotionally supportive environment to young children. Often, early childhood educators take on a parenting role, giving children a foundation in morals and values through discussions with children or through modelling appropriate behavior. Early childhood educators have the capacity to play an influential role in the development of young children, yet public policy makers and governments undermine the significance of the early educator's position in young children's lives. In the process of establishing relationships with children, early educators can boost or crush a child's self-esteem depending on their ability to encourage, interact with, and support a child's development. The role of an educator involves complex responsibilities. They need to ensure that children are safe and have their primary needs cared for. They are responsible for providing an environment that is stimulating and emotionally nurturing.

Educators are expected to build positive relationships with children, integrating a respectful approach based on the child's ability without shaming or demeaning children. Educators should promote learning by creating developmentally appropriate opportunities within a cultural context. Although early childhood education work is challenging, the desire to make a difference in the lives of children and families is cited as a primary motivator for early educators (Beach, Bertrand, and Cleveland, 1998). The relationships among caregiver, child, and parent is encouraged and rewarded. The success of developing their relationship is dependent on the educator's ability to effectively integrate the family and cultural background in the program curriculum, while maintaining an integrated approach to anti-discriminatory education practices.

Early Childhood Education Training: George Brown College

In a city like Toronto, where the majority of the population is comprised of new immigrants and refugees, developing a solid understanding of the principles of anti-racism education is particularly relevant, but these issues often get lost in diversity training or anti-bias education rhetoric. Students are challenged to make the transition from what has historically been the dominance and normalcy of the white, middle-class, Christian heterosexual family to the diversity that exists in the college classroom and early childhood settings. All of a sudden they are working alongside peers in Hijab, single mothers, students who speak English as a second language, and students living in poverty. They are working with faculty who are white, black, gay, and straight. Although the learning environment is focused on working with children and families, students are also forced to negotiate a new understanding of difference. This is particularly true of students who have attended homogenous high schools and have had limited exposure to social relationships outside their own family and community.

Students in the early childhood education program are required to undertake core mandatory courses that address foundations in child development and program curriculum in an integrated approach that includes working with a diversity of children and families. In order to successfully complete course requirements and to meet course outcomes outlined by the Ontario government's Colleges Standards Accreditation Committee, students in the early childhood education program must demonstrate their ability to work in a diverse child care community (Ministry of Education, 1996). Combined with academic course work, students are required to spend fifty percent of their time in field placement working with a variety of age groups in different early childhood settings.

At George Brown College, the Early Childhood Education Program provides a two-year Early Childhood Education Diploma that prepares graduates to work with children between the ages of six weeks and twelve years in a variety of early childhood services and family support programs. The program is guided by four principles of early childhood education including (George Brown College, 1999):

- knowledge of child development
- an inclusive, anti-bias approach
- family-centred practice
- a play-based curriculum

The students are evaluated on their ability to integrate anti-bias principles in field practice and are expected to meet specific course outcomes related to the integration of diversity. For example, in an effort to expand their understanding of a variety of family structures, students in the "Working with Families" course, are expected to complete a research paper on marginalized families such as adoptive families, aboriginal families, lesbian and gay families, and so forth. Course content takes a variety of approaches to interpret anti-racist principles, including both an integrated approach and a topic-specific approach depending on the course design and faculty preference on how to discuss the issues.

The Learning Process in Young Children

It is often assumed that children do not begin to learn until the formal school years. Parents are fascinated by their babies' ability to say "mama" or "ball," and easily communicate with their babbling young toddlers. However, they are often resistant to accept the tremendous amount of learning that takes place in the first three years of life. Although in these early years children learn thousands of words, understand the difference between trusted adults and strangers, learn how to self-regulate and demonstrate long attention spans if interested in their surroundings and interactions, there is general resistance by the public to acknowledge the importance of the early childhood years. The early years are critical in the development of intelligence, personality, and social behavior, and the effects of early neglect can be cumulative. There are critical points in children's development where it is important to ensure that they have experiences that support their growth and development. New research in brain development shows that much of the brain is already formed at birth, and during the first two years of life most of the growth of brain cells occurs. In the pre-school years, most of the structuring of neural connections are made and have the most significant impact on the child's learning ability. Clearly research supports the assertion that it is also important to ensure that the caregivers are supportive of healthy emotional and physical development (Evans, 2000).

There are common characteristics in how children develop, although children vary when they reach developmental milestones. There is also significant research that demonstrates the value of play in learning, although the definition of play varies depending on the perspective of the researcher, theorist, or participant (Gestwicki, 1999). The very idea of children learning through play is a foreign concept to many parents as they recall their own experiences of schooling as being formal with children sitting in rows of desks. Adapting to the nature of early childhood programs in the West, where children are encouraged to explore messy sensory experiences, engage in conversations whenever they please, and select their own play activities is a significant leap in expectations for many families. The provision of care is an interactive relationship between parent and caregiver, yet this fundamental principle is rarely explained to parents in the introductory orientation sessions organized for families considering group-based childcare. If in fact it is explained, there is very little room for the parents to voice their opinions and perhaps explain their own understanding of how children learn.

Piaget believed that learning in children takes place through constructivist processes that build knowledge and skills through a slow, continuous process of construction that keeps modifying the understanding of the world around them based on new information that each child brings to the situation. As children play, Piaget believed they encounter (assimilate) new things or ideas. However, Vygotsky emphasized and recognized the social significance of play and believed that the increasingly complex mental activities of the child were derived from social and cultural contexts. By engaging with members of their society, children learn to think and behave in ways that reflect their community's culture (Gestwicki, 1999).

A Review of *Developmentally Appropriate Practice*

In order to recognize the importance of how children relate to their community culture, it becomes critical that early childhood programs are culturally inclusive and respectful of the traditions practised by the children's families. According to Gestwicki (1999), as children shift from being emotionally attached to their primary caregivers to becoming more autonomous, "the process of identification plays a key role in their relationships and social development . . . children move to wanting to be like the important adult in their lives. Much of the identification process is on an individual and personal basis, though the larger culture certainly influences messages about valuing certain identifications." (166) Although the development of the individual is important, "the ideology of individualism also takes our attention away from group relations and statuses, directing it instead toward equal opportunity to achieve upward mobility" (Sleeter, 1994).

In an effort to explore group identification, Gestwicki explains "[P]reschool children identify themselves as members of families and their larger culture. Over time, children show signs of being influenced by societal norms and attitudes toward the group of which they are members" (Gestwicki, 1999, 166). She acknowledges that research indicates that children are aware of their racial/cultural identity by the age of four, and have absorbed attitudes toward their own and others' racial identity, yet does not identify the power differential that exists between the dominant white race and minoritized groups. Gestwicki further explains that "in a society with as much cultural diversity as ours, children learn about their cultural identity in an environment of diversity. Clearly this is a social/emotional issue that deserves attention" (Gestwicki, 1999, 166). Although Gestwicki states that cultural identity deserves attention, it remains problematic that it is left hanging without exploring how educators are equipped to handle diversity or cope with the diverse population of children they work with and how they may feel about having to work within this cultural context. There is no recognition of the challenge to be constantly aware of differences and to acknowledge the impact of these differences from a historical perspective.

Gestwicki further suggests that "it is important that teachers become personally aware of prejudices that have influenced their own development and understand the ways that messages of bias are passed on to children. Rather than teaching explicit multicultural curriculum to preschool children, teachers should examine all interactions, materials, and experiences to ensure that they convey attitudes of respect for all people" (Gestwicki, 1999, 172). Although Gestwicki is right to suggest that educators must shift away from teaching "explicit multiculturalism," the accompanying photos in the book show dolls that represent different races and a poster with "welcome" translated into many languages (Gestwicki, 1999, Figures 11–5 and 11–6, 172). When students are exposed to Gestwicki's example of how to avoid explicit multiculturalism, they walk away thinking that in fact it is perfectly acceptable to post welcome signs in a variety of languages. Gestwicki misses the opportunity to reflect on the avoidance of explicit multiculturalism through the anti-racist lens and the promotion of early childhood work as proactive opportunities to discuss and examine how the dominance of the male gender, white race, Western culture, and heterosexuality embed themselves in early childhood programming. Textbook content that address issues related to racial and cultural difference have to recognize the significance of nonverbal messages. These messages are passed on to educators, who may leave with an understanding that multilingual welcome signs are a sufficient effort toward integrating an anti-bias approach to early education. The visual representations in *Developmentally Appropriate Practices* are predominantly of white children and adults, although there is an effort to include representations of black children in the photo captions.

Gestwicki advocates a pluralist approach to early education explaining that, "the classroom should become a microcosm of the pluralistic society the children do and will continue to live in, always emphasizing the similarities among people more than the differences. The teacher should focus on the people in the child's world of today, not a historical world. The goal with pre-schoolers is not to teach history, but to inoculate them against racism" (Gestwicki, 1999, 172). However, the author does not consider the reality of the child's home environment, which may include discussion on past oppression and will likely include daily experiences of discrimination. Ignoring the history and the reality of racism in today's world serves no purpose except to ignore the truth.

Derman-Sparks (1998) suggests "the pre-school years lay the foundation for children's development of a strong, confident sense of self, empathy, positive attitudes towards people different from themselves, and social interaction skills. However, pervasive institutional and interpersonal racism and other forms of oppression in our society sabotage healthy development in these areas. Early childhood teachers and parents must help children learn how to resist" (Derman-Sparks, 1998, 194). Although Gestwicki draws from the work of Derman-Sparks, encouraging early educators to review *Anti-Bias Curriculum: Tools for Empowering Young Children*, the discussion on cultural and racial identity is generally limited to programming ideas and a basic overview of what caregivers should not do. For the most part, early childhood teachers are encouraged to "examine all pictures and books to ensure that they realistically portray the diversity of the individual classroom and community, provide toys, materials and activities which children can identify (themselves)" (Gestwick, 1999, 176). Gestwicki (1999), similar to other early childhood research in anti-bias approaches, misses the opportunity to discuss a more comprehensive approach to multicultural education.

Nieto (1995) argues that multicultural education without an explicit focus on racism nullifies the discriminatory practices in educational settings. In an assimilationist approach to multicultural education, teachers offer bits of cultural studies instead of presenting the privileged status of dominant groups. Although Gestwicki's work attempts to pay attention to the needs of families from a variety of diverse backgrounds, an in-depth analysis of history, value judgments, and program practices could be strengthened.

Partnerships: Families and Communities in Canadian Early Childhood Education

In the opening paragraph of *Partnerships: Families and Communities in Canadian Early Childhood Education,* Wilson writes "this book has been developed as a resource for faculty, students, and teachers in early childhood environments to encourage the development of positive and respectful relationships with all types of families. Our Canadian experience is unique, and this book attempts to celebrate the diverse nature of our population while outlining strategies for culturally sensitive and inclusive practice" (Wilson, 2001, 1). In an effort to simplify the task, I have chosen to focus my discussion on the chapter titled "Building Effective Partnerships." In this chapter, Wilson focuses on how to develop successful relationships with families, and the benefits and barriers to effective partnerships and strategies for supervisors and teachers. Most of the pictures in the chapter represent children and adults from a variety of cultural and racial backgrounds. Certainly the photos depict a diverse community, although there are few representations of children or adults with disabilities. The author seems to have selected photographs that show children from many races enjoying their time together, and for the most part the pictorial representations are of happy children.

Wilson describes partnerships with families as an integral part of the role of an early childhood educator, recognizing that the child care center operates within a community—never in isolation, influenced by a larger macrosystem of political, economic, and social issues. Wilson misses the opportunity to explain and explore how political, economic, and social barriers can prevent families from effectively participating in the partnership process, or if in a position of privilege, can enable families to build partnerships. Wilson clearly states the benefits of developing effective partnerships, citing from a variety of appropriate research sources, including references to American multicultural resources such as the work of Gonzalez-Mena who says, "Culture is invisible. It has been said that one moves in one's culture the way a fish moves through water" and that "we may be unaware of how much our culture influences our actions, our thoughts, our very perceptions" (Gonzalez-Mena as cited in Wilson, 2001, 74).

She argues, "early childhood programs must adapt and respond to the needs of families, as opposed to requiring that families adapt and respond to the programs" (Wilson, 2001, 74). Although Wilson accurately describes the demanding factors of work and family responsibilities, and limitations in language proficiency that may inhibit parental involvement, she could go a step further to discuss the dominant cultural values often connected to parent involvement in educational programs. Delpit (1988) argues that parent-school relations are socially constructed, idealizing the white, middle-class experience. The notion of *parent*, however, cannot be separated from considerations of race, class, gender, and sexuality. Schools (and early childhood environments) cannot disregard power relations, community cultures, and differing locations of parents/families when it comes to parental involvement. Tools, resources, and considerations of time and place are significant in evaluating how individuals are able to fulfil their roles and responsibilities as parents, guardians, caregivers, family members, and community workers.

Wilson intentionally utilizes the term *family* instead of *parent* to describe the primary caregiver(s) in a child's life. This demonstration of inclusion is positive and indicative of many different cultural definitions of who is the parent.

> "The question of who/what is defined as a parent or family in parental involvement has required some rethinking. Within certain cultural communities, the family is the larger community and any related adult is considered a parent with responsibility for education. The myriad of examples of community involvement in schooling has meant that a working definition of *parental involvement* is able to rupture white, middle-class assumptions and challenge the idea of simply inserting parents and communities into hegemonic structures of schooling. It is therefore important for critical educational research on home/family learning strategies and community-based educational outlets to articulate the different histories and contexts of conventional discourses that highlight a perceived lack of minority family/community involvement in schooling (Wilson, 2001, 82).

Wilson emphasizes the need to work with families in an equal partnership viewing families as a source of support and knowledge. She sees the partnership as constantly evolving, including a need to review and rethink approaches. In order to successfully build on partnerships, Derman-Sparks argues, "teaching from an anti-bias perspective means seeking to respect and support each child's and parent's background and reality while introducing a working concept of diversity that challenges social stereotypes and discrimination. However, respecting parents does not necessarily mean acquiescing to all their beliefs" (Derman-Sparks, 1998, 194). This is particularly true of creating inclusive environments for children with gay parents, be they male or female. The recent debate in Surrey, British Columbia, on the inappropriateness of including children's books related to lesbian and gay family life, such as *Heather Has Two Mommies* or *Asha's Mums* exemplifies this problem. According to a recent CBC radio program, gay and lesbian parents are raising an estimated 250,000 children (Wilson, 2001). To ignore the reality of lesbian and gay families feeds into both the subtle forms of homophobia and the more obvious frenzy against lesbians and gay families by fundamentalists who cite the Bible and the Koran in an effort to legitimize clear forms of discrimination.

In addressing challenges to partnerships, Wilson discusses work and family demands, differing educational philosophies, exclusionary practices, and racism as barriers to building effective relationships with parents. Wilson cites the work of Phillips and James in describing the reality of racism in educational institutions. Teachers are often reluctant to examine their own biases and attitudes toward diversity in families and how institutional racism is prevalent in education. Phillips argues, "we must explore the stereotypes we have learned that are racist and ethnocentric and develop strategies for changing what we believe about ourselves and others. Too many of us still unconsciously treat light-skinned children better than dark-skinned ones and the working mother better that the one on welfare" (Phillips as cited in Wilson, 2001, 36).

Exploring these challenges in a training environment includes difficult discussion on the reality of who holds the power in educational institutions and why they do. It includes questioning the cultural dominance of white middle-class values and the heterosexist assumptions that are made. In describing what she names as the "culture of power," Delpit (1988) explains that issues of power are enacted in the classroom through the power of the teacher over the students, and the power of publishers of textbooks and of the developers of the curriculum to determine the view of the world presented. Those with power are frequently least aware of or least willing to acknowledge its existence. Those with less power are often most aware of its existence.

Critical Education

As a lesbian middle-class woman of South Asian heritage, I am often shocked at the lack of understanding with respect to racial and cultural differences. My background frames the person I am, the food I eat, the way I move, and the way I work. I expect people to acknowledge my gender and my race and all the complexity it brings. I understand that personal location contributes to the production of meanings (Dei, 1999) and acknowledge that I occupy a simultaneous position of oppression and power by virtue of my race and gender, but also by way of my socioeconomic background and my teaching position in an institution of higher learning. It is with this framework that I approach my work with students from a diverse population representing every race, a cross-section of languages, and a variety of socioeconomic backgrounds. The early childhood community remains predominantly female, and the limited male students add to the complexity of the student population.

Teachers need to recognize the connection between multicultural education and critical pedagogy. Kincheloe and Steinberg (1998) address the social justice implications of multicultural education or critical multiculturalism. They refer to how racism, sexism, and class bias are economically, politically, educationally, and institutionally produced. Teachers can help students overcome these social barriers by engaging them in exploring different ways of resisting oppression. As an educator in a community college environment, I encourage students to challenge their understanding of the norm. In class discussions, when I raise various forms of discrimination or prejudice, students often respond by talking about the importance of helping children get along and learning to accept all people regardless of difference. When I challenge their common perceptions of people living on the street, new refugees or gays and lesbians, students are offended by my assumptions of their biases. It is not until I acknowledge my own biases that they are prepared to discuss their biases more openly. I share my childhood experience of being raised in a South Asian family that had no social connections with black people except in the form of family servants and nannies, and how that experience influenced my first relationships with black families that I worked with in early childhood environments. In order for students to articulate and understand systemic barriers, it is the responsibility of educators to create opportunities for transformation. Kincheloe and Steinberg (1998) argue that in order for students to experience such a transformative process, teachers must have already experienced it themselves.

Although it is challenging to apply American literature to the Canadian context, the principles of anti-discriminatory practices are universal. There are many resources available on how to develop inclusive programming, yet there is very little discussion about the distribution of power in the early childhood sector and the limited number of women of color in management positions. Many early childhood educators in Toronto are women of color who are immigrants to Canada. However, inclusivity and the sharing of power from a management perspective are limited. Many of the center supervisors and boards of directors of nonprofit child care are white, including the people in change of those programs that serve a predominantly immigrant or refugee community, although staff and parents utilizing early childhood programs are representative of the changing face of Toronto. Coming to terms with the significant discrepancy between the power of white women and the limited power of women of color is a challenge to the early childhood community.

Last year, I had an opportunity to attend a workshop on the delivery of early childhood training programs at the Association of Canadian Community Colleges conference in the Yukon. The facilitator discussed the challenges of working with participants in the remote areas of the Yukon and the Northwest Territories, including the "problems of abuse and alcoholism" in First Nations communities. In keeping with the silence that surrounds the role of white peo ple in oppressing First Nations communities, the facilitator continued to add to the negative perception that many of the problems that face First Nations communities are a result of their inability to make change, without taking any responsibility for contributing to the ongoing barriers facing the First Nations people including the isolation, poverty, and limited access to treaty rights. Typically I remained silent, adding to the problem rather than shifting toward solutions. In an effort to develop programs that were suitable for First Nations students, Yukon College in partnership with the federal government had designed a series of early childhood education workshops as a precursor to a college diploma. However, when asked how many of the workshop participants would complete a college diploma in early childhood education, the facilitator responded, "this would not happen with these students," feeding into the cycle of oppression experienced by First Nations people. Although the program was developed with inclusive principles in place, the institutional racism was apparent.

Schools can play a significant role in the formal education of students. They also play a role in helping young people understand how power differentials can support or negate students' learning. Freire (1970) said, "there is no neutral education (12)." Every class or teaching moment can either support or dismiss the success of student learning. There are few examples of innovative and inclusive approaches to working with aboriginal people whose traditions include a very clear understanding of the importance of family. For example, in an effort to respond to First Nations training needs, the Cowichan Project in partnership with the School of Child and Youth Care at the University of Victoria developed a Generative Curriculum Model by including more recognition of elders and a higher profile for children and their families (Beach, Bertrand, and Cleveland, 1998). The active involvement of elders has improved the students' retention rate and helped the program meet the need for trained early childhood education staff. The Generative Curriculum and its flexible model helps to address the shortage of First Nations people who are trained early childhood educators (Beach et al., 1998).

Similar to school-based classrooms, the increasing racial diversity of college courses means that the everyday classroom interactions of students and instructors are not only richer in variety, but more complex (Dei et al., 1999).

Inadequate attention is paid to the life experience of students who struggle to translate their life experience into theoretical concepts. In academic settings, more credence is given to theoretical approaches rather than lived experience. The diversity in Canadian population is illustrated in the variety of languages represented, where 32% of the population reports a home language other than English or French, and that an average of 225,000 immigrants and refugees enter Canada every year (Bernhard and Gonzalez-Mena, 2000). "Teachers, in particular, are faced with the task of helping one another, and their students, to engage positively, negotiating fairly, and intellectually come to understand 'difference' in their classrooms" (Dei, 1997, 3). I saw this particular notion in play when the discussion on diversity was conducted in the "Teaching in Institutions of Higher Education" course in graduate studies at the Ontario Institute for Studies in Education (OISE). The students made many assumptions about cultural differences and displayed what seemed like a high level of ignorance on how gender impacts women's lives (class discussion, June 2001). I was surprised at comments such as "I did not realize I was oppressed, until I came to OISE." It was said with humor, but I think there was a level of seriousness to the comment that I found particularly meaningful. The way we struggle with understanding our own oppression makes understanding other people's differences and oppression more challenging. The class discussion facilitated an opportunity for everyone to speak, but some of the most offensive comments came from white male students who were able to comment on cultural differences and the impact of gender without acknowledging their own privileged position. The instructors and other students attempted to challenge their notions, yet I walked out of that class thinking that there is much work to do in understanding the reality of cultural and racial differences. I was particularly concerned because those students plan to teach or pursue leadership careers in institutions of higher learning.

In a challenge to teachers working with the urban poor, D. Corson (1998) suggests that a good place to begin reform is teacher education itself, which means that the circle turns back fully to the selection of those responsible for orienting teachers in their professional practice. Clearly a more strategic process in the discourse of anti-racism education needs to develop so that students with early childhood diplomas do not continue to limit their experience to simulated or mock celebrations of Diwali and Hanukkah. Instead of focusing on festivals, a greater emphasis is needed on the diverse child-rearing practices that go beyond the dominant Western understanding of child development.

In early childhood training programs, the provision of appropriate care-giving practices is central to the consideration of quality childcare. There is a growing body of evidence documenting the diverse practices that exist in infant and toddler care giving (Bernhard, 2000; and Gonzalez-Mena, 1995). Further, there is a developmental recognition that children are aware at a very young age that color, language, gender, and physical ability are connected with privilege and power. This is exemplified by the patterns in play activities, when boys refuse to play with girls, or a child refuses to hold the hand of a black class-mate because he insists it is "dirty" (Derman-Sparks, 1989). In addition to understanding a variety of culturally based care-giving practices, early childhood educators need to be prepared to work with these situations and feel comfort-able in resolving childhood definitions of racism or sexism in a developmen-tally appropriate manner. The Ontario government's College Standards and Accreditation Council has established program outcomes including one that "graduates will demonstrate the ability to support the development and learn-ing of individual children, within the context of family, culture and society" (Ministry of Education, 1996).

In an effort to meet government program outcomes and often driven by a desire to treat all students equally, faculty members prefer to take on a "color-blind" position, assuming that students of all racial and socioeconomic back-grounds are deemed equal in their ability to achieve success, and proposing that all students have the same level of support and preparedness for postsecondary studies. However, to ignore the students' racial or socioeconomic background is to deny the reality of their existence. A Native American student described the alienation she experienced when she first entered a graduate nursing pro-gram: "the class is white and all the rest of us are other" (Steffan-Dickerson, Neary, and Hyche-Johnson, 2000, 136). The further "presumption that stu-dents come to us having already learned the disciplinary standards of reading, writing and evaluation, would of course be an example of how we assume stu-dents should have had a fairly upper middle class background" (Nelson, 1996, 165). This is particularly illustrated in work with students who do not speak English as their first language, but most course work in postsecondary insti-tutions assumes students are skilled in the dominant language.

Educators in institutions of higher learning need to place themselves in a position of risk by helping students critique the prevailing silence about racism and the business-as-usual approach to racial politics (Lawrence, 1997). In my own work, a critical approach to the reality of racial dominance in institutions of higher learning has enabled me to develop an alternative vision of working with students from a variety of racial and ethnocultural backgrounds. In the early childhood department at George Brown College, only three of the four-teen full-time faculty members are not white. In *Looking White People in the Eye*, Razack (1998) writes that the emphasis on cultural diversity too often descends in a multicultural spiral to a superficial reading of differences that makes power relations invisible and keeps the dominant cultural norms in place. Cultural sensitivity, to be acquired and practised by dominant groups, replaces, for example, any concrete attempt to diversify the teacher population.

In preparation for thesis completion, Patricia Corson (1998) interviewed fourteen early childhood faculty members, all of whom identified as white. In a planned focus group of five faculty members, the majority considered themselves to be experts in diversity and all were white. White authors have written many of the popular publications on diversity and anti-bias programs in early childhood education. David Corson (1998) and others are nationally renowned authors who may identify as culturally different, but are predominantly white (Chud and Fahlman, 1995; Derman-Sparks, 1989; Hall and Rhomberg, 1995; Kilbride, 1997). In a position of power (Arber, 2000), the authors represent members of dominant groups, yet do not acknowledge their position of privilege.

Students' education, outside the prescribed learning environment, needs to be integrated further. There is very little connection made between the wealth of knowledge that exists in the changing early childhood workforce and new students entering training programs. Perhaps this would pose a greater challenge in smaller, rural communities that have predominantly homogenous populations, but in urban areas such as Toronto, students come from different parts of the world and live in a range of socioeconomic circumstances, which requires a more public voice. An opportunity needs to be provided to the students and the teachers working in the early childhood sector when it comes to sharing expertise on anti-racist approaches related to work with children and families. This notion has forced me to look at my own oppression and my own privilege and how they interact in my work as a teacher.

In early childhood programs, there is ongoing debate on whether to utilize an integrated approach to teaching anti-bias education principles or to develop specific courses on antiracist education. While there is an emphasis on integrating anti-bias principles into education, in practice it proves to be an effective approach to addressing these issues because it is left up to the interpretation of the instructors. A key problem in making a shift toward anti-racist education is that the general evidence testifies convincingly that no real change happens unless teachers internalize it on a very deep level. Changes do not happen without teachers, and teachers do not institute changes unless they understand them and believe in them (Gaine, 2000).

When students are asked how they integrate anti-bias approaches in field placement, many discuss the Spanish music they shared or how they made fruit salad with "exotic" fruit. When I consider challenges that students have faced during the years I have taught early childhood education, I think they would benefit from a course that specifically deals with anti-racist principles and practices that are relevant to early childhood environments, in addition to an integrated approach. Similarly, anti-racism awareness training for social workers allows them to examine their individual attitudes and how they shape behavior. It also helps social workers see the connection between individual and structural elements in racism, and how personal changes can contribute to addressing the needs of non-dominant groups (George, 2000).

David Corson (1998) has suggested a model that includes several courses on self-discovery, cross-cultural competence, critical thinking skills, and a general anti-bias framework. Although well intentioned and innovative, existing institutions are scrambling to maintain course hours for existing requirements, let alone a commitment to new courses. Introducing a shorter specific course would give students a foundation for integrating anti-racism education principles and practices throughout the program, while recognizing the limitations and inability to give full attention to anti-racism principles and practices.

In an effort to be inclusive and to encourage a pluralist approach to education, we have lost the opportunity to challenge the dominant culture and seem unable to equip students for putting anti-racism education principles into practice. Although there is some progress being made, in my opinion, there is no consistency in how students understand and practice antiracist principles. The shift from an anti-bias perspective to anti-racist education is a difficult one that will create tension and a questioning of how valuable and relevant it is in early childhood programs. The implications for making the shift will affect the way early childhood programs are delivered, the content in ECE courses, who gets hired and in what position, and the review of program and government policies. Although institutions have made an attempt in the past to develop employment equity policies, when the current provincial government removed the legislation, there was no deliberate effort on the part of large institutions to maintain the policy. Evaluating hiring policies and practices through an anti-racist lens means analyzing how many of the recent hires have not been representative of the dominant majority. Whether it is at the early childhood educator level or at the faculty level, are child-care programs and community colleges making an effort to recruit a diverse range of individuals? If in fact students and graduates are still struggling with integrating anti-racist principles in their practical work with children and families, ECE training programs need to complete a review of course content and method of delivery. Implications for teaching include questioning, in a deliberate way, the explicit and implicit messages concerning human development (Bernhard, 1998). With the apparent expertise in place, it is not necessary for early childhood educators to limit themselves to a tourist approach to programming.

Anti-racism education is about exploring and rupturing power relationships among the majority and the minoritized. In Toronto the face of the majority has changed, yet educational institutions are slow to respond to the change. Early childhood educators should be able to articulate the principles of anti-racist education and be able to put them into practice.

REFERENCES

Arber, R. 2000. "Defining Position within Politics of Difference: Negotiation Spaces 'In Between.'" *Race, Ethnicity and Education* 3(1): 45–62.

Beach, J., Bertrand, J., and Cleveland, G. 1998. *Our Child Care Workforce: From Remuneration to Recognition-More Than a Labour of Love.* Ottawa: Human Resources Steering Committee.

Bernhard, J. (1998, June). "Recognizing the Authenticity of Cultural Diversity and Racial Equity: Beginning a Discussion and Critical Reflection on Developmentally Appropriate Practice." *Canadian Journal of Research in Early Childhood Education* 7(1): 81–90.

Bernhard, J., and Gonzalez-Mena, J. 2000. "The Cultural Context of Infant and Toddler Care in Infants and Toddlers." In *Out of Home Care*, (Eds.), D. Cryer and T. Harms. Baltimore: Brookes Publishing.

Chud, G., and Fahlman, R. 1995. *Honouring Diversity within Child Care and Early Education. Instructor's Guide.* Victoria: B.C. Centre for Curriculum and Professional Development.

Corson, David. 1998. *Changing Education for Diversity.* Philadelphia: Open University Press.

Corson, Patricia. 1998. *Anti-Bias Education in Early Childhood: Preparing Teachers for Diversity.* Toronto: Ontario Institute for Studies in Education of the University of Toronto.

Dei, G. 1996. *Anti-Racism Education: Theory and Practice.* Halifax: Fernwood Publishing.

Dei, G. 1997. *Restructuring 'Drop Out': A Critical Ethnography of the Dynamics of Black Students' Disengagement from School. Toronto: University of Toronto Press*

Dei, G. 1999. "Knowledge and Politics of Social Change: The Implications of Anti-Racism." *British Journal of Sociology in Education* 20(3): 395–409.

Dei, G., James, I. M., James-Wilson, S., and Karumanchery, L. 2001. "Rethinking Inclusive Schooling: Theoretical and Philosophical Foundations." In *Removing the Margins: The Challenges and Possibilities of Inclusive Schooling.* Toronto: Canadian Scholars' Press.

Delpit, L. D. 1988. The Silenced Dialogue: Power and Pedagogy in Educating Other People's Children." *Harvard Education Review 58*, 208–298.

Derman-Sparks, L. 1989. *Anti-Bias Curriculum: Tools for Empowering Young Children.* Washington: National Association for the Education of Young Children.

Derman-Sparks, L. 1998. "Activism and Preschool Children." In *Beyond Heroes and Holidays,* (Eds.), E. Lee et al. Washington: Network of Educators of Americas.

Evans, J. 2000. "Working with Parents and Caregivers to Support Children from Birth to Three Years." In *Coordinators Notebook*, No. 24. Toronto: The Consultative Group on Early Childhood Care and Development.

Freire, P. 1970. *Pedagogy of the Oppressed.* New York: Seabury Press.

Gaine, C. 2000. "Anti-Racist Education in 'White' Areas: The Limits and Possibilities of Change." *Race, Ethnicity and Education* 3(1): 65–79.

182 | *Critical Issues in Anti-racist Research Methodologies*

George Brown College. 1999. *Field Placement Handbook: Early Childhood Education Program-ECE First Year Students*. Toronto: George Brown College

George, U. 2000. "Toward Anti-Racism in Social Work." In *Canadian Context in Anti-Racism Feminism* (Eds.), George Dei and Agnes Calliste. Halifax: Fernwood Publishing.

Gestwicki, C. 1999. *Developmentally Appropriate Practice: Curriculum and Development in Early Education*. Albany, NY: Delmar Publishers.

Gestwicki, C., and Bertrand, J. 2001. *The Essentials of Early Childhood Education*. Toronto: Thompson Nelson.

Gonzalez-Mena, J. 1995. *Multicultural Issues in Child Care*. New York: McGraw Hill.

Hall, N., and Rhomberg, V. 1995. *The Affective Curriculum: Teaching the Anti-bias Approach to Young Children*. Scarborough: Nelson Canada.

Kilbride, K. M. (Ed.). 1997. *Include Me Too. Human Diversity in Early Childhood*. Toronto: Harcourt Brace and Company.

Kincheloe, J. L., and Steinberg, S. R. 1998. "Critical Multiculturalism: Rethinking Educational Purpose." In *Changing Multiculturalism*. Buckingham, PA: Open University Press.

Lawrence, S. 1997. "Beyond Race Awareness: White Racial Identity and Multicultural Teaching." *Journal of Teacher Education* 48(2): 108–117.

Ministry of Education. 1996. *Early Childhood Education Program Standard*. (College Standards and Accreditation Council.) Toronto: Queen's Printer for Ontario.

Nelson, C. E. 1996. "Student Diversity Requires Different Approaches to College Teaching Even in Math and Science." *American Behavioral Scientist* 40(2): 165–175.

Newman, H. 1989. *Heather Has Two Mommies*. Boston: Alyson Wonderland.

Nieto, S. 1995. "From Brown Heroes to Holidays to Assimilationist Agendas." In *Multicultural Education: Critical Pedagogy and the Politics of Difference*. Albany: State University of New York Press.

Razack, Sherene. 1998. *Looking White People in the Eye*. Toronto: University of Toronto Press.

Sleeter, C. 1994. "*White Racism*" Spring, 5–9. Multicultural Education.

Steffan Dickerson, S., Neary, M. A., and Hyche-Johnson, M. 2000. "Native American Graduate Nursing Students' Learning Experiences." *Journal of Nursing Scholarship* 32(2): 189–196.

Tabors, P. O. 1998. "What Early Childhood Educators Need to Know: Developing Effective Programs for Linguistically and Culturally Diverse Children and Families." *Young Children* 53(6), 20–26.

Wilson, L. 2001. *Partnerships: Families and Communities in Canadian Early Childhood Education*. Toronto: ITP Nelson.

Yeates, M., Mckenna, D., Warberg, C., and Chandler, K. 2001. *Administering Early Childhood Settings*. Toronto: Prentice Hall.

Chapter Nine

NUZHAT AMIN

Voices of Minority Immigrant Women

LANGUAGE, RACE, AND ANTI-RACIST FEMINIST METHODOLOGIES

Introduction

In this chapter, I explore the challenges of conducting anti-racist research in the field of applied linguistics, which is dominated by colonialist ideologies of who is a legitimate speaker of English, who can be a valid English-language teacher, and who is the final authority on pedagogies in English language teaching (ELT). Eurocentric theories embedded in the imperialist worldview that white people from the predominantly English-speaking countries of the First World have more ownership of English than non-white people from the Third World inform the theories and research conducted in this field. Many of these linguistic concepts are clustered around the binaries *native Englishes* (which refers to the Englishes spoken in the core English-speaking countries of the First World, for example, England, Canada, and the United States) and *non-native Englishes* (which refers to the varieties of English spoken outside these First World societies). The "native speaker of English" then, is a code phrase for white speakers of English from the core English-speaking countries of the First World (Paikeday, 1985), while the phrase "non-native speaker of English" refers to speakers of English from the rest of the world. Native speakers of English are positioned in applied linguistics as speaking standard, good, real English with a standard accent; in this binary, non-native speakers are viewed as speaking non-standard, deficient, inferior English with a non-standard, inferior accent. As such, First World linguists are perpetuating a caste system

(Kachru, 1997) among speakers of English based largely on race, ethnicity, and national origin; a caste system that has been provided pedagogical and linguistic justification backed by empirical research by some native-speaking researchers. Despite challenges by many critical non-white scholars and researchers (e.g., Braine, 1999; Canagarajah, 1999; Kachru, 1992; Nayar, 1994), and a few white scholars (e.g., Phillipson, 1992; Pennycook, 1992; Paikeday, 1985), concepts and ideologies epitomized by these binary divisions continue to circulate in ELT. ELT, then, is a site where discourses of colonialism, racism, and sexism intersect to produce and mark women and men from the Third World as permanent Others when they speak what was once the language of the colonizers—English—but what is now very much an institution of the former British and American colonies and also a dominant language of countries without a history of British and American colonialism. This continuing hegemony of ELT by white First World researchers and scholars raises a number of ethical and methodological questions, including the following: Who gets to produce knowledges in the interrelated fields of applied linguistics and ELT? What is the worldview of these researchers? And why are the voices of non-white speakers of English in the First World and the Third World, which point to the racist and colonialist underpinnings of ELT and applied linguistics, not being heard?

I take the position in this chapter that applied linguistics is a site where, with a few exceptions, First World researchers are complicit in the continuing linguistic hegemony of the First World over the Third World through the native-speaker-of-English concept, and that this concept does not have a sound linguistic basis; rather, it is a linguistic manifestation of nativist discourses that position non-white women and men living in First World societies as non-native to the nation (Amin, 2000). I also posit that the native speaker concept is a gendered phenomenon, and that this trope negatively impacts the lives of non-white women living in the First World, and especially those women who work as teachers of English as a second language (ESL). I will first address my location as a researcher and producer of knowledges in the area of minority women's exclusion along the axes of language, race, and gender, and then take a look at the status of English in the world at the beginning of the twenty-first century. After that, I will give details of my research on minority immigrant women who teach ESL and discuss some of the methodological issues and concerns that arose for me while conducting my research. Finally, I will look at the implications of conducting research in fields where the voices of members of subordinate groups are silenced.

The Researcher

Simon and Dippo (1986) urge that we researchers should recognize "our implication in the production of data and thus must begin to include ourselves . . . in our analyses of the situations we study" (200). Similarly, Lather (1991) stresses the importance of positionality and reflexity in postmodern research when she notes that researchers should account for the ways in which "our invested positionality shapes our rhetoric and practice" (xvii). This theoretical view compels me as the researcher to make transparent my location and my investments in this study. My decision to conduct research on minority immigrant ESL teachers' encounters with the native-speaker concept and nativism is informed by my location as a middle/upper-class Pakistani heterosexual woman who has participated in the English language, first from a position of relative power in postcolonial Pakistan where I grew up, and subsequently from a position of less power in Canada where I immigrated as an adult and where I have experienced a degree of Otherness vis-à-vis standard native English and standard accent.

At decolonization, the upper classes of the British colonies became the new oppressors of their countries, and these classes had, and continue to have, great investments in English. I belong to this class and to one such family in urban Pakistan. This class maintained power and status by giving importance to family name, pedigree, old money, and family occupation. English was, and remains, an obvious marker of this class difference. The English taught at the convent schools that I attended for fourteen years in Karachi was modelled on British native-speaker English; the ideal here was clearly Received Pronunciation (RP), emblematic of which was the BBC (British Broadcasting Company). We were supposed to speak only English, and local languages were looked down on or laughed at. Those girls who shone in the English class had a reputation of being intelligent and cultured; those who did well in Urdu were either ignored or identified as being from a lower class. However, within the walls of the convent schools it was made clear that native speakers were the real and true speakers of English, and Pakistanis could never make such a claim. We understood that only white people were native speakers. I went on to do two master's degrees in English at Karachi University—in literature and then language. During the latter program, the native speaker was no longer a phantom presence, but a flesh-and-blood person, embodied by the visiting white scholars who flew into Karachi to give a few talks. A white man headed the language laboratory that we frequented for our phonetics course; hence, during this program the association of the native speaker with whiteness became even stronger.

186 | *Critical Issues in Anti-racist Research Methodologies*

I would describe my initial language-related experiences in Canada in the late 1970s as difficult, as I was constructed as Other to the norm of native-speaker English and native-speaker accent. As an ESL teacher of adult immigrants in Toronto, I experienced similar Otherness. I have taught ESL to adults in Toronto in both credit and non-credit courses in programs run by community colleges and by school boards. There were many differences in these programs in terms of goals, duration, and curriculum. The students in these programs varied in terms of age, gender, ethnicity, linguistic background, level of education, ability in English, and length of stay. A common thread in these very different teaching situations was that many of the students murmured the term *native speaker* with awe. I received the message that however hard I might work at preparing competent lessons, my teaching could not be as good as that of a native speaker. The discomfort of having to use tapes with native-speaker accents for students to model themselves on, the ignominy of students storming out of class and demanding a "real" English teacher, the embarrassment of having to rely on supervisors to pacify angry students with an unconvincing "All our teachers are very qualified." All these encounters with linguistic nativism had an extremely negative effect on my identity formation, as I felt that my years of experience as an announcer and news reader in English on Radio Pakistan and my two master's degrees in English seemed to be wiped away overnight by being identified as a speaker of non-native/non-standard English. My different experiences of English, especially the connotation that the native speaker can lay more claim to being fully proficient in English than a non-native speaker ever can, inform this study.

Theoretical Perspectives

Englishes in the Third World

In order to ground my discussion of native-non-native speaker issues, in this section I will give a comprehensive background on the status of English in the former British and American colonies and its current status as a world language. English was introduced in the British colonies as a "vital appendage of British colonial rule, one that was to be used as an instrument of oppression, alienation, and marginalization of the indigenous peoples" (Dissanayake, 1993, 337). In the decolonization era, Britain and the United States followed deliberate policies of economic imperialism all over the world, and this economic imperialism is tied to English (Pennycook, 1992; Phillipson, 1992; Tollefson, 1991), so that after decolonization, English remained a dominant language in the former British and American colonies and also became entrenched in countries without a history of British or American colonization, such as China,

Japan, and Surinam. In sum, at the beginning of the twenty-first century, English is a dominant language of the middle and upper classes in Third World countries. Although there are more non-native speakers of English than native speakers, (Kachru, 1992, estimates that there are four non-native speakers for every native speaker), the power to decide what is standard, correct, good English continues to rest with native speakers or the original "owners" of English, that is, the countries where English was a dominant language before it was introduced in the Third World. Phillipson (1992) divides English users into "core English-speaking countries" (for example, England and Canada) and "periphery-English countries" (for example, Pakistan and Ghana), thus foregrounding the power inequality between these two groups of English users. Phillipson explains his division thus: Countries such as Pakistan and Ghana are peripheral in the sense that "norms for the language are regarded as flowing from the core English-speaking fountainheads" (25) and the "target in language teaching is English as it is spoken in one of the core English-speaking countries" (25). In order to reveal the bias in First World researchers' studies of non-native Englishes, I need to make the distinction between native and non-native Englishes more specific than Phillipson's core-periphery division. Phillipson's distinction, although useful in foregrounding the power inequality between the two spheres, elides distinctions between those periphery countries such as India, Kenya, and Jamaica, which have indigenized varieties of English (IVEs) that have been institutionalized in local settings, and those countries such as Poland and Russia, which are not making claims to having such a variety. IVEs such as Caribbean English, Filipino English, Indian English, and Nigerian English are distinct varieties of English (see, for example, Kachru, 1990; Lowenberg, 1992; Phillipson, 1992; Sridhar and Sridhar, 1992); these Englishes have a clear colonial past and are also referred to as Third World Englishes (see, for example, Kachru, 1986; Fairman, 1986). This division is along racial lines. The population of core English-speaking countries is predominantly white, while the population of the former British and American colonies is predominantly non-white, and hence I also use the terms *white Englishes* for native Englishes and *non-white Englishes* to refer to non-native Englishes.

The important characteristics of IVEs are first, they have their own rules and norms, and second, as they are used daily in particular settings, they have developed new linguistic features at all linguistic levels, and these linguistic innovations have become de facto norms for English usage in those countries as these linguistic innovations have become nativized (Lowenberg, 1992, 108–109). For researchers in applied linguistics, the main issue regarding IVEs is whether they are different or deficient varieties of English. Historically, native speakers have decided whether a variety of English is valid, but as a number of linguists have pointed out, the rules they use to decide on the validity of a particular variety of non-native English are culturally and linguistically biased (see, for example, Kachru, 1992; Sridhar and Sridhar, 1992). Kachru (1992) takes the position that any deviation from mother English in the IVEs has been termed not a difference but a mistake or error by native speakers of mother English, for the norm they use is that of English as used in native contexts. Similarly, Lowenberg (1992), in an indictment of core countries' marginalization of IVEs, says that, although there have been many advances in English language testing, relatively little attention has been paid to the variability inherent in the linguistic norms for English that are generally tested. He argues that when identifying these norms, "most researchers in testing appear to assume implicitly that the benchmark for proficiency in English around the world should be the norms accepted and used by 'native speakers' of English" (108). Lowenberg takes the position that such an assumption is not universally valid. This non-acceptance of Third World Englishes is clearly grounded in First World linguists' stand that there is only one English, not several Englishes (see Phillipson, 1992, 26). Quirk (1990), an extremely influential player in the native-non-native Englishes debate, dismisses any attempt at acceptance of these new varieties of English and insists that standard British English should be the norm internationally. Kachru (1991) points out that Quirk's insistence that standard British English be the norm internationally is unrealistic and misguided as it ignores the reality of world Englishes.

In this section I have shown the biases inherent in the evaluations of Third World Englishes by First World researchers, who use native Englishes as the benchmark for correct, standard, and good English, and hence conclude in their research that the Englishes of the Third World are nonstandard and deficient. I, on the other hand, take as the theoretical underpinning of my research that the native speaker of English construct is a linguistic manifestation of nativist discourses, which have historically constructed non-white women as being non-native to the nation-state in First World societies. Hence I consider the native speaker concept to be an interlocking oppression that works in concert with racism and sexism to oppress and marginalize non-white women. This brings me to a discussion of how race, gender, and non-native speaker status intersect to produce minority immigrant women as Other.

Race, Gender, Accents, and New Racisms

This section will focus on the social organization of race in "inner circle" countries and the parallel processes by which minority immigrant women become constructed as non-native to the nation and non-native speakers of English in the field of ESL. But first, let me spell out how I am using the concept of race in this chapter. Dei (1996) emphasizes that race is a socially constructed category that "lacks any sound scientific validity" (41). A number of theorists echo Dei's views (e.g., Brah, 1996; Frankenberg, 1993; Miles, 1989, 1993; Ng, 1981, 1990) and call attention to the organization and arrangement of racial relationships of domination and subordination. Like Dei, they consider race to be a set of social relations in which they emphasize the simultaneity of the impact of race, class, and gender in shaping the lives of women of color, rather than its production out of the single axis of gender domination or patriarchy. They thus emphasize the interconnectedness of all oppressions. Brah (1996), for example, specifies that racism, like ethnicity, nationalism, and class, represents a gendered phenomenon (154). McCarthy and Crichlow (1993) make a similar point when they say that minority women and girls have radically different experiences of racial inequality than do their male counterparts because of the issue of gender (xix). Within this understanding of race as a set of social relations, let me now look at the encounters of minority immigrant women with racism. Ng's (1981, 1990) work is useful here in that she looks at the social processes whereby a person comes to be labeled as an immigrant and as ethnic (Ng, 1981, 101). According to Ng (1990), although the term *immigrant women* refers to women with a particular legal status, in everyday life only certain groups of women are seen to be "immigrant women" by members of society, and these are "visible minority" women, women who do not speak English or who speak English with an accent (other than British or American), and women who work in low-paid menial jobs (21). Ng concludes that the "common usage of the word embodies class, ethnic and racial biases" (21) and that it is almost synonymous with "visible minority women" (22). Ng indicates how racism and sexism as systems of oppression and domination produce minority women as Other (22). A marker of being an immigrant woman and of being non-native to inner circle societies is an immigrant woman's race. This experience of Otherness is reproduced in ESL through the imagining of the native speaker as white; in both sites race is socially organized to produce Otherness. I argue that the concept of the native speaker as white pervades all aspects of ESL programs as it influences the teaching, classroom materials, and relations between the teacher and learners. Let me now look at how a minority immigrant woman teacher's race impacts on her *lived experience* in ESL, in which case, as Rockhill and Tomic (1995) state, the referent is "White, Anglo, male" (210). Here I need to discuss the findings of an earlier study for which I interviewed five minority immigrant women teachers of adult ESL students. The findings of the study indicated that these teachers believe that some ESL students make the assumptions that (a) only white people can be native speakers of English and (b) only native speakers know "real," "proper," "Canadian" English (see Amin, 1997). The findings of my study regarding race concur with those of Leung, Harris, and Rampton (1997) who, building on Rampton's earlier (1990) research, argue that there is an "abstracted notion of an idealised native speaker of English from which ethnic and linguistic minorities are automatically excluded" (546).

I have so far established that ELT, which is dominated by native speakers, continues to construct the white native speaker as the norm and as the referent of the ESL classroom, thus positioning the minority teacher as Other, an obvious marker of her Otherness being her race. I will now look at another way that native speakers maintain their hegemony in ELT, by constructing First World accents as the standard, thus positioning minority immigrant women as having accents that are deviant from the norm of the Canadian ESL classroom. While the native speaker-dominated ESL classroom maintains that First World accents are the norm and that all accents that are different from this norm are non-standard and therefore deficient, the theoretical underpinning of my research is that accents, like race, are socially organized, are a linguistic manifestation of nativism, and constitute a new and effective form of racism. I need to first lay out what *accents* symbolize in our society. Matsuda (1991) states: "Everyone has an accent, but when an employer refuses to hire a person 'with an accent,' they are referring to a hidden norm of non-accent . . ." (p. 1361). Matsuda then explicates this norm of non-accent: "People in power are perceived as speaking normal, unaccented English. Any speech that is different from that constructed norm is called an accent" (1361). In the course of her work as a law professor in the United States, Matsuda listened to a number of stories about people who had been born outside the United States and had been denied a particular job in the country because of having a "heavy accent"; she concluded that "accent discrimination is commonplace, natural, and socially acceptable" (1348). Lippi-Green (1997) takes this line of argument further when she says that at present "accent serves as the first point of gatekeeping" into American society because it is no longer legal to discriminate on the basis of ethnicity, race, and homeland, and hence "accent becomes a litmus test for exclusion" (64). She thus establishes that accents are a legal and acceptable form of exclusion of certain groups of people who do not have the constructed norm of accent. Which groups of people? Lippi-Green states: "It is not *all* foreign accents, but only accents linked to skin that isn't white, or which signals a third-world homeland, that evokes such negative reactions" (238–239). Now let me look at native-speaker discourses on accents, and at a particular accent as being among the set of characteristics that are socially held to represent the native speaker. Brutt-Griffler and Samimy (1999) argue that "national origin and accent" are crucial characteristics that are socially held to represent those of the native speaker (416). I would go one step further and say that a native speaker is imagined as having a white accent. Here I am drawing on my 1994 study, which indicated that accents associated with First World countries such as Britain, the United States, and Canada have a higher status than accents associated with non-white countries such as India, Kenya, and Singapore (see Amin, 1994).

Native-Speaker Construct as Gendered Phenomenon

When designing my study, I kept in mind the fact that in the context of ESL, it is mainly women who are impacted by the native speaker concept. Racism, colonialism, and Canada's immigration policy intersect to produce a class of immigrant women who will become ESL instructors in part-time, low-waged jobs with few if any benefits and little job security. I will now take a brief look at the group of women who immigrate to Canada from Third World countries, who are potential ESL teachers. Bolaria and Li (1988) argue that since the end of World War II, many Third World countries have been subsidizing the accumulation of capitalist countries by supplying them with many highly trained workers (10). These writers look at the brain drain in light of the domination of First World societies over Third World societies, and add that global disparities allow First World countries to have access to an international labor pool. These countries play an important role in regulating the flow of international labor and facilitating the transfer of professional and skilled labor, especially through their ideological and educational domination over many parts of the world (209). Within this understanding of the social organization of migration, let me now look specifically at immigration policies and practices regarding non-white women. Since the early 1970s, Canada has been increasingly recruiting immigrants from the professional classes in Third World countries. As I pointed out earlier in this chapter, English is a dominant language among the middle and upper classes in many Third World societies, especially in the former British and American colonies, and hence many of the women who come to Canada have high proficiency in English. Among them are schoolteachers and university teachers who might become ESL teachers.

How and why do these women become ESL teachers? First, as Anderson and Lynam (1987) point out, although employment prospects are particularly grim for those women who are not fluent in English or French, a woman's education in her country of origin does not necessarily stand her "in good stead in the Canadian labour force" (67), and many women who were professionals in their home countries/countries of immigration experience "downward career mobility" on their arrival because (a) their credentials from the Third

World are not recognized, (b) there are few chances of becoming re-qualified in their professions, and (c) economic necessity makes them accept low-paying, dead-end jobs (67–68). Women with teaching qualifications and degrees from the Third World have difficulty in getting their work experience and degrees recognized (Ng, 1990) and in getting the required accreditation to teach in public schools. Competition is high for these positions as schools offer teachers "enviable working conditions, with long-term stability, reasonable pay, good benefits, and solid union protection" (Power Analysis, 1998, 62). ESL outside the public school system is so far not regulated, and degree requirements are less rigorous. A number of organizations offer Teaching English as a Second Language (TESL) certificate programs, and hence it is possible for immigrant women who are proficient in English to take a TESL course and then find part-time ESL work. The second reason why minority immigrant women decide to become ESL teachers is that, just like women with less English, they bear primary responsibility for reproductive labor, defined as "the various physical, emotional and educational tasks involved in bearing and raising children, as well as those which go into sustaining the material and emotional well-being of adults" (Nestel, 1996, 1). Working immigrant women, like Canadian-born women, have a double day and bear primary responsibility for child-care and household work in their families. Hence the relatively flexible hours of part-time work and teaching evening classes make such employment comparatively attractive for these women as they can juggle child care and housework with their paid work in ESL.

A few statistics will establish that ESL is a gendered field. The overwhelming majority (86%) of teachers in the federal Language Instruction for Newcomers to Canada (LINC) and provincial ESL programs in Ontario are women (see Power Analysis, 1998, i). The average age is 45.1 years. About 94% of teachers in the Power Analysis study had formal ESL qualifications, nearly 80% had a university degree, and 87% had taken at least one professional development course related to ESL (iv). The typical teacher had 9.3 years of ESL teaching experience (iv). It is clear that the typical ESL teacher has university education and a good deal of experience teaching ESL. Does this imply that teachers in government-funded ESL programs are permanent employees, have benefits, and earn a good wage? The answer is no. The Power Analysis study found that only 29% of LINC/ESL teachers were permanent employees; the majority (67%) were on contracts, which generally lasted for the school year. The rest were working without any contract (62). Nearly 40% of the teachers had no benefits. As opposed to their counterparts teaching in the regular school/college system, most ESL teachers had no collective bargaining agreement (62). It becomes apparent, then, that in the context of Canada, the native-speaker concept is a gendered phenomenon, as the majority of ESL teachers are women and these women teachers experience the socio-political and financial implications of being constructed as deviant from the standard on the basis of their non-native speaker status, race, gender, and Third World homeland. However, the critical literature by non-native speakers is male dominated (see, for example, Braine, 1999; Canagarajah, 1999; D. Liu, 1999; J. Liu, 1999), does not explore the gendered experience of being constructed as a non-native speaker, and hence suggests that the experience of minority men and women non-native speakers is similar. I will discuss this point in the next section, which addresses the methodology of my study.

Methodology Matters

From 1998 to 1999 I conducted interviews with eight minority immigrant women who had taught or were teaching Settlement ESL, that is, ESL for adult immigrants in government-financed programs. The purpose of my research was to explore how nativism, in particular the concept of the native speaker, is manifested in the context of ESL and how minority immigrant women teachers of ESL negotiate this linguistic manifestation of nativism.

I ground my study methodologically in the following three research traditions: (a) feminist ethnography (e.g., A. Cameron, 1990; Conway, 1996; Gluck and Patai, 1991; Haraway, 1988; Kirby and McKenna, 1989; Lather, 1991; Maguire, 1987; Oakley, 1981; Personal Narratives Group, 1989), (b) critical ethnography (e.g., Anderson, 1989; Sheper-Hughes, 1992; Simon and Dippo, 1986), and (c) anti-racist ethnography (e.g., D. Cameron, 1992; Connolly, 1992; Essed, 1987, 1991; hooks, 1991, 1994; Spivak, 1987). Although these are seen as distinctive traditions, I consider them to be ideologically similar. When designing my study on nativism, and also during the process of data collection and interpretation/analysis, I kept in mind the following principles of critical research from the above-mentioned traditions: First I was mindful that I, as the researcher, am not in any way outside the research, and that I am implicated in the production of data and also the findings (Simon and Dippo, 1986; Lather, 1991). Second, when deciding on an appropriate form of data collection, I kept in mind that I wanted to give voice to groups that have been marginalized and suppressed (Spivak, 1987; Personal Narratives Group, 1989). Once I decided that semistructured interviews with minority teachers would be the ideal form of collecting data for my study, I was mindful of how to conduct interviews on egalitarian principles, so that the interviews would be dialogues between two people of relative equality (Essed, 1991) and where the researcher regards her subjects as coparticipants rather than as data collection instruments (Oakley, 1981). And last, throughout this project I was self-conscious of the power differential between me, as the researcher, and the teachers as subjects of my study, and tried to mitigate this power at every stage of the study (Essed, 1991; Lather, 1991; Oakley, 1981).

The Sample: Women at the Center

I previously indicated that, in the context of Canada, the native-speaker concept is a gendered phenomenon, as the majority of ESL teachers are women, and these women teachers experience the socio-political and financial implications of being constructed as deviant from the standard on the basis of their non-native speaker status, race, gender, and Third World homeland. However, the critical literature by non-native speakers is male dominated (see, for example, Braine, 1999; Canagarajah, 1999; D. Liu, 1999; J. Liu, 1999). I consider the significance of this whole body of work for applied linguistics to be profound in that these researchers have used their access to the academy and knowledge production in order to make visible the continuing linguistic domination of the First World over the Third World through native-speaker ideologies. But it does not explore the gendered experience of women ESL teachers and hence makes invisible, or at least suggests that the experience of minority men and women non-native speakers is similar. Referring to the gendered nature of knowledge production, the Personal Narratives Group (1989) says that traditionally knowledge, truth, and reality have been constructed as if men's experiences were normative, and that in fact being human meant being male (3). Listening to women's voices, they add, has been crucial to feminist reconstruction of their understanding of the world (4).

The absent voices of women from the Third World who experience linguistic nativism in the First World exemplifies the point made by feminist researchers (e.g., Haraway, 1988; Lather, 1991) that subordinated groups have always had their experiences constructed and given meaning by dominant groups. It is against this history of social injustices that the Personal Narratives Group (1989) encourages researchers to seek out the narratives of non-dominant groups. While emphasizing the use of personal stories as a valuable form of data collection, the Personal Narratives Group also points to the importance of getting the insights of subordinate groups on issues that affect them:

> Personal narratives of non-dominant social groups (women in general, racially or ethnically oppressed people, lower-class people, lesbians) are often particularly effective sources of counterhegemonic insight because they expose a viewpoint embedded in dominant ideology as particularist rather than universal, and because they reveal a reality of life that defies or contradicts the rules. (7)

Just as the literature by non-native speakers concerning the native speaker is dominated by male writers, much of the critical literature on Settlement ESL is written from the perspective of white women teachers (e.g., Goldstein, 1991, 1994; Peirce, 1993, 1995; Rockhill and Tomic, 1995), and here, as in the above-cited literature on the native speaker, the voices of non-white teachers are missing. I decided to give voice to the teachers who directly experience linguistic manifestations of nativism by having as my participants minority women teachers who teach ESL rather than, say, non-white male teachers or white supervisors of the programs where these women teach.

I next need to address my rationale for choosing as participants women who had taught or were teaching Settlement ESL. There are two reasons for this. First, that is the field within ESL with which I have the most experience, and hence I would be able to engage with the narratives at an experiential level. Second, I thought the Settlement ESL classroom for adult immigrants would be the ideal site for my exploration into how the discourses of native speaker and nativism would manifest themselves because of the association of native speaker and nativism with nation. Hence, the research participants in the study were visible minority immigrant women who were teaching or had taught Settlement ESL to adults. The women I interviewed were originally from China, Goa, Egypt, India, Iran, Kenya, Jamaica, Pakistan, and Surinam. I wanted participants from different racial and ethnic backgrounds because adult ESL classes in Ontario are taught by teachers from a variety of racial and ethnic backgrounds (see Power Analysis, 1988, 55). In addition, I wanted to emphasize that the experiences of minority women from different ethnic and national backgrounds would have dissimilarities: English is a global language, but women participate in it differently in different countries, depending on class, culture, and the linguistic conditions of their particular society, and these histories inform their negotiation of native-speaker ideologies and their pedagogies. Settlement ESL teachers in Ontario are from a variety of age groups (see Power Analysis, 1988, 55). Hence, in order to provide a strong profile of immigrant ESL teachers' lives, I tried also to find women of different ages and at different stages of their careers; therefore some of the participants were comparatively new in the profession, for example, Violet had been teaching for only a year and had taught ESL for a few months as a volunteer, while Iffat had worked for 30 years in this field and had recently retired. My participants' ages ranged from the late thirties to the sixties. Most of the women self-identified as being from the middle and upper-middle classes. I asked the women to identify their class location, but I did not ask them for the criteria by which they were ascribing a certain class status to themselves. All the women had university education. At the time of the interview they were living in Toronto.

Feminist Anti-racist Interviews

I gave a great deal of thought to what would be a good way to capture the teachers' gendered experience of nativism in Ontario's ESL programs for adult immigrants. A questionnaire sent to between 50 and 80 ESL teachers would not have provided the complex and intricate information that I was looking for about the participants' *lived* experience of linguistic nativism. Semi-structured interviews seemed to be the most appropriate way to capture the voices and acts of ESL teachers from the Third World teaching in First World classrooms, and to investigate their encounters with nativism. In addition to the interviews, I considered observing the teachers in the classroom to see how they interacted with students, what their pedagogies were, and what kinds of racism students manifested. But I decided against classroom observation for the following reasons: (1) my study was about the teachers' perceptions of how they experience nativism; and (2) from my own experience in ESL teaching, I know that many of the students who do not want to be in a minority teacher's classroom leave after the first class, when they see that their teacher is not a "Canadian."

I began my interviews with two minority teachers whom I identified with the help of the Toronto and Ontario affiliates of Teachers of English as a Second Language (TESL Toronto and TESL Ontario). The rest were chosen through "snowball" sampling (Bogdan and Biklen, 1992, 70), where the first few participants suggested colleagues and friends who would be willing to be interviewed. I now address the interview process. I first conducted an initial short phone interview in which I established that the women met the requirements for participants. As I was investigating the experience of visible minority immigrant women/immigrant women of color, I wanted as participants, *only* visible minority immigrant women/immigrant women of color. In the phone interview I asked potential participants if they identified as visible minorities and accepted their self-definition. The other requirements for participation in this study were that the women should have immigrated to Canada as adults and that they should have ESL teaching experience with adults in state-funded programs and not in private schools.

In order to present the women as fully formed subjects, I asked the women to talk about their participation in English in three sites: (1) in their home country (2) in Canada but outside ESL, and (3) as ESL teachers. Prior to conducting the interviews, I wrote out a list of topics that I wanted to discuss with the participants in each of these sections. In the first section I tried to establish how much English the participants used in their home countries, in both public and private spheres, and the status of English in relation to indigenous languages. For example, was English privileged over other languages in the school? At home? If so, in what situations? I also tried to find out how much the participants held up the native speaker as the norm in their home countries. In the second section we discussed how and why the participants came to Canada and their impressions of their immigration experience. While the questions were focused on the participants' language-related experiences, I also asked them how and why they became ESL teachers. In this context, I asked them about how they went about settling themselves, getting their degrees and work experience from outside Canada accredited and validated, looking for work, and what kind of training they had to get in order to become ESL teachers. Section 3, that is, ESL, was divided into two subsections: (1) students' perceptions of an ideal ESL teacher in terms of race, native-speaker status, and their attitudes to their minority teacher, and (2) the participant's response to the stereotypes and racism that she might have experienced in ESL; an integral part of this subsection was a discussion of the participant's pedagogy.

My interviews were open-ended, and this format was conducive to dialogue, as was the relative equality between the participants and me. Essed (1991) states that most social scientists "study down" rather than "study up," and points out that feminist social scientists strongly encourage research among equals because such research represents the ideal conditions for a non-hierarchical relationship between researcher and informants—shared experiences, social equality, and natural involvement with the problem (67). By way of example, Essed adds that it has been repeatedly shown that black women are reticent about discussing their experiences of white racism with a white interviewer. I could lay claim to a few similarities and commonalities with the subjects in my study. First, all my participants save Fayza, like myself, were proficient in English when we immigrated to Canada. Second, the teachers and I were visible minority women who immigrated to Canada as adults and had experience in teaching Settlement ESL. Third, we shared, to varying degrees, a history of native-speaker hegemony. However, at this juncture I need to trouble my qualified claim of social equality with my participants. Building on Patai (1991) and the Personal Narratives Group (1989) among others, Conway (1996) points out that the social relations of unequal material privilege that often regulate the relations between the researcher and researchee ensure that it is the privileged researcher who benefits most from research, through career-building and academic achievement (Conway, 1996, 72–73). Throughout the interview process, I was cognizant that there was a power differential between the participants and myself as the researcher, and that I would reap immediate material benefits from the study, in that it would help in the completion of my doctorate at a First World university, which in turn would give me more access to knowledge production in my area of research.

But despite the power differential embedded in researcher-researchee relations, at times a mutual learning relationship developed between the researcher—me—and the women because of our similarities. I found the interview process enlightening: I was surprised at the different positions that my participants took on native-non-native speaker issues; and these different positions, analyses, and interpretations made me rethink my own understanding of the significance of the native speaker in ESL, what a native speaker symbolizes to minority women teachers, and what constitutes resistance to inequities in ESL. These varying positions made me realize that despite our similarities, my participants and I had different interpretations of native-non-native speaker issues. It was possible for these differences to be aired only because of the relative equality between my participants and me. Although the participants did not get the immediate tangible rewards from the study that I did, it seems that their work felt the effect of the research experience (see Patai, 1991). Some of my participants informed me that they had so far not given much thought to terms and concepts such as first language, mother tongue, native speaker, accent, Canadian; that their TESL training had not troubled these terms at all; and that the interview process was a catalyst in their problematizing these concepts, which in turn would inform their pedagogies.

Sharing the Narratives

Feminists are bringing issues of exploitation of participants to the forefront of academic discussion (Gluck and Patai, 1991; Lather, 1991; Oakley, 1981). I have stated that there was relative equality between my participants and me. However, I was conscious that as the researcher, one associated with a university, I had the power to decide what to use of the interviews. I kept in mind Oakley's (1981) caution that we should look at our participants not as data but as participants, and be self-conscious about how we use the information that they have given us about themselves (46–58), information which might make their identities obvious to readers and thus be potentially harmful to their careers. The participants were therefore informed in a clearly written letter about the objectives and parameters of the study, and were told that they could withdraw from the study after seeing the transcripts of their interviews. I was mindful not to run with the data, not to take the steamship home (Patai, 1991). Once I had transcribed the transcripts in full, I tried to mitigate the power differential at this stage of the process by inviting my participants to look at the transcripts and to correct and delete any information that they did not want to be made public. Several of the participants chose to carefully go over the transcripts and made minor corrections. One participant was horrified when she read the transcript of her interview. Although she did not deny saying what was in the transcript (the interview was tape recorded and transcribed in full), she felt that she had revealed too many details and these should be removed as she felt she would be identified and this might adversely affect her career. She deleted large amounts of material from the transcribed copy of her interview and left approximately 30 pages of material from the original transcribed copy of 70 typed pages.

While I was anxious to lessen the power that I had as the researcher who would finally choose which aspects of the narratives to present in my thesis, I was also mindful that my participants had classes to teach, lessons to prepare, and parental responsibilities (all the participants had children) and might not want an extra burden; hence I did not make it a condition of their participation that they had to go over their transcripts. Here, I took my lead from Gluck and Patai (1991), who observe that despite feminist desires for methodology that attempts to share power between the researcher and her subjects, researchers should also guard against burdening participants with what might be the researcher's desire for affirmation (92). Hence, after a great deal of self-reflection, I decided not to send the subjects copies of my analyses of their interviews. At face level, this does not seem like anti-racist or feminist methodology, but this was a carefully thought-out decision and was based on two related but separate moments. First, for an earlier study that I conducted in 1994 with a smaller group of ESL teachers, I sent copies of my analyses to the participants and requested their feedback. I did not hear back from any of the participants. Second, I have been a participant in a few studies where I felt that it was important that the voices of women of color be heard, and hence, despite the pressures of graduate school and responsibilities involved with child rearing and mothering, I agreed to be a participant. However, in one such study, the researcher, a white anti-racist feminist activist, came back to me several times for feedback on her analyses. I respected her desire to not misinterpret my words and not misrepresent my narrative, but the study became a burden for me. For these two reasons, I decided not to send the subjects copies of my analyses of their interviews. As mentioned before, some of the participants were new immigrants and thus going through time-consuming and emotionally difficult immigration-related experiences. For example, Tasneem's husband was still living in Saudi Arabia and she had to settle her son and herself without her husband's help. She was teaching a few hours of ESL and also looking for more work. She was also involved in her son's school. Violet was devoting a great deal of time to getting her degrees from Jamaica recognized, and to settling her children at school and in their new neighborhood. All the participants were mothers and hence had mothering responsibilities in addition to their paid ESL work.

Concluding Remarks

I have in this chapter explored the challenges of conducting anti-racist feminist research in applied linguistics, a field that continues to be dominated by colonialist ideologies of white native speakers as "owning" English, ideologies that construct visible minority women and men from the Third World living in the First World as speakers of non-standard English. Despite challenges by critical non-white scholars and a few white scholars, the concepts and ideologies epitomized by these binary divisions continue to circulate in ELT, and intersect with racism and sexism to produce non-white immigrant women as permanent Others. I have posited that the native-speaker concept is a gendered phenomenon in the context of Canada, as the majority of ESL teachers in government-funded programs are women, and the native-speaker concept affects the material lives of minority women teaching in these programs.

What are the methodological implications of my study? Here I turn to Dei (1996), who says that one of the collective responsibilities of anti-racism activists "is the engagement in political action to address questions of social inequality" (123). Dei adds that the responsibility in the struggle for justice and equality is different for those who wield power and those who are subordinated. Those who wield power should use their power to address domination and injustice, while those who have less power "have a duty to resist their domination and to demand that responsibilities be fulfilled" (123). First World linguists, minority ESL teachers (the participants in my study), and I, the researcher, are situated differentially along the continuum of power. I will look at the responsibilities of these three different agents in the struggle for justice.

The professional organization, Teachers of English to Speakers of Other Languages (TESOL), which is dominated by First World scholars, should first, actively dismantle the native speaker-non-native speaker dichotomy as it is perpetuating a caste system among speakers of English. Second, like Kachru (1992), I consider the Quirk-like stance that dominates ELT and dismisses acceptance of non-native Englishes (see Quirk, 1990) to be misguided and unrealistic as it ignores the reality of world Englishes; with Kachru, I ask for a dialogue on world Englishes. I see TESOL's role in such an initiative to ensure that the unequal power relations between the First World and the Third World, which are a big factor in the stigmatization of Third World Englishes, are not reproduced.

Minority immigrant women ESL teachers have much less power than white linguists in our society; hence, to use Dei's framework, they have a duty to resist their domination. How can they do that? The narratives of the participants in my study indicated that they set up a counter-discursive paradigm in their classrooms that decentered the native speaker of English, and that they were more successful in their teaching when they foregrounded their non-native speaker status rather than following the native-speaker norm. As a minority immigrant woman with an accent that identifies me as having a Third World homeland, I am subordinated in this society by nativist discourses that construct me as Other. However, I consider myself to wield power in that I have access to a white academy, and through this white academy I have access to knowledge production. As an anti-racist activist and researcher, I have a political responsibility to rupture imperial knowledges in applied linguistics and in the teaching of ESL. To cite Dei (1996) again, we anti-racist workers are engaged in a "political and academic task to produce, interrogate, validate and disseminate alternative and sometimes oppositional forms of knowledge" (124). Throughout my doctoral program, and now as a university teacher, I have used this position of power to produce and disseminate counter-hegemonic and anti-imperialist knowledges on the challenges minority immigrant women ESL teachers face along the axes of race, gender, non-native speaker status, and non-standard accent. As an anti-racist researcher, I consider that I have a social responsibility to make public the multifarious ways in which minority women teachers offer resistance to practices of domination. The narratives of the participants in my study are narratives of resistance, of counter-hegemonic knowledges and paradigms; they thus rupture imperialist and colonialist knowledges on minority immigrant women and are a major initiative toward decolonizing the academy.

REFERENCES

Amin, N. 1994. Minority Women Teachers on Ownership of English. Unpublished master's. Ontario Institute for Studies in Education of the University of Toronto, Toronto.

Amin, N. 1997. "Race and the Identity of the Nonnative ESL Teacher." *TESOL Quarterly 31*, 580–583.

Amin, N. 2000. *Negotiating Nativism: Minority Immigrant Women ESL Teachers and the Native Speaker Construct.* Unpublished doctoral dissertation, Ontario Institute for Studies in Education of the University of Toronto, Toronto.

Anderson, G. 1989. "Critical ethnography in education: Origins, current status, and new directions." *Review of Educational Research, 59*(3), 249–270.

Anderson, J., and Lynam, J. 1987. "The Meaning of Work for Immigrant Women in the Lower Echelons of the Canadian Labour Force." *Canadian Ethnic Studies, 19*(2), 67–90.

Bogdan, R. C., and Biklen, S. K. 1992. *Qualitative Research for Education: An Introduction to Theory and Methods* (2nd ed.). Boston: Allyn & Bacon.

Bolaria, S., & Li, P. (Eds.). 1988. *Racial oppression in Canada*. Toronto: Garamond.

Brah, A. 1996. *Cartographies of Diaspora: Contesting Identities*. London & New York: Routledge.

Braine, G. 1999. "From the Periphery to the Center: One teacher's journey." In G. Braine (Ed.), *Non-native Educators in English Language Teaching*. Mahwah, NJ: Erlbaum, pp. 15–27.

Brutt-Griffler, J., and Samimy, K. 1999. "Revisiting the Colonial in the Postcolonial. Critical Praxis for Nonnative-English-Speaking Teachers in a TESOL Program." *TESOL Quarterly 33*, 413–431.

Cameron, A. 1990. "The Operative Principle Is First." In L. Scheier (Ed.), *Language in Her Eye* Toronto: Coach House Press, pp. 64–71.

Cameron, D. 1992. "Respect, Please! Investigating Race, Power, and Language." In D. Cameron, et al. (Eds.), *Researching Language: Issues of power and Method*. London: Routledge.

Canagarajah, S. 1999. "Interrogating the 'Native-Speaker Fallacy': Non-Linguistic Roots, Non-Pedagogical Results." In G. Braine (Ed.), *Non-native Educators in English Language Teaching*. Mahwah, NJ: Erlbaum, pp. 72–92.

Connolly, P. 1992. "Playing It by the Rules: The Politics of Research in 'Race' and Education." *British Educational Research Journal 18*(2): 133–154.

Conway, S. 1996. *The Experiences and Perspectives of Single Mother Students in University: Stories Lives Tell from the Margins*. Unpublished master's dissertation, Ontario Institute for Studies in Education of the University of Toronto, Toronto.

Dei, G. 1996. *Anti-racism Education: Theory and Practice*. Halifax: Fernwood.

Dissanayake, W. (1993). Perspective 1. *World Englishes 12*, 336–341.

Essed, P. 1987. *Academic Racism: Common Sense in the Social Sciences*. (CRES Publications, no. 5) Universiteit van Amsterdam: Centrum voor Etnische Studies.

Essed, P. 1991. *Understanding Everyday Racism: An Interdisciplinary Approach*. Newbury Park, CA: Sage Publications.

Fairman, T. 1986, July. "Prestige, Purity, and Power." *English Today 7*, 13–16.

Frankenberg, R. 1993. *White Women, Race Matters: The Social Construction of Whiteness*. Minneapolis: University of Minnesota Press.

Gluck, S., and Patai, D. (Eds.). 1991. *Women's Words: The Feminist Practice of Oral History*. New York: Routledge.

Goldstein, T. 1991. *Immigrants in the Multicultural/Multilingual Workplace: Ways of Communicating and Experience at Work*. Unpublished doctoral dissertation, Ontario Institute for Studies in Education of the University of Toronto, Toronto.

Goldstein, T. 1994. "We Are All Sisters." *TESL Canada Journal 11*(2); 30–45.

Haraway, D. 1988. "Situated Knowledges: The Science Question in Feminism and the Privilege of Partial Perspective." *Feminist Studies, 14*(3): 575–599.

hooks, b. 1991. *Yearning, Race, Gender, and Cultural Politics*. Boston: South End Press.

hooks, b. 1994. *Teaching to Transgress*. New York: Routledge.

Kachru, B. B. 1986. "The Power and Politics of English." *World Englishes 5*, 121–140.

Kachru, B. B. 1990. *The Alchemy of English: The Spread, Functions and Models of Non-native Englishes* (2nd ed.). Oxford: Pergamon.

Kachru, B. B. 1991. "Liberation Linguistics and the Quirk Concern." *English Today 25*, 3–13.

Kachru, B. B. (Ed.). 1992. *The Other Tongue: English across Cultures* (2nd ed.). Urbana: University of Illinois Press.

Kachru, B. B. 1997. "English as an Asian Language." In M. L. S. Bautista (Ed.), *English Is an Asian Language: The Philippine context* (pp. 1–23). Manila, Philippines: Macquarie Library.

Kachru, Y. 1994. "Monolingual Bias in SLA Research." *TESOL Quarterly 28*, 795–800.

Kirby, S., and McKenna, K. (1989). *Experience, Research, Social Change*. Toronto: Garamond.

Lather, P. 1991. *Getting Smart: Feminist Research and Pedagogy with/in the Postmodern*. New York: Routledge.

Leung, C., Harris, R., and Rampton, B. 1997. "The Idealised Native Speaker, Reified Ethnicities and Classroom Realities." *TESOL Quarterly 31*, 543–560.

Lippi-Green, R. 1997. *English with an Accent: Language, Ideology, and Discrimination in the United States*. London: Routledge.

Liu, D. 1999. "Training Non-native TESOL Students: Challenges for TESOL Teacher Education in the West." In G. Braine (Ed.), *Non-native Educators in English Language Teaching*. Mahwah, NJ: Erlbaum, pp. 197–210.

Liu, J. 1999. "From Their Own Perspectives: The Impact of Non-native Professionals on Their Students." In G. Braine (Ed.), *Non-native educators in English Language Teaching*. Mahwah, NJ: Erlbaum, pp. 159–176.

Lowenberg, P. 1992. "Testing English as a world language: Issues in assessing non-native proficiency." In B. B. Kachru (Ed.), *The Other Tongue: English across Cultures* (2nd ed.) Urbana: University of Illinois Press, pp. 108–121.

Maguire, P. 1987. *Doing Participatory Research: A Feminist Approach*. Massachusetts: Center for International Education.

Matsuda, M. 1991. "Voices of America: Accent, Antidiscrimination, Law, and a Jurisprudence for the Last Reconstruction." *The Yale Law Journal 100*, 1329–1407.

McCarthy, C., and Crichlow, W. 1993. "Introduction." In C. McCarthy & W. Crichlow (Eds.), *Race, Identity, and Representation in Education*. New York: Routledge, pp. xiii–xxix.

Miles, R. 1989. *Racism*. London: Routledge.

Miles, R. 1993. *Racism after 'Race Relations'*. London: Routledge.

Nayar, P. B. 1994. Whose English Is It? *TESL-EJ 1*(1), F-1. [Online serial]. URL http://berkeley.edu/-cwp.

Nestel, S. 1996. "Immigration, Proletarianization, and Racialization: Constructing the Nursing Labor Force in Ontario." Unpublished research paper, Ontario Institute for Studies in Education of the University of Toronto, Toronto.

Ng, R. 1981. "Constituting Ethnic Phenomenon: An Account from the Perspective of Immigrant Women." *Canadian Ethnic Studies 13*(1): 97–107.

Ng, R. 1990. "Racism, Sexism, and Visible Minority Immigrant Women in Canada." In *Zeitschrift der Gesellschaft fuer Kanadastudien. 10 Jahrgang, Nr. 2* (pp. 21–34). Neumuenster, Germany: Karl Wachholtz Verlag.

Norton, B. 1997. "Language, Identity, and the Ownership of English." *TESOL Quarterly 31*, 409–429.

Oakley, A. 1981. "Interviewing Women: A Contradiction in Terms." In H. Roberts (Ed.), *Doing Feminist Research*. London: Routledge & Kegan Paul, pp. 30–61.

Paikeday, T. 1985. *The Native Speaker Is Dead*. Toronto: Paikeday Publishing.

Patai, D. 1991. "U. S. Academics and Third World Women. Is Ethical Research Possible?" In S. Gluck and D. Patai (Eds.), *Women's words: The Feminist Practice of Oral History*. New York: Routledge, pp. 137–153.

Peirce, B. N. 1993. *Language Learning, Social Identity, and Immigrant Women*. Unpublished doctoral dissertation, Ontario Institute for Studies in Education of the University of Toronto, Toronto.

Peirce, B. N. 1995. "Social Identity, Investment, and Language Learning." *TESOL Quarterly 29*, 9–31.

Pennycook, A. 1992. *The Cultural Politics of Teaching English in the World*. Unpublished doctoral dissertation, Ontario Institute for Studies in Education of the University of Toronto, Toronto.

Personal Narratives Group. 1989. *Interpreting Women's Lives: Feminist Theory and Personal Narratives*. Bloomington: Indiana University Press.

Phillipson, R. 1992. *Linguistic imperialism*. Oxford: Oxford University Press.

Power Analysis. 1998. *Study of ESL/EFL Services in Ontario*. Toronto: Power Analysis, Inc.

Quirk, R. 1990. "Language Varieties and Standard Language." *English Today 21*, 3–10.

Rampton, B. 1990. "Displacing the 'Native Speaker': Expertise, Affiliation, and Inheritance." *ELT Journal 44*, 97–101.

Rockhill, K., and Tomic, P. 1995. "Situating ESL between Speech and Silence." In J. Gaskell and J. Willinsky (Eds.), *Gender in/forms curriculum: From enrichment to transformation*. New York: Teachers College Press, pp. 209–229.

Samimy, K., and Brutt-Griffler, J. 1999. "To Be a Native or Non-native Speaker: Perceptions of 'Non-native' Students in a Graduate TESOL Program." In G. Braine (Ed.), *Non-native educators in English language teaching*. Mahwah, NJ: Erlbaum, pp. 127–144.

Sheper-Hughes, N. 1992. *Death without Weeping: The Violence of Everyday Life in Brazil*. Berkeley: University of California Press.

Simon, R., and Dippo, D. (1986). "On Critical Ethnographic Work." *Anthropology and Educational Quarterly 17*, 195–202.

Spivak, G. C. 1987. *In Other Worlds: Essays in Cultural Politics*. New York: Methuen.

Sridhar, S. N. 1994. "A Reality Check for SLA Theories." *TESOL Quarterly 28*, 800–805.

Sridhar, K., and Sridhar, S. N. 1992. "Bridging the Paradigm Gap: Second-Language Acquisition Theory and Indigenized Varieties of English." In B. B. Kachru (Ed.), *The other tongue: English across cultures* (2nd ed. Urbana: University of Illinois Press, pp. 91–107.

Tollefson, J. W. 1991. *Planning Language, Planning Inequality*. New York: Longman.

Chapter Ten

JUDY HUGHES

Analyzing Women's Experiences

RACE,
SOCIAL DIFFERENCE,
AND VIOLENCE
AGAINST WOMEN

Pursuing anti-racist research is not about collecting information on race. It is an expressly political project aimed at creating knowledge about the social relations and practices of domination, white supremacy, and exploitation for the purposes of challenging and changing these systems. This project demands as much from the experience of the researcher as it does from the experience of the researched. Throughout this paper, I will suggest that individual identity and the social differences rooted in these identities are centrally important to understanding and explaining women's experiences of oppression and marginalization. In suggesting this approach, I have created a difficult and challenging role for myself as a translator of other women's experiences, as a navigator of multiple and complex social differences, and as a self-proclaimed authority on what is/will be considered important and researchable from women's lives and experiences. This will be an especially challenging experience as I come to this research from a dominant and privileged position as a white, English-speaking, Western woman.

This chapter represents my attempt to understand and clarify the role of race and social difference as I research, theorize, and write about issues related to violence against women. I come to researching violence in women's lives as a former counsellor and advocate for abused women. Pursuing research in this area allows me to continue to be an advocate and to maintain my personal commitment toward eliminating violence in women's lives. Entering with this agenda is exhilarating in that it provides me with the space to describe how women's experiences of violence and abuse are shaped and constrained by dominant discourses, processes, and social relations, and ultimately to create knowledge useful in changing these oppressive structures.

Beginning with this agenda is also problematic because it allows me to position myself as a savior or a more liberated champion of other women (Razack, 2000), and it requires that I navigate across difference and the different experiences of women from the position of a dominant, white researcher. In this chapter I have two goals: (1) to explore how women's differing identities of race, class, age, sexual orientation, culture, ethnicity, and class create and shape women's experiences of violence and abuse, and (2) to interrogate my own positioning as a white dominant (woman) researcher exploring the experiences of other women.

This chapter is an exploration of women's experiences of abuse and violence from their intimate partners through a feminist, anti-imperialist, discursive framework. Exploring women's experiences through a feminist lens allows me to begin with the assumption that women's lived experiences are valuable, and that grounding inquiry in these experiences leads to valuable knowledge about oppression and violence. Anti-imperialism is the recognition of the power relations of hegemonic, imperialist structures of knowledge production wherein knowledge produced about minoritized groups often results in either universalized accounts that ignore important social differences (see Mohanty, 1991) or essentialized accounts that exaggerate difference to segregate women's experiences (Essed, 1996; Razack, 2000). Maintaining a focus on race and social difference is vital to ensuring that complex analyses (not universalizing accounts) are created to describe women's experiences and vital in exposing the hegemonic, imperial systems that create difference.

Why use women's experiences of violence and abuse as a means of understanding difference? This approach is important because women's experiences of violence are shaped and created by differences based on ethnicity, race, religion, sexual orientation, level of ability/disability, culture, language, and life experience. Too often in theorizing, writing, and research on violence against women, social differences among women and the social and historical context that creates and sustains these differences are ignored in favor of distorting and imposed definitions and explanations of violence. I want to suggest here that understanding women's experiences of violence from their intimate partners requires knowing how social differences impact, shape, create, and in turn are shaped and created by, social differences among women. Individual experiences of intimate violence must be understood as being directly connected with individual identity, and must be analyzed where they intersect with identities of race, gender, sexual orientation, class, and ability/disability. These intersections must be used creatively to reflect difference, yet also used to connect social differences to the oppressive structures and social relations of privilege and subordination.

I begin by exploring the difficulties and limitations inherent in studying difference, particularly from a white, dominant position. Next, I review the literature on violence against women with the aim of exposing how inadequate conceptualizations of difference distort the understanding of women's experiences of violence and oppression. Then, I propose a process for researching women's experiences of violence in intimate relationships that seeks to avoid constructing imposing and imperial accounts of women's experiences by: (1) beginning inquiry in how women themselves understand and articulate their own experiences of intimate violence/oppression; (2) viewing women not as passive victims of violence/oppression adhering to a narrow restricted sense of self based on a feminine ideal, but as active agents able to resist instances of violence/ oppression, despite being controlled and held powerless by these same forces; (3) building analyses that expose and subvert social and cultural stereotypes of abused women (particularly stereotypes of abused women from minoritized groups), and expose and subvert the process, practices, and social relations that create and sustain these myths and stereotypes; and (4) create linkages among women's diverse experiences to suggest strategies for social change. Last, I suggest that white women locate their own sites of privilege and subordination in relation to the lives other women in order to avoid constructing imperialist accounts of other women's experiences.

White Women and the Study of Difference

Issues related to researchers' subjectivity and subject locations usually revolve around discussions of the racial or ethnic identity of the researcher and the researched and how these identities influence the ability of the researcher to gain access to study participants or the research setting (Egharevba, 2001; Rhodes, 1994) or how white, European subject locations can impact or distort research accounts (Anderson, 1993; Egharevba, 2001). Wisdom suggests that dominant researchers situate themselves in their research, but this requires more than just the articulation of a dominant subjectivity and acknowledgment of an accompanying privilege.

Boushel (2000) suggests that white researchers need to carefully consider many questions before beginning research on minoritized groups, such as who is likely to benefit from the research, what will be the advantages and disadvantages of the research for both the dominant and oppressed groups, and to whom the research will be accountable. The challenge is that the interests and purposes of dominant researchers in researching minoritized groups cannot be naively or innocently considered. Researching minoritized groups carries the danger that the information collected will not be used to disrupt dominant discourses or alter existing power relations, but will serve to further reinforce negative ideas and stereotypes. These questions suggest that in using the experiences of other women to pursue social justice and social transformation, I will need to locate my own sites of privilege and subordination so that I am accountable for the descriptions and explanations I produce about the lives of minoritized women.

As a white, Western, and heterosexual woman, I come to this research with an identity and accompanying privileges that are often invisible. The invisibility of the privilege afforded to white, Western women has allowed this group to construct understandings of women's experiences that either ignore the reality that the experiences of white, middle-class, Western women are not the universal experiences of all women (Mohanty, 1991) or attempt to simply graft the experiences of women of color or women from Third World countries onto these Eurocentric universal explanations of women's experiences (West, 1999). In both cases, the white, middle-class, First World woman remains the authorial subject within analyses of women's oppression. Such analyses do little to disrupt existing social and power relations. Indeed, these analyses can reinforce dominant stereotypes and even produce their own set of power relations. Creating disruptive analyses and knowledge requires that as dominant researchers we place ourselves in our accounts of the lives of Others and that we continually recognize the limits of what we can claim to know about the lives of those in minoritized positions.

For dominant white researchers, being accountable for the knowledges we produce requires that we produce analyses/knowledge about the lives of others that have the potential to disrupt, denaturalize, and, ultimately change dominant discourses, practices, and structures that lead to multiple forms of violence/oppression. In such analyses, difference cannot be ignored, as examining difference is important for understanding how women's experiences are created and shaped through dominant discourses and social relations. Yet, the danger is that difference will be naively conceptualized as essentialized differences that segregate women's experiences into separate categories, or that difference will be acknowledged simply as a means of taming difference, rather than as a mechanism to challenge the system of domination and subordination that creates and sustains social difference.

Conceptualizing Difference

In research and academic writing, social difference is ignored when information on race and difference is not included in research studies or resulting analyses. Difference can also be ignored through reliance on essentialized or total-itizing notions of difference, such as the universal woman in Western feminism or a Marxist homogenous working class (Rutherford a, 1990). Often, the abil-ity to ignore difference and create essentialized discourses is a function of power, as in Western feminism. Totalizing descriptions can also be created as by-products of waging battles against oppressive structures or practices where strategic essentialism is employed to privilege certain silenced or marginalized perspectives. For example, essentialized notions of the "properly white and middle-class abused woman" and the "physically beaten and battered wife" were used by the women's movement in North America to garner attention, sympathy, and funding for the issue of violence against women (Ashcroft, 2000; Lee, 2000). Phelan (1993) also describes how the construction of a nat-ural or authentic lesbian identity is a kind of strategic essentialism that is nec-essary to provide an identity with which lesbians can measure and justify their experiences as lesbians and as a place to counter arguments against heterosex-ist and homophobic constructions of lesbianism as aberrant or unnatural. Viewed in this manner, essentialism is necessary and even understandable because, as Phelan states, "when one is presented with a stigmatized identity, it makes sense to challenge the stigma surrounding that identity" (773).

Thus, strategic essentialism can be useful at times to allow silenced or mar-ginalized discourses to be heard. However, social difference must be under-stood as locations created out of subordination and prejudice and not as naturally occurring, fixed, and pre-existing spaces. Relying solely on preexist-ing categories of social difference is simply a containment of difference as it leads either to the notion of fixed, bounded categories of differences of race, class, and sex, which ignore the rich complexity of differences within each of these categories; or this leads to the flawed understanding that different forms of oppression are separate from one another and can therefore be arranged hier-archically in relation to one another (i.e., black women are more oppressed than white women, black lesbians more oppressed than both black women and white women, and so on) (Rutherford a, 1990). Put another way, although we can-not rely on ready-made categories or identities that we can slip into or use to understand difference in others and ourselves, we need not abandon categories completely, but use them strategically and maintain "caution and humility in their use" (Phelan, 1993, 799).

Another means of conceptualizing difference is by replacing it with diver-sity and engaging in a celebration that reduces differences to those of a cultur-al or ethnic nature, and focusing on differences in food, clothing/dress, holidays, and traditions. Here, difference is acknowledged through the cele-bration of diversity, but with the ultimate effect of containing and trivializing difference. Acknowledging difference through the celebration of diversity is not useful as an antiracist approach to research because the focus on cultural differences ignores the existence of multiple oppressions and works to hide the system of domination and privilege that creates and defines cultural differences. Further, a view of culture is created that ignores how cultures are formed and managed in the Canadian context through the manufacture of traditional, time-bound cultures. Minoritized cultures are only tolerated as long as they maintain this status as traditional entities and do not challenge the authority/superiority of the dominant culture (Bannerji, 2000). Acknowledging difference in this manner does not create understandings of difference that challenge racist and other oppressive practices; rather the celebration of diversity only masks Eurocentric norms, values, and interests (Bhabha as cited in Rutherford, 1990 b).

To be useful as a tool for challenging dominant power relations, difference must not be ignored, tamed, essentialized, or understood as a way to segregate; difference should be employed as a creative means to challenge and change the social relations that create privilege and dominance for some and subordination and repression for others. Viewed in this way, social difference is a means to uncover and interrogate what is taken for granted or considered natural and as a means to challenge what is regarded as other or different. In the stratified multiracial and multiethnic context of Canadian society, any study of difference must include a focus on race as race represents the socially and historically created categories that, based largely on skin color, create and maintain privilege for some and penalty for others. To accomplish this questioning through antiracist research, the problem of difference must be recast as the problem of privilege and dominance (Brooks, 1988). A focus on race and difference within anti-racist research should be a means to expose racism, racial domination, and white supremacy (Maynard, 1994; Razack, 1998; Sypnowich, 1993; Winant, 2000).

Difference and Violence against Women

Violence is so prevalent in Canadian society that it can invade women's lives in a variety of forms, including the violence of poverty, stranger sexual assault, everyday covert and overt racist and sexist behaviors and practices, and unequal economic relations between northern and southern hemisphere countries. Here I restrict my discussion of violence to the physically, emotionally, sexually, and financially abusive behaviors directed at women by female and male partners in the context of intimate relationships, which can sometimes involve violence from caregivers and other family members, such as fathers, mother-in-laws, aunts, and brothers.

The literature on woman abuse is immense, spanning empirical research, theoretical writing, and disciplinary boundaries. Social differences among women based on ethnicity, race, religion, sexual orientation, level of ability/disability, culture, language, and life experience are rarely included or considered as important. Current debates in this literature focus either on attempts to establish underlying causes or explanations for why men abuse women (Chornesky, 2000; O'Neil, 1998; O'Neil and Harway, 1997) or attempts to better define and measure violent behaviors (DeKeseredy, 2000; Schafer, 1996). Social differences appear only as isolated discourses of violence against women in specific communities, such as Native communities (Hamby, 2000; McGillivray and Comaskey, 1999), violence in lesbian relationships (Burke and Follingstad, 1999; Carlson, 1992), or violence against so-called ethnic minority and immigrant women (Agnew, 1998; Razack, 1998).

Studying women's experience of violence without consideration of social differences among women suggests that there is a supposed norm or center (Maynard, 1994) with *difference* specified as the experiences of other women, such as black women, women of color, immigrant women, and disabled women. The resulting decontextualization and universalizing of women's experiences of violence leads to a focus on individual experiences and personality (see Chornesky, 2000; Heise, 1998; O'Neil, 1998; O'Neil and Harway, 1997), which ignores the impact of oppressive social structures and power relations embedded in racism, ableism, ageism, and so on. Gender itself has been eliminated and ignored as an important variable in some research studies as researchers attempt to be gender neutral. Women's and men's experiences of violent behaviors are then compared without reference even to the difference that gender itself makes in patriarchal/sexist contexts (see Johnson, 1995; McFarlane et al., 2000). Analyses based on socioeconomic class are also infrequently considered and, when used, often serve to pathologize the experiences of lower-income families as rates of violence in families experiencing poverty/unemployment are compared to rates in higher-income families or used as an justification or rationale for men's violence toward women (see Heise, 1998). Particularly absent in these accounts are the experiences of lesbian women, which places emphasis only on how and why men abuse women (see Carlson, 1992).

Often, information is collected on the manifestation of violent behavior in culturally or ethnically specific ways to argue for culture- or ethnic-specific services (Agnew, 1996) or to provide much needed information to white, dominant culture researchers and service providers about the values and traditions of other ethnic and cultural groups (Lee, 2000; Sorenson, 1996). Yet ignoring race in favor of ethnicity or culture leads theorizing and research away from the supposed "universal" abused woman, only to create other essentializing discourses of women's experiences. For example, Sorenson (1996) interviewed women and men from four ethnic groups (African Americans, Anglo-Americans, Asian Americans, and Mexican Americans) about their knowledge and experiences of intimate violence. Results of these interviews were grouped according to ethnicity in an attempt to examine commonalties and differences among these four ethnic groups. Although Sorenson notes the effects of racial/cultural stereotypes, the central focus remains on discussion of differences in cultural patterns of violent behaviors, and thus on the behavior of the women and men belonging to these ethnic groups. Beginning as Sorenson does with collecting information on ethnicity and violence suggests that there is something in the culture of various ethnic groups (traditions, patterns, history) that functions to erase the impact of historical and current racism and white supremacy in the lives of women experiencing abuse and violence.

Beginning with culture and ethnicity also obscures important differences among women of the same cultural or ethnic group. Agnew (1996) explains how the "invisibility of middle-class women in accounts of women from Africa, Asia, and the Caribbean reinforces the stereotype of these women as victims," rather than identifying them also as social workers, counselors, community activists, and volunteers actively struggling against racism and sexism" (103–104). Descriptions of culturally specific violence against women, without recognition of important differences among women within these ethnic categories, constructs South Asian women as passive, helpless victims of not only predominately male violence, but as cultural victims of timeless, homogenized practices and beliefs (Agnew, 1996).

Homogenized discourses on violence against "immigrant" women-largely described as women of color, non-English speaking, and lacking information on Canadian laws, values, and social programs (Agnew, 1996; Sorenson, 1996) also constructs immigrant women as almost completely helpless and even complicit in the abuse they experience from intimate partners, and ignores the historical struggles against patriarchy waged by these women in their countries of origin and within the north. Ignoring the reality that white, English-speaking women are also immigrant women, and holding the use of this term for women from particular racial and ethnic groups, reinforces dominant racist stereotypes of non-white women from so-called Third World countries. If abused, these women are then depicted as backward because of their culture or ethnicity, ignorant because of language barriers, and then further described as requiring intervention to acquaint them with more liberal, Canadian laws and values (Agnew, 1996; Razack, 1998). This focus on ethnicity and culture recreates the difficulties faced by immigrant women of color as a problem originating within ethnicity or culture, rather than "as the result of colonial and postwar economic and political policies of the north, or as a reflection of current north/south relations" (Essed, 1996, 35).

Violence against women with disabilities is rarely if ever considered within the abuse literature demonstrating a lack of social concern about the abuses experienced by these women, as though abuse against women with disabilities was quite natural and expected (Calderbank, 2000). Often, women with disabilities are described as helpless, dependent, demanding, and burdens to their caregivers, and thereby deserving of or responsible for the violence directed at them (Asch and Fine, 1995; Calderbank, 2000). Women with learning disabilities are especially susceptible to having their experiences of violence and abuse minimized or even denied (Calderbank, 2000). As with ethnicity and culture, beginning with a focus on disability suggests that there is something essential about women with disabilities that causes them to be abused, rather than focusing on ableism and social indifference as the causes of this violence.

The abused woman created through this literature is a woman who is raceless, classless, ahistorical, transgeographical, ageless, nondisabled, and of undetermined sexual orientation, whose experiences of violence can be unproblematically applied to all women (West, 1999). Although differences due to culture, class, sexual orientation, and disability are equally ignored in this literature, race tends to be especially invisible as, when it is considered, it usually refers only to the experience of black women (West, 1999) or it is ignored in favor of a focus on culture or ethnicity. Limiting discussions of race and violence against women to the experience of black women or more generally women of color, and not analyzing the experiences of white women as racialized experiences, segregates the experiences of white women and women of color, which maintains the experiences of white (mostly middle-class) women as the supposed center or norm of all abused women's experiences. Further, focusing on culture and ethnicity rather than race serves to hide how race (based mainly on skin color) and the resulting racist beliefs, practices, attitudes, and institutions shape the experiences of violence and abuse of women of color. These racist beliefs and practices create difficulties in attempting to speak about violence and abuse experienced by women of color, as speaking out can serve only to fuel dominant racist and colonial beliefs about certain racial and cultural groups (Bannerji, 2000). Focusing on race and analyzing all women's experiences of violence and abuse as racialized experiences displaces the experiences of white, middle-class women as the supposed norm of all women's experiences and reminds researchers that race and racism impact all women's experiences.

Researching Women's Experiences of Violence in Intimate Relationships

Researching women's experiences of violence and abuse requires a focus on complex differences due to gender, class, ability/disability, sexual orientation, culture, and so on, yet these differences must not be used as independent or explanatory variables in myopic searches for differences and commonalties in the experiences of different abused women, such as comparing rates of violent behavior between heterosexual and lesbian relationships (see Burke and Follingstad, 1999; Carlson, 1992) or in pointless comparisons of the experiences of different ethnic groups (see Sorenson, 1996). Whether women's experiences are collected as narratives or stories in qualitative research or collected as numbers indicating the extent or severity of violent and abusive behaviors, these experiences must be understood as connected to raced, gendered, classed, disabled identities and analyzed as they occur in particular social, historical, political, and economic contexts. Social differences can then be used as analytic tools to bring the focus not onto difference for its own sake, but to interrogate social difference created by interlocking systems of sexism, ableism, racism, ageism, and so on.

Individual Identity and Experience

Although largely ignored or negated in the dominant literature on violence, difference based on identities of race, sexual orientation, age, class, gender, and ability/disability are integral to understanding women's experiences of violent behavior as these behaviors are experienced in racist, sexist, heterosexist, and ablest social contexts. Where difference or othered identities are ignored in research studies on abuse, the social historical context wherein abuse takes place is also ignored, which creates the appearance that experiences of violence are devoid of any social, historical, or political meaning. Although abuse is experienced as deeply personal events often occurring in the woman's own home, women's personal histories and experiences of violence and abuse must be understood and analyzed as they intersect individual and collective identities of race, gender, age, ability/disability, and sexuality, and as they occur in a social context that privileges some identities and penalizes others.

Beginning with women's experiences in the intimate moments of their everyday lives provides a means to search out difference that comes closest to describing actual, lived experiences of oppression. Inherent then to each woman's description of abuse and violence are differences stemming from her own unique personal history and her subject location, representing her individual and collective identity. Narratives of violence and abuse can be read as texts that demonstrate the ways by which individual and collective identities are created, recreated, shaped, negotiated, and renegotiated in relation to the social and historically constructed forces of classism, racism, sexism, ableism, and so on. These experiences are also sites of difference within difference that disrupt essential, homogenized discourses and sites of tangible moments of resistance and agency that question and challenge generalizations based on race, class, ability/disability, and so forth.

Identities are unique to us as individuals, but identities are not fixed or frozen; rather they are created and shaped as we interact with others across multiple contexts. Identities are also about how some bodies become marked as different or other. As D'Auost (1996) describes in the following quote, unique individual identities are shaped by the power relations embedded in changing social contexts:

> I learned that no matter how I identify myself to me (a Deaf lesbian or otherwise) the names which others call me affect the way they treat me. If men think I am straight, some will probably try to pick me up; if lesbians think I am straight, they probably won't. If hearing people think I am hearing, they generally do not understand my need to lip read; if Deaf people think I am hearing, they disbelieve my Deafness because of my good speech. If people think I am white, they treat me worse or better (depending on what their map of white means). I also learned that race is really about color. If people think you don't look white, then you are not (to them) white. If they think you look white, then you are (to them) . . . I have learned to live with the mapping imposed on my experiences. (156–157)

The risk or danger of analyzing and researching women's experiences of violence through different or othered identities is that these identities are not born innocently, but are conceived through struggles and privilege (Razack, 1998). While some identities are invisible, other identities are inundated by social, cultural and racial stereotypes that name these identities as inferior and abnormal (Egharevba, 2001; Hamby, 2000; Vernon, 1999).

Although othered identities are created and shaped by the social and historical forces of racism, sexism, and ableism, these identities can also be powerful sites of resistance and agency. Conceived in this manner, subjected identities are not constructed as pathological, but can act as powerful critiques of the "cultural master narrative of normalcy, wholeness, and the feminine ideal" (Thomson, 1997, 241). Anderson (2000) describes how Native women's processes of reclaiming a Native identity challenge negative stereotypes based on racist beliefs and act as powerful moments of resistance for Native women. Similarly, O'Toole (2000) describes how lesbian women with disabilities can construct their own identities in opposition to heterosexist discourses that construct lesbian women's sexuality as deviant and ablest discourses that describe persons with disabilities as asexual. Resisting and contradicting social, cultural, and racist stereotypes requires a focus on oppressive structures and practices that impose oppressive identities onto minoritized groups, because it is the structures themselves that are oppressive and not the raced, classed, sexed, and disabled identities (Robinson, 1999).

Focusing on systems of domination and oppression that construct stereotypes exposes these stereotypes as myths and helps researchers to avoid rather than reinforce these myths. For example, black women's reluctance to contact the police when they have been abused by black male partners cannot be described as a *failure* on the part of black women to protect themselves from abuse, but rather as black women's responses to a history of slavery, racial domination, and white supremacy (West, 1999). Similarly, depiction of violence against women in Native communities should not be described in reference either to alcoholism or the intergenerational transmission of abuse and violence; rather violence in Native communities must be described as resulting from a history of abuse and stigmatization brought about by European colonization (McGillivray and Chomaskey, 1999).

Power/Resistance

Describing acts of resistance and agency against oppression and oppressive forces must be balanced with descriptions of the difficulties, challenges, and pain created by various oppressions. Otherwise, there is the danger that oppressed identities will be romanticized, and oppression will be viewed as a virtue (Sypnowich, 1993), especially by members of the dominant culture/group who read these accounts. Both Anderson and O'Toole point out the difficulty in resisting oppression and reclaiming identity because "liberation is not free. The cost of liberation is sometimes oppression in other forms. There are difficulties as well as joy" (O'Toole, 2000, 216).

Romanticizing the experiences of oppressed individuals fuels dominant narratives by suggesting that minoritized individuals and groups change themselves rather than suggesting that change be focused on societal transformation. This has often been the case for persons with disabilities, as their lives are valorized if they struggle to fit into able-bodied society. Disability as a virtue leaves the privilege of being able-bodied uninterrogated and unrecognized. Valorized descriptions of abused women as survivors are generally only constructed for women who separate from their abusive partners, but the focus on eliminating violence against women should not be on having woman after woman leave abusive partners, but in searching and eliminating the forces that create and sustain intimate violence. Even after women leave their abusive partners, difficulties, challenges, and pain remain, such as single motherhood and poverty or even increased poverty. For many women, the challenges of racism, ableism, heterosexism, ageism, and classism also remain.

Viewing difference as created through oppressive/dominant social relations and as a site of resistance to challenge dominant discourses is central for anti-racist praxis and research. Indeed, analyses of social differences that focus on the social and historical creation of difference, acknowledge the role of agency and resistance in recasting and reclaiming marginalized and different identities, and critique of the normalizing gaze and assumptions of Eurocentric thought, research, and knowledge is critical for anti-racist research.

Collective Identities

To work effectively with social difference, researchers must navigate the particularities of abused women's personal histories and experiences of violence, while maintaining a simultaneous focus on how experiences are also shaped by collective identities based on membership in minoritized groups. To recognize the particularities of women's experiences is to resist the temptation to inscribe all abused women with the same experience, and to resist the allure of taming difference through developing essentialized notions of women's experiences. Thus, complexity is necessary to adequately capture individual, particular experiences of oppression and violence, yet these unique experiences have to be envisioned as they occur within the raced, classed, sexed, and ableist social contexts that shape collective and group experiences.

Hamby (2000) presents a complex understanding and analysis of violence against Native women through examining how gender relations between women and men in distinct tribal social organizations prior to contact with white Europeans were shaped by colonial imposition, poverty due to loss of traditional lifestyle, and racism. This is not an analysis of violence that creates a homogenized, ahistorical, Native, abused woman, but an account that examines Native women's experiences of violence and abuse through analyses of patriarchy and male dominance, European colonialism, economic and class differences, and racism. Similarly, both Asch and Fine (1995) and Calderbank (2000) present complex analyses of the experiences of women with disabilities that take into account the varying influences that impact these women's experiences of abuse and violence, such as the type and extent of physical and intellectual disability, socioeconomic/class status, degree of caregiving required, and degree of personal autonomy of each individual woman.

Such accounts of violence against women are important in abandoning the notion that difference can be managed by creating fixed, knowable categories within which to fit the experiences of women (Razack, 1998). These more complex understandings also allow for the violence that is experienced by individual women and groups of women to be analyzed as a part of the context within which it occurs, and recognizes that because of existing power relations, the severity and consequences of experiencing violent behaviors in intimate relationships is different for different women.

This is not to suggest, however, that the experiences of socially, historically excluded groups should not be written and theorized as separate, essentialized experiences. West (1999) directly asserts that because of the dominance of analyses of white women's accounts of violence in the abuse literature, separate analyses of the emotional and spiritual consequences of intimate male violence for black women are necessary because of a history of slavery, domination, and racial oppression. Calderbank (2000) also clearly states that because of social indifference toward persons with disabilities, accounts of their experiences of violence and abuse are absent in research on abuse, and therefore the meaning of abuse in the lives of persons with disabilities must be examined separately. Strategically employing essentialized discourses based on the experiences of silenced and marginalized groups can create powerful political moments capable of exposing the privilege inherent in the silences (Phelan, 1993), and of creating spaces to seek justice and equity through anti-racist research.

Creating Linkages

Strategies for change must not only be inclusive of difference, but must also be accountable in recognizing how all oppressions are interlocked in social relations of privilege and subordination (Razack, 1998). Viewing oppression based on intersectionality between various oppressions creates a picture of oppression and social difference as fixed spaces or locations within oppressive and discriminatory systems, and posits an understanding of individuals as either oppressed or oppressors. Within this paradigm, oppressions are evaluated based on how far or close each is located to being white, middle-class, able-bodied, and heterosexual. Thus, individuals are assumed to be more oppressed if they hold membership in one oppressed group that intersects with membership in another oppressed group, and it is further assumed that these experiences of multiple oppression intensify the experiences and consequences of oppression and discrimination (Robinson, 1999).

Understanding oppressions as created and sustained in a complex, interlocking system of domination and subordination similarly recognizes that the consequences and severity of oppression and discrimination are different for individuals in different groups or for individuals who are multiply oppressed. However, this paradigm recognizes that the consequences of oppression are not stable or fixed depending on membership in particular groups, but rather the consequences of oppression resulting from membership in one oppressed group can be mediated by the privilege resulting from membership in another group (Robinson, 1999). This interlocking notion of oppression presents a view of oppression and discrimination as located within complex social relations that can result in privilege and subordination.

For persons with disabilities, Vernon (1999) describes how social relations of privilege and subordination shape this group's experiences of stigma and oppression, which are "modified or exacerbated depending on the presence or absence of other social identities and whether they conform to or deviate from the established and valued norm" (395). That is, all persons with disabilities share a common oppression because of being persons with disabilities in an able-bodied world. However, the stigma of having a disability can be modified or exacerbated by privilege or penalty due to gender, race, age, sexual orientation, and/or class. Analyses of experiences of violence against women must similarly locate abused women within the power relations of privilege and subordination. Abused white women are oppressed by patriarchy and sexism, but can be simultaneously privileged by race and class; abused black women experience sexism and racism, but can also be privileged by class and level of ability or disability; and abused lesbians with disabilities experience heterosexism and ableism, but may also be privileged by class or race.

Disruptive analyses that maintain this level of complexity, open up possibilities to create linkages between various oppressions. Indeed, the complexity of difference within difference and the very interlocking nature of multiple oppressions require that all oppressions and the social systems of domination, white supremacy, and exploitation that sustain these oppressions be challenged simultaneously. To work to eradicate violence against women is also to work to challenge and eradicate patriarchy, sexism, racism, ageism, classism, ableism, and heterosexism. These oppressive forces exist in the lives and experiences of all women, and certainly in the lives and experiences of all abused women, as these forces intersect women's experiences of violence. Strategies for social change must recognize and "take account of the whole oppressive structures of our society and be careful to challenge all forms of oppression wherever it is found" (Vernon, 1999, 396). Challenging all forms of oppression creates linkages between oppressions that are experienced by various groups and begins the search for common ground for social justice and strategies for social transformation.

Situating the (White Woman) Researcher

It is not enough here to stop at creating linkages between women's experiences of violence and describing how the social relations and practices of domination, white supremacy, and exploitation structure groups of women's experience in relation to other groups' experiences. As researchers and authors, as women, we need to situate ourselves in our research; state who we are and our purposes for researching the lives and experiences of other women. This is the challenge I have set for myself to engage in anti-racist research from the position of a white dominant (woman) researcher for the purpose of discovering/uncovering the practices and processes that imprison women in violent relationships, and develop knowledge that has the potential to transform these practices and processes. To accomplish this, I will need to navigate across difference and attempt to understand the experiences of other women that are quite different from my own experiences and challenge myself to see the "world through the experiences of others" (Anderson, 1993, 52).

Boushel (2000) describes the experience of researching across difference as a difficult process for dominant white researchers:

> My own experience as a White Irish woman exploring these issues suggests that the process is likely to be one of 'spiral learning,' constantly self-challenging and frequently evoking feelings of confusion, avoidance, anxiety, inadequacy and irritation, as well as more noble emotions. (85)

The confusion, anxiety, and fear produced by this process stems from the recognition that there is no firm ground or foundation on which tone can stand and claim to know and understand the experiences of all other women or even the experiences of all abused women. Even deciding to study violence in the lives of other women is problematic for researchers without personal experience of violent and abusive relationship(s) in their own lives. For instance, is it possible for researchers without experiential (lived) knowledge of intimate violence and abuse to understand the confusion, fear, and uncertainty of moving in and out of (an) abusive relationship(s)? Further, in understanding across social difference, can white women understand the experiences of racism that women of color face on a daily basis? Can heterosexual women understand lesbian women's experiences of homophobia and heterosexism? There are no places of safety because the analyses that we build of the lives and experiences of other women implicate us not only as researchers/authors, but also the racial, ethnic, cultural, disabled, and sexual groups we attempt to represent in our work. If we produce understandings that reinforce dominant oppressive stereotypes, then we do more harm than good.

For researchers in dominant positions, the task of seeing through the experiences of others requires giving up the privilege of easy knowing and taken-for-granted assumptions about others. This process of giving up privilege does not involve getting to know and understand the Other better, but is rather a process of knowing ourselves and continually interrogating how our own privilege allows us to remain silent, innocent, and invisible, never have to question (unless we choose to) the meaning of whiteness, of being heterosexual, or of being able-bodied. The self that emerges in this ongoing questioning of privilege is not silent, but rather this is a self that is aware of its own location or subjectivity in relation to others, and humble about the limitations and incompleteness of what can be known from this position (Phelan, 1993). Phelan describes this self as the "postmodern self":

> This self, aware of its own contradictory and ongoing construction, is a more humble self than that of modern theories. It knows itself to be a product as well as initiator of local politics and, thus, possessed of only incomplete knowledge. That we must act is certain; that we do so without full knowledge is equally certain. (784)

Combating violence, abuse, patriarchy, racism, sexism, homophobia, heterosexism, and ableism in women's lives requires that I seek to understand women's experiences of oppression and then act on these understandings. Being aware that I enter this work from a dominant position as a white researcher requires also that I recognize the limitations of what I can know and remain vigilant in ensuring that the analyses I produce about other women's lives and experiences disrupts, rather than reinforces, imperial hegemonic knowledge (Razack, 2000).

Conclusion

Abuse and violence are caused by and will persist within any society whose dominant social relations are based on hierarchy and dominance, and where dominant discourses and ideologies have the power to create positions of privilege and subordination based on different locations in this social hierarchy. In this paper, I have described how women's experiences of violence and abuse cannot be understood without analyzing where these experiences intersect with identities of race, class, gender, sexual orientation, age, and ability/disability. Intersections between experience and identities of difference must be used creatively to demonstrate how the consequences and severity of oppression are different for different individuals and groups, yet maintain connections to the social relations and oppressive structures that create and sustain all oppressions. Used in this way, difference is a creative tool to resist homogenizing discourses, create linkages and common ground between oppressions, and provide strategies and opportunities for social change.

NOTE

I would like to thank Shirley Chau, Pamela James, George Dei, and an anonymous reviewer for helpful comments on earlier drafts of this chapter.

REFERENCES

Agnew, V. 1996. *Resisting Discrimination: Women from Asia, Africa, the Caribbean and the Women's Movement in Canada*. Toronto, Ontario, Canada: University of Toronto Press.

Agnew, V. 1998. "Tension in Providing Service to South Asian Victims of Wife Abuse in Toronto." *Violence against Women* 4(2): 153–179.

Anderson, K. 2000. *A Recognition of Being: Reconstructing Native Womanhood*. Toronto, Ontario: Second Story Press.

Anderson, M. L. 1993. Studying across Difference: Race, Class and Gender in Qualitative Research. In J. H. Stanfield and D. M. Rutledge (Eds.), *Race and Ethnicity in Research Methods* (pp. 39–52). Newbury Park, CA: Sage Publications.

Asch, A., and Fine, M. 1995. Beyond Pedestals: Revisiting the Lives of Women of Disabilities. In M. Fine (Ed.), *Disruptive Voices: The Possibilities of Feminist Research*. Ann Arbor, MI: University of Michigan Press.

Ashcroft, C. 2000. "Naming Knowledge: A Language for Reconstructing Domestic Violence and Systemic Gender Inequity." *Women and Language XXIII*(1): 3–10.

Bannerji, H. 2000. *The Dark Side of the Nation: Essays, on Multiculturalism, Nationalism, and Gender*. Toronto, Ontario, Canada: Canadian Scholars' Press Inc.

Boushel, M. 2000. "What Kind of People Are We? 'Race,' Anti-racism and Social Welfare Research." *British Journal of Social Work 30*, 71–89.

Brooks, G. 1988. Now You See Her, Now You Don't. In E. Spelman (Ed.), *Inessential Woman: Problems of Exclusion in Feminist Thought*. Boston, MA: Beacon Press, pp. 160–167.

Burke, L. K., and Follingstad, D. R. 1999. "Violence in Lesbian and Gay Relationships: Theory, Prevalence and Correlational Factors." *Clinical Psychology Review 19*(5), 487–512.

Calderbank, R. 2000. "Abuse and Disabled People: Vulnerability or Social Indifference." *Disability & Society 15*(3): 521–534.

Carlson, B. 1992. "Questioning the Party Line on Family Violence." *AFFLIA: Journal of Women and Social Work 7*(2): 94–110.

Chornesky, A. 2000. "The Dynamics of Battering Revisited." *AFFLIA: Journal of Women and Social Work 15*(4): 480–501.

D'Aoust, V. 1996. Which Map Is Not Whose Territory? In S. Tremain (Ed.), *Pushing the Limits: Disabled Dikes Produce Culture*. Toronto, Ontario, Canada: Women's Press, pp. 172–187.

DeKeseredy, W. S. 2000. "Current Controversies on Defining Nonlethal Violence Against Women in Intimate Heterosexual Relationships." *Violence against Women 6*(7): 728–746.

Egharevba, I. 2001. "Researching An-'other' Minority Ethnic Community: Reflections of a Black Female Researcher on the Intersections of Race, Gender and Other Power Positions on the Research Process." *International Journal of Social Research Methodology 4*(3): 225–241.

Essed, P. 1996. *Diversity, Gender, Color and Culture* (I. Orlow-Kein, Trans.). Amherst, MA: University of Massachusetts Press. (Original work published in 1994.)

Hamby, S. 2000. "The Importance of Community in a Feminist Analysis of Domestic Violence among American Indians." *American Journal of Community Psychology* 28(5): 649–669.

Heise, L. L. 1998. "Violence against Women: An Integrated Ecological Framework." *Violence against Women* 4(3): 262–290.

Johnson, M. P. 1995. "Patriarchal Terrorism and Common Couple Violence: Two Forms of Violence against Women." *Journal of Marriage and the Family* 57(2): 257–295.

Lee, M. Y. 2000. "Understanding Chinese Battered Women in North America: A Review of the Literature and Practice Implication." *Journal of Multicultural Social Work* 8(3/4): 215–241.

Maynard, M. 1994. The Dynamics of 'Race,' Gender and the Concept of 'Difference' in Feminist Thought. In H. Afshar and M. Maynard (Eds.), *The Dynamics of 'Race' and Gender: Some Feminist Interventions*. Bristol, PA: Taylor & Francis, pp. 9–25.

McFarlane, J., Willson, P., Malecha, A., and Lemmey, D. 2000. "Intimate Partner Violence: A Gender Comparison." *Journal of Interpersonal Violence* 15(2): 158–169.

McGillivray, A., and Comaskey, B. 1999. *Black Eyes All of the Time: Intimate Violence, Aboriginal Women, and the Justice System*. Toronto, Ontario, Canada: University of Toronto Press.

Mohanty, C. T. 1991. Under Western eyes: Feminist Scholarship and Colonial Discourses. In C. T. Mohanty, A. Russo, and L. Torres (Eds.), *Third World Women and the Politics of Feminism*. Bloomington, IN: Indiana University Press, pp. 51–77.

O'Neil, D. 1998. "A Post-Structural Review of the Theoretical Literature surrounding Wife Abuse." *Violence against Women* 4(4): 457–490.

O'Neil, J., and Harway, M. 1997. "A Multivariate Model Explaining Men's Violence toward Women: Predisposing and Triggering Hypothesis." *Violence against Women* 3(2), 182–203.

O'Toole, C. J. 2000. "The View from Below: Developing a Knowledge Base about an Unknown Population." *Sexuality & Disability* 18(3): 207–224.

Phelan, S. 1993. "(Be)coming Out: Lesbian Identity and Politics." *SIGNS* 18(4): 765–790.

Razack, S. 1998. *Looking White People in the Eye*. Toronto, Ontario, Canada: University of Toronto Press.

Razack, S. 2000. Your Place or Mine? Transnational Feminist Collaboration. In A. Calliste and G. J. S. Dei (Eds.), *Anti-racist feminism: Critical race and gender studies*. Halifax, Nova Scotia: Fernwood Publishing, pp. 39–53.

Rhodes, P. J. 1994. "Race-of-interviewer Effects: A Brief Comment." *Journal of Sociology* 28(2): 547–558.

Robinson, T. L. 1999. "The Intersections of Dominant Discourses across Race, Gender, and Other Identities." *Journal of Counseling & Development* 77, 73–79.

Rutherford, J. 1990a. A Place Called Home: Identity and the Cultural Politics of Difference. In J. Rutherford (Ed.), *Identity: Community, culture, and difference*. London, England: Lawrence & Wishart Limited, pp. 9–27.

Rutherford, J. 1990b. The Third Space: Interview with Homi Bhabha. In J. Rutherford (Ed.). *Identity: Community, culture, and difference*. London, England: Lawrence & Wishart Limited, pp. 207–221.

Schafer, J. 1996. "Measuring Spousal Violence with the Conflict Tactics Scale: Notes on Reliability and Validity Issues." *Journal of Interpersonal Violence* 11(4): 572ff.

Sorenson, S. B. 1996. "Violence against Women: Examining Ethnic Differences and Commonalties." *Evaluation Review* 20(2): 123–145.

Sypnowich, C. 1993. "Some Disquiet about 'Difference'." *Praxis International* 13(2): 99–112.

Thomson, R. G. 1997. Disabled Women as Powerful Women in Petry, Morrison, and Lorde: Revising Black Female Subjectivity. In D. T. Mitchell and S. L. Snyder (Eds.), *The Body and Physical Difference: Discourses of Disability.* Ann Arbor, MI: University of Michigan Press, pp. 240–266.

Vernon, A. 1999. "The Dialectics of Multiple Identities and the Disabled People's Movement," *Disability & Society 14* (3). 385–398.

West, T. C. 1999. *Wounds of the Spirit: Black Women, Violence and the Resistance Ethics.* New York: New York University Press.

Winant, H. 2000. "Race and Race Theory." *Annual Review of Sociology 26,* 169–185.

Chapter Eleven

SAMINA JAMAL

Critical Ethnography

AN EFFECTIVE WAY TO CONDUCT ANTI-RACISM RESEARCH

Introduction

In this chapter, I attempt to examine the various approaches of conducting anti-racism research. The article takes note of the decline of positivism in social science research and the increasing popularity of qualitative research, one example of which is critical ethnography. I feel the success of critical ethnography as a qualitative research methodology can be attributed to the fact that it takes into account the diversity and individuality of human nature. In this article I also attempt to highlight the importance of disclosing the researcher's positionality to reduce (if not entirely eliminate) the biases and his or her own prejudices, which is done in order to add greater reliability, authenticity, and credibility to a study. The positionality of the authors as to who they are and where they are coming from, is a very important consideration. According to Andrew Gitlin and Robyn Russel (1994, 181) "[V]alidity and reliability are the criteria that set the standards on which research is judged." An example that comes to mind is that of the authors of *The Feminist Classroom*, Maher and Tetreault (1997), who had originally organized their data around four themes: mastery, voice, authority, and positionality. The authors reanalyzed their data and discovered that their positionality was of utmost importance in understanding their own whiteness. They sought to acknowledge and fully understand their own positions as white researchers and interrogate their social position of privilege in comparison to their subject, which in some ways made them oppressors as well as allies. This chapter examines various approaches to conducting anti-racism research.

Philosophical Context

It is my belief that in spite of the great strides that anti-racism policies have made over the last few decades, the issue of race continues to impact on an individual's educational opportunities and life chances. Differences in class, gender, and sexuality also continue to affect our academic and occupational opportunities, as well as our social mobility.

An increased awareness regarding all such differences allows us to more critically analyze the different ways in which policy makers in the field of education truly understand the impact of these factors on the process and outcomes of education for the young. Such awareness would represent a big step forward in the area of social change. More specifically, an anti-racist approach, whether confined to the educational sector or across the broader social environment should highlight rather than underestimate or deny the impact of such differences.

According to David Corson, in his book entitled *Language, Diversity and Education* (2000), human science disciplines have, over the years, undergone a significant transformation, taking into account increasingly divergent views concerning social life. Corson further points out that positivism was based on the belief that human actions are predictable rather than random; the implication being that the knowledge one gains in studying human actions in one culture can be transported to other cultures as well a principle that continues to be upheld in much current research. The author also notes the following limitations of positivism: (1) the different ways in which people's minds work were not adequately taken into account by positivist social scientists in their theories, and (2) the role played by meaning and interpretation was not sufficiently respected.

I agree with Corson and argue that the positivist's philosophical view that reality consists essentially in what is available to the senses, is flawed. In my view, this is only a part of the bigger picture because reality also depends on values, beliefs, and language all of which vary from people to people and from culture to culture. In short, the positivist view fails to take into account such diversity, which is clearly a social reality.

When Burrell and Morgan (1979) examine the philosophical assumptions that are the basis of various approaches to social science, they developed four sets of assumptions related to ontology, epistemology, human nature, and methodology. Ontological assumptions are about the very essence of the phenomena being investigated. The question before social scientists is whether the reality being investigated is external to the individuals or the product of an individual's consciousness. The second set of assumptions is epistemological in nature. These are assumptions concerned with the form of knowledge that can be obtained and how true and false can be sorted out. The third set of assumptions concerns human nature and the relationship between humans and their environment. The two conflicting views are that on one extreme, human beings and their experiences are the products of the environment, while on the other, they have a more creative role when men have choices and are free to create and control their environment. These assumptions result in different methodologies. Social scientists who consider the social world as a hard objective reality will probably focus on analyzing relationships and regularities; they will search for universal laws that can explain and govern the reality being observed. Social scientists who stress the subjective experience of individuals as being paramount have a totally different approach. Their main concern is to develop an understanding of how an individual creates, modifies, and interprets the world. Burrel and Morgan's analysis differentiates the two opposing views as voluntarism/determinist and radical change/status quo, which can also be called sociology of regulation or sociology of change. Voluntarism implies that the individual or agency has control over his environment and life chances, as opposed to determinism, which gives all powers to the external world. The concept of status quo implies that society is a joint creation for the overall good of the majority, and is inherently created to continue smoothly for the benefit of all. Radical change implies that society is a forced creation, made on the basis of coercion, and that change for the better requires radical change. Anti-racism research creates awareness in the consciousness and mind of people about their marginalized conditions, implying that there should be a radical change for the better.

Race, Ethnicity, Privilege, and Anti-racism

According to Dei and James (1998), the race of a person constitutes a defining principal of identification and identity formation. They argue that identity cannot be defined in isolation because it is relational, and that identity acquires its meaning from both what it is and from what it is not. They contend that to create an identity, one must be perceived as identifiable, or must be identified with someone else. Hence, according to these authors, identity constitutes a marker of difference and differentiation among individuals and groups. They further note that racial identities are important in the fight against educational and social injustice. For example, a look at Toronto today shows how the city has been divided into zones based on racial and ethnic identities. This is because the minorities are becoming aware that while difference can be cause of interest to those who want to experience other cultures through ethnic food or ethnic music, it can also be a cause of discrimination against those who are different from the majority. This grouping together on the basis of racial and ethnic identification is an attempt on the part of minorities to empower themselves and give special privileges to those belonging to a particular group because of their ethnic and cultural similarities.

To view a fuller picture of what racism is all about, one must first understand the concept of privilege and all that it implies. *Privilege* is defined in the *American Heritage Dictionary of the English Language* as a "special advantage, immunity, permission, right or benefit granted to or enjoyed by an individual, class or caste." By extension, one understands that race is also related to privilege.

According to Lopez (1995)

> The characteristics of our hair, complexion, and facial features still influence whether we are figuratively free or enslaved. Race dominates our personal lives. It maintains itself in our speech, dance, neighbors, and friends?our very ways of talking, walking, eating and dreaming are ineluctably shaped by notions of race. (192)

It is a fact of life that our race has an impact on nearly every facet of our lives, influencing our economic prospects and careers. The race-conscious market screens and selects us based on the particular stereotypes we are identified with. Racism poisons the atmosphere of trust that one needs in order to live in peace and harmony.

According to Claudia Card (1999)

> If "race" may have internal, external, and interactive aspects, "racism" suggests first and foremost a negative external view, that is, a negative view held toward members of another group. Like "sexism," "racism" refers to oppressive behaviors, policies, and attitudes ranging from institutional murder to unwitting support of insensitive practices by the well intentioned. (258)

Here it is important to differentiate between race and ethnicity. Although these concepts are closely linked, they carry different shades of meaning. While one's ethnicity is often considered to be something positive, one's race arouses suspicion. While both terms suggest birthplace and birthright, the term *ethnic* usually suggests geographic origin, whereas the term *race* suggests a biological inheritance.

According to James (1999), "[T]he terms ethnic population, ethnic food and ethnic music are used often. In some cases, ethnic is used to describe Italians, Portuguese, Ukrainians and others. It is also used as stereotype. The term ethnic is sometimes used interchangeably with race and immigrant and culture to try to socially define or locate people" (49).

John Stone (1995), citing Max Weber, defines ethnic groups as "human groups (other than kinship groups) which cherish a belief in their common origins of such a kind that it provides a basis for the creation of community" (396). Theodorson defines an *ethnic group* as, "[A] group with a common culture, traditions and a sense of identity which exists as a subgroup of a larger society. The members of an ethnic group differ with regard to certain cultural characteristics from the other members of their society" (cited in Isajiw, 1974, 113).

A common notion among Canadians is that ethnicity is how people choose to identify themselves, and that ethnicity is of little concern to society in general. In reality, however, ethnicity is not dependent on individual choice but is defined by society as a whole. According to James (1999), "ethnicity gives individuals a sense of identity and belonging based not only on their perception of being different, but also on the knowledge that they are recognized by others as being different" (p. 49)

According to Claudia Card (1999), "'Ethnicity,' as distinct from 'race,' suggests culture, especially folk culture. [It is] . . . produced by people who share a history that is usually tied to a geographical territory" (259).

While racism tends to be more dangerous, ethnicity can also be used as the basis of discrimination, with equally detrimental effects, engendering a sense of feeling singled out and highlighting the unfair privileges enjoyed by the dominating class but denied to the ethnic, thereby leading to social fragmentation and disharmony that can often take on dangerous turns (as we currently witness in the rise of aggressive nationalism in many parts of the world). Our history provides many examples of such racism in Canadian society and education. Deeming aboriginal culture as inferior, the early Europeans settlers made it a mission to "civilize" its members. According to Davies and Guppy (1998), "Racism has been understood historically as an attribute of individuals, a belief that people of other biological types are inferior" (p. 130).

The analysis of racism is embedded in understanding anti-racism. According to Dei (1999),

> Anti-racism . . . deals with race, difference and interlocking oppression. Thus anti-racism works with race and the intersection of social difference (class, gender, sexuality, race, and ethnicity). As a 'socio-political construction' (Omi and Winnant 1993; Lopez, 1995) race may be regarded as a social relational category, defined by socially selected physical characteristic." (p.96)

The essential theme that emerges is the effort to bring effective change in individuals and institutions. The anti-racist educational work aims to change the world.

Research is a process and can be understood as a series of activities that have a beginning and an end. Experienced researchers develop a style of their own for doing research. Most research shares three phases in common. According to Gary Anderson (1998):

> Research in education is a disciplined attempt to address questions or solve problems through the collection and analyses of primary data for the purpose and description, explanation, generalization and prediction . . . [R]esearch is fundamentally a problem solving activity, which addresses a problem, tests a hypothesis or explains a phenomena. (6–7)

A research method is a way to approach a research question or problem. According to Gary Anderson, methodology is comparable to fine cooking in which there can be a variety of approaches to cooking a product. The product you prefer is a matter of personal taste, and is related to what you intend to do with it. However in research, as in baking bread, certain essential ingredients are common, such as the need for data though its exact nature can vary from one approach to another, as does the method by which it is processed. Regardless of the type of research, the methodology chosen is dictated by the question the research addresses and the approaches the researcher takes.

The decision to use a certain methodology is strongly connected to the research area, and more precisely to the central research question. Some methodologies may be more suitable and effective for a particular kind of research. The methodology portion of a research report is a separate section discussing what the researcher did. A methodology describes the general approach or procedure, the framework, the research question, sources of data, instruments, methods of analysis, and limitations.

Qualitative research is a social science research that gives results that cannot be obtained by statistical procedures or simple quantification. Although the data may be quantified or measured, the analysis is qualitative. Generally speaking, qualitative research has to do with people's lives, their stories, and behavior. It is very useful in examining organizations, relationships and social movement. Qualitative research produces data that is descriptive, for example, of a person's own spoken or written words or observable behavior. Qualitative researchers use methods that involve participant's observations, unstructured interviews, and life histories.

The important characteristics of qualitative research include involvement with the people being studied; for example, a researcher investigating handicapped children should have an appreciation and understanding of the difficulties faced by such children and those close to them. Another important characteristic is that the subjects in qualitative research are studied over a period of time, and the emphasis is on the process and the way things change. Qualitative research is also unstructured and the research strategy is such that the relationship between the theory and the research is allowed to emerge, whereas quantitative research simply aims to confirm the relationship between the theory and the research findings.

According to Bouma and Atkinson (1995), "Quantitative research is structural, logical, measured, and wide. Qualitative research is more intuitive, subjective and deep" (208). Some subjects lend themselves to qualitative research, while others are better investigated using quantitative approaches. Sometimes a combination of the two methods proves to be the most effective. It can be seen from the above that qualitative research is more appropriate where we are trying to understand the nature of people's experiences. It can be useful in understanding situations and phenomena about which we know little, and allow us to gain new insights on issues about which a lot is already known.

According to Foster (1991), the positivistic psychometric paradigms based on psychology are fast giving way to qualitative research methods. The move toward qualitative research is noticeable in the increasing number of courses being taught and the increasing number of students who are relying on qualitative methods. Qualitative researchers focus on developing a relationship of trust with those they are studying, and this kind of research involves close contact between the researchers and the subject. Researchers can either study a setting as it exists or they can motivate action by intervening in the lives of the subjects, and in this way become catalysts for change. According to Foster (1991), Newberg initiated a cross-school restructuring program and his research was undertaken to promote change. Foster (1991) further states, Kawakami and Edwards initiated book-reading projects in the communities they studied. In qualitative research fieldwork, the techniques utilized to gather data could be of many different kinds, from in-depth interviews to observation. Sometimes multiple techniques are utilized, such as interviews, observation and document analysis. The use of multiple sources of data for qualitative research is called triangulation, which increases the reliability of the research, and allows data to be compared and confirmed in more than one way.

Effective research allows participants to formulate their own answers through open-ended interviews. Though more time-consuming, such interviews encourage subjects to express feelings and ideas in their own words, resulting in more in-depth accounts.

According to Foster (1991) Participants in such studies are usually tape-recorded; sometimes they are even videotaped. For example, the data presented in Edward's study included videotaped sessions, which helped the researchers examine and study the way in which parents interacted with children during book reading. Another factor that differentiates qualitative research from quantitative research is that in qualitative research, instead of seeking to confirm or deny a given hypothesis, the hypothesis is allowed to evolve from the evidence collected. Qualitative research takes into account that different people in the same environment and situation can often hold different views of the same setting. Qualitative researchers therefore share their discoveries with those being studied in order to ensure that findings are reflective of their subject's opinions.

In recent years, a number of anti-racism studies have been based on critical ethnography, which is essentially a form of qualitative research. The term *ethnography*, according to *Oxford Dictionary*, refers to "the scientific description of peoples and cultures" (305).

According to Simon and Dippo (1986), the term *ethnography* does more than simply describe a research method. Ethnography is similar to producing knowledge; the focus is on both the actual practices and the viewpoints of people in an organized set of social relations. It needs to be stressed that an ethnographic inquiry must be understood as a concept research practice that is constructed with the intention of producing a particular kind of knowledge. The fact that knowledge is power and acquiring knowledge empowers individuals and societies cannot be overemphasized. Ethnographic studies, which are a means of producing knowledge, tend to shift the balance of power in favor of those who initiate such studies. Ethnographic studies can be classified as classical or critical.

Classical Ethnography

This type of ethnography involves a paradigm based on a set of rules for data collection and methodology, and definite procedures for presentation of data that ensures the findings are scientific and acceptable. There are three types of classical ethnography (discussed below), and all share the fact that researchers experience extended exposure to the respondents. For example, if a school or educational institution is to be studied, it must be studied over a period of at least one year. The ethnographer must be involved and at the same time detached enough to be objective.

It is common in classical ethnography to place students in unfamiliar settings in their own society. The researcher must be able to record, categorize, and code what is observed (take field notes), and determine what categories of behavior will be studied, how observations will be recorded, and how results will be cross-checked. Another question concerns the criteria against which the descriptive adequacy of the completed ethnography will be judged.

Classical ethnography falls into three categories based on the research style: (1) holistic, (2) semiotic, and (3) behavioral.

Holistic Ethnography

According to Peggy Reeves Sanday (1979), the holistic form of classical ethnography is the oldest style. The central theme is consistency; According to Peggy Reeves Sanday (1979), Benedict (1934) said in "Patterns of cultures," each culture selects from an infinite variety of behavioral possibilities a limited position that conforms to a configuration. According to Peggy Reeves Sanday (1979), Radcliffe-Brown (1952, 9) divided the social system into three units:

- social structure, the way people maintain an orderly social life
- ecology, the way a society adapts to its environment.
- Culture, how a person develops habits, attitudes, and traits that make him suitable for the social structure.

Holistic ethnography involves the historical processes whereby certain behaviors become acceptable or deviant in a culture which traits are emphasized and which are not.

Semiotic Ethnography

Semiotic ethnography takes into account the viewpoint of the native population. The researcher must gain access to the subjects' thoughts, put ourselves in their shoes, and see things from their point of view. to the researcher must think like the respondents, while holding on to his/her own opinions as well. The semiotic style is also called *ethnoscience.*

This school of thought believes that culture is located in the minds and hearts of men. According to Peggy Reeves Sanday (1979), Goodenough (1971), the premier researcher in scientific ethnography, defines culture as the things one needs to know in order to live in a way acceptable to the individual society in which one lives.

Behavioral Ethnography

Behavioral ethnography involves studying participants' behavior based on observations. Peggy Reeves Sanday's 1979 research comparing the "six" culture study of child rearing and child behavior associated primarily with Whiting (1963) explored this approach. According to Sanday, "the purpose of the six culture study was to explore cross-culturally the relation between different pat-

---

Author: the third line below "Semiotic Ethnography" does not make sense—"their point of view. to the researcher . . ." Please advise how to fix this. Thanks.

tern of child rearing and subsequent difference in personality" (536). The researcher does not seek to uncover meaning or to diagnose the whole. Participation, observation, and recording of data are the three standard techniques.

As can be seen from the descriptions given above, the classical ethnographic approaches are not geared to bring about social change, which is why classical ethnographic studies have not been a popular choice for doing anti-racism research. In contrast, critical ethnography research that aims to emancipate participants from unfair social oppression has been a very popular choice when it comes to anti-racism research. For any ethnographic work to be considered critical, it must meet these three conditions.

1.   It must employ an organizing problematic that defines the data and analytical procedures in a way consistent with the project.
2.   The work must be conceived as a starting point for changing the conditions of oppressive and unfair moral and social regulations.
3.   The work must acknowledge and discuss the limits of its own claims.

Critical Ethnography

Critical ethnography emerged in Britain as part of the interpretivist movement. Its main goal is to free individuals from the sources of domination and repression, which is the primary reason why such studies have been very popular in anti-racism research. Critical ethnography is in its formative stage, and grew out of dissatisfaction with the social accounts given for the structures of society like race and class, in which real human actors had no role. By giving priority to the agency, a critical ethnography study focuses on both the relationship between social structures and individuals, and on the importance of the accounts of the individuals in interpreting their world. In other words the world cannot be transformed unless it is properly interpreted. A useful work of critical ethnography can be a means of creating increased awareness about the oppressed conditions of particular group members, with the aim of bringing about a positive change in their lives. Such a study can be a starting point in influencing policies or bringing the focus of international organizations on pressing social problems. A case in point was a critical ethnography study by Benedicta Egbo titled "Gender, literacy and life chances in Sub-Saharan Africa" (1954), which addresses the importance or lack of international focus on the lives of women in rural Nigeria. Critical ethnographers view classical ethnographers as too neutral in their approach. On the other hand, classical ethnographers criticize critical ethnographers for being too biased. In the field of education, ethnography is the result of two independent trends: epistemology and social theory. The epistemology movement was a shift in research paradigm that was an attempt to break from the quantitative method. According to Anderson (1989), " of all the qualitative research traditions available ethnography most captured the imagination of researchers in the field of education (Atkinson, Delamont. and Hammersley, 1988; Jacob, 1987)" (250).

According to Anderson (1989), "although ethnographies of schooling have been done by small groups of anthropologists for some time, the ethnography movement began in the field of education during the late 1960s and early 1970s. The works of Cusik (1973), Henry (1963), Jackson (1968), Ogbu (1974), Rist (1973), Smith and Geoffery (1968), Smith and Keith (1971), Wolcott (1973), and others provided examples of the genre that later educational ethnographers would emulate" (250).

According to Anderson (1989), "other studies that explored the concepts of race, gender and class in students' subcultures include those of Angus, 1986b; Aggleton, 1987; Aggleton and Whitty, 1985; Brah and Minhas, 1985; Corrigan, 1979; Humphries, 1981; Jenkins, 1983; and Macpherson, 1983" (257).

Critical ethnography owes a great debt to the interpretive movement in the fields of anthropology and sociology. The main result of the interpretive movement was to emphasize the human actors and their interpretive and negotiating capacities as the center of the analysis. A critical ethnographer raises serious questions about the role of schools in the social cultural reproduction of social classes, gender roles, and social and ethnic prejudice. Their focus on the human agency appeals to neo-Marxists and feminists. Critical ethnography's goal is to generate insight, explain events, and seek understanding. Critical ethnographers are concerned with unmasking dominant, social structures and the vested interests they represent, with a goal of transforming society and freeing individuals from the sources of domination and repression.

The most critical issues facing critical ethnographers are the validity or trustworthiness of their accounts, issues such as self-reflection (reflection on the researcher's own biases), the biases of the respondents; and even the reflectivity of the reader of the ethnographic account.

Compared to classical ethnography, critical ethnography

- is more interpretive
- is a new development because many things cannot be explained by classical study
- has as its main goal to free individuals from the sources of domination and repression

- focuses more on the classroom, and
- considers reflectivity and validity issues that are not part of classical ethnography.

Critical ethnography examines power relations materially and historically, in terms of what is legitimated and available to different segments of society. Qualitative research method and qualitative data is vital to critical ethnography work because it provides access to the actual practices of social actors, including the way people talk, the language they use, and their gestures and actions. Another important aspect of any critical ethnography work is that a major aim of such a study is to bring about social change in favor of the oppressed. Anti-racism is an emotional issue that, over the last few decades, has been crying out for change. To get to the root of the issues that at times may be subtler, researchers must build a bond of trust with subjects. This is an important reason why critical ethnography studies have proved highly effective in conducting anti-racism research.

In the global village scenario where we find ourselves today, where there is a great deal of emphasis on social equality, a research study that reveals, and through a disciplined process highlights, racism and the discrimination that goes hand in hand with it, will encourage social change. Because critical ethnography aims to bring about social change, it seems to be the most effective research strategy for anti-racism research. The growing number of highly effective and acclaimed anti-racism studies based on the critical ethnographic approach proves the effectiveness of critical ethnography in anti-racism research.

Taking into account my own position as a woman who grew up in a very orthodox patriarchal society in Pakistan and later immigrated to a far more emancipated society, I feel strongly that qualitative research is a far more effective way of doing anti-racism research. In just five years of being away from the land of my childhood, I feel out of touch with the reality of the life of women back home. For this reason alone I feel that qualitative research, in this case a critical ethnography study, would be the only credible and effective method of doing research on women in my homeland. It would involve close contact and long-term exposure to the subjects being studied and would produce knowledge of the exact circumstances of their day-to-day existence and firsthand experiences of the problems and challenges they face. It is easy for me to see that quantitative research on a subject like this could be very misleading for example, quantitative research on the numbers of women working as professionals in rural Pakistan. The low numbers of working women, which to the Western view may appear unfair, unjust, and exploitative, could actually represent a very different reality. As an example, a more in-depth ethnographic study might reveal that given the taboos, discrimination, and harassment involved for women working outside the home in orthodox, patriarchal, rural Muslim societies, the professional, working, educated women are less privileged than women who have strong, stable marriages where their husbands take care of their economic needs. I know that many women in my part of the world turn to a professional career as a last resort, when they are struggling to survive due to a tragic loss or a failed marriage. In contrast to the reality in the West, a woman living as a housewife with little education and no career of her own may be in a more privileged and respected position than educated career women.

Another example that I feel bears testimony to the greater effectiveness of qualitative research in anti-racism studies is my experience as a new immigrant to Canada. Most information disclosed the world over about the reality of life is quantitative, such as where the largest numbers of immigrants are welcomed every year or where per capita income is far higher than in most immigrants' country of origin. These black and white figures hide many gray realities, which can only be revealed by experiencing life firsthand as immigrant; realities like the frustration and disappointment of the majority of immigrants who are unable to find employment in their areas of expertise. And there are other subtle but bitter realities; although these people may be wealthier than they were back home, many immigrants find themselves at the bottom of the economic ladder. I believe these realities could be far more effectively revealed by critical ethnographic study, whereas it would be far easier to hide and bury these subtle forms of racism under statistics and numbers, which are the basis of quantitative studies.

REFERENCES

Aggleton, P. 1987. *Rebel without a cause*. London: Falmer.

Aggleton, P. and J., and G. Whitty. 1985. "Rebels without a cause? Socialization and Subcultural Style Among the Children of the New Middle Classes." *Sociology of Education*. 53: 60–72.

Anderson, G. 1989. "Critical Ethnography in Education: Origins, Current Status and New Directions." *Review of Education Research*. 59 (3): 249–270.

Anderson, G. 1998. *Fundamentals of Educational Research*. New York: Falmer Press, Taylor and Francis.

Atkinson, P. S. Delamont and M. Hammersley. 1988. "Qualitative Research Traditions: A British Response to Jacobs." *Review of Educational Research*. 58: 231–250.

Benedict, R. 1934. *Patterns of Culture*. New York: Houghton Mifflin.

Bouma, G. D., and Atkinson G. B. J. 1995. *Social Science Research*. Oxford: Oxford University Press.

Brah, A. and R. Minhas. 1985. "Structural Racism or cultural difference: Schooling for Asian Girls." In G. Weiner (Ed.) *Just a Bunch of Girls*. Milton Keynes, England: Open University Press.

Burrel, G., and Morgan, G. 1979. *Sociological Paradigms and Organizational Analysis*. Aldershot: Heinemann, pp. 1–37.

Card, C. 1999. "Race, Racism and Ethnicity." In Leonard Harris (Ed.), *Key Concepts in Critical Theory Racism*. New York. Humanity Books, pp. 257 266.

Corrigan, P. 1979. *Schooling the Smash Street Kids*. London: Macmillan.

Corson, D. 2000. *Language, Diversity and Education*. NJ: Lawrence Erlbaum.

Cusik, P. 1973. *Inside High School: The Student's World*. NewYork: Holt, Rinehart and Winston.

Davies, S., N. Guppy. (1998). "Race and Canadian Education." In V. Satzewich (Ed.), *Racism and Social Inequality in Canada*. Toronto: Thompson Educational Publishing, pp. 131–155.

Dei, G. J. S., James, I. M. 1998. "Becoming Black." *Race, Ethnicity and Education* 1 (1): 91–108.

Egbo, B. 2000. *Gender, Literacy and Life Chances in Sub-Saharan Africa*. Clevedon: Multilingual Matters Ltd.

Foster, M. 1991. "Introduction: Qualitative Investigations into Schools and Schooling." In Michele Foster (Ed.). *Readings on Equal Education*. (Volume 11) New York: AMS Press, Inc., pp. 1–9.

Gitlin, Andrew, and Robyn Russel. 1994. "Alternative Methodologies and Research Context". In

Gitlin, A. (ED.) *Power and Method*. New York: Routledge, pp. 181–203.

Goodenough, W. 1971. *Culture, Language and Society*. Reading, MA: Addison-Wesley Modular Publications, No. 7.

Henry, J. 1963. *Culture against Man*. new York: Randon House.

Humphries, S. 1981. *Hooligans or rebels?* Oxford: Martin Robertson.

Isajiw, W. W. 1977. "Definitions of Ethnicity" 1 (2): 111–124 *American Journal of Sociology*. 1(2): 111–124.

Jackson, P. 1968. *Life in Classrooms*. New York: Holt, Rinehart and Winston.

Jacob, E. 1987. "Qualitative Research Traditions: A review." *Review of Educational Research*. 57(1): 1–50.

James C. E. 1999. "Race, Ethnicity and Cultural Identity." In C. James (Ed.). *Seeing Ourselves, Exploring Race, Ethnicity and Culture*. Toronto: Thompson Educational Publishing, pp 39–63.

Jenkins, R. P. 1983. *Lads, citizens and ordinary kids: Working Class Youth Lifestyles in Belfast*. London: Routledge and Kegan Paul.

Lopez, I. J. 1995. "The Social Construction of Race." In R. Delgado (Ed). *Critical Race Theory: The Cutting Edge*. Philadelphia: Temple University Press.

Macpherson, J. 1983. *The Feral Classroom*. London: Routledge and Kegan Paul.

Maher, F., and Tetreault T. 1997. "Learning in the Dark: How Assumptions of Whiteness Shape Classroom Knowledge." *Harvard Educational Review* 67 (2): 321–349.

Ogbu, J. 1981. "School Ethnography: A Multi-level approach." *Anthropology and Education Quarterly*. 12:3–29.

Omi, M., and Winnat, H. 1993. " On the Theoretical Concept of Race." In C. McCarthy and W. Crichlow (Eds.), *Race Identity and Representation in Education*. New York: Routledge, pp. 3–10.

Oxford Dictionary. 2001. 3rd ed. Oxford: Oxford University Press.

Radcliffe-Brown, A. R. 1952. *Structure and Function in Primative Society*. London: Oxford University Press.

Reeves Sanday, Peggy. 1979. "The Ethnographic Paradigms." *Administrative Science Quarterly* 24 (4): 527–538.

Rist, R. C. 1973. *The Urban school: A Factory for Failure*. Cambridge: M. T. Press.

Simon, R,. and Dippo, D. 1986. "On Critical Ethnographic Work." *Anthropology and Education Quarterly* 17, 195–202.

Smith, L. M. and W. Geoffrey. 1968. *The Complexities of an Urban Classroom*. New York: Holt, Rinehart and Winston.

Smith, L. M. and P. M. Keith. 1971. *Anatomy of Educational Innovation*. New York: John Wiley.

Stone, J. 1995. "Race, Ethnicity and Weberian Legacy." In J.H. Stanfield II (Ed.) *Theories of Ethnicity. Sage*, 391–406.

Whiting, B. 1963. (Ed.) *Six Cultures*. New York: Wiley.

Wolcott, H. 1973. *The Man in the Pricipal's Office: An Ethnography*. New York: Holt Rinehart and Winston.

Chapter Twelve

ANDREW C. OKOLIE

Toward an Anti-racist Research Framework

THE CASE
FOR INTERVENTIVE
IN-DEPTH INTERVIEWING

Introduction

Critical social science scholarship is increasingly recognizing the need for people to speak for themselves, to relate their experiences themselves, to tell their own stories and have these interrogated and validated. Accompanying this is the question of who should listen to, record, and report those stories, and what these stories and narratives can/should be used for. Thus it is increasingly being argued that those who share an experience are better positioned to be accorded the authority to speak to those experiences (Smith, 1992, 1987; Barron, 2000). It can be taken to the extreme to mean that outsiders *cannot* or *should not* study insiders, but the real implication is that only a group can speak *for* itself although others can speak *about* it.

Others have, however, raised objections arguing that it is absurd to suggest that members of a group have qualities that better qualify them as researchers of that group. They even suggest that the non-member may, in fact, be better positioned to study the group since the nonmember has no stake or "baggage." They therefore insist that anyone can study any group, anywhere, and that the real issue is competence, objectivity, and value neutrality. This line of reasoning was clearly articulated long ago in Robert Merton's lengthy essay, "Insiders and Outsiders" (1971). More recent ones include Patai (1994) and Hammersley (1995).

These issues are relevant to anti-racist research. There are the challenges of articulating a research framework suitable for anti-racism, the question of objectivity and value neutrality in research, and the question of what research is (or can be used) for. The latter refers to whether research can exist for its own sake or for social action.

From an anti-racism perspective, we experience and interpret the world differently given our varying social locations, environments, lived experiences, and worldviews. These different locations and experiences also help shape our identities because they affect how others relate to us and our interpretation of those relationships. Therefore anti-racist (and most critical) scholars reject the positivist and even Weberian notions of objectivity and value neutrality, but they do recognize that the results of research should be grounded in reality, so that efforts to uplift people, especially people's struggles to liberate themselves, would be based on reality and, therefore, be more useful. The real issue then is how to capture that reality through research.

This chapter attempts to provide a justification for an anti-racist research framework and contributes to the discourse on how anti-racist research may fruitfully be done. It also makes a case for researchers who share an experience with research subjects to research that experience, but it rejects the notion of racial exclusivity in research. Some of the ideas come from the author's own experiences interviewing a variety of subjects in Nigeria, who share some kind of identity or experience with the author variously as, African Canadian, Nigerian, Igbo, and townsfolk. I argue for *interventive in-depth interviewing* as a necessary component of an anti-racism research framework. This refers to deep, probing interviews in which the researcher goes beyond mere collection of facts or stories and narratives. Rather the researcher, in addition, intervenes in order to get at the subjects' interpretation of their experiences, tries to interpret those interpretations, puts them in their wider sociohistorical and political context, and feeds them back to the subjects as information arranged and presented in a theoretically framed manner. It is a dialectical process in which the giving back of information to the subjects is embedded in the researchers' questions. I argue that this can *best* be done when researchers interview their own people, people with whom the researchers share one or more of such identities as race, ethnicity, country of origin, class, or gender. It is an interviewing technique that suits contexts of interlocking and intersectionality of oppression/identities. I shall demonstrate the need for more researchers from within affected groups and communities, and challenge some of the standards that have been used to evaluate field research that claim objectivity and value neutrality (with their positivist biases). I conclude with a discussion of the promises and perils of members of minoritized groups conducting research on and having the authority of expert on the minoritized.

This discussion of interventive interviewing draws from the pioneering work of Marx in *Enquête Ouvrière* (cited in Bodemann, 1978), an earlier call by Michal Bodemann (1978) for its utilization in research among the working classes, and more recently work by other scholars such as Cuadraz and Uttal (1999), Dei (1996, Dei et al., 2000), Stanfield (1994), and Scheurich and Young (1997).

The Limits of Positivism

The sociology of the capitalist epoch[1] was born in positivism. Positivism aims at the application of natural science methods to the study of social phenomena. Auguste Comte (1875), one of its founders, called for positive science, by which he meant that sociologists should employ the methods of the natural and physical sciences. To him, all phenomena are subject to invariable laws. Positive philosophy has a universal character, and all disciplines must adopt it.

Positivists deal with facts as *things*. According to Comte, scientific theories are a series of logical facts, and only by *observing* these facts well can we arrive at the knowledge of logical laws. He was against introspection and insisted on the *classification* of these facts as zoologists and botanists do after studying the things themselves. Emile Durkheim (1964) gave positivism its most elaborate early treatment. Social facts, to him, are things and should be regarded as such. They are sui generis and constrain individuals. He rejected introspection as well as psychological reductionism, arguing that knowledge of facts cannot come from purely mental activity; their conception requires data from the outside, derivable from observations and experiments. Social life creates a moral quality different from individual wishes and opinions. It is these observable facts that should be classified, *described,* and *analyzed*; unobservable ones should be ignored, he argued. Positivism emphasizes random sampling and representativeness or statistical generalizability, the larger the sample the better. Positivists often experiment, trying to see the effects of specific variables on others. Control groups are typically used in order to better isolate the variables responsible for specific effects. In the natural sciences, the emphasis is on the generation of universal laws. The higher the generality, the more virtuous it is considered to be.

Positivism, with its emphasis on evidence, impassioned data collection, and disinterested analysis, shaped more than a generation of social scientists and still dominates in mainstream social science in North America, especially for those who study "social problems."

Opposed to the positivist method is the *historical-sociological* method prominent in the works of Karl Marx and Max Weber. Marx and Weber, while not entirely free of positivist influences, did emphasize human agency, with Weber more explicitly insisting on interpretive understanding of social action, a theme that the symbolic interactionist perspective later elaborated upon. Marx, however, made his politics more explicit and stressed the importance of the subjective intervention of the researcher in data collection for the sake of social praxis. The historical-sociological method enjoins us to go back to history and examine individual socio-historical phenomena as unique, unrepeatable constellations of factors. They should be seen in their individuality. As Irving Zeitlin (1994) explains, here history is not data to be used to prove the present, but helps indicate the uniqueness of phenomena and seeks explanations for them. These unique individual phenomena are then compared with other phenomena to help indicate and explain the similarities and differences between them. Thus Marx, in analyzing the capitalist mode, had to study other modes in history. This enabled him to understand the specific features of the capitalist mode that mark it out from other modes and shows the divorce of producers from their means of production, pervasive commodification, private appropriation of social wealth, profit motive as the driving force of production, and so forth. Other modes may have had some of these features, but none had them in this combination (1954). Weber (1961, 1968) did the same and, in addition, saw rationalization as a distinguishing characteristic of the modern epoch.

When they employ comparison, historical sociologists employ *ideal types*. This means using extreme cases far from reality, and then trying to see how far reality approximates them. Thus Weber's bureaucracy is an ideal type, and Marx's characterization of modes of production capitalist, feudal, slave may be seen in this light (Weber, 1968, 1949; Zeitlin, 1994).

Historical sociologists also aim at explaining. Here all the inner interconnections of phenomena are analyzed. Thus in trying to explain capitalism's origin, both Marx and Weber examined several interrelated processes in Western Europe at a particular historical period, processes that culminated in the separation of agricultural producers from their land and their proletarianization and (for Weber) Calvinism (1958). As Marx explained in the "Afterword" to the second German edition of *Capital*, (volume 1), the researcher must examine the material in detail, analyze its different forms of development, and trace out their inner connections in order to be able to adequately describe the actual movement (1954, 28).

Unlike positivism, this approach does not aim at the establishment of general laws except as a means to a more detailed study. The emphasis is on historical specificity, not supra-historical theory. Marx had occasion to quote approvingly from an article in *The European Messenger* that discussed his method. The article said that Marx denies the existence of general laws of economic life applicable to all times. Marx's aim, it continued, was to investigate the special laws that regulate the origin, existence, development, and death of a given social organism and its replacement by another (1954, 28). Marx made the same point in the "Preface" to the first German edition of *Capital* (volume 1) and in two separate letters he wrote regarding the applicability of his analysis to Russia. One letter was addressed to Vera Zasulitch (1953, 411–412), the other (which was never sent) to the editors of *Otechestvennye Zapiski* (1982, 109–110).

One does not have to agree with Marx's and Weber's conclusions in order to see the superiority of their approach to positivism. The natural sciences deal with different subject matter. Positivism hardly recognizes the creative potentials of humans; they are simply objects responding to the constraints of social facts. Analysis of social processes is thus reduced to description and counting without any attempt at understanding (from the actors' viewpoint) what they are doing and why, their interpretations of their lived experiences, or their conception of possible courses of action. Bernd Baldus (1990) and Joseph Bryant (1990) have, respectively, pointed to positivism's inability to account for the somewhat chaotic character of certain social processes and inability to recognize the cultural, temporal, and spatial specificity of social processes. Its rejection of history is also unacceptable. How else would we know how societies have transformed? How else, for instance, would we know how racism and anti-racist struggles evolved, including people's perceptions and experiences of it?

Fieldwork, including interviews, is an essential tool in the study of social phenomena. They have found that on issues to which people have deep emotional attachment, and in order to go beyond the "official" answers, researchers need to conduct in-depth interviews. Racism/racial oppression is one such issue. But it is also recognized that personal preferences may enter into interpretations of phenomena. Consequently, Weber (1949) specifically admonished social researchers against mixing intellectual activity with politics. He called for "ethical neutrality" and "objectivity," by which he meant that the researchers/teachers should prevent their value judgments, biases, and prejudices from affecting their work so that their findings would be acknowledged as valid even by someone who does not share their ethical standards. Value judgment, to Weber, meant practical evaluations of the goodness or badness of a phenomenon.

Weber agreed that people have value judgments and that that it is noble that the teachers make clear their value judgments and try to distinguish for their audiences (and to themselves) statements of theirs that are logically deducible or empirically observed facts and those that are statements of practical evaluation. However, he doubted whether scholars should, on the basis of their position, assign to the universities and thereby to themselves the universal role of moulding human beings, or of imparting ethical, aesthetic, cultural, or other attitudes. The valuable influence of the academic lecture hall, he insisted, lies in specialized training by specially qualified persons. The emphasis, according to him, is on the inculcation of intellectual integrity.

His worry was that the professor has the privilege of being free from outside control, hence the need for specialization. The teacher should not have "the right to carry the marshal's baton of statesman or reformer in his knapsack" (1949, 5). Rather s/he should fulfill a given task in a professional fashion, recognize facts even if they are personally embarrassing, distinguish them from his/her own evaluation, and subordinate himself/herself to his/her task. Clearly unwilling to see the personal as political in a meaningful way, Weber insisted that personal questions must not be mixed with specialized factual analysis if science is to remain a vocation. But he recognized the influence of people's social locations and values on their perception of social facts. Contrary to a jurist who said he would not hire an anarchist to teach law, Weber would hire him/her because the anarchist's convictions can enable him/her see the weaknesses in the basic assumptions of legal theory, which cannot be seen by those who take them for granted.

While recognizing that sociology emerged in response to practical problems, Weber insisted that an empirical science should not provide binding norms and ideals from which immediate practical activity can be derived. It should rather focus on the analysis of ends and means, indicating which means are more appropriate to the attainment of a given goal as well as the consequences of using those means. To Weber, an empirical science should not tell people what they *should* do, but what they *can* do.

Many other scholars have challenged these claims to objectivity and value neutrality. Many of them insist that such claims are actually a ruse, a mask for a social science of the status quo (e.g., Bottomore and Nisbert, 1979; Gouldner, 1970; Code, 1991; Stanfield, 1994; Scheurich and Young, 1997). It is easier to claim ethical neutrality and objectivity than to practice them. The history and character of dominant Eurocentric social science scholarship proves how unrealistic Weber's admonitions are. It is a mark of privilege not to worry about what one's research is used for and not to speak out against oppression in one's work. What should the anarchist do about the knowledge of the weaknesses of the dominant legal theory, act to change them or merely explain them? The validation of a researcher's findings on the basis of their acceptance, even by those who do not share the ethical standards, underestimates the role of values, ideologies, and racial constructions (and other vested interests) in human affairs. As anti-racist scholars know too well, *who* says something is often as important as *what* is said. And to urge teachers/researchers not to pass moral judgments in their work on social phenomena (such as racism/racial oppression, sexism, or classism) is not just a mark of privilege; it is absurd.

The reality is that knowledge production and dissemination are value-laden, and they are political (Banks, 1993; Dei, 1996; Dei et al., 2000; Webb, 2001). Researchers may then acknowledge and make explicit their biases and politics or pretend to be objective and value-neutral. The social researcher is not neutral. She or he has some theoretical constructs about the workings of the social world and the functioning of social oppression, including the relational character of oppressions. The choices that researchers make about what to study, what data are to be collected, and how, are influenced by these among other factors. Questions asked of the subjects do not just gather facts, they also embody the researcher's theoretical constructs and assumptions about the nature of reality, how to interpret that reality and moral evaluations of that reality. Thus Marx's insistence that social praxis, especially for the liberation of the dominated, requires the conscious political intervention of the researcher in the research process. The researcher should frame questions in ways that not only try to get factual information but also help to conscientize the subjects. I shall return to this theme presently.

Anti-racism is not just a critical approach to understanding racial oppression; it is also a theoretically informed strategy to end racial oppression. So it cannot pretend to be a neutral science and does not claim to be an objective science devoid of biases, values, and politics. Choosing to be neutral in an inequitable society is a political position in support of the dominant. As Code (1991, 70) asks, "Out of whose subjectivity has this ideal [of objectivity] grown? Whose standpoint, whose values does it represent?" And anti-racism cannot be a science for science's sake. It is an anti-systemic, emancipatory theory and practice with the following, among other key differentiating features:

1. Anti-racism is unapologetically political. It deals with a subject matter—race/racism—that many would rather avoid like a plague. The subject matter is one that anti-racism researchers have a negative value judgment on and would like to see abolished. The researchers do not adopt a neutral, moral stance toward racism. Anti-racism will make some people uncomfortable and empower others. So in a way anti-racist researchers are activists and, therefore, potentially carry the marshal's baton of the reformer, as Weber polemicized. But does it make them any less scientific? No, unless we dismiss Weber's social scientific contributions because of his Eurocentrism, nationalism, and his belief that the bourgeoisie was the force for change and stability, evident in his writings (Bottomore and Nisbert, 1979). In any case, as H. Schwartz and J. Jacobs

(1979) argue in their critique of positivism, there is no consensus on what constitutes the scientific method. Anti-racist research has to rupture the taken-for-granted meaning of science by, for instance, including such elements as emotions and spirituality, which mainstream science conveniently thinks away.

2. There is another subject matter-related issue. Anti-racism researchers are dealing with a phenomenon that is both subjective and objective/structural. Racism is individual and group, personal and systemic, and part of the world-view and common sense of the society. In short, it is supported by structures and institutions in society and is embedded in the ontological, epistemological, and axiomatic systems of the dominant group. It can be observed objectively, but it is also so subjective that its very existence can be denied not just in interpersonal interaction, but with respect to institutions and organizations. Some of the common statements heard from a variety of white and non-white Americans and Canadians include, "There is no racism here," "we are an equal opportunity employer," "I am not racist," "Amy's best friend is black," "I have not experienced racism; everybody treats me equally," "there is only one race, the human race," "We have a policy against all forms of discrimination," to cite only a few. Racism can be denied by both members of the dominant group and the racially minoritized. This poses different challenges from the ones mainstream researchers typically deal with. (For example does the anti-racist researcher refuse to record these denials? And how should they be interpreted and explained? How can the researcher get behind the "official" line and the personalization of racism in order to reach its location in institutions and the worldviews and common sense of the society? (Scheurich and Young, 1997). Why is racism so invisible and yet so visible? (See Apple, 1999). Positivism will be of limited help here. Merely collecting people's opinions and experiences won't help much either.

Unlike positivism, anti-racism is reflective and self-reflexive. While positivists see themselves as value neutral, objective professionals distanced from their subjects, anti-racist researchers are conscious of their position and subjective positioning relative to the subject matter of research. They examine their work, biases, and relationships with the subjects and other groups and institutions, as well as the taken-for-granted assumptions about reality, how to know it, and how to evaluate it. So there is no distance from what is being studied in the way positivists speak of it. Anti-racist researchers see themselves as implicated in what they study (and see other researchers as such) and, therefore, cannot be distanced from what they study. In this sense, to be truly objective requires an acknowledgment of the researcher's subjectivity and its implications for the research.

3. Anti-racism centers race. Its research, while recognizing the interlocking and intersectionality of different forms of oppression, such as race, class, and gender, is focused primarily on race as the entry point. This is a political choice born out of the tendency for race to be marginalized or ignored in anti-oppression discourses and practice. Anti-racism understands that how one form of social difference affects people is linked to the other forms as well, and that ending one of these forms of oppression will not necessarily end the others. Structures of domination affect individual lives differentially at different points in their lives (Cuadraz and Uttal, 1999, 178). For example, a Chinese homosexual male living in North America experiences oppression differently. Black women here also experience oppression differently from black men.

But anti-racism recognizes different saliences of the various forms of oppression for different bodies. That understanding will shape the work of the anti-racism researcher.

4. Anti-racism, by being emancipatory, seeks to empower the subjects of research rather than simply seeking information from them in a disinterested or domineering way. The anti-racist researcher recognizes and is guided by a notion of multiple knowledges and ways of knowing. The subject is also a knower and teacher just as the researcher. The researcher sees the knowledge and ways of knowing of the subject as worthy of interrogation and useful in thinking about and designing strategies for his/her emancipation. This is different from dismissing the subject's knowledge and ways of knowing as inferior and unworthy in the hierarchy of knowledges that have been erected by the dominant Euro-American-centered model or positivism's separation of researcher-subject and subject-knower.

5. Since anti-racism is about the emancipation of the racially minoritized, the holistic way in which most people of color construct their worlds and relationships with others and with nature has to guide research. This includes spirituality, conception of time and space, relationship with ancestors, and so forth. Anti-racist research will seek to uncover the varying ways in which non-European societies construct and make sense of their worlds with a view to teasing out elements in them that can help in empowering and emancipating them.

6. Since most people of color had (and have) oral traditions (even in places where written traditions existed) qualitative research, structured around oral communication, has to be the dominant approach, especially when the issue is how they experience and construct their world and the things in it. But anti-racism research need not be exclusively qualitative, as Stanfield (1994) seems to suggest. It should not be about completely replacing the quantitative with the qualitative. After all, as Stanfield himself says this should not be

about creating a new baby in order to bury the old, but to reflect the plurality of North American society and the world, including ways of knowing.
Studying the minoritized should be done for more reasons than understanding how they construct their world; it should also be about how their world
constructs them. We cannot underestimate the power of numbers even for the
oppressed. Some statistics are sometimes necessary, if only to highlight some
of the objective consequences of the world in which they find themselves. The
rate of completion of schooling, racial composition of faculty, school administrators and other support staff, income differentials by race, police brutality,
rates of arrests, composition of juries, rates of conviction and incarceration for
different racial groups, and lengths of sentences for similar offences for different racial groups are all issues where numbers are necessary (although not sufficient) for anti-racist research and praxis. Interventive in-depth interviews can
then help give meaning to those numbers, reveal what the statistics fail to reveal,
put all of them in context, and help to conscientize the subjects.

7. Anti-racist researchers do not assert intellectual independence from
what is being studied and in trying to uncover "truths." To them, intellectual independence is a mark of privilege. If researchers, as the rest of society, are
subject to the same socialization processes, including schooling and media portrayals that create and denigrate the "Other," it is reasonable to assume that
their priorities, questions, and emphases are shaped by these portrayals and
common sense. Given this reality, it does not surprise anti-racist researchers that
most of the contemporary social science scholarship on racial/ethnic relations
by dominant scholars tends to focus on the mere celebration of difference while
avoiding a discussion of power and privilege. Much of such scholarship also
tends to insist that equality of opportunity exists and is adequate to address previous and current racial discrimination.

Therefore there is a need to seek a methodological framework most suitable for anti-racist research, and address questions of validity and reliability in
a politically meaningful way. How can anti-racist researchers approach issues
of objectivity, value neutrality, and such other ethical, moral, and methodological issues as who is qualified to study whom and for what purpose? To what
extent can those standards apply to anti-racist research?

Toward an Anti-racist Research Framework

Sociological theory and practice have, since the nineteenth century, been
involved in creating "Others," inferiorizing, delegitimizing, and excluding
them. Those others include the non-Euro-American peoples, women, homo-
sexuals, and the disabled. Because of Eurocentric sociology's roots in the

Enlightenment, capitalist industrialization, and liberal political struggles for the rights of the emerging middle class, societies that were not doing exactly the same were deemed unworthy of even being studied by sociology or political science. That "inferior" task was left for anthropology and it did a "good" job of discovering how "primitive" these societies were. When the "Others" are to be studied using sociological tools, it is typically only done within Euro-American societies (e.g. the inner cities and slums under urban sociology). They are studied as pathological urban social problems. (These include crime, delinquency, drug use and trade, homelessness, overcrowding, teenage pregnancy, dropping out of school, mental illness, alcoholism, and so forth. Often these pathologies are seen to result from race, peculiar cultures, family organization, libidinal irresponsibility, etc.). So they suffered the same fate as their kin in the "primitive jungles" of Africa, Asia, South America, and the South Pacific.

Some questions are in order here to help frame the discourse. To what extent are the tools designed for the study of the Western rational, atomized, industrial, colonizing/dominating society suitable for other societies? Can the tools used to study the "self" be used to study the "Other"? Can the same tools and methods used for the study of the dominant be used, in an unmodified form, to study the dominated and vice versa? Can the same tools used to study one's "inferiors" be used to study one's equals? In research, are we likely to ask the same question of the dominant as the oppressed, and can we reasonably expect to elicit answers from the oppressor and the oppressed that are similarly unencumbered? Can we expect the dominant to ask the oppressed similar questions as the dominated would ask the dominant if they had the opportunity? And would the dominant give to the dominated similar answers as they would give to a fellow dominated? How would the oppressive environment within which both live differentially affect the questions asked and the answers given? To what extent can anti-racists still conduct research under the cloak of objectivity when the social environment is so skewed and the power differentials so acute that the research environment can hardly be a neutral one? How can those long denied a voice be able to regain their voice if the researcher does not explicitly try to facilitate the process? Is it reasonable to expect the oppressor to willingly grant that voice when the denial and silencing of that voice are themselves often also denied?

People of color see and relate to the world differently because of their different differential social locations and lived experiences. Seeing the world from the cotton and sugar cane fields and from the kitchens and backyards of white masters and madams reveals a different world from that presented by looking at the world from the parlors, stock exchanges, corporate boardrooms, and the big corner offices in government and university buildings. To be sure, people of color are differentiated by race, nationality, culture, class, gender, and sexual orientation, but within Euro-American contexts race is most salient for them. For example, people of African descent are often seen and treated as black before they are seen and treated as Jamaican, Nigerian, Canadian, homosexual, and male or female.

The relative absence of objectivity and value neutrality in mainstream social research, beyond rhetoric, is not sufficient to dismiss the issues that they raise. But anti-racist work cannot be meaningfully carried out under the constraints imposed by such notions as objectivity and value neutrality, sampling and representative samples, and comparison or control group. They were created and promoted under different intellectual, epistemological, ontological, and axiomatic grounds. The assumptions implicit in those notions are hardly valid when viewed against the research that dominant Euro-American scholars have done for centuries that exclude, inferiorize, oppress, and dehumanize blacks, aboriginal peoples, women, and others. The scholars who carry out those researches have not been immune against the social influences around them, such as their socialization in racialized, classed, and gendered societies, as well as the hierarchy of knowledges and ways of knowing.

Stanfield (1994) and Scheurich and Young (1997) make the point that researchers are not immune against their socialization and the common sense that dominates their world. They are influenced by their time and the ideas, ideologies, and prejudices of their group(s). Thus Euro-American scholars described Africans and others as having no (or inferior) history, religion, and political systems before European incursions into their societies. They were mainly shaped by the positivist knowledge system and the ideology of European superiority, which is what they typically legitimated (and still legitimate) to the detriment of others. This is contrary to the insistence of anti-racism that knowledges and ways of knowing are multiple and that there should not be a hierarchy. Therefore anti-racist research should not aspire to standards set by the dominant Euro-American-centered scholarship but has not met with respect to the minoritized. Euro-American-centered scholarship has often been biased rather than objective, has often not acknowledged the impact of its privileges and power, and has often not studied the minoritized as victims and resisters of oppression. For example, the positivist emphasis on objectivity, sampling, control group, and impassioned data collection, may be unable to capture just how racially biased a piece of legislation or classroom practice that professes equality can be. It is often unable to show how inequitable the "equal" treatment of people can be. True objectivity requires that politics is recognized where it exists, that bias is recognized where it exists, that oppression and exploitation are seen as such, and that victims and resisters are seen as such. This is not the kind of objectivity recommended by the positivists.

A knowledge system that tunes out other knowledges and ways of knowing that have served other people for centuries without even the benefit of interrogating them is hardly objective. A research method that promotes only particular truths while disparaging and delegitimizing others is hardly value-neutral. A research method and knowledge system that pejoratively dismisses that which it cannot explain as mere myth or narrative (negatively defined) can hardly be considered unbiased and complete. Anti-racist workers, therefore, rightfully regard with some skepticism the universal claims of a knowledge system that has ignored, dismissed, delegitimized, and inferiorized other knowledge systems as it erected a racial hierarchy that privileges whites over others. The social science of modernity has been shown by many critical theorists including postmodernists, poststructuralists, and anti-colonial theorists as, in many respects, mere representations of Euro-American knowledges and knowledge systems. It is an incomplete system.

Should this mean that the dominant Euro-American knowledge system be dismissed as irrelevant? Or should we find a way to take elements from that style of knowing while refusing to be constrained by it; while not allowing it to dictate all that the anti-racist researcher can and should do? At the very least, positivism's injunctions must mean that anti-racist researchers need to be careful in order not to allow their biases to prevent them from allowing the voices of subjects to be heard as they speak. My experiences doing research among Toronto's blacks showed that what is required is a different approach; one that combines traditional interviewing methods with other techniques. It should be a method of data collection that takes away the pretensions toward value-free research, and that treats the research subjects as subjects who are deeply and negatively affected by the issues under investigation rather than passive providers of research data. It should treat subjects as people who have not had a voice (but *should* have a voice), and should be centered rather than marginalized (Smith, 1992, 1987; Barron, 2000).

Anti-racist researchers must position themselves and make explicit their biases and politics, rather than hide behind objectivity and value neutrality while trying to elevate one partial way of looking at the world over others. They have a responsibility and reason to show more respect for the rights of subjects. They understand that their subjects' experiences of the world are shaped by their place in that world and that they are therefore different. Their research is on people who have been told for generations by Euro-American scholars that they are inferior and have been treated as such. They want that ended and so they are *not* neutral. Consequently, they have to do their work in a way that is not unnecessarily encumbered by the methodological restrictions of the dominant, masked as objectivity.

Therefore anti-racist research must seek to assist the subjects to recover their voices and dignity, to tell their stories and narrate their experiences, hopes, and fears. These stories and experiences may be individual, but they are likely connected to wider socio-historical and structural factors, especially if they cut across individuals (the intersection of biography and social structure). On the question of contextualizing, Stanley and Wise (1981, 156–173) point out that there is a disjuncture between individual accounts and theoretical constructions. Therefore, individual accounts should not be automatically construed as representing the group's experiences until commonalities appear among individual accounts. Cuádrez and Uttal (1999) point out that data collection methods that would suit the analyses of race, class, and gender must emphasize subjectivity, process, and experience and also be capable of adequately accounting for the large social, structural, and ideological forces that shape people's lives. They call on researchers to interpret the subjects' answers, including the subjects' interpretation of their lived experiences. So the anti-racist researcher needs to go beyond merely listening to these narratives to interpret and contextualize them.

But we need to go beyond that. Anti-racist research should also intervene to feed back information to the subjects beginning with their questions. This can be done with what I have called *interventive in-depth interviewing*. Interventive in-depth interviewing in anti-racism research should combine in-depth interviewing with interventive fieldwork as defined by Bodemann (1978). It stresses that the researcher frames the interview questions in a theoretically grounded manner that not only seeks factual information, but also informs the subjects in a theoretically framed manner in order to help conscientize them. In interventive in-depth interviewing the researcher probes deeply into the subjects' experiences and how they make sense of their worlds. The researcher also attempts to interpret those narratives and explanations, and put them in their wider socio-historical and structural contexts. Oral history is an important source of data, and the researcher deals with the whole persons of the subjects, including their spirituality and relationships with others and with nature. Traditional in-depth interview studies do not always do that.

As early as the nineteenth century, Karl Marx showed clearly that survey research by dominant [bourgeois] scholars and officials targeting the working class tended to be biased in favor of the capitalist class and the state. For example, he argued, bourgois scholars typically assumed that the situation of the working class was natural and that only reforms were necessary or possible. Those assumptions are still made today in researches involving the dominated. Marx showed with survey questionnaires of his own that a researcher interested in the liberation of the working class can and must ask different kinds of questions. The workers' lived experiences were connected to wider socio-historical and political forces in carefully framed questions that sought but also gave information to the workers in ways that linked their personal troubles with wider structural issues. From Marx's example we see that the real issue is not whether questionnaires are used or not, but what kind of questions are asked and to what of kind of uses the researcher puts the questionnaires. To Marx, questionnaires must do more than merely collect data from politically disemboweled subjects; they are also a means of feeding theoretical information to the subjects. The emancipatory researcher would have to intervene in the research process and make that intervention explicit and central.

As Michal Bodemann (1978) explains, unlike the surveys done up to the 1880s Marx addressed his enquiry directly to the workers themselves. To Marx, only the workers "can describe with full knowledge the evils which they endure; only they and not providential saviours can energetically apply remedies to the social ills which they suffer" (Marx in Bodemann, 1978). Marx's questionnaire, the *Enquête,* as well as the *Preambule* to it, clearly show that the survey had two objectives. One was to present the workers' own description of their social condition to the public. The other was to increase the consciousness of the working class with the questionnaire itself through the use of a systematic catalog of questions. So the *Preambule,* unlike most research questionnaires, explicitly states the purpose of the questionnaire. It was seeking factual information from workers, but it was also didactic and political. The following selection from the questions clearly shows that some sought factual information, while others (sometimes sarcastically) sought to conscientize the workers by familiarizing them with such theoretical constructs as relative surplus value, wage, exploitation, and so forth. They did this by drawing from the workers' everyday experience.

> 46. What kind of work contract do you have with your employer? Are you engaged by the day, by the week, by the month, etc?
> 48. In the event of the contract being broken, what penalty is imposed on the employer if it is his fault?
> 49. What penalty is imposed on the worker if it is his fault?
> 26. In case of accidents, is the employer obliged *by law* to pay compensation to the worker or his family?
> 27. If not, has he ever paid compensation in any way to those who have met with an accident while working to enrich him?
> 43. Are the machines cleaned by workers specially employed for this work, or are they cleaned gratuitously by the workers who are employed on them during their ordinary working day?

45. How much time do you lose every day in getting to work and in returning home?
76. Indicate changes in the *price of the commodities* which you produce, or of the services which you provide, and indicate for comparison whether your wage *has changed at the same time*, or whether it remained the same (in Bodemann, 1978, 408–209, Marx's emphasis).

It is clear from this sample that Marx was not just trying to gather and present factual information, but was also encouraging the workers to put their troubles in their wider social context, including understanding the source of their troubles. As Michal Bodemann (1978, 409) points out, questionnaires and opinion polls are political, pretensions to the contrary notwithstanding. The researcher chooses the problem, structures the questions, and thereby constrains the range of possible answers. In Bodemann's view, what the *Enquête* admonishes us to do "is to gather 'experiences' and to immediately feed back these experiences as *information*: ordered and presented in a theoretical framework." Objectivity and value neutrality are little more than part of the professional ideology of academics. It is their claim of standing above the fray while, in fact being right in it.

Anti-racist researchers can certainly draw from this and design interview questions that not only gather factual information, but also help the racially minoritized to theoretically articulate their oppression. For the anti-racist researcher, the workers in Marx's *Enquête* and their experiences of exploitation can easily be replaced by racial minorities, and their mostly menial jobs and experiences of racial oppression. They can also be replaced by minoritized students, and the employers/employment situation replaced by teachers and the existing structure and practices of schooling.

Of course anti-racist researchers can adopt elements from some of the research methodologies employed in the social sciences generally. They can observe racism, classify types of racism, and compare racial oppressions across time and space. They can even engage in statistical analysis of, for instance, racial representations in the media or racism in the justice system. But these are insufficient. Subjective meanings and interpretations are central because anti-racism does not just deal with the objective observable phenomena, but also their hidden forms, people's subjective meanings. And these have to be placed in their wider historical, socioeconomic, and political context. This means that elements of the historical-sociological method are critical and that the findings have to be useful to the subjects.

Therefore, anti-racist researchers will benefit more from the historical sociological method and such field research techniques as the focused interview (Merton, Fiske, and Kendall, 1956), conversational dialogue (Fishman, 1978), and key informant technique (Tremblay, 1982) than quantitative analyses and random sampling. But these are not enough. Their interviews with subjects must be in-depth and interventive if they are to be true to their intellectual and political obligations. Anti-racist research does not just deal with "social facts"; it is also about how people interpret those facts, how the researcher interprets those interpretations, contextualizes them, and assists the subjects in developing theoretical understandings of their lived experiences. Like Marx's proletariat the racially oppressed do not need any providential saviors; only they can apply the remedies. Mao Tse-Tung may have been alluding to this interventive strategy when he talked about "teaching the masses clearly what we have received from them confusedly" (in Bodemann, 1978, 410).

So how the researcher frames questions is critical in shaping the subjects' understanding of their experiences. They may be gendered, classed, and sexed. The researcher also needs to remember that the voices are likely to have been somewhat polluted and affected by power relations. "We want electricity, tarred roads, a new church or tax cuts" or "let's just get along" may simply be reflecting pollution and local power relations. But that interpretation has to be done with, rather than for, the people in a space that is safe, free, and sensitive to the power relationships involved.

So it is problematic to simply stop at asking people what their experiences are or what accounts for them or what they want. We have to theorize with the people and acknowledge that we do so and show how we do it (Fine, 1994). That way the subjects learn from the researcher as the researcher learns from the subject. This will help the researcher avoid appropriating or misappropriating the subjects' knowledges. To ask supposedly neutral questions of people who have been bombarded and continue to be bombarded by racist ideology (some of it presented as science) and oppression, will not further the cause of anti-racism. As Cuadraz and Uttal (1999) point out, contextualizing and interpreting help link biography to history: Personal troubles, with the help of the researcher, are then linked to wider structural forces and events. As C. Wright Mills rightly pointed out, "Social science deals with problems of biography, of history and of their intersections within social structures" (1959, 143). By seeking information and giving theoretical information back, anti-racist researchers would be engaged in grounded theorizing and political praxis.

The interventive in-depth interviewing method poses some challenges for the anti-racism researcher. Of course the researcher cannot control or predict what answers interviewees will give to his/her questions. For instance, they may fail to articulate structural issues in their answers or even deny them (e.g., the impact of racism). Interviewees may also not recognize how different forms of oppression intersect to subjugate them (e.g., race, class, gender). The multiplicity of identities and social structures also poses a challenge. Cuadraz and

Uttal (1999) suggest that the researcher has to figure out how to address structural issues and how to analyze the multiple ways in which individual biography intersects with social structures, while at the same time explaining each of these multiple social structures. These, in my view, clearly speak to the need to work theoretical constructs into some questions, even as other questions seek factual information. It also speaks to the need to interpret the data rather than assume that they speak for themselves. The researcher's theoretical understandings would help. This will also help the anti-racism researcher to avoid authenticating or certifying every story or narrative of the dominated.

The anti-racist researcher should be mindful of the power that she or he has vis-à-vis the subjects. There should be no patronizing, condescending attitudes and actions, and no attempts to tie the subjects in knots with closed-ended questions. Issues around oppression and resistance are not always captured by yes or no, strongly/somewhat agree/disagree answers. As an example, a black student accompanied one of my students to one of my classes. After watching Jane Elliot's film, *Blue Eyed*, for about 40 minutes in a small class where he was the only minoritized body, he turned and asked me where and when the movie was made. I told him what I knew and asked him why? He responded that it is because he did not experience the kind of racism in the movie while he was growing up in the United States. But when the wrap-up discussions toward the end of the movie veered toward some of the everyday racism that minoritized bodies face, he turned again and, this time, narrated how he was pulled over by a police officer and was asked to spell his name even before he finished pronouncing it. And it was a simple two syllable English name. Clearly his response to a "yes" or "no" question as to whether he had experienced racial discrimination would not have caught this, especially as he watched his white friend in obvious discomfort as the movie progressed.

Research designed to gather information from minoritized students about their schooling experiences, for instance, should pay attention to who the students are, their diversity, how they define themselves, and their perception of how others define them. What do they, their parents, and communities see as their problems? What do they think the priorities should be in dealing with their educational problems? The researcher should think these through with them. The researcher is not approaching it from the position of ignorance. The researcher knows something and has some theoretical constructs that will help in framing the questions and in the dialogue.

The researchers must heed Rosalie Wax's advice not to interview only those who like and trust the researcher. Hostile or "neutral" people may be a good source of research data and need to be studied as well (1952, 34–37).

It is worth repeating that whatever the relative merits of the interventive in-depth interview, the idea should not be to reject outright every technique employed by the research orthodoxy. It is not about replacing one hegemonic way of knowing with another. Rather it is to take elements from them that still allow for the freedom to capture the uniqueness of the experiences and worldviews of the racially minoritized, and to politically intervene bringing them to conscienceness. It is to promote multiple readings of the world; about telling and analyzing the stories that otherwise would not be told or correctly analyzed; about giving voices to those denied same for so long and suggesting ways to end racial oppression.

The requirement to feed back information to the subjects also means that anti-racist researchers must learn to and practice communicating in a language that the subjects can understand. The suffocating and opaque language of many critical theorists, which anti-racists often employ, must be avoided. The writings of anti-racist researchers must be accessible to those they claim to work for, rather than only sophisticated professional academics.

Anti-racism research must be guided by the key principles of anti-racism theory and practice as articulated by George Dei and others (Dei, 1996; Dei et al., 2000; Thomas, 1984; Lee, 1985). Given its explicitly and unapologetically political and intellectual character, anti-racism researchers must constantly be aware of their political responsibility while noting that interventive interviewing is not a licence to embellish stories or narratives to suit their value preferences. They should make certain their subjects to reject any notions of inferiority of their knowledges to other knowledges and ways of knowing. They should also help their subjects to realize that they have agency and can resist (and have been resisting) oppression. By assisting the subjects and audience of the research to make the connections between personal troubles and wider socio-historical and structural issues, the researcher is also able to make apparent the interlocking nature of oppressions and the ways in which different oppressions intersect in the individual's identity and experiences.

Anti-racism researchers, unlike dominant researchers should not study their subjects as pathologies, as problems needing solutions. It is their oppression and marginalization that are the problems. The problems that seem to be more prevalent among them are unemployment, petty crime, school disengagement, drugs, violence, and teenage pregnancy. Mainstream researchers have focused on these issues, but they are, for the most part, the consequences of oppression and marginalization. So they are the products of racialized society's pathologies. It is the latter that should be the primary focus if long-term solutions are to be found to those problems. Anti-racist researchers must understand that, in general, their subjects are victims of a racialized and inequitable social order who should not be re-victimized. They should seek to create spaces for anti-racist discourses and praxis with a view to ending racism. For that reason, studying the subjects' narratives and experiences is only one part; the other part is studying how they are oppressed, inferiorized, delegitimized, and marginalized. Merely understanding the consequences of oppression is inadequate. The causes of oppression, *how* oppression works, and how it is per-petrated are critical issues if oppression is to be fully understood and ended. That understanding will help the researcher to frame questions and understand the rationale for certain answers given by subjects, as well as solutions to problems that people may be dealing with. It will help researchers to get beyond the official layer to locate what they are not being told or what the sub-jects may be overlooking.

Anti-racist research must look at the whole persons of the subjects includ-ing their spirituality. As George Dei and others explain, spirituality refers to per-sonhood and a person's place in this world. It refers to how people make connections between the body and the soul, the sense of wholeness, the rela-tionship between the person and the environment including fellow beings. A person's understanding of the self, connections to family, community, and envi-ronment are all aspects of a person's spirituality. In this context there is a need to examine how a group's spirituality affects its experience of oppression, and how racial oppression affects its spirituality (Dei et al., 2000; Gadgil, Berkes and Folke, 1993; Vardey, 1996; Kolander and Chandler, 1990, cited in Dei et al., 2000).

Done properly, the interventive in-depth interview not only provides deep and detailed understanding of social processes and discovers new concepts, cat-egories, and issues (Cuadraz and Uttal, 1999, 162), but also has the potential for conscientizing the subjects. It becomes an exchange rather than merely a one-sided extraction of information from hapless subjects. This will compen-sate for sample size, representativeness or statistical generalizability, and con-trol groups (Cuadraz and Uttal, 1999). Anti-racist researchers that deem comparison essential can engage in a different kind of comparison. Using Weber's and Marx's ideal types, for example, they can compare existing racial-ized, classed, and gendered societies or classrooms with an "ideal type," where difference is not just acknowledged, but people are treated equitably to ensure equitable outcomes for all groups. That way they can show, for instance, how inequitable current societies and classrooms are and identify what can be done to make existing societies/classrooms more equitable.

Concluding Remarks: Insiders and Outsiders

So who is better positioned/qualified to conduct this type of research and have the authority of the expert on anti-racism, the racially minoritized scholars or white scholars or both? This "insider/outsider" debate has been around since the minoritized began to challenge the dominant Euro-American-centered and sexist scholarship on themselves. Of course, the terms insiders and outsiders can be flipped depending on the situation. For our purposes here, insiders are members of the subject group, the racially minoritized groups being studied. The outsiders are members of the dominant group. I think that we can make a case for having more minoritized studying the minoritized without going to the absurd length of calling for racial exclusivity in research, but positioning is very critical. We need to know who is researching whom, the researchers' social location and political preferences, and what these results/findings are used for.

Robert Merton's (1971) claim that outsiders can bring new insights, while sensible on the surface, is actually disingenuous, for it hides the reality of power relations and inequitable access to resources in the research enterprise. Who has been making decisions about who studies whom or what? What chances do minoritized scholars have of getting financial backing to study whites and whiteness, for example, from the point of view of the dominated? Would dominant scholars accept that non-whites should study them so as to enable them understand themselves better? How well would African or Chinese anthropologists' studies of white North Americans be received? Studies of the minoritized by minoritized scholars have not even often been well received by the dominant scholars except when they express views considered acceptable to the dominant. The term *moderate* has been reserved for those scholars who conduct "acceptable" research. We must not forget why insiders insist on being considered more qualified, namely the biased and dehumanizing job of studying them being done by the outsiders who also happen to have more power.

As I already indicated, anti-racism researchers do not assert intellectual independence from what is being studied and in trying to uncover "truths." They cannot afford to. One may ask "independence from what?" from the researchers' socialization, social class, race, gender, or the commonsense ways of making sense of the world that characterize their groups? Can I be independent of the effects of my skin color on the research subjects? Do I have a choice in the matter? There are still things that researchers cannot control; the effects of the color of their skin or their gender on how they are perceived are among subjects; the effects of centuries of oppression, exclusion, and marginalization; and the prejudices of many dominant scholars.

Attention should really be focused on the promises and perils of the minoritized studying their own so as to better understand and deal with them. First the potential perils. One is the sense of powerlessness that the subjects sometimes feel in relation to the researcher. Being minoritized themselves, the researchers may be seen as powerless to do anything about the issues being researched. The subjects know where real power lies. They may have been studied several times earlier by those with the real power with nothing to show for it, in their assessment. While this has little to do with the researcher's competence and integrity, this perception and that legacy of dominant group research may affect the answers given to the insider anti-racist researcher. This realization may encourage the insider researcher to exaggerate the potential effects of the research in order to secure better cooperation from the subjects. The researcher must resist this. The researcher must make sure that the subjects do not read unrealistic promises into the research process. The subjects should not be duped into cooperating with the researcher.

Another peril is the legacy of colonial oppression and racism. Sometimes it is easier for the dominant researcher to gain access to information in the minoritized community and institutions than the "native" researcher given the legacy of colonialism and the existing resource and power inequities. Related to the above, the anti-racism researcher may also be treated with contempt by the subjects relative to a dominant researcher, as I experienced while interviewing Nigerian President Olusegun Obasanjo in 1992 (then a retired military head of state), and some other subjects. Anti-racist researchers may also (as is often the case) have fewer resources relative to dominant researchers and so may not be able to induce responses or to show gratitude for same, thereby hampering future relations, including research cooperation. But this may also be an advantage. At least it ensures that the answers that they get are not induced by rewards or promises of it.

There is also the challenge of researchers getting people's frank opinions on issues when they and the researcher "know" each other and each other's experiences (and perhaps opinions) so well. The subjects may not feel free to speak frankly to the researcher. There is also the risk of the insider anti-racist researcher becoming part of the story, being "sucked in" to the extent that impedes the gathering of factual information. For instance, how much sympathy, if any, should the researcher exhibit during an interview, especially when the culture encourages the subjects to expect it? The researcher should be able to express the culturally expected sympathy while keeping his/her gaze on the purpose of the research, which is to gather and give information that will help bring about real changes in people's situation. The other challenge is the risk of the insiders becoming native informants when they study themselves. They may simply become data collectors or intellectual "spies" who further empower or merely entertain the dominant.

But there are important advantages in members of minoritized groups studying their own. In every conversation, in every culture and social group, there are the unspoken words, the gaps that the other party in the conversation is expected to fill. This is similar to what ethnomethodologists call *etceteras*. How does the researcher respond to *etceteras* (phrases such as "you know what I mean")? Would such phrases be used to the same extent with a stranger-researcher? What will the stranger-researcher make of them if they are used? What would be lost if they are not used because the researcher is an outsider? There is also the body language that the cultural stranger cannot capture: the nods, the winks, the rubbing of the eyelids or hands, all of which make sense to the "initiated" but not to the outsider. Some early anthropologists tried to get around some of these challenges (especially the whole question of manifest and latent functions of social practices) by residing for a year or more in the societies that they studied. But few people would really believe that the length of stay completely wipes out the "stranger among us" tag. Often people just know what cannot be said or done in the presence of the stranger, however well intentioned, friendly, or assimilated.

Then there are the emotions, the anger, the passion, the sympathy, the pleading, the "not again" and "they don't care" that I hear from subjects, which I do not hear when I interview people who have little investment in the issues and/or are strangers to the issues/locales. I doubt that outsider researchers experience the same to the same extent. The sharing of that identity with the researcher encourages the subjects to express those emotions, which should constitute part of the data or, at least, help give meaning to the data or put them in context. It is mainly because of this shared identity that anti-racist researchers have more political investment in ending racism. To them, neutrality in the face of oppression amounts to complicity in that oppression. They cannot afford to approach their work merely as "professionals" *just doing a job*. Anti-racist researchers know from history books (written mostly by Euro-Americans) that conquerors rarely write the history of the conquered in glowing lights. The best that the conqueror often offers is how noble and blissful the conquered were in their "savagery" and "stupidity."

There are ethical and moral questions as well. If outsiders cannot know insiders as well as insiders know themselves, is it fair to rely on outsiders' knowledge of insiders for policies that affect the insiders? Of course, this may be countered with a claim that outsiders do not need to know the minoritized as well as the insiders in order to study them, but is it right that outsiders become the experts on insiders when the insiders do not even have the capacity to become experts on the outsiders? Also, to what uses would these knowledges be put? Anti-racists cannot afford to do research for its sake, but to help end their racial subjugation. The insider is more likely to be concerned about the effects of research on subjects.

Is the research on insiders less valid because insiders carried it out? Should it be more valid only when outsiders, who often have more power and resources, including publication outlets, carry it out. Shulamith Reinharz (1979) argues rightly that we should do research that is relevant/useful to the group being studied, and therefore closeness to the group/subject is critical. In anti-racism the insider is often the closest to the issue/subject. If field researchers emphasize rapport, familiarity with subjects/issues, then that is also a case for the primacy of the insider. Resistance against it seems rather more political than anything else.

Also Denzin (1978) notes that people tend to draw conversations to themselves bringing in gender, race, class, and so forth. And according to Pamela Fishman (1978), men bring more power into conversations. We also know that the dominant bring more power into conversations with the dominated as black persons who have attended labor union meetings and black feminists who attend feminist meetings in North America know. This certainly speaks to the need for insider researchers. The dominant is often the one that names, certifies/decertifies, and qualifies/disqualifies the dominated. The dominant has historically cornered the market for the study of the dominant and the dominated, yet the dominant has not seen this near monopoly in the study of themselves and the "Others" as intellectually, ethically, and morally problematic. But these are the kinds of charges being levelled against the dominated studying the dominated.

Few would doubt that feminist scholarship, especially by women, has enriched the social sciences, and our understanding of society and the classroom. But it has not done enough to recognize and act upon the recognition that gender is raced and classed.

What these promises and challenges mean is that, although there are definite advantages of the insider doing research on the minoritized, there are challenges that call for caution, preparation, and commitment. They also mean that the dominant scholars can and will continue to study the racially minoritized. But such dominant scholars must state their positions and positioning and recognize that they are approaching the work from positions of privilege and power, and that their work may indeed be limited by their outsider/

powerful/dominator position. More importantly, they must problematize the processes and structures that put them in the position to study the minoritized, make the political commitment necessary to gain a deeper understanding of the experiences of the minoritized, and be willing to bear the risks associated with doing anti-racist work. Therefore, in some cases it may be necessary for the subjects to play a role in the decision to have themselves studied by outsiders. But it will be a disservice to the subjects to accord the work of outsiders more recognition than those of the insiders mainly because the outsiders have more power and resources to impose their will on the rest.

NOTE

1.   I make this distinction because of the existence of insightful and quite sophisticated sociological analyses that predate this era by thousands of years, such as those of Ibn Khaldun. See, for example, Khaldun (1950).

REFERENCES

Apple, M. 1999. "The Absent Presence of Race in Educational Reform." *Race, Ethnicity and Education* 2(1): 9–16.

Baldus, B. 1990. "Positivism's Twilight?" *Canadian Journal of Sociology* 15 (2): 149–159.

Barron, C. L. 2000. *Giving Youth a Voice: A Basis for Rethinking Adolescent Violence.* Halifax, NS: Fernwood.

Bodemann, M. 1978. "A Problem of Sociological Praxis: The Case for Interventive Observation in Field Work." *Theory and Society* 5, 387–420.

Bottomore, T., and R. A. Nisbet (Eds.). 1979. *A History of Sociological Analysis.* London: Heinemann.

Bryant, Joseph. 1990. "Positivism Redivivus? A Critique of Gerhard Lenski's Uncritical Proposals for Reforming Sociological Theory." Unpublished manuscript. Department of Sociology, University of Toronto.

Code, L. 1991. *What Can She Know?* New York: Cornell University Press.

Comte, A. 1875. *The Positive Philosophy* (trans. Harriet Martineau, vol.1). London: Trubner and Co.

Cuadraz, G. H., and L. Uttal. 1999. "Intersectionality and In-Depth Interviews: Methodological Strategies for Analyzing Race, Class, and Gender." *Race, Gender and Class* 6(3): 156–186.

Dei, G. S. J. 1996. *Anti-Racism Education: Theory and Practice.* Halifax: Fernwood Publishing.

Dei, G. S. J., et al. 2000. *Removing the Margins: The Challenges and Possibilities of Inclusive Schooling.* Toronto: Canadian Scholars Press.

Denzin, N. K. 1978. *The Research Act: A Theoretical Introduction to Sociological Methods.* New York: McGraw-Hill.

Durkheim, E. 1964. *The Rules of Sociological Method* (trans. George Catlin). New York: Free Press.

Fine, M. 1994. "Dis-stance and Other Stances: Negotiations of Power Inside Feminist Research." In A. Gitlin (Ed.), *Power and Method: Political Activism and Educational Research*. New York: Routledge, pp. 13–35.

Fishman, P. M. 1978. "Interaction: The Work Women Do." *Social Problems 25*, 397–406.

Gadgil, M., F. Berkes, and C. Folke. 1993. Indigenous Knowledge for Biodiversity Conservation. *Ambio 22*, 151–156.

Gouldner, A. 1970. *The Coming Crisis of Western Sociology*. New York: Basic Books.

Hammersley, M. 1995. "Research and Anti-Racism: A Critical Case." In M. Hammersley, *Politics of Social Research*. London: Sage Publications, pp. 66–84.

Khaldun, I. 1950. *An Arab Philosophy of History: Selections from the Prolegomena of Ibn Khaldun of Tunis (1332–1406)*, (trans. and arranged by C. Issawi). London: John Murray.

Lee, E. 1985. *Letters to Marcia: A Teacher's Guide to Anti-racist Education*. Toronto: Cross Cultural Communication Centre.

Marx, K. 1954. *Capital* (vol. 1). Moscow: Progress Publishers.

Marx, K., and F. Engels 1953. *Selected Correspondence*. Moscow: Foreign Languages Publishing House.

Mbiti, J. 1990. *African Religions and Philosophy*. Oxford and Portsmouth, NH: Heinemann.

Marx, Karl 1982. "Pathways of Social Development: A Brief against Suprahistorical Theory." In Hamza Alavi and Teodor Shanin (Eds.), *An Introduction to the Sociology of Developing Societies*. New York: Monthly Review Press.

Merton, R. 1971. "Insiders and Outsiders." In A. R. Desai (Ed.), *Essays in Modernization of Underdevelped Societies*. Bombay: Thacker.

Merton, R. K., M. Fiske, and Kendall, P. L. 1956. *The Focused Interview*. Glencoe, IL: Free Press.

Mills, C. W. 1959. *The Sociological Imagination*. New York: Oxford University Press.

Patai, D. 1994. "When Method Becomes Power." In A. Gitlin (Ed.), *Power and Method: Political Activism and Educational Research*. New York: Routledge, pp. 61–73.

Reinharz, S. 1979. *On Becoming a Social Scientist: From Survey Research and Participant Observation to Analysis*. Brunswick, NJ: Transaction Books.

Scheurich, P., and Young, M. 1997. Colouring Epistemologies: Are Our Research Epistemologies Racially Biased? *Educational Researcher 26*(4): 4–16.

Schwartz, H., and Jacobs, J. 1979. *Qualitative Sociology: A Method to the Madness*. New York: The Free Press.

Smith, D. E. 1987. "Sociology from Women's Experience: A Reaffirmation". *Sociological Theory 10*(1): pp. 88–98.

Smith, D. E. 1992. *The Everyday World as Problematic: a Feminist Sociology*. Boston: Northeastern University Press.

Stanfield II, J. H. 1994. "Ethnic Modeling in Qualitative Research", in Norman K. Denzin and Yvonna S. Lincoln. *Handbook of Qualitative Research*. Thousand Oaks, CA: Sage Publications.

Stanley, L., and Wise, S. 1981. "Back into the Personal or Our attempt to construct Feminist Research." In *Theories of Women's Studies*. University of California Berkeley: Women's Studies.

Thomas, B. 1984. "Principles of Anti-racist Education." *Currents 2*(3): pp. 20–24.

Tremblay, M. 1982. "The Key Informant Technique: A Non-Ethnographic Application." In Robert G. Burgess (Ed.), *Field Research: A Sourcebook and Field Manual*. London and Boston: G. Allen & Unwin.

Vardey, L. 1996. *God in all Worlds: An Anthology of Contemporary Spiritual Writing*. Toronto: Vintage.

Wax, R. H. 1952. "Field Methods and Techniques: Reciprocity as a Field Technique." *Human Organization* 11: 34–37.

Webb, P. T. 2001. "Reflection and Reflective Teaching: Ways to Improve Pedagogy or Ways to Remain Racist," *Race, Ethnicity and Education* 4 (3). 150–156.

Weber, M. 1968. *Economy and Society* (trans. Guenther Roth and Claus W. Wittich, 3 vols.). New York: Bedminster.

Weber, M. 1949. *The Methodology of the Social Sciences* (Trans. and Eds. E. A. Shils and H. A. Finch). New York: Free Press.

Weber, M. 1958. *The Protestant Ethic and the Spirit of Capitalism*. New York: Charles Scribner's Sons.

Weber, M. 1961. *General Economic History* (Trans. Frank H. Knight). New York: Colliar Books.

Weber, M. 1968. *Economy and Society* (Trans. Guenther Roth and Claus W. Wittich, 3 vols.). New York: Bedminster.

Zeitlin, I. M. 1994. *Ideology and the Development of Sociological Theory*. 5th ed. Englewood Cliffs, NJ: Prentice-Hall.

Chapter Thirteen

GURPREET SINGH JOHAL

Order in K.O.S.

ON RACE, RAGE, AND METHOD

> We cannot live life without our lives.
> —Audre Lorde, *Sister Outsider*

This paper continues dialogues that started long before I entered this world. It is a journey to discover a knowledge of self (KOS) that may bring order to life. It is an attempt to nurture a self that is not separated from the rest of life. The knowledge of self ensures that we will never ignore the connection that brings all of us together in the family of life. Many people before me have given voice to their experiences; many have not. Their lives are examples for us all. Their actions have motivated many, including myself, to attempt to carry on what they did not think twice about doing. These people—our mothers, fathers, sisters, brothers—whether by blood or in blood, continue to carry us on their shoulders. Without them, not a word would appear on the following pages. I am constantly reminded, nourished, and empowered by what these people have accomplished. The eras in which they lived were intensely difficult, yet they never hesitated to do what was needed to get things done. Never did they relinquish or shy away from the primary motivator in their lives—love. I will never be able to understand the experiences of these people in the most difficult times of their lives. I do not know the lived experiences of chattel slavery, indenture, genocide, or rape. All I know is what I have gone through. The historical moments of slavery, colonialism, and imperial conquest have passed, but their legacies continue. This chapter attempts to situate discussions of systems of oppression within a contemporary neocolonial framework that is based on the historical legacies of enslavement, forced migration, and extermination of people of color by colonial forces.

What is to be made of people of color and those of the First Nations, who express their sorrow against occupied settler states such as Canada and the United States? What is to be made of the collective rage that some people simply can not control? I will attempt to situate these questions in an analysis of the trajectories of rage. Historically, *black rage* is a term used to describe the potential dynamite that is the black underclass of the United States, but are there other readings of this term? How can the language of rage be used to empower oppressed peoples? It is critical that there is conceptual clarity between the rage of the oppressor and that of the oppressed. Where does one begin to discuss the roles of love and hate in all of this? To borrow from a popular Tina Turner song of some years ago—"What's love got to do with it?"

Survival is of the utmost concern in a neocolonial era. How does one survive today? How did folks survive in the past? Is there a way to nurture a *pedagogy of rage* as a possible vehicle for resistance? What would a pedagogy of rage entail? Are there some key points that we may be able to rely on when attempting to make connections with others? What are the roles of embodiment, voice, militancy, memory, and survival in the articulation of a pedagogy of rage?

We live in a world in which we, as people of color and First Nations communities, are constantly forced to fit into models that cannot accommodate our various shapes, sizes, and differences. There are plenty of people with good intentions in the world, who just can not seem to understand the fact that they engage in oppressive acts and behaviors. When they are told what they are doing, a frown usually appears, accompanied by denials. We need to get beyond the issue of intent and choice and move into the realm of accountability and responsibility. One way to roust people from their comfort zone is an angry articulation of their complicity in systems of oppression, but can this be done in a way that does not recenter the dominant gaze?

Trajectories of Rage

Black rage is the rage of the oppressed.
—P. Harris, *Black Rage Confronts the Law* (1997)

Black rage is often depicted in mainstream discourse as a pathological condition of an under-privileged segment of society. No one more explicitly articulates this than Price Cobbs and William Grier in their widely discussed book *Black Rage* (1968). These two black psychologists used a Freudian viewpoint to convince readers that rage was merely as sign of powerlessness. By calling it a pathology and explaining it away, they failed to see it as a potentially healthy, healing response to oppression and exploitation.

My primary motivation for writing this chapter is an attempt to articulate the necessity of rage for all oppressed peoples in attempting to counter systems of oppression that dominate their everyday lives. By rescuing rage from the pathologizing lens of mental disorder, I hope to demonstrate how rage can be utilized to maintain health and well-being. Mainstream portrayals of black rage often construct nihilistic accounts of black youth alienated and angry for no apparent reason. Black rage in this sense is seen as a normative aspect of a pathologized and impoverished black urban culture. I hope to rupture such depictions of angry behaviors because they do not take into account the systems of oppression that are in operation.

Mainstream depictions of black rage utilized in media discourses operate under the aegis of common sense (Campbell, 1995). Common sense invokes notions of the familiar and normative. One contemporary example of how common sense is operationalized in the imagination of mainstream media discourses are those involving criminality and militancy, which are often intertwined with race, gender, class, age, and ability. This is most often seen as an underclass made up of youths of color who are recognized as the enemy from whom those of the bourgeois utopia are to be protected. According to mainstream media discourses, the irrational rage of this group must be policed and contained. Legislation must be strengthened to teach this collective of inconsiderate troublemakers a lesson. Stiffer penalties, new laws, increased policing, zero tolerance policies, and/or medication (such as Ritalin), are some commonsense strategies that are routinely deployed when authorities attempt to deal with pathologized black rage. This example illustrates the material ramifications of a pathologized, decontexualized rage.

Public focus on black rage and the attempt to trivialize and dismiss it, must be subverted by public discourse about the pathology of white supremacy and the madness it creates. We need to talk seriously about ending all forms of oppression if we want to see an end to rage. White supremacy is frightening. It promotes mental illness and various dysfunctional behaviors on the part of whites and people of color. White supremacy is the real and present danger—not black rage. These whom mock and trivialize rage do so because they do not want rage against the status quo to assume the form of strategic resistance.

Hailing the rage of the oppressed is a conscious and deliberate attempt to make rage synonymous with a sense of interconnectedness and self-love. By linking rage to a passion for justice, we may be able to conceptualize the catalyst of rage. A passionate ethical commitment to justice serves as the catalyst for rage. The fire inside oneself fuels rage—it is a necessary element for every form of struggle against oppression. It is an act of love of self as well as of the collective movement toward freedom.

Such an understanding of rage urges one to not see oneself as a perpetual victim. This tone must move away from a sense of isolated hopelessness and meaninglessness that often has led to what Cornel West has described as "nihilism" (West, 1994). *Nihilism,* according to West, "is the lived experience of coping with a life of horrifying meaninglessness, hopelessness, and (most important) lovelessness" (23). This sense of victimization carries great costs for the oppressed; anger becomes internalized and is directed at oneself and those closest to oneself. The internalization of oppression is a symptom of a disconnected self. Once disconnected, the rage of the oppressed becomes dangerously self-destructive.

The oppressor often welcomes victimization. For example, victimization negates white guilt because it comforts the oppressor. bell hooks (1995) suggests that it comforts whites because it is the antithesis of activism. The internalization of victimization leaves the oppressed powerless and unable to assert agency on their own behalves. hooks notes that, "when we embrace victimization, we surrender our rage" (18).

bell hooks speaks of "constructive healing rage" (18), and notes that this form of rage leads to self-recovery, which is a necessary precursor to establishing clarity. It burns one's psyche with such an intensity that it creates clarity. This form of rage is a fundamental component of the political process of decolonization. For the oppressed, confronting rage forces one to grow and change. It allows one to intimately understand that rage has the potential not only to destroy but also to construct. It is a necessary aspect of the resistance struggle. Rage can act as a catalyst inspiring courageous action. hooks notes:

> By demanding that black people repress and annihilate our rage to assimilate, to reap the benefits of material privilege in white supremacist capitalist patriarchal culture, white folks urge us to remain complicit with their efforts to colonize, oppress, and exploit. (16)

hooks further states that the political process of decolonization not only allows for one to see clearly but that it is also a way to freedom for both the colonized and the colonizer. Individuals who have decolonized their minds make it possible for rage to be heard and used constructively by working together. Malcolm X serves as a primary figure in the clear defiant articulation of this form of rage. He unabashedly called for black people to claim their emotional subjectivity by claiming their rage.

The following statement by hooks allows one to begin viewing rage as productive. Her words speak to the urgency and necessity of reclaiming rage: "As long as black rage continues to be represented as always and only evil and destructive, we lack a vision of militancy that is necessary for transformative revolutionary action" (19).

Paul Harris (1997) offers a critique of the mainstream utilization of black rage. His usage of the "black rage defense" in the U.S. court system

> refutes the idea that there is a lower class of people inherently criminal and can be written off by society. It tries to educate people about the oppressive structures and behaviours in society that produce and increase criminality. It has been said that ignoring race is a privilege that only white people have. This defense forces whites, for a critical moment in time, to give up that privilege and think about the consequences of a system of white supremacy. (275)

Harris also states that

> [although] the usage of the term evokes violent, aggressive images, the black rage defense encompasses a broader view of African American life than just rage and violence. It includes pride in one's heritage. It explains hopelessness and sheds light on the darkness of fear and abuse. Most of all, it says to the American legal system: You cannot convict me without hearing who I am and what has shaped me. I was not born with an M-1 carbine in my hands. My childhood dreams did not include robbing a bank. (37)

Harris notes that black rage is the rage of the oppressed. It is cultivated in an oppressive environment. In the neocolonial era, all those who suffer from white supremacy, capitalism, patriarchy, and homophobia are oppressed. As stated at the outset of this chapter, my focus is on bodies of color in relation to whiteness. Therefore, as much as white people across differences of class, gender, sexuality, ethnicity, or religion may be oppressed in relation to the dominant white middle-class heterosexual male subject, they hold a pigmentary passport of privilege that allows sanctity as a result of the racial polity of whiteness. This is a luxury that people of color do not have. This is the central issue upon which I am focusing my analysis in this paper. A pedagogy of rage insists upon an unconditional commitment to justice. Justice is not something that is only available to a select group of beings on this planet. As much as systems of oppression attempt to ensure justice as "just us," a pedagogy of rage is an instrumental catalyst of opposition.

Resentment versus Rage

> The rage of the oppressed is never the same as the rage of the privileged. One group can change their lot only by changing the system; the other hopes to be rewarded within the system.
>
> —bell hooks, *Killing Rage*

The rage of the oppressor is not the rage I wish to utilize for any transformative project. This form of rage is anger motivated by fear. It is a fear of the loss of dominant status or privilege in relation to the oppressed. Flipping the tired, all-too-often quoted Lord Acton statement that "power corrupts and absolute power corrupts absolutely" on its head, Aung San Suu Kyi offers another reading of power and corruption. Rather than focus on power itself, and thus, in the process, deny any agency to the power of resistance to the oppressed, her emphasis simultaneously relies on the loss of power and the unhealthy state of perpetual victimhood experienced by the oppressed. She states the following: "It is not power that corrupts but fear. Fear of losing power corrupts those who wield it and fear of the scourge of power corrupts those who subject to it" (1995, 182). Thus the fear of the oppressor should be seen as a form of resentment towards those who threaten the dominant status of this all-knowing subjectivity.

White resentment has often been equated with black rage in mainstream discourses. The justification of white vigilance to maintain white officialdom, and the pathologization of black rage to demonstrate innate threats to white civility have been readily documented by scholars such as Patricia Williams (1991) and Paul Harris (1997). I will consider their respective contributions to my analysis later in this section. First I want elaborate on my point concerning white resentment.

The discourse of resentment, according to Cameron McCarthy (1998), is "[T]he practice of defining one's identity through the negation of the 'other'" (84). The following quote taken from Jamaica Kincaid's *Lucy* (1990) exemplifies my usage of resentment within the context of its treatment as victimhood: "How do you get to be the sort of victor who claims to be the vanquished also?" The fear of "encirclement by difference" is that motivates the dominant subject's claim to victimhood. A loss of autonomy, as well as a loss of property, generates the fear and subsequent anxiety of the dominant subject. Both the material and representational aspects of whiteness are seen to be at stake for those who feel they must defend their sovereignty against social difference. McCarthy articulates the negation of social difference by white resentment in the following passage, "The middle class declares there are no classes except itself, no ideology except its ideology, no party, and no politics, except for the politics of the center, the politics of the middle, with a vengeance" (91).

In order to comprehend the functioning of white supremacy, we must be able to see its material relationship to the environment in which it is produced. As C. W. Mills's *Racial Contract* (1997) has demonstrated, occupying the moral center is vital to the reproduction of whiteness. The aggressive manner in which this is accomplished is seemingly justified due to the overall commitment to racial polity. Thus white resentment is seen to be a defense of whiteness. And since whiteness is a set of power relations, then resentment is "[a] power with its own material and discursive logic" (McCarthy, 1998, 92).

Whiteness offers white people material as well as symbolic benefits. Many have become so accustomed to the benefits and privileges associated with whiteness that such rewards seem natural. This naturalization has led to seemingly innate biological and cultural characteristics of civility. In the minds of white people, they have earned everything they have achieved through their personal hard work and merit. The "wages of whiteness" have been translated into beads of perspiration and have resulted in comfortable positions within the racial polity (Roediger, 1991). George Lipitz (1998) notes that white people hold a "possessive investment in whiteness" due to the fact that

> [w]hiteness has a cash value: it accounts for advantages that come to individuals through profits made from housing secured in discriminatory markets, through the unequal education allocated to children of different races, through insider networks that channel employment opportunities to the relatives and friends of those who have profited most from present and past discrimination, and especially through intergenerational transfers of inherited wealth that pass on the spoils of discrimination to succeeding generations. (vii)

Lipitz argues that whites are encouraged to invest in whiteness, to remain true to an identity that provides them with resources, power, and opportunity. As a form of property, whiteness is something that is invested in, but is also a means of accumulating property and keeping it from others. Patricia Williams (1991) has commented on the harsh realities that result from this form of investment. The symbolic obliteration of any threat to the property of whiteness is that which Williams refers to as "spirit murder" (74). The fear and anxiety associated with the loss of this form of personal property translates into actions justifying hate toward the threat of the Other. This fear brings with it an intense paranoia and a constant obsession with safety. The growing number of gated communities in Canada and the United States is but one example of the obsession with safety. This form of resentment cannot be equated with the rage of the oppressed because of its reliance on a distant Other who must be dominated to ensure the survival of self.

The rage of the oppressed, on the other hand, is a rage motivated by love of self, justice, and the ecology that binds all living things on this planet together. Once again I turn to the words of bell hooks in guiding an understanding of the politicization of love. Love, hooks (2000) notes, drawing on the work of M. Scott Peck, is

> the will to extend one's self for the purpose of nurturing one's own or another's spiritual growth . . . The desire to love is not love itself. Love is as love does. Love is an act of will—namely, both an intention and an action. Will also implies choice. We do not have to love. We choose to love. (4, 172)

hooks's insistence on thinking of love as an action rather than a feeling is one way in which "anyone using the word in this manner automatically assumes accountability and responsibility" (2000, 13). I will touch upon the issue of accountability and responsibility later in this section. First I want to explain the usage of love in the context of the rage of the oppressed. The nurturing of oneself and another's spiritual growth must be seen as antithetical to preservation of power and domination over others. The necessity of self-love, derived from self-assertiveness and self-regard, should not be seen as the same as the narcissistic hedonism that flourishes within the realm of possessive individualism. The possessive individual requires a subordinate and distant other in order to secure an understanding of a dominant self. On the other hand, as hooks states, self-assertiveness is "the willingness to stand up for myself, to be who I am openly, to treat myself with respect in all human encounters" (58). This form of self-assertion should be seen as a claiming of one's humanity in the wake of ongoing attempts at subjugation via objectification by systems of oppression. Self-regard connotes a sense of self-acceptance. One is only able to accept the Other if one is first able to accept oneself. This is based on seeing one's interconnection with others in a manner that sees everyone as part of a larger composite of life. The path of self-love requires much nourishment and healing in an era of ongoing systems of oppression.

Erich Fromm, quoted in hooks, notes that "the principle underlying capitalistic society and the principle of love are incompatible . . . Our society is run by a managerial bureaucracy, by professional politicians; people are motivated by mass suggestion, their aim is producing more and consuming more, as purposes in themselves" (72). And as Mills's *Racial Contract* has shown us, white supremacy is a vital aspect of maintaining this operating system. Artist Barbara Kruger, notes bell hooks "Created a work proclaiming 'I shop therefore I am' to show the way consumerism has taken over mass consciousness, making people think they are what they possess" (2000, 72). The link made by George Lipitz is crucial to demonstrate the "possessive investment" in whiteness that many whites think they "naturally" hold. While the zeal to possess intensifies, so does the sense of spiritual emptiness. The words of Aime Cesaire (1972) articulate this sense of emptiness, "It is not the head of a civilization that begins to rot first. It is the heart" (28).

Love cannot simply be of self but must be seen in terms of connections to others. This is based on an understanding of self beyond the narrow confines of the individual. "The choice to love is a choice to connect—to find ourselves in the other" (hooks, 2000, 93). Love must be seen, as bell hooks notes, "as an active force that should lead us into greater communion with the world . . . loving practice is not aimed at simply giving an individual greater life satisfaction; it is extolled as the primary way we end domination and oppression" (76). In this sense, love must not be seen as a highly individualistic marginal phenomenon. Love must be seen as a social activity. Nurturing a pedagogy of rage would have to center around what hooks describes as a "love ethic" (87). She suggests that, "A love ethic presupposes that everyone has the right to be free, to live fully and well. To bring a love ethic to every dimension of our lives, our society would need to embrace change" (87). The development of a love ethic in this sense is fundamental in addressing the issue of fear. If fear is a primary source of personal and societal corruption as Aung San Suu Kyi notes, then radical change is seen to be a grave threat to upholders of the status quo, and a nihilistic sense of isolation and helplessness is the greatest threat to those who suffer from subjugation. A love ethic is the primary beacon to guide one out of both predicaments, for love is the ability to see and act in a manner that connects all. It also forces one to become accountable and responsible for one's own actions or lack thereof.

Taking accountability and responsibility for one's actions urges a person with privilege to resist aiding and abetting oppression. It also ensures that the oppressed dos not remain in a state of perpetual victimhood. The oppresseds' own actions are the key to defying that which has been imposed on them. This notion of love as action is a tie that binds the privileged to the oppressed. This is the point at which an understanding of the connections between systems of oppression becomes crucial. As I mentioned earlier, people of color must ensure that all the differences among us do not become subsumed under a generic subjectivity that assumes the mantle of innocence. My point here is to make explicit the fact that many people of color have been and are complicit in ensuring the personal progress of white people. Mills's *Racial Contract* articulates this as a situation in which whiteness offers rewards to some people of color at the expense of others. This can be seen in the following examples: (1) people of color attempt to secure bourgeois respectability, but actually succeed in aiding in the oppression of other communities of color; (2) men of color, operating under the aegis of patriarchy to secure male dominance also aid in the oppression of women of color; (3) people of color operate with naturalized heteronormative discourses of sexuality and thus demonize queer members of the community. In all cases one must work within the framework of whiteness to secure a spot on the mantle of the status quo (Fellow & Razack, 1998). We, as people of color, must recognize that although we are all oppressed by the system of white supremacy, our privileges may come at the expense of other people of color. Nurturing the rage of the oppressed requires a love ethic that allows people of color, differentially privileged and oppressed, to individually experience the collective pain of all people of color. This is not an easy task due primarily to the personal and collective efforts that are a prequisite for the cleansing of the colonized mind. As Malcolm X said, we "have to change our own mind . . . We got to change our own minds about each other. We have to see each other with new eyes. We have to come together with warmth . . ." (as cited in hooks, 1995, 146). We must be able to make connections across *our stories,* to see how patriarchy is vital to reproducing the notions of nation that hold women of color hostage—Radhika Mohanram (1999) documents how women of color come to embody the space of the nation in discourse of national liberation; thus one responsibility of men of color is to constantly disrupt the gendered roles ascribed to them by the cultures of occupied settler societies in Canada and the United States. We must see how naturalized narratives of heterosexuality are necessary for the reproduction of white supremacy via dominant discourses of family values. People of color must challenge these naturalized discourses and interrogate our own complicity in heteronormative practices that continue to marginalize queer people of color. How natural is heterosexuality? As natural as whiteness I presume. The pain of one of us is the pain of all of us. We must recognize our pain and name it as such. Then can we begin to see how others are also suffering.

bell hooks (1994) reminds us that, "It is not easy to name our pain, to make it a location for theorizing" (74). Patricia Williams (1991) writes that even those of us who are aware are made to feel the pain that all forms of domination (homophobia, class exploitation, racism, sexism, imperialism) engender:

> There are moments in my life when I feel as though a part of me is missing. There are days when I feel so invisible that I can't remember what days of the week it is, when I feel so manipulated that I can't remember my own name, when I feel so lost and angry that I can't speak a civil word to the people who love me best. There are the times when I catch sight of my reflection in store windows and am surprised to see a whole person looking back . . . I have to close my eyes at such times and remember myself, draw an internal pattern that is smooth and whole. (228)

The rage of the oppressed is fueled by a love that is articulated by actions of resistance. In this neocolonial era, love of self is a grave threat to the existing systems of oppression. Love is a form of political resistance that is so powerful because once ignited it can never be extinguished. Che Guevara and Paulo Freire's utilization of the concept of revolutionary love is well documented in Peter McLaren's (2000) text on the pedagogy of revolution. Revolutionary love is born of dialogue, reciprocity, self-reflexivity, and collective historical memory. McLaren notes:

> The commitment of revolutionary love is sustained by preventing nihilism and despair from imposing their own life-denying inevitability in times of social strife and cultural turmoil. Anchored in narratives of transgression and dissent, love becomes the

foundation of hope. In this way, love can never be reduced to personal declarations or pronouncements but exists always in asymmetrical relations of anxiety and resolve, interdependence and singularity. Love, in this Freirean sense, becomes the oxygen of revolution, nourishing the blood of historical memory. It is through reciprocal dialogue that love is able to serve as a form of testimony to those who have struggled and suffered before us, and whose spirit of struggle has survived efforts to extinguish it and remove it from the archives of human achievement . . . while we often abandon hope, we are never abandoned by hope. (172)

The reclaiming of the self from the objectifying forces of systemic oppression forms the foundation that is the pedagogy of rage. An outright refusal of subperson status enscripted upon our bodies of color by white supremacy is unconditionally demanded by a pedagogy of rage. The process of reclaiming ourselves from the dominant gaze is a pedagogy of rage.

Pedagogy of Rage

[S]urvival is not an academic skill.–Audre Lorde, *Sister Outsider*

In this section I do not propose a cohesive or exhaustive framework for engagement with the pedagogy of rage, but I do wish to emphasize a few key points that may nurture our personal and collective rage. My usage of the concept of pedagogy concerns the need for people of color to maintain the ability to be simultaneously reflexive and proactive. All of our personal and collective mechanisms for resistance and methods of negotiating the oppressive conditions we find ourselves in should be constantly nourished. The following sections outline points that may aid in the nourishing endeavor. But before I continue, I wish to emphasize the following: If it has not been made clear, the point of my writing this paper is tell those folks who cringe, become flustered, resent, and/or react to instances when the rage of the oppressed does not flinch when looking them in the eye—we ain't gonna make this easy for you. We are not going to sugarcoat our experiences of violence, pain, and anger. We will only talk to you if you are willing to listen to the language of our tongues. We do not feel you require the luxury of a translator. So you best believe we gonna come at you and unleash our fury if you present yourself as the all knowing, or when you want to give us your opinion about our lives, or when you say you've acknowledged your subject-position and then continue to do what you have always done. Nah, we ain't sugarcoating our shit for you.

Reclaiming our WHOLE selves

We refuse to be what you want us to be, we are what we are, and that's the way it's going to be.

—Bob Marley, *Babylon System*

There is a space reserved for bodies of color within the imagination of whiteness. It is the space for the token, the spokesperson, the exotic, and the threat. The first three have limited space and have room for just a few. When the first three are filled, the last space is used as a holding area for the rest of us. All of these spaces grant partial visibility to people of color, yet all require that those who are chosen to enter leave "that which is not desired at the door" before they are granted entry. The only subject that does not require a separation from self in this imagination is the somatic norm whose reality is reflected in this sphere. The somatic norm is exemplified in the notion of the bourgeois subject (white, middle-class, heterosexual male). (For further elaboration, the notion of the bourgeois subject is taken up by Sherene Razack, 1998.) Those who wish entry into this sphere are required to convert themselves. The process of conversion holds that moral, cognitive, and aesthetic requirements are to be met before one is accepted into their respectively allocated space.

In light of an established authoritative moral code in occupied settler states such as Canada and the United States, people of color and First Nations communities have traditionally been viewed as incapable of morality and passing the innate threat of a "return to nature." Thus both the bleeding heart liberal model of the white man's burden and the conservative model of incantations of national tradition have been utilized to ensure that people of color and First Nations communities become equipped with the "proper tools" necessary to achieve "success" today. Fundamental to this moral code is the establishment of a dominant gaze within the eyes of the converted. The dominant gaze becomes internalized, and thus one must be able to see oneself through a negation of self, in part through imperial eyes.

The subperson status ascribed to nonwhites by the system of White Supremacy is deemed a result of cognitive inferiority because nonwhites lack sufficient rationality to make them fully human. The capacity for cultural development—civilization—is denied to bodies of color. Thus invites the intervention of those who are capable of culture. The lack of nonwhite cognition must be verified by white cognition to be accepted as valid. According to the requirements imposed on bodies of color, the capability of mastering white Western culture must be proven before partial membership is granted in the epistemic community.

The aesthetic dimension for the norming of the individual involves a specific norming of the body. Judgment of moral worth is often conflated with judgment of aesthetic worth in mainstream discourses. Notions of beauty and ugliness are based on the white body as the somatic norm. To the extent that these norms are accepted, people of color (whose features are most removed from this norm) will be the most alienated. bell hooks (1995) has categorized the requirements imposed upon the black body by white supremacy as a process of dissimulation. She describes dissimulation as, "the practice of taking on any appearance needed to manipulate a situation—[a] form of masking that black folks have historically used to survive in white-supremacist society. As a social practice it promoted duplicity, the wearing of masks, hiding true feelings and intent" (143). While this strategy of survival is often necessary in daily relations with white supremacy, it undermines the bonds of love and intimacy necessary to cultivate health. Himani Bannerji (1995) discusses her own experiences of dissociation—the violent moment of rupture between the private and public self (102–103). She is forced by the social relations required in academia to place her role as pedagogue over her personal well-being. The acts of dissociation and dissimulation are techniques of survival in social relations of violence and alienation. However, these are moments when the attempt to avoid violence is replaced with an act of violence upon oneself. Although these acts of dissimulation and dissociation are necessary at the moment, they should not become overvalued as comfortable places of being. The violence inherent in such personal practices takes its mental toll, often leading to nihilistic behavior. Andrien Katherine Wing (1997), reflecting on Patricia Williams usage of the term spirit-murder, aptly summarizes this point in the following passage, "To me, spirit murder consists of hundreds, if not thousands, of spirit injuries and assaults—some major, some minor—the cumulative effect of which is the slow death of the psyche, the soul, and the persona" (28).

On the other hand, when these acts are recognized as subversive or moments of protest motivated by an unrelenting rage and vision of a larger collective goal, then they may be analogized as "a stream moving on its way, a little tributary to join what I dream of—a real socialist revolution, feminist, antiracist, marxist, [queer], anti-imperialist" (Bannerji, 1995, 106).

The refusal of space allocated to bodies of color within the imagination of whiteness is vital to the assurance of mental, physical, and spiritual well-being. We should never have to adjust ourselves to fit into an unilinear, white male paradigm to be seen as successes or as failures in this world. We are a mutually constituted, "multilayered, multiplicative wholeness . . . multiple of each of our parts yet holding one indivisible being" (Wing, 1997, 31). For the oppressed to claim full visibility—not just the partial visibility granted to us by whiteness—we must understand our experiences as, "characterized not only by oppression, discrimination, and spirit murder, but by strength and love and transcendence as well" (32).

Tongues Untied

> Until I am free to write bilingually and to switch codes without having always to translate, while I still have to speak English or Spanish when I would rather speak Spanglish, and as long as I have to accommodate the English speakers rather than having them accommodate me, my tongue will be illegitimate.
>
> — Gloria Anzaldua, "How to Tame a Wild Tongue"

There are always going to be consequences and judgments of our actions as we continue to struggle to survive in the neocolonial world. The most important judges of our actions should be those who love us—ourselves and those with whom we share true love. True love is unconditional and extremely difficult to attain because to achieve it, much effort is required by all parties involved. For ourselves, we must attempt to live fully, without relying on the outside world for a measuring stick to gauge self-worth. We can travel to the ends of the earth only to discover that what we have been searching for is located within. Living fully implies speaking the truth as one knows it, that is, we find our true selves by living fully in the present. Thich Nhat Hanh, quoted in bell hooks's, *All About Love*, notes the following:

> To return to the present is to be in contact with life. Life can be found only in the present moment, because 'the past no longer is' and 'the future has not yet come' . . . Our appointment with life is in the present moment. The place of our appointment is right here, in this very place. (hooks, 2000, 204)

We must untie our tongues and speak the truth of what we feel. Worrying about the future or ramifications resulting from our actions of the present often results in constant fear and anxiety. Recall Aung San Suu Kyi's comments regarding corruption resulting from the scourge of power. This often leads to a lack of respect or recognition for those of us whose resistance is articulated in acts of love.

> A most insidious form of fear is that which masquerades as common sense or even wisdom, condemning as foolish, reckless, insignificant or futile the small, daily acts of courage which help to preserve [one's] self-respect and inherent human dignity. (Suu Kyi, 1995, 184)

Often the actions that our own mothers engage in everyday are not seen as resistance within the lens of patriarchy. Nurturing acts by women are not seen to be a choice but rather an inherent marker of women's role in the world. All anger against white supremacy articulated verbally by people of color in general is seen to be a marker of inherent bestial emotions. These outbursts or over-reactions are not seen to be calculated acts of intolerance but rather markers of mental disorder or irrationality. The dominant discursive frame of the neocolonial era will always attempt to give form to our experiences and actions. This should not control the form of engagement we wish to pursue at any particular moment.

> Moving from silence into speech is for the oppressed, the colonized, the exploited, and those who stand and struggle side by side, a gesture of defiance that heals, that makes new life, and new growth possible. It is that act of speech, of "talking back" that is no mere gesture of empty words, that is the expression of moving from object to subject, that is the liberated voice. (hooks, 1990a, 340).

Militant Mindedness

> That victim who is able to articulate the situation of the victim has ceased to be a victim; he, or she, has become a threat.
> —James Baldwin, *Notes from a Native Son*

Under the shield of everyday morality, which Mills has described as fundamental to the reproduction of whiteness and the racial contract, white supremacy is able to maintain, often righteously, the conditions of systemic violence (Mills, 1997). People of color experience the violence of whiteness on a daily basis. Whether it is physical or symbolic, the assault leaves the victim materially wounded. The physical and psychological wounding of people of color has effects for the assailant in the form of the reproduction of dominant subjectivity (whether it is state or citizen); as well as for the assaulted, in the form of the reproduction of subpersonhood. However, it is only when the assaulted attempt to respond to their condition as being a result of systemic forces that the term *violence* is invoked. Lewis Gordon comments on labeling of the resistance of the oppressed as violence by an oppressive regime:

> In an oppressive regime, bent upon its own theodicean preservation—where evil can only be accounted for through the existence of bad individuals or groups, not the system—any efforts towards systemic change will be regarded as violent. Consequently, to meet the system's criteria for nonviolence, one must ensure preservation of the system itself. (Gordon, 1997, 154)

Therefore, the only forms of resistance that a neocolonial regime will accept as nonviolent are those that preserve the status quo. However, Malcolm X's (1970) articulation of the nature of violence in the neocolonial era is one that is vital to an understanding of a pedagogy of rage:

> This [racist element in the State Department] is the element that became worried about the changing Negro mood and the changing Negro behaviour, especially if that mood and that behaviour became one of what they call violence. By violence they only mean when a black man protects himself against any attack of a white man. That is what they

mean by violence . . . Because they don't even use the word violence until someone gives the impression that you're about to explode. When it comes time for a black man to explode they call it violence. But white people can be exploding against black people all day long, and it's never called violence. I even have some of you come to me and ask me, am I for violence? I'm the victim of violence, and you're the victim of violence. But you've been so victimized by it that you can't recognize it for what it is today. (176).

Mills's *Racial Contract* demonstrates the necessity for violence in containing and regulating bodies of color in the neocolonial era. Occupied settler states such as Canada and the United States take pride in their "liberal democratic" institutions as upholding traditions of democracy and justice. However, the historical legacy of the suppression of people of color and First Nations—centered movements in these occupied territories illustrates that democracy and justice are reserved for those who wish to serve and maintain the system as is. One only has to look at the contemporary history of the state's response to the American Indian Movement at Wounded Knee in 1973, the Philadelphia police's response to the MOVE organization in 1979 and 1985, the Canadian army's response to Oka and Gustafson Lake in 1990 and 1995, to see the intimate workings of systems of oppression in the neocolonial era. Mainstream media discourses, the penal system (lawmakers, and police agencies, and the government) all worked collectively to censor and contain any threat to the racial order of things. Censoring and/or containing militant responses to the workings of whiteness, ensures that there will be no revolutionary effort to gather that rage and use it for constructive social change. However perpetual incidents of violence serve as harsh reminders compelling us to take a stand, speak out, and choose whether we will be complicit or resist. Silence in the face of assault is complicity.

Lorraine Hansberry (quoted in bell hooks, 1990b) echoes the necessity of militant mindedness when she wrote in 1962:

> The conditions of our people dictates what can only be called revolutionary attitudes . . . Negroes must concern themselves with every single means of struggle: legal, illegal, passive, active, violent and nonviolent. They must harass, debate, petition, give money to court struggles, sit-in, lie-down, strike, boycott, sing hymns, pray on steps–and shoot from their windows when the racists come cruising through their communities . . . the acceptance of our present condition is the only form of extremism which discredits us before our children. (186–187)

A pedagogy of rage recognizes the necessity of militancy given the extreme techniques of containment and control utilized in the neocolonial era. The violence we experience on an ongoing basis requires us to defend ourselves as well as our loved ones. Within this context, pacifism (the acceptance of one's condition as inevitable and unchangeable) must be seen as a pathology (Churchill and Ryan, 1998). One cannot turn one's cheek when there is no other cheek left to turn. Once again I turn to the words of Malcolm X: "I don't believe in any form of unjustified extremism, but I believe that when a man [or woman] is exercising extremism, a human being is exercising extremism, in defense of liberty for human beings, it's no vice. And when one is moderate in the pursuit of justice for human beings, I say [s]he's a sinner" (1970: 144). The history of these occupied lands is of extremism. Any attempt to pursue societal progress through institutional reform in moderation is regress. From the time of the colonial occupation of these lands, the spaces occupied have been extreme. People operating under the aegis of whiteness, have misused their power (or selfishly utilized it at the expense of people of color and First Nation's communities). Their tactics of spatial management are extreme. The only way to counter this abuse is through change; the only way change is going to come is via extreme methods.

Walking with the Spirits of Our Ancestors

'When memory dies, a people dies.'
What if you create false memories?
That's worse. That's murder.
—A. Sivanandan, *When Memory Dies*

We must be willing to remember and attempt to walk in the footsteps of all those who have spilled their blood to clear the path for us. We must resist the neocolonial distortions of *our stories*. Memory is a key site of resistance that requires constant nourishment in an era in which we are inundated with mainstream discourses that offer false memories, camera tricks, and rose-colored lenses through which to view our pasts. Toni Morrison (1990) captures this sentiment:

'But let us drop a veil over these proceedings too terrible to relate' . . . In shaping the experience to make it palatable to those who were in a position to alleviate it, they were silent about many things, and they 'forgot' many other things. (301)

Having said this, we must be wary of Frantz Fanon's warning against retelling of our past as a golden unified era (Fanon, 1963). We, as people of color and First Nation's communities, across all our differences—gender, sexuality, culture, religion—do not share a mythical past. We do have a shared history, albeit differentially experienced, of being oppressed in the colonial and neocolonial eras. We must extrapolate our histories of shared struggle, as well as those moments in which we were complicit in another's oppression. In short, we must be willing to dialogue as long lost siblings who have found each other after being separated by a system bent on keeping us apart.

The pain that our forebears bore so that we are able to sit and communicate together today cannot be lost. We must tap this collective spirit so it may flow through our veins now. We must be willing to sacrifice without any hesitation or fear of death. We must see death as a part of life; something to welcome and move toward. What's the point of life if one is unwilling to risk comfort for the betterment of self and others collectively? There's a poster of a revolutionary martyr that has hung on the wall in my family home for a number of years. The caption on the poster reads: "A physical death I do not fear. But a death of consciousness is a sure death." The living dead are all among us. They are those who value personal profit and property over the well-being of life on this planet. Remembrance of our past and critical awareness of the present are vital in ensuring that we are able to form a collective consciousness. For the oppressed, the trauma associated with the pain and suffering of the past must be coupled with love in the present. Only then will it be possible to tap our collective rage and struggle for the future. I recall an Orwellian saying that has been floating around in my head for some time: "Those who control the present, control the past. Those who control the past, control the future." A pedagogy of rage nurtures a struggle for positioning in the memory war of the neocolonial era.

Surviving Together

> I am from an island whose history is steeped in the abuses of Western imperialism, whose people still suffer the deformities caused by Euro-American colonialism, old and new. Unlike many third world liberationists, however, I cannot claim to be a descendent of any particular strain, noble or ignoble. I am, however, "purely bred," descendent of all the parties involved in that cataclysmic epoch. I despair, for the various parts of me cry out for retribution at having been brutally uprooted and transplanted to fulfill the profit-cry of "white" righteousness and dominance. My soul moans that part of me that was destroyed by that callous instrument . . . the gun, the whip, the book. My mind, echoes with the screams of disruption, desecration, destruction.
> —Rose Villafane-Sisolak, quoted in Anzaldua *Making Face, Making Soul*

The need for a person to recognize whatever form of privilege they hold in relation to another is vital to nurturing a pedagogy of rage. We must work together if we are to see any change in the way things work in the neocolonial era. Therefore, anyone who holds privilege, whether it is skin color, gender, sexuality, class, ability, or age, must recognize their privilege as such and take responsibility for it.

Lip service alone is not going to cut it. Simple recognition without any firm commitment to material and/or personal change is politicking the chameleonesque movements that allow a person of privilege to appear progressive and caring about someone else's well-being at one moment in time and space, yet fail to act when moments of potential rupture arise in their space of personal comfort. Politically correct attitudes tell people what they want to hear without revealing what lurks within: "I hear and feel your pain and support you, but won't do anything to help you if it means forsaking anything." One cannot simply acknowledge one's privilege and continue to do what one has always done. Action is the only way to measure the commitment of the privileged in their attempt to denaturalize their position. You can not call yourself an ally if you expect the world to continue to revolve around you. Thinking about others and changing the things one always has done is a part of the process of loving that is necessary for spiritual connections to be made. This is fundamental to any talk of transgression or hybridity. Actions change in response to the need for a solidarity in which the survival of each depends on the survival of all. We must get away from an emphasis on voluntarily giving up privilege. Understanding of privilege will only occur through experience and struggle against the system of oppression that provides that privilege.

The issue of unlearning privilege is the same as unlearning racism, sexism, or any other aspect of the "ism schism." You cannot do it? It is a fallacy to think that one can unlearn one's privilege. Yvonne Brown (1997) articulates this point:

> It is a fallacy that you can unlearn racism [or any other 'ism], there is at yet no learning theory which says this is possible. Once you have learned racist attitudes and behaviours, they are available in memory to be retrieved when the socio-economic conditions are fertile to act these out. However to know about and understand all aspects of racism gives the individual choices in behaviour and the bases for critical thinking in all social and personal situations. (Brown, 1997)

To get beyond the issue of guilt and resentment, persons with privilege must take responsibility for all of their actions or lack thereof. They must understand and take responsibility for a structure they did not create but from which they still benefit. They cannot expect those who have suffered under this privilege to show them how to do this. This is a personal journey that will eventually bring people together in the struggle against systems of oppression that dehumanize all who are involved. Treason to bourgeois respectability (whiteness, patriarchy, heteronormativity, capitalism) is loyalty to humanity. Once again I invoke the words of Malcolm X (1970):

> And in my opinion the young generation of whites, blacks, browns, whatever else there is, you're living at a time of extremism, a time of revolution, a time where there's got

to be a change. People in power have misused it, and now there has to be a change and a better world to be built, and the only way it's going to be built is with extreme methods. I for one will join in with anyone, I don't care what color you are, as long as you want to change this miserable condition that exists on this earth. (1970, 182)

Conclusion

Before any lasting and meaningful solidarity and alliance can be made among white people, people of color, and First Nations communities, many of us must be willing to acknowledge our own complicity in the oppression of others. This willingness will only be possible if one has done the work necessary to avoid relying on privileges bestowed upon them. The possessive investment in a dominant subjectivity will have to be dispossessed, but it must be made clear that any acknowledgment and rescission of privilege is not a single, one-time deal. It is part of an ongoing process of decolonization. It will not be complete until the various systems of oppression operating in the neocolonial era are dismantled. As long as systems of oppression continue to exist, various privileges associated with these systems will be available to those who wish to cash in their investment. It is not enough for one to simply acknowledge the fact they now understand what it means to have privilege. They must be willing to shut their mouth, perk up their ears, and demonstrate via their actions what it is they feel they now know.

My rage will never allow me to turn my cheek during moments when I am in a position to be an ally to someone else or when I am a direct recipient of the violence of the neocolonial era. Depending on the circumstances, I will choose my course of action, but never will my rage be extinguished. It burns with such intensity that it is unlikely I will ever comprehend it fully. This is because the source of my rage is not only the ongoing attempt to respect myself in the wake of an onslaught of constant violence but an irrevocable bond with those who have brought me this far. I must associate with those with whom I can dialogue, build a community, and critically interrogate my own complicity. These souls help to replenish the personal energy I need to keep moving in life. I know I must walk carefully, methodically, and maintain my focus at all times. I can do this because of my love for myself and others, and my ongoing demonstration of respect for all those who continue to carry me through the realm of material madness in the neocolonial era. The spirits of our ancestors have led us this far. The least we can do is carry on with what they knew to be true—a truth that is located within. A truth that emerges from a knowledge of the interconnected self and brings a grounded order in KOS.

REFERENCES

Anzaldua, G. 1990. "How to Tame a Wild Tongue." In R. Ferguson, M. Gever, T. T. Minh-ha, and C. West (Eds.), *Out There: Marginalization and Contemporary Cultures.* New York: New Museum of Contemporary Art.

Anzaldua, G. 1990. *Making Face, Making Soul: Haciendo Caras.* San Fransisco: Aunt Lute Foundation.

Baldwin, J. 1955. *Notes from a Native Son.* Boston: Beacon Press.

Bannerji, H. 1995. *Thinking Through: Essays on Feminism. Marxism, and Anti-Racism.* Toronto: Women's Press.

Brown, Y. 1997. "A Framework for Thinking and Acting Critically About Racism." Unpublished Document. University of British Columbia.

Campbell, C. P. 1995. *Race, Myth and the News.* London: Sage Publications.

Cesaire, Aime. 1972. *Discourse on Colonialism.* New York: Monthly Review Press.

Churchill, W., and Ryan, M. 1998. *Pacifism as Pathology: Reflections on the Role of Armed Struggle in North America.* Winnipeg: Arbeiter Ring.

Dei, G. J. S. 1999. "The Denial of Difference: Reframing Anti Racist Praxis." *Race, Ethnicity and Education* 2(1): 17–38.

Fanon, F. 1963. *The Wretched of the Earth.* New York: Grove Weidenfeld.

Fellows, M. L., and S. Razack. 1998. "The Race to Innocence: Confronting Hierarchical Relations among Women." *Journal of Gender, Race and Justice 1,* (2): 335–352.

Gordon, L. R. 1997. *Her Majesty's Other Children: Sketches of Racism from a Neocolonial Age.* New York: Rowman and Littlefield.

Grier, W. and Cobbs, P., 1968. *Black Rage.* New York: Basic Books.

Harris, P. 1997. *Black Rage Confronts the Law.* New York: New York University Press.

hooks, b. 1990a. "Talking Back." In R. Ferguson, M. Gever, T. T. Minh-ha, and C. West (Eds.), *Out There: Marginalization and Contemporary Cultures.* New York: New Museum of Contemporary Art.

hooks, b. 1990b. *Yearning: Race, Gender, and Cultural Politics.* Toronto: Between the Lines.

hooks, b. 1994. *Teaching to Transgress.* London: Routledge.

hooks, b. 1995. *Killing Rage.* New York: Owl Books.

hooks, b. 2000. *All about Love: New Visions.* New York: William Morrow and Company.

Kincaid, J. 1990. *Lucy.* New York: Farrar, Straus and Giroux.

Lipitz, G. 1998. *The Possessive Investment in Whiteness: How White People Profit from Identity Politics.* Philadelphia: Temple University Press.

Lorde, A. 1983. *Sister Outsider.* Freedom, CA: Crossing Press.

Malcolm X. 1970. *By Any Means Necessary.* New York: Pathfinder Press.

Marley, B. 1979. "Babylon System" from the album *Survival.* Universal Records.

McCarthy, C. 1998. *The Uses of Culture: Education and the Limits of Ethnic Affiliation.* New York: Routledge.

McLaren, P. 2000. *Che Guevara, Paulo Freire, and the Pedagogy of Revolution.* New York: Rowman and Littlefield.

Mills, C. W. 1997. *The Racial Contract.* Ithaca & London: Cornell University Press.

Mohanram, R. 1999. *Black Body: Women, Colonialism, and Space.* Minneapolis: University of Minnesota Press.

Morrison, T. 1990. "The Site of Memory." In R. Ferguson, M. Gever, T. T. Minh-ha, and C. West (Eds.), *Out There: Marginalization and Contemporary Cultures.* New York. New Museum of Contemporary Art.

Razack, S. 1998. "Race, Space and Prostitution." *Canadian Journal of Women and the Law 10*(2): 338–376.

Roediger, D. R. 1991. *The Wages of Whiteness: Race and the Making of the American Working Class.* London: Verso.

Sivanandan, A. 1997. *When Memory Dies.* London: Arcadia.

Suu Kyi, Aung San. 1995. *Freedom from Fear.* London: Penguin Books.

West, C. 1993. *Race Matters.* New York: Vintage Press.

Williams, P. J. 1991. *The Alchemy of Race and Rights.* Cambridge: Harvard University Press.

Wing, A. K. 1997. "Brief Reflections towards a Multiplicative Theory and Praxis of Being." In A. K. Wing (Ed.), *Critical Race Feminism: A Reader.* New York: New York University Press.

Contributors

Nuzhat Amin's research interests are interdisciplinary and focus on minority women, language, and power. She has published in *TESOL Matters*, *TESOL Quarterly*, *Canadian Woman Studies*, and *Resources for Feminist Research*. She is coeditor of *Canadian Woman Studies: An Introductory Reader* and *Feminism and Education: A Canadian Perspective*, Vol. 2. She has taught at the University of Guelph, Brock University, McMaster University, and the Ontario Institute for Studies in Education of the University of Toronto. She is currently an assistant professor in the School of Education, C.W. Post Campus of Long Island University.

Paula Butler has worked as a church bureaucrat, adult educator, and social justice activist. She is currently completing her doctoral studies at the Ontario Institute for Studies in Education of the University of Toronto.

Beverly-Jean Daniel has worked in the public school system for several years as an advocate for minority youth. She is currently employed in the Department of Sociology at Ryerson University in Toronto. Her research interests include teacher education, critical pedagogy, antiracism education, and African Canadian feminist epistemologies.

George J. Sefa Dei is professor and chair of the Department of Sociology and Equity Studies in Education at the Ontario Institute for Studies in Education of the University of Toronto. His research and teaching interests are anti-racism education, domination studies, Indigenous knowledges and anti-colonial thought.

Louise Gormley's lived experiences of family and mothering are situated in Mexico, Taiwan, and Canada. She often reflects upon her work as an English as a Second Language teacher in Japan and Taiwan. She believes that in an environment of critical and supportive dialogue, the fields of anti-racist and comparative education can learn something from each other.

Judy Hughes is a former counselor and advocate for abused women and their children. She is now a Ph.D. candidate at the Faculty of Social Work at the University of Toronto.

Zeenat Janmohamed is currently teaching in the Early Childhood Education Department at George Brown College in Toronto. She has been involved in community development in the child care sector and has participated in international early childhood work in Bosnia and Kosovo.

Gurpreet Singh Johal is a Junior Fellow in the Center of Criminology at the University of Toronto. He is currently completing his Ph.D. work in the Department of Sociology and Equity Studies in Education at the Ontario Institute for Studies in Education of the University of Toronto.

Karen Max is an activist who has worked in the area of violence against women for the last eight years. She has worked in women's shelters in both British Columbia and the Yukon. The focus of her current research is the development of strategies for white educators to work as allies in the area of aboriginal education and its connections to anticolonial, anti-racist, and feminist approaches to adult learning.

Andrew C. Okolie obtained his bachelor's and master's degrees from the Universities of Jos and Port Harcourt, both in Nigeria, and his doctorate in sociology from the University of Toronto, Canada. His current research focuses on anti-racist education, knowledge production, and sustainable development in Africa as well as identity constructions in post-colonial societies. He taught anti-racist education at the Ontario Institute for Studies in Education of the University of Toronto as well as a University of Toronto sociology course for "at risk" Toronto-area high school students from communities that are underrepresented in tertiary education until July 2004. He has worked with the Toronto-based Inter-Church Coalition on Africa and groups within Toronto's black community.

Renu Sharma's work focuses on transcending ideologies of holistic education, which give consideration to the emotional and spiritual dimensions of teaching and learning. Her most recent works include *Spirituality in Education: Synergy of Mind, Body and Soul* (2001), *Spirituality in the Workplace* (2000), *Theorizing Spirituality* (2002), and *Spiritual Rationality* (2002). She has received her BA and MA from the University of Toronto where she is currently a PhD candidate.

Amar Wahab is a Caribbean-Canadian scholar working on diversity issues in both Trinidad and Canada. At present he is an instructor at Ryerson University (Toronto) and a SSHRC Postdoctoral Fellow at University of Warwick.

Index

Studies in the Postmodern Theory of Education

General Editors
Joe L. Kincheloe & Shirley R. Steinberg

Counterpoints publishes the most compelling and imaginative books being written in education today. Grounded on the theoretical advances in criticalism, feminism, and postmodernism in the last two decades of the twentieth century, Counterpoints engages the meaning of these innovations in various forms of educational expression. Committed to the proposition that theoretical literature should be accessible to a variety of audiences, the series insists that its authors avoid esoteric and jargonistic languages that transform educational scholarship into an elite discourse for the initiated. Scholarly work matters only to the degree it affects consciousness and practice at multiple sites. Counterpoints' editorial policy is based on these principles and the ability of scholars to break new ground, to open new conversations, to go where educators have never gone before.

For additional information about this series or for the submission of manuscripts, please contact:

Joe L. Kincheloe & Shirley R. Steinberg
c/o Peter Lang Publishing, Inc.
275 Seventh Avenue, 28th floor
New York, New York 10001

To order other books in this series, please contact our Customer Service Department:

(800) 770-LANG (within the U.S.)
(212) 647-7706 (outside the U.S.)
(212) 647-7707 FAX

Or browse online by series:

www.peterlangusa.com